REPRESENTING RESISTANCE

Recent Titles
in Contributions to the Study of Mass Media and Communications

Developing Sanity in Human Affairs
Susan Presby Kodish and Robert P. Holston, editors

The Significance of the Printed Word in Early America: Colonists' Thoughts on
the Role of the Press
Julie Hedgepeth Williams

Discovering Journalism
Warren G. Bovée

Covering McCarthyism: How the *Christian Science Monitor* Handled Joseph R.
McCarthy, 1950–1954
Lawrence N. Strout

Sexual Rhetoric: Media Perspectives on Sexuality, Gender, and Identity
Meta G. Carstarphen and Susan C. Zavoina, editors

Voices in the Wilderness: Indigenous Australians and the News Media
Michael Meadows

Regulating the Future: Broadcasting Technology and Governmental Control
W. A. Kelly Huff

Native American Speakers of the Eastern Woodlands: Selected Speeches
and Critical Analyses
Barbara Alice Mann, editor

Mass Media in 2025: Industries, Organizations, People, and Nations
Erwin K. Thomas and Brown H. Carpenter, editors

Manufacturing the Gang: Mexican American Youth Gangs on Local Television News
Raúl Damacio Tovares

Giving Meaning to the World: The First U.S. Foreign Correspondents, 1838–1859
Giovanna Dell'Orto

Brown and Black Communication: Latino and African American Conflict and
Convergence in Mass Media
Diana I. Rios and A. N. Mohamed, editors

REPRESENTING RESISTANCE

MEDIA, CIVIL DISOBEDIENCE,
AND THE GLOBAL JUSTICE MOVEMENT

EDITED BY ANDY OPEL
AND DONNALYN POMPPER

Contributions to the Study of Mass Media and Communications,
Number 66

Westport, Connecticut
London

Library of Congress Cataloging-in-Publication Data

Representing resistance: media, civil disobedience, and the Global Justice
  Movement/edited by Andy Opel and Donnalyn Pompper.
    p.   cm.—(Contributions to the study of mass media and communications,
  ISSN 0732–4456; no. 66)
  Includes bibliographical references and index.
  ISBN 0–313–32385–2 (alk. paper)
  1. Anti-globalization movement. I. Opel, Andrew, 1964–
    II. Pompper, Donnalyn, 1960–   III. Series.
  JZ1318.R47 2003
  303.48'2—dc21   2003045598

British Library Cataloguing in Publication Data is available.

Library of Congress Catalog Card Number: 2003045598
ISBN: 0–313–32385–2
ISSN: 0732–4456

First published in 2003

Praeger Publishers, 88 Post Road West, Westport, CT 06881
An imprint of Greenwood Publishing Group, Inc.
www.praeger.com

Printed in the United States of America

The paper used in this book complies with the
Permanent Paper Standard issued by the National
Information Standards Organization (Z39.48–1984).

10 9 8 7 6 5 4 3 2 1

To all of the concerned, engaged world citizens who courageously challenge authority to give voice to the marginalized.

Contents

Introduction:
An Emerging Paradigm?

> If globalization continues to be conducted in the ways that it has been
> in the past, if we continue to fail to learn from our mistakes,
> globalization will not only not succeed in promoting development but
> will continue to create poverty and instability.
>
> —*Joseph E. Stiglitz*
> Globalization and Its Discontents *(2002, p. 248)*

Never before in world history have masses of diverse peoples around the
globe taken to the streets in protest, united by a common goal: To challenge
government policymakers and multinational corporations who threaten
their unique way of life. Media coverage of dissent at mass demonstrations
staged on nearly every continent in recent years has moved the term "globalization" from the pages of policy journals to the kitchen table. While
social movements of the 1960s legitimized protest as a political tactic, the
advent of new technologies has reconfigured the face of civil disobedience.
Internet technology has coined "new activism," for social activists are able
to circumnavigate traditional, mainstream, corporatized media and appeal
directly to the people in promoting their causes, raising funds, and recruit-
ing members. In fact, globalization may be approaching paradigmatic status, supplanting Cold-War dominant ideology as the "largest story of our
times" (Rosenberg, 2002, p. 29).

Globalization's critics have tapped into their internal resources—multiple
generations, classes, and orientations—from cyber-savvy college students
taking on overseas sweatshops, to glamorous fashion models-turned animal

rights activists, to anthropologists decrying cultural imperialism's effects on remote tribes.

This book brings together an outstanding group of international authors who examine globalization as the defining force shaping the world today.

WHAT IS GLOBALIZATION?

In the past fifty years—predominantly during the 1990s—an unprecedented 153 regional trade agreements have been notified to the General Agreement in Trade and Tariffs (GATT) or the World Trade Organization (WTO) in an effort to erase trade barriers and enhance free trade (Alphabetti, 1998). Similarly, International Monetary Fund (IMF) and World Bank reforms have redefined global trade (Chossudovsky, 1997). There seems to be no universally accepted definition of "globalization."[1] It has been characterized as a "sinister" word—a technocrat's "euphemism" (Frank et al., 2000, p. 420). Largely inspired by U.S. policymakers after World War II in order to secure the world power's economic clout, globalization is designed to restructure economies worldwide by opening vast channels for the unfettered exchange of goods, information, and ideas across borders. Others equate globalization with internationalization, or "free trade." All in all, globalization promises the unification of a global economy replete with legislated international trade agreements to benefit all countries and elevate underdeveloped nations.

A "globalization" definition that we feel best captures the scope and tone of the debate comes from sociologist Anthony Giddens (1990): "[T]he intensification of worldwide social relations which link distant localities in such a way that local happenings are shaped by events occurring many miles away and vice versa" (p. 64). Indeed, an explosion of global exchange in recent years has had enormous ripple effects. From the 2001/2 economic crisis in Argentina, to the Enron Corp. meltdown, to the local shelves of Wal-Mart lined with imported goods, globalization is omnipresent.

Change of such magnitude that touches the daily lives of people the world over has engendered bipolar reaction divided along political lines. Hence, critics seek opportunities to expose "myths" surrounding globalization, as summarized by Martin Feil (2002, p. 25):

Myth 1: The economic progress that has occurred in the twentieth century is a consequence of globalization.

Myth 2: Consumers of the world are better off as a consequence of globalization.

Myth 3: Globalization represents the only method whereby underdeveloped and developing countries can become developed countries.

Myth 4: Globalization is inevitable.

Myth 5: Losers from the globalization process can be compensated.

Myth 6: Globalization will result in a borderless world economy with borderless
factories delivering a global market to those companies who have established a competitive advantage as a consequence of their efficiency, scale,
and use of technology.

Because we also consider the positions of those who oppose globalization, we view it as more than simply the "increasing economic integration
of countries around the world" (IMF, 2002). Overall, critics charge that a
handful of greedy multinational corporations in search of profits have
assumed control, sanctioning exploitation of poor countries and victimizing
women and children. Specifically, globalization is blamed for economic crisis and disease in South America (Rosenberg, 2002), labor abuses in Asia
and Central America (Klein, 1999; Ross, 1997), and irreparable environmental damage to planet Earth—including climate change and global
warming (Gare, 1995).

WHAT IS GLOBAL JUSTICE?

Perhaps globalization's earliest and most vocal critic during the early
1990s was populist U.S. presidential candidate and captain of industry,
Ross Perot. He cautioned that the North American Free Trade Agreement
(NAFTA) would devastate the U.S. economy by encouraging U.S. companies to move operations to Mexico in order to take advantage of compara-
tively cheap labor. Speaking in soundbites, Perot's colorful metaphor of "a
giant sucking sound" caused by employment and dollars rushing from the
United States to Mexico, was picked up by the news wires and fed to mainstream news outlets across the continent.

As a positive alternative to the term "anti-globalization," some have chosen the name "democratic globalization" (DeLuca & Peeples, 2002), while
others prefer "global justice movement" (Wallach, 2002). Environmentalists, union members, human rights activists, and a host of others have cried
out against globalization, and these diverse perspectives are the driving
force behind the hybrid coalition that has emerged as the global justice
movement. Thus, regardless of terminology invoked, the coalition remains
the same. Overall, the emphasis is on alternative, viable policy changes as
opposed to only resisting current practices. Activist and global justice
movement organizer Lori Wallach (2002) defines "global justice" as "a
movement of democracy and diversity" that seeks to regulate global trade
in such a way so as to level the playing field between emerging economies
and multinational corporations. Thus, global justice activists expose the
negative impact of globalization and promote equitable global labor and
environmental rights and standards (Cavanagh, 1997).

Another, perhaps unintended, effect of globalization that critics emphasize is the declining role of the nation-state in tandem with the rise of the

multinational corporation. Although nation-states continue to exert power in the areas of immigration and domestic governance, increasingly they are pressured by the workings of two institutions empowered to make globalization a reality—the IMF and World Bank initiatives, and economic restructuring policies created by the WTO. Thus, national and natural resources are ripe for foreign investment, regardless of the democratically expressed will of the people.

In particular, social justice groups and concerned citizens lament that even though the WTO was created for trade ministers worldwide to negotiate agreements, meeting room doors have been closed to representatives of poor countries or from public interest groups worldwide (Rosenberg, 2002). Similarly, the IMF and World Bank are charged with lending funds to countries in economic recession, but characterize this with a thinly veiled paternal management role used to control developing nations' day-to-day affairs (Rosenberg, 2002). Consequently, meetings of the WTO and IMF/World Bank have provided global justice activists with a highly visible forum to promote their agendas and stage demonstrations in order to capture the attention of policymakers and the news media.

WHY EXAMINE MEDIA'S ROLE?

The power of media to represent dissent, shaping our collective conscious and attitudes toward political issues, is examined in two significant ways in this book. The news media and the new media continue to play a major role in providing a forum for debates surrounding global trade policy.

First, the drama of masses demonstrating in parades awash with colorful costumes, violence among protesters and police, and the charisma of celebrity spokespersons has proved a powerful combination for the worldwide manufacture of news about global justice issues. Even though protest movements rooted in economic and labor disputes have dominated political landscapes in India, Asia, and Latin America for many years, more recent meetings of the WTO, IMF, and World Bank have perhaps attracted the greatest amount of news media coverage.

Mainstream and alternative media coverage of specific meeting sites and protests has taken us beyond our living rooms to Seattle and Washington, D.C., in the United States; Prague in the Czech Republic; Sydney, Australia; Barcelona, Spain; Genoa and Rome in Italy; and Quebec City, Ottawa, and Calgary in Canada. Even though corporatized news media extensively covered trade negotiations and civil disobedience surrounding WTO and IMF meetings, reportage has focused almost exclusively on the *spectacle and violence* that erupted. Meanwhile, the *substantive issues* raised by street activists have received little or no mainstream news media attention.

Indeed, mass mediated visuals of ideologically opposed groups linked in solidarity to challenge a new global economy have flooded the public sphere in recent years—including pictures of organized union workers walking arm in arm with environmentalists. In the wake of bloody battles between laborers like Pacific Northwest loggers and radical EarthFirst! activists organized to save the lands of the endangered spotted owl during the 1980s, such an unexpected liaison years later is difficult to image. Hence, a lack of awareness and confusion surrounds the globalization debate—even affecting celebrity journalists. For instance, seasoned ABC news political analyst and journalist Cokie Roberts asked the director of Public Citizen's Global Trade Watch, Lori Wallach, during a brief interview on ABC's *This Week* in 2001: "It's gotten to the point where any time there are global meetings, world leaders meeting, we have a sense that the protesters are going to be there, and there's not much sense of exactly what you're protesting" (Solomon, 2001). Such ignorance and low level of sophistication by a leading journalist on a national television network—about a movement that had been visible on the global stage for over two years—is indicative of media representations of participatory democracy in action.

Not since the social unrest of the civil rights movement and Vietnam antiwar demonstrations have people taken to the streets to resist hegemonic institutions. Yet, the complexity of globalization has proven to be a major hurdle for the public and the media as they attempt to grasp the economic, political, cultural, and social ramifications of a set of policies and practices.

As this volume's chapters affirm, the dominant, mainstream news media consistently failed to accurately articulate the messages of the people in the streets. The basic mantra of "fair trade not free trade" most often was corrupted and presented as "for or against free trade," thus positioning policymakers and multinational corporations "for" free trade against protesters, who were "against" free trade. Thus, the anti-globalization frame was invoked throughout mainstream news reportage, suggesting that protesters were actually hurting the marginalized populations they claimed to support. The failure to explain the difference between fair and free trade has resulted in a significant knowledge gap.

However this is not to say that media coverage of globalization and its critics has been or continues to be monolithic. Whether in the streets or on the op-ed pages of daily newspapers, the globalization debate continues to generate a wide variety of opinions from economists, public interest groups, labor unions, environmentalists, and others.

Only recently have the media assumed a less-moderate stance by finally confronting the litany of injustice around the world—global environmental issues, worker's rights, the preservation of domestic jobs, human rights abuses, corporate takeover of state industries, and increased access to natural resources, to name a few. An example of an evolving media response to globalization is a *New York Times Magazine* cover story, "The Free-Trade Fix." In contrast to most other newsworkers' treatment of globalization issues, the coverage articulates many of the protesters' concerns.

In closing, Rosenberg (2002) predicts that globalization can continue only if it ". . . ceases to be viewed as an end in itself, and instead is treated as a tool in service of development: a way to provide food, water, housing, and education to the wretched of the earth" (p. 75).

Another example of the increasing mainstream visibility of issues as raised by global justice activists is the publication of *Globalization and Its Discontents,* a book by the former chief economist for the World Bank and Nobel Prize winner, Joseph E. Stiglitz. In his book, Stiglitz (2002) calls for a major reevaluation of the economic policies driving globalization, asking us ". . . to think once again about how decisions get made at the international level—and in whose interests" (p. 22). Hence, high profile, highly credible pieces such as this legitimize the chants in the street and at the same time force journalists to reconsider their representations of dissent.

Second, this book examines communication technology developments and their application in arenas of dissent. One of the ways that the free-fair trade knowledge gap has been bridged is through the use of alternative media. While the dominant, corporate media outlets continue to focus on spectacle and the hackneyed "for or against" free trade news frame, hundreds of diverse activist groups have adopted a range of creative tools to get their voices heard—from pre-demonstration self-defense training to elaborate costumes and street skits. Furthermore, many of these groups organize and maintain extensive Internet websites, articulating contested policies, as well as proposing solutions. Grassroots media have responded with "Indy Media Centers," where independent writers, photographers, and videographers submit material and distribute it via the Internet. These "Indy Media" sites foster vast databases of first-person accounts from those who participate in the demonstrations. In many cases, Indy Media Centers emerged in tandem with global justice protests, yet as the protests have moved on, these websites have remained, continuing to provide an outlet for alternative media and independent news. Such realities offer a stark contrast to representations of chaos and anarchy portrayed by mainstream news media.

Representing Resistance: Media, Civil Disobedience, and the Global Justice Movement fills a void in scholarly attention to the intersection of media and the globalization paradigm shift. This edited collection features three main sets of essays.

Part One: "Gathering in the Streets: Civil Disobedience and Global Justice in the Third Millennium" features five essays that examine the metamorphosis of traditional performance techniques introduced in earlier eras to creative strategies that maximize mainstream media's attention to the sensational and visual. Hundreds of diverse activist groups have adopted a range of creative tools to get their voices heard. However, effectiveness of these techniques varies since police and other authorities increasingly use force to squelch protesters' First Amendment civil liberties. Louise Leclair's essay locates the roots of contemporary "Carnivals against Capital" in pre-

Christian and pre-Industrial times. Next, Audrey Vanderford examines the protest tactics and garb of the Italian protest group, *Ya Basta,* who see their costumed bodies as counteracting the invisibility and powerlessness fostered by the forces of capital and the state. Åsa Wettergren examines the relatively undefined protest strategy of "culture jamming," and finds a pluralistic and ambivalent field of activists who are ambitious in their efforts to create new creative forms of collective action. He then draws connections between "culture jamming" and the social justice movement. Andy Opel resurrects an obscure environmental protest incident from 1997 that involves pepper spray, and goes on to make connections between the changing nature of police responses to civil disobedience and the way that these responses are represented through the media. Finally, Pat Gillham and Gary Marx analyze police and protester interactions during large demonstrations against the WTO meeting in Seattle in 1999. Together, these essays describe the context within which protest takes place—changing practices and strategies used to overcome institutional barriers to public participation in global policy decisions.

Part Two: "Representing Resistance: The U.S. Media and the Global Justice Movement" includes six essays that critique mainstream news media coverage of civil disobedience organized to protest globalization forces. The institutionalized mass media apparatus plays a central role in producing and maintaining hegemonic power structures with far-reaching effects on popular opinion and sociocultural beliefs. These essays demonstrate the limited range of commercial news media representations of the global justice movement and the barriers that such limitations impose on participatory democracy. Ilia Rodríguez explores the role of print news media in the production of knowledge about globalization during the early 1990s—at the time this construct emerged in the public discourse. Anne Marie Todd examines the dynamics of a U.S. political ritual, the Democratic National Convention, and the demonstrations that accompanied the 2000 event as framed in U.S. newspapers. Nancy Snow offers a first-person account of her involvement in the global justice movement regarding image and strategy. Next, Emma Miller argues that citizens of the South have been locked into poverty by policies that favor the rich and powerful. Her case is supported through an examination of the Western media coverage of social protest in the global South. Karin Wahl-Jorgensen taps into discourses about the global justice movement, as represented in the British daily press' coverage of the 2001 May Day Protests. Finally, Donnalyn Pompper examines the roles celebrities play in the global justice movement and suggests ways activists can work within the traditional, hegemonic mass media apparatus. Thus, these essays illustrate not only the limitations associated with activists' attempts to penetrate traditional media, but offer strategies for amplifying voices of dissent within the institutional media structure.

Part Three: "Organizing Online: The Internet, Technology, and the Global Justice Movement" offers five essays that document the sophistication of electronic organizing used to coordinate social movement organizations' protests. In particular, groups are "becoming the media," determining their own media representations through Indy Media Centers, listservs, news groups, and other new media forms. First, Sasha Costanza-Chock uses the case study approach to develop a framework for careful analysis of online activism. Various tactics of electronic contention are described and distinctions are made among conventional, disruptive, and violent strategies. Next, Ted Coopman offers a nuanced analysis of the terms, "alternative media" and "free media," citing activists' use of new communication technologies and anarchist organizational techniques to overcome the endemic obstacles of traditional alternative media. Jeff Shantz contrasts sensational news media depictions of anarchists with detailed descriptions of real-world constructive anarchist projects that model hierarchical, peaceful, and creative social relations. Dorothy Kidd argues that the growing Indy Media Center network constitutes a new kind of communications commons, which survives against and within an encroaching global capitalist enclosure of information and democratic discussion. Next, John Downing focuses on the emergence of non-Western Indy Media Centers (IMC). In particular, he suggests that IMCs establish international political connectivity of a kind not tied in most cases to a specific political party or sect, and therefore, are much more open to debate and the working through of different emphases and strategies. These essays capture an exciting moment in the emergence of independent and alternative media and the possibilities that media play in the process of resistance for social transformation.

This volume is intended to capture the early work on this important subject, providing a seminal resource for scholars and practitioners. Altogether, these essays illustrate the here-and-now impact of globalization. We consider this book, written for our university students and colleagues, as a means to elevate the voices of global justice activists. We see our edited collection and the ideas, values, issues, and data offered as rich in scope and bold in tone.

NOTE

1. For example, see Hutton and Giddens, 2001; and Scholte, 2000.

REFERENCES

Alphabetti spaghetti: Are regional trade agreements a good idea? (1998, October 3). *The Economist, 348*(8088), 19–21.

Cavanagh, J. (1997). The global resistance to sweatshops. In A. Ross (Ed.), *No sweat: Fashion, free trade, and the rights of garment workers* (pp. 39–50). London: Verso.

Chossudovsky, M. (1997). *The globalization of poverty. Impacts of the IMF and World Bank reforms*. London: Zed Books.

DeLuca, K., & Peeples, J. (2002). From public sphere to public screen: Democracy, activism, and the 'violence' of Seattle. *Critical Studies in Media Communication, 19*(2), 125–151.

Feil, M. (2002, Winter). Some important myths about "globalisation." *National Observer—Australia and World Affairs*, 25–31.

Frank, M., Hornblower, M., Thigpen, D. E., & Zagorin, A. (2000, April 24). The new radicals. *Time, 155*(16), 42.

Gare, A. E. (1995). *Postmodernism and the environmental crisis*. New York: Routledge.

Giddens, A. (1990). *The consequences of modernity*. Palo Alto, CA: Stanford University Press.

Hutton, W., & Giddens, A. (Eds.). (2001). *On the edge. Living with global capitalism*. London: Vintage.

International Monetary Fund. (2002, January). Globalization: Threat or opportunity. [online]. Available: http://www.imf.org/external/np/exr/ib/2000/041200.htm#II. Accessed 9/16/02.

Klein, N. (1999). *No logo*. New York: Picador USA.

Rosenberg, T. (2002, August 18). The free-trade fix. *New York Times Magazine*, 29–33, 50, 74–75.

Ross, A. (1997). Introduction. In A. Ross (Ed.), *No sweat: Fashion, free trade, and the rights of garment workers* (pp. 9–37). London: Verso.

Scholte, J. A. (2000). *Globalization. A critical introduction*. London: Palgrave.

Solomon, N. (2001, June). Scrutiny overdue for "white bloc." *Z Magazine* [online]. Available: http://www.zmag.org/ZMag/articles/june01solomon.htm.

Stiglitz, J. E. (2002). *Globalization and its discontents*. New York: W. W. Norton & Co.

Wallach, L. (2002, February 4). *Whither globalization and its architects in a post-Sept 11, post-90s-bubble world*, a roundtable discussion on globalization. Recorded February 4, 2002 at The Community Church of New York, New York City. Transcript [online]. Available: http://www.citizen.org/ trade/ issues/wef/articles.cfm?ID=7318.

Part One

Gathering in the Streets: Civil Disobedience and Global Justice in the Third Millennium

Carnivals against Capital: Rooted in Resistance

Louise Leclair

The first "Carnival against Capital" took place in London, England, in June 1999. Since then, major protest carnivals have been held in Washington, D.C., Sidney, Davos, Prague, Quebec City, Genoa, Barcelona, Rome, and, simultaneously, in Calgary and Ottawa. Protests in support of global justice—some with similar characteristics to the aforementioned events—have been taking place in India, Asia, and Latin America for many years. More recently, carnivals against global injustices have arisen at the local level. From the fight over the control of seeds to the fight over adequate food, housing, water, and the control of currency, ordinary people have been using the carnivalesque to resist injustice around the world.

In this chapter I will focus on the carnival as it has been used in large protests organized in North America and western Europe since 1999. The chapter examines how the carnival came to be used at the end of the twentieth century and traces some of the currents that link the contemporary Carnivals against Capital to the early carnivals, held in hundreds of autonomous communities of what is now western Europe. For the purposes of this exploration, I define "carnival" as the primary location or "mediation site" (Martin-Barbero, 1993, p. xiii) for the expression or communication of "popular culture."[1]

THE POWER OF THE PEOPLE

"There ain't no power like the power of the people 'cause the power of the people won't stop."[2] I first heard these words chanted in the streets of

Seattle on a crisp and sunny Sunday afternoon in December 1999. The "millennium round" of the World Trade Organization—(WTO) was scheduled to open in downtown Seattle the following day, and a giant Carnival against Capital had been organized in protest. It was a time dominated by music, laughter, and a recognition of the sacredness of Earth and its inhabitants. Thousands of people dressed as monarch butterflies or turtles, cornstalks or whales. Radical cheerleaders and porters carrying giant effigies of corporate world leaders—from the chairman of the International Monetary Bank to the president of the United States—met in celebration with the residents of a working-class Seattle neighborhood.

People had been arriving in the west-coast U.S. city for weeks, setting up a temporary community in a ramshackle warehouse—what came to be known as the "convergence center"—to prepare for protests that would take place before and during the WTO talks. Propelling the activities of this temporary community was a collective force to which every participant contributed, whether in the daily activities of training, food preparation, and sharing spiritual practice; the production of props and costumes; or the provision of medical, legal, and emotional support.

There had been considerable mainstream media coverage of the direct-action training many activists participated in during the months leading up to Seattle. However, little media attention had been paid to the issues to be discussed at the WTO talks or to the decisions world leaders would be making during the millennium round, decisions that could adversely affect the lives of ordinary people around the world. In North America, mainstream media presented no serious international perspective on the ongoing impacts of the WTO or those of its partners, the World Bank and the International Monetary Fund. As Michel Chossudovsky later reported in an article entitled "Seattle and Beyond," published in *Covert Action Quarterly*, "The global media giants fabricate the news, overtly distort the course of world events, and mask the truth. This precludes a collective understanding of the workings of an economic system that destroys people's lives" (Chossudovsky, 1999). It was significant, then, that in Seattle—as in Geneva and London—an alternative people's conference was held in advance of the high-level talks. Aimed at stimulating public discussion, the gathering brought together activists from around the world to scrutinize WTO-proposed policies and to discuss the global issues ignored in the advance mainstream media coverage of the WTO meetings.[3] If adopted, the official policies on the WTO table would, among other things, make it easier to privatize water and other natural resources, encourage experiments in the genetic modification of seeds, and endorse corporate attempts to patent everything from naturally occurring organisms to growing processes—all redefined in international bureaucratic parlance as "intellectual property."

In street gatherings surrounding the convergence center, these issues of vital importance to worldwide ecological balance and the survival of communities became the subject of myriad forms of creative, public exploration. It was clear from the outset that the coming days' events would represent a departure in protest style from what North Americans were used to. The air was filled with the sounds of singing and with the powerful rhythms of marchers pounding on makeshift drums made of plastic bottles, garbage cans, cardboard shields, and even the backs of those walking in front of them. Hands and feet served as rhythmic instruments. In the middle of the road, on sidewalks, in parks, what seemed to be spontaneous storytelling and dancing erupted, encouraging everyone to join in. Pageants featuring huge puppets impersonating authorities or representing the oppressed moved through the streets re-creating scenes of repression both contemporary and ancient, in particular that of indigenous peoples and of women.

Participants expressed fears about the attempts by international corporations to patent and control the distribution of seeds for crops cultivated over centuries by the peasants and small farmers of the world. Wearing costumes that reflected their concerns, people told stories about corn being poisoned as a result of genetic experiments and about the plight of butterflies, bees, turtles, and birds affected by pesticides. It was an occasion of intense education for thousands of participants and onlookers. The events during day one of the Seattle Carnival against Capital succeeded in publicly communicating more information about the life-and-death issues to be discussed behind closed doors during the WTO meetings than months of corporate-driven mass mediated stories leading up to the talks.

The next morning, at the crack of dawn, thousands of people gathered in Seattle's market area. They grouped themselves according to a four-color designation; the colors indicated the degree of direct action individual protesters would be prepared to undertake during the expected confrontations with police. Each group set off from a different starting point, but by 7 A.M. all four groups had converged in and around the vicinity of the Seattle convention center, blocking all means of entry to the WTO delegates whose discussions and decision-making authority excluded them.

Protesters were met by double lines of black-clad police sporting helmets and armed with billy clubs and pepper spray. The police, surprised by both the number of protesters and their high level of organization, had failed to block some entrances to the convention center in advance. The protesters closest to the convention center, prepared for civil disobedience, sat down and "locked down"—a term used to describe the process by which protesters link their bodies together, creating a wall of resistance. Some protesters linked arms directly in front of the convention center entrances, and it was at one such entrance that tear gas and pepper spray were first used. The police gradually escalated their use of these substances, eventually supplementing their arsenal with rubber bullets. Throughout the day demonstrators foiled various police attempts to keep them away from the meeting site by changing tactics: breaking up into groups of up to approximately 200, for example, and marching in different directions, led by pipers and drummers. Small groups of ski-masked "Black Bloc" protesters targeted well-known corporations such as Starbucks and the Gap,[4] for direct action via property damage, while other independent affinity groups remained locked down at key intersections of the city, staged performances on the roof edges of buildings, or interrupted traffic with banner drops that denounced the world control, by a few, of land, food, and human and natural resources. Thousands of others linked arms and chanted, "The whole world is watching." Police declared the city center under curfew from 5 P.M. onward. By 8 P.M., the final protesters had been driven from the downtown core back to the neighborhood where, just thirty-six hours earlier, the carnival's focus had been on laughter, storytelling, and community.

What came to be known as the "Battle in Seattle" galvanized thousands of North American grassroots activists. The repercussions were felt around the world. As Alejandro Bendana from Nicaragua's Center for International Studies told CBC (Canadian Broadcasting Corporation) Radio on November 18, 2001, "People in Third World countries watched what was happening in Seattle on their small black-and-white TV sets and knew that their struggles were being fought in North America, too" (Bendana, 2001).

THE WORLD OF RESISTANCE TURNED "UPSIDE DOWN"

The impetus for the Carnivals against Capital came first from Chiapas, Mexico, in 1995. The Zapatistas sent out an international call for a global resistance movement to fight the most recent version of transnational corporatization—neoliberalism—and the response was overwhelming. In the summer of 1996, people in struggle from all over the world came to the free zone in the jungles and mountains of southeastern Chiapas for the first Intercontinental Encounter for Humanity and against neoliberalism.

In spite of the rainy season, the encuentro attracted over 4,000 people. It was held over five days in five different Zapatista towns. Each day's intense and often heated discussions were invigorated with cultural offerings by those in attendance, including:

Gorgeously beribboned and silver-plaited Tzeltaleras of Garrucha [who] danced cumbias far across the muddy compound. . . . A German duo tootled Irish jigs for the Tzeltal children as they stood pressed against a wall mural that depicted the deadly military incursion on the "ejido" in January 1994. (Ross, 2000)

It was during this first international encuentro that a group calling itself Peoples' Global Action (PGA) was formed to launch "a worldwide coordination network of resistance to the global market, a new alliance of struggle and solidarity" (PGA, 2003).

The PGA's first event was held in May 1998 in Geneva, Switzerland, during a WTO summit. The first action to be organized under the title "Carnival against Capital" took place in London, England, in June 1999. Both events were timed to coincide with meetings of the G8 leaders.

British PGA organizers described the event in advance publicity as "an international day of action, protest and carnival aimed at the heart of the global economy" (PGA-London, 1999). The London actions were enlivened by masks, music of various kinds, and effigies of the neoliberal leaders and satirical performances. The carnival began with the distribution of decorative eye masks[5] as protesters exited different tube stations on their way to a main gathering point. The gathering point exploded with color as masked participants arrived from several directions. One group of carnival-goers was joined by city workers who danced and reveled in protest around a McDonalds fast-food restaurant. Another group built a brick wall to block entry to the London Financial Futures and Options Exchange building, making the point that there was no future in the financial system—"No future in futures." Since the London event, both the name "Carnival against Capital" and the carnival model have been used at major sites of protest against neoliberalism: Seattle in 1999, Sydney and Barcelona in 2000, Quebec City and Genoa in 2001, Rome, Barcelona, Ottawa, and Calgary in 2002.

What led PGA organizers to link the concept of carnival to political protest? Although hippie fairs established in the 1960s and 1970s promoted alternatives and eschewed consumerism, these had disappeared from the North American scene by the 1980s. Politics, spirituality, and protest of any kind seem markedly absent from the contemporary carnivals such as those identified with Venice, New Orleans, and Quebec City. The most prominent aspects of these theatrical, artistic, and musical spectacles are drinking and general license. Politics and spirituality are similarly absent from community and regional fairs, which have become commodified versions of earlier agricultural fairs.

Yet political protest and spirituality were integral elements of European carnivals from the very beginning of the spread of Christianity. Songs, dance, theatre, masks, and satire employing huge puppets and various forms of pageantry were expressions of resistance used by the common people to thwart those in power who were disdainful of their long-held beliefs and rituals. In reintroducing these elements into carnival, contemporary activists are unearthing these deep roots.

THE ROOTS OF CARNIVAL

Historically, carnival was a place where what was important in popular culture could be freely expressed. It embodied people's own rituals, as opposed to the liturgical rituals and other activities imposed by the state and the church as Christianity began to take hold. The songs, satire, masks, puppets, and pageants of carnival became a means for ordinary people to communicate ideas and express themselves in ways ordinarily frowned upon by an increasingly vigilant clergy.

Although my examples in this chapter will be taken primarily from the several centuries leading up to the Industrial Revolution in Europe—roughly the eleventh to the sixteenth centuries—it is important to begin by noting that the link between carnival and resistance predates Christianity. Carnival initially reflected people's resistance to the earliest of European societal transformations—from the autonomous, collective activities of small communities of people to societies based on hierarchy and authority (Bakhtin, 1970; Muchembled, 1979). The transition started about 3500 B.C. and continued for centuries as Christianity gained ascendancy, with carnival reaching its pinnacle in the Middle Ages, between the twelfth and four-teenth centuries (Bakhtin, 1970). "In a social order that has neither classes nor government, both the serious and the comical aspects of human spirit were, according to all evidence equally official—one might say" (Bakhtin, 1970, p. 14).[6]

In earlier, egalitarian European civilizations—those existing before the introduction of class hierarchies—laughter and satire held as important a place in people's ritual practices as the praise and glorification of those in command. There was no need for an independent space (carnival) where people could laugh at the figures of authority, since laughing was consid-ered one of the most primeval of human rituals (Baktin, 1970).

Russian cultural historian Mikhail Bakhtin (1970) explains that as late as the decline of the Roman Empire, the satirization of a returning conqueror was an integral element of the public celebration greeting his return. Similarly, funerals afforded the opportunity for people to both mourn and ridicule the deceased (p. 14). Spirituality infused both celebrations and peo-ple's daily lives. Rianne Eisler (1987) describes life in Minoan and other early civilizations:

For many thousands of years, everything was done in a sacred manner. Planting and harvesting fields were rites of spring and autumn, celebrated in a ritual way. Baking bread from grains, molding pots out of clay, weaving cloth out of fibers, carving tools out of metals—all these ways of technologically melding culture and nature were sacred ceremonies. (Eisler, 1987, p. 32)

The thousand-year rise of the Christian church in Europe was strongly related to the church's ability to co-opt these pre-Christian rituals and, over time, to bring all noninstitutional spirituality within the sphere of the church's control. Christian ideas were inserted into the lives of what was a primarily rural population via holy day festivals. Many Christian festivals were designed expressly to coincide with the ages-old cyclical rituals that people observed. As the church's influence grew, carnival became the one place where people's own rituals, their popular culture, could be practiced relatively freely.

Although carnival was tolerated until the end of the Middle Ages, the church hierarchy always railed against it. While the festivals in which carnivals were positioned may have had Christian affiliations, for example, honoring a saint, or been positioned during a period recognized by the church, such as the Feast of All Souls, in reality they were "not uniquely, not even essentially, Christian" (Muchembled, 1979, p. 50). For both church and the people, carnival evoked a time of less authority:

In the carnival, laughter is not just entertainment and pleasure, but an expression of opposition and challenge to the seriousness of the official world with its ascetic penance for sin and its identification of value with higher things. The laughter of the people . . . is a victory over fear; because it emerges in the effort to make laughable and subject to ridicule all that causes fear. . . . Laughter connects with freedom. (Martin-Barbero, 1993, p. 66)

The antics of fools, buffoons, and huge puppets were an expression of social criticism during carnival. In addition, the fertility and cleansing rituals observed by young and old, the shared stories and songs, the healing sought through natural processes, magic and witchcraft, and communications with dead ancestors all created, during these carnival periods, a sense of security in otherwise insecure lives. The spaces created by carnival during the festival cycles and the language used during carnival were central to people's physical and spiritual survival. In the face of harsh economic conditions and an increasing repressive political and religious climate, carnival "provided the cement that held the collectivity together" (Muchembled, 1979, p. 60).

In writing about this period French scholar, Robert Muchembled (1979) divided the year into six parts. He refers to these as "ambivalent" festival periods, connected to both the sacred (religious) and the profane (pre-Christian) (pp. 50–51). Each festival cycle had its own set of "carnivalesque" practices and rituals, from youthful parties and rampages to community games and inter-village competitions, long parades and pageants though the villages, and bonfires, storytelling, and communications with the dead. Every festival was concerned in some way with "fertility, emotional discharge, the active participation of societal age groups, and the redefinition of society" (Muchembled, 1979, p. 58).

The rites of the spring festivals during April and May highlighted youth, sexuality, and agriculture. During these and other festivals, authority and authority figures were always a favorite target among youth:

A period of license, Carnival loosed all human passions. As at the time of the Feast of Fools, young people attacked established values, wore disguises and played practical jokes on adults or on other inhabitants of the village. (Muchembled, 1979, p. 57)

It took the church until the end of the Middle Ages to notice that one group of young people, in northern France, had renamed Shrove

Tuesday—the day before Lent begins and one during which they celebrated the "pleasures of the table"—Saint Pansard (Saint Fat Belly Day) (Muchembled, 1979, p. 57). One account of the Feast of the Innocents describes how clerics, "wearing masks . . . sometimes wearing female dress, danced in the choir of the church during mass, singing obscene couplets" (p. 140). Another account tells of "spontaneous" winter carnivals that were organized quickly during times when the weather was particularly cold to dispel people's fear, discomfort, and sense of uncontrollable danger. The larger-than-life puppet hosts reigning over the community would help send the dangers of winter packing through "joy, dance, fire and an impromptu feast (Muchembled, 1979, p. 131). Carnival would chase away "fears born of subjection to authorities, to the king and to the Church" (Muchembled, 1979, p. 131).

The sacred and the profane coexisted in carnival until the end of the Middle Ages, around the end of the thirteenth century. As that period drew to a close, "popular culture" was increasingly viewed as a threat to the church and to the rising nation-states of Europe. From about the eighth century onwards both church and state had been solidifying their strength through military buildup and political expansion.

Around the end of the fourteenth century, a period of collusion between the two major authorities occurred. The autonomy that was symbolized by carnival clashed head-on with these dual forces: the elite, exclusive spiritual approach of the Christian church, and the individual pursuit of wealth that was the lynchpin of the ascending dominant political, economic, and social system—capitalism. This period, the "several hundred years of the evolution of mercantilism during which the modern nation-state took shape" (Martin-Barbero, 1993, p. 86) was marked by the systematic erosion of ordinary people's ways of knowing, working, learning, healing, praying, and even having fun. This period in European history was characterized by the centralization of political, economic, and social power. It was a period identified with the displacement, by clocks and technology, of cyclical time in daily life. It was also a period of witch burnings. At the same time, regulations governing what people were allowed to do within carnivals was tightened. Pageants came under the control of the church, theatre was banned from the streets, and masks became taboo. The destruction of autonomous carnivals was an indication of how deeply people's independence was undermined during this major period of privatization, commodification, and centralization of control.

This transformation, which by the end of the eighteenth century would profoundly change people's lives, had begun in England, Germany, Spain, and Portugal around the end of the thirteenth century. It would spread far and wide as the new empires set out to conquer people and amass wealth from the resources in the rest of the world. All across Europe people were driven from the land by the appropriation of common grazing areas and by the introduction of technology aimed at production control, which effectively ended rural cottage industries.

The process of "enclosing the commons"—removing land from common ownership and turning it into private property—had started long before the fourteenth century; between 1300 and 1500 thousands of people were evicted from their holdings and much common land was fenced off for private sheep-grazing lands (Goldsmith et al., 1992).

For millions of new urbanites, life would be controlled by factory production schedules—at least for those lucky enough to find work. Clocks came to replace the natural cycles identified with seasons, weather, and regular activities. Schools aimed primarily at inculcating youth with the social, moral, and religious tenets of church and state came to replace the family and the community as the focal points for passing along "the memory of the collective" (Martin-Barbero, 1993, p. 66; Muchembled, 1979, p. 44). Church liturgy and moral code took up all the space in holy day festivals. And both carnival and women's traditional practices became the site of 200 years of intense repression in Europe.

The villages and towns that had possessed considerable independence were gradually lost, leaving a void in both urban and rural communities. In the absence of people's now-forbidden traditions, there was nothing "to provide a coherent explanation of the world" (Martin-Barbero, 1993, p. 15). Expressions of popular culture, once based in the carnivals associated with cyclical festivals, now came to play their resistance role in a new venue.

As people were faced with dictate after dictate that curbed their ability to speak or perform in public, they took to the streets in defiance, developing mime when the use of speech was banned from street theatre, carrying placards bearing slogans instead of shouting, sending anonymous, threatening letters to the rich filled with magic and blasphemous verse. With the cleansing bonfires of St. John's Day prohibited, people turned to setting garbage and barrels on fire. The songs and chants that ridiculed the wealthy clerics and kings rang out in anger instead of laughter. Once banned, the freedom-giving activities of the carnival intensified in the streets and the fields and the dark of night, as revolts and uprisings became common by the seventeenth century. People greeted the theft of their commonly held land with peasant revolts, food riots, and the storming of shops, castles, and even churches. Throughout England, Germany, and southern Europe, peasants scoured the countryside, destroying enclosures and leveling fences (Goldsmith et al., 1992, p. 132).

The trials and murder of millions of witches throughout southern Europe also reached their pinnacle in the seventeenth century. The role that women had played in the transmission of traditional knowledge, and women's obstinate rejection over centuries of official religion and culture (Martin-Barbero, 1993, pp. 90–91) were inextricably tied to their fate on pyres and gallows and to the destruction of their communities (Muchembled, 1979, p. 62).

Though the witches were not exclusively women, their treatment represented both convincing evidence of Christianity's ages-old misogyny and a frontal attack on popular culture, since women were "the receptacle of popular culture . . . the memory of the collective" (Martin-Barbero, 1993, p. 66).

Communal decision making was thwarted as church and state authorities sowed seeds of mistrust within communities, and women became the catalysts for, and the objects of, one of the most far-reaching waves of cultural repression in history. Just as humor and satire had, in an earlier period of social transformation, been moved into the "underground" represented by carnival, so too were women forced to conceal their vital importance in the workings of the community.

Witch burning was a key feature of church and state repression. Muchembled (1979) identifies a geographic pattern in this repression (pp. 241–242) suggesting that it was most brutal in those areas of Europe (both Protestant and Catholic) where popular resistance to the enclosures was strongest. As food riots and massive street demonstrations became commonplace in the cities and towns of southern Europe, displacing the autonomous carnivals and burnings of the powerful in effigy became a common act of defiance. Today the effigy burnings are interpreted by some scholars as a retaliatory public act for the witch burnings (Martin-Barbero, 1993, p. 93).

THE GROWTH OF RESISTANCE

For centuries, much state and church repression of common people's expressed frustration was explained away, even justified by historians, as the actions of authorities simply subduing out-of-control crowds. But by burning fields and factories and organizing noisy processions filled with buffoonery, people were reacting to more than economic conditions. The resistance embodied in these actions represented a revolt against the overpowering—the hegemonic—forces being imposed by church and state. The changes were imposed first regionally, then nationally. They affected every aspect of life, from the languages people spoke to the way they prayed, dressed, and dined. In a very broad sense, people were waging "a struggle against new forms of exploitation" (Martin-Barbero, 1993, p. 93).

The accusation that Luddites and others rising in opposition against all technology is both simplistic and demeaning. In fact these people were fighting against "technologies that would crush their livelihoods and overturn the traditional modes of work and community and market places that had endured for centuries" (Sale, 1999, p. 313).

The struggle of ordinary people to maintain cultural autonomy in the face of the strengthening connections between Christianity, the state, and the growing phenomena of capitalism was not exclusive to Europe. As capitalism and Christianity were exported to different parts of the world colonial powers continued to use the co-optation of popular culture, along with other forms of repression, to overcome popular resistance to their theft of communal lands and natural resources.

Although England, Germany, Spain, Portugal, and France were the first sites of contestation between dominant forces and the traditional social and cultural practices on which community autonomy was historically based, the link between carnival and resistance was maintained as the process of enculturation spread to Africa, India, the Americas, and Asia. In what is now known as Latin America, the Roman Catholic Church was engaged in a mission to eradicate communal and spiritual practices not invented or controlled by the church. Phillip Wearne, in his book *Return of the Indian* (1961), quotes a Mayan "refugee" on the subject of the colonizer's rejection of communal rights: "They kill us because we work together, eat together, live together and dream together" (Wearne, 1996, p. 72).

In Latin America as in Europe, the co-optation of peoples' rituals by the church and state resulted in the establishment of carnivals, a subversive space where popular culture could be expressed. Here, as in Europe, the church reluctantly allowed some space for local ritual practice. In his book about the Chiapas rebellion, sociologist Neil Harvey (Harvey, 1998) explores how the Catholic church attempted to co-opt the autonomy of the indigenous people of Chiapas in this way. However, the church failed to understand the deep resistance at play.

The situation allowed for the persistence of indigenous religious practices, although they were expressed in a new Christian form. The fiestas were organized in each village by religious associations, or cofradias, identified with particular saints. The Dominicans appear to have been highly pragmatic in allowing the cofradias some local autonomy in exchange for their devotion to Christianity. However, it was this ambiguity of Ladino-Indian relations that permitted native leaders to establish a space of resistance to Spanish rule, culminating in outright rebellion. (Harvey, 1998, p. 39)

Even today, the most famous pre-Lenten extravaganza in Brazil continues to contain ambivalent elements, pockets of resistance to the spiritual dominance of the Christian church. In contemporary Mexico and Guatemala, ritual celebrations like the Day of the Dead bear an uncanny resemblance to the clandestine activities of early European All Souls celebrations. Masks, parades, pageants, satire, music, rhythm, songs, and carnivals there maintain a connection with the notion of autonomy, the natural cycles, and concern for the earth and all its creatures. It is significant that today's revival of the "carnival" should originate from Chiapas, which originally was part of Guatemala and is a location that "has experienced an Indigenous rebellion every fifteen years since the Conquest of 1524" (Goldsmith et al., 1992, p. 135).

TWENTY-FIRST CENTURY RESISTANCE
IN THE GLOBAL JUSTICE MOVEMENT

Like the early European carnivals, Carnivals against Capital are mediation sites for what ordinary people have to say about the world and the way it should be managed. The participants in these contemporary carnivals use the carnivalesque as a means of communicating their political views and supporting direct action, just as peasants and serfs did in Middle Ages Europe and indigenous peoples did in South America after "contact." The Carnivals against Capital represent contemporary resistance to "transformations" arising from collusion between dominant forces rather than from autonomous community decision making. This time both the carnivals and the resistance they embody are taking place on an international scale.

Young people play as important a role as ever in using carnival as a means of criticizing the "establishment." PGA and other groups have reinvented carnival with the express purpose of critiquing and opposing corporate globalization. The five hallmarks of the PGA, most recently revised at a meeting in Cochabamba, Bolivia, in February 2002, reflect what has always been at the heart of the carnival: resistance. PGA rejects capitalism, imperialism, and feudalism as well as all the bureaucratic elements that promote a destructive form of globalization. All forms of domination and discrimination are rejected in favor of embracing dignity for all human beings. PGA supports and promotes confrontation with existing undemocratic organizations, since it considers transnational capital the real policymaker. PGA calls for direct action and civil disobedience in support of the struggles of social movements. The five hallmarks highlight PGA's advocacy of forms of resistance that maximize respect for life and the rights of those who are oppressed. Finally, the network promotes the construction of local alternatives to global capitalism. The entire PGA philosophy is based on decentralization and autonomy (PGA, 1988).

The origins of the Carnival against Capital lie in the earliest European forms of resistance to hierarchical authority. Today, those who seek total control over, and personal gain from, Earth and its resources threaten our lives and livelihoods just as they did in the Middle Ages. Fuelled by people's inexhaustible creativity, carnivals will remain a potent force for expressing and igniting dissent. As the slogan has it, "The power of the people won't stop."

NOTES

1. Popular culture refers to all aspects of the lives of ordinary people. It speaks to class and to the way in which people view their own class and those in power. Martin-Barbero links popular culture to hegemony. In doing so he draws upon the work of Ginzburg, de Certeau, the Frankfurt School, Gramsci, E. P. Thompson, and others. Martin-Barbero, J. M. (1993). *Communication, culture and hegemony: from the media to mediations* (Fox, E., White, R. A., Trans.). London, Newbury Park, New Delhi: Sage, pp. 62–97).

2. The author first heard this chant in the streets during the millennium round of talks held in Seattle in December 1999.

3. For more discussion see, a Citizen's Guide to world trade published by the working group on the WTO/MAI, July 1999. Available at http://depts.washington.edu/wtohist/Research/academic.htm#top10

4. Starbucks and the Gap are just two of many corporations that are criticized for both domestic and international labor practices.

5. The masks, in addition to contributing to the carnivalesque atmosphere, were a symbol of protest against an existing British anti-IRA law prohibiting face masks to be worn in public.

6. Author's translation.

REFERENCES

Bakhtin, M. (1970). *l'oeuvre de Francois Rabelais et la culture populaire au Moyenne Age et sous la Renaissance*. Paris: Gallimard.

Bendana, A. (2001). *Sunday Edition: Critics' Panel* [radio program]. Toronto: Canadian Broadcasting Corporation. Available: www.cbc.ca.

Chossudovsky, M. (1999). *Seattle and beyond: Disarming the new world order*. [on-line] Available: http://www.nadir.org/nadir/initiativ/agp/free/seattle/chossudovsky.htm [July 7, 2003].

Committee, P. G. A. (1998). *Bulletin #1*. People's Global Action [online newsletter] Available: www.nadir.org/nadir/initiativ/agp/en/PGAInfos/bulletin1.htm [June 1, 2001].

Eisler, R. (1987). *The chalice and the blade: Our history, our future*. San Francisco, CA: Harper & Row.

Goldsmith, E., Hildyard, N., Bunyard, P., & McCully, P. (1992). Whose common future? *The Ecologist, 22*, 123–210.

Harvey, N. (1998). The Chiapas rebellion: The struggle for land and democracy. Durham, NC: Duke University Press.

Martin-Barbero, J. M. (1993). *Communication, culture and hegemony: From the media to mediations*. (Elizabeth Fox & Robert A. White, Trans.). London, Newbury Park, New Delhi: Sage.

Muchembled, R. (1979). *Popular culture and elite culture in France 1400–1750*. Baton Rouge and London: Louisiana State University Press.

PGA-London. (1999). *Statement of purpose* [online newsletter]. Available: http://bak.spc.org/j18site/ [June 2001].

PGA (2002). *Hallmarks of peoples global action* [online newsletter]. Available: www.nadir.org/nadir/initiativ/agp/free/pga/hallm.htm [April 3, 2002].

——— (2003). *What is PGA?* [online] Available: http://www.nadir.org/nadir/initiativ/agp/en/

Ross, J. (2000). *The war against oblivion: Zapatista chronicles 1994–2000*. Monroe, Maine: Common Courage Press.

Sale, K. (1999). The achievements of General Ludd. *The Ecologist, 29*(5), 310–313.

Wearne, P. (1996). *Return of the Indian: Conquest and revival in the Americas*. Philadelphia, PA: Temple University Press.

2

Ya Basta!—"A Mountain of Bodies That Advances, Seeking the Least Harm Possible to Itself"

Audrey Vanderford

On September 26, 2000, over 10,000 demonstrators from all over the world converged on Prague to protest the annual World Bank/International Monetary Fund (IMF) Meetings. As had occurred at every major international meeting in the few preceding years, they came to challenge global capitalism, corporate domination, and the policies of these institutions—policies many link to poverty and environmental degradation worldwide. The activists promised to close down the meeting as they had done when the World Trade Organization met in Seattle in 1999. The Czech government responded by banning all public demonstration for the duration of the event. The irony of this was not lost on protesters: In 1989 the "Velvet Revolution" saw massive nonviolent demonstrations lead to the downfall of Czechoslovakia's communist regime. Again in 2000, Wenceslas Square was to be the locus of protest. This time, however, the leaders of the Czech Republic, including once dissident playwright now President Václav Havel were on the inside of the meeting site looking out at a new era of protests. Against a police force some 11,000-strong, protesters marched toward the Congress Center, a fortress overlooking the city that was built during the Soviet occupation to withstand both siege and nuclear disaster—a symbolic reminder of the past.

The protesters planned for the march to the Congress Center to split into three groups, blue, yellow, and pink, designating the range of tactical styles each agreed to utilize. The blue group consisted almost entirely of anarchists and others prepared to use violent confrontation and property destruction. The pink group, headed by a samba band, maintained a commitment to nonviolent civil disobedience. The yellow group also planned to use nonviolent tactics; however, like the blue group, they intended to confront and push beyond the police line. Despite these distinctions, all three marches clashed with police, who met them with tear gas, concussion grenades, and billy clubs. Some protesters pried cobblestones from the streets, launching them at windows and police. The new McDonalds in Wenceslas Square was ransacked. Violent confrontation raged for two days, and by the time the World Bank/IMF ended their meeting—one day early— over 900 protesters had been jailed. Activists' calls for another "Carnival against Capitalism" were being characterized in the mainstream press as "violent protest," but some of the demonstrators hoped that their performances in the streets of Prague would draw attention to the opposition to the World Bank and IMF, as well as to the brutal police tactics used to protect global capitalism.

This chapter focuses on one of the groups to attract the most attention in Prague—*Ya Basta*, a network of activists and groups drawn mostly from Italy's Social Centres.[1] Ya Basta (Spanish for "Enough!") comprised almost the entire yellow group en route to the Congress Center, making headlines even before the protests began when some 1,200 members journeyed by train to Prague. Held up at the Czech border for almost two days as persona non grata, Ya Basta finally were admitted after international media learned of the story. Ya Basta already had made a name for themselves at previous European demonstrations and were renowned for their costumes and their tactics. And again in Prague, the media documented the group's creative confrontations.

Ya Basta fashion their own "armor" out of recycled materials, stuffing foam padding around their bodies and transforming cardboard and plexiglas into protective wear and shields. Wearing helmets, goggles, and gas masks, Ya Basta's handmade apparel provides protection from the onslaught of teargas and batons. According to one activist, Ya Basta use "all things that [are] visible and clearly for defensive purposes only. We wanted people to understand on which side lay reason, and who started the violence" (Wright, 2000, p. 3). This chapter will examine the costume and armory of Ya Basta, arguing they create these colorful and imaginative objects to draw attention to their bodies—a form of symbolic and utilitarian resistance.

Although Ya Basta's techniques seem innovative, there exists a long tradition of using costume and material culture in street theatre and protest. From the Middle Ages, theatre and festivals have fostered a certain liminality in moments of symbolic and social transgression, often responding to political issues with puppets and parody. According to Mikhail Bakhtin (1984), oppositions and symbolic inversions are abundant in the celebratory atmosphere of these festivals; the laughter of carnival overcomes the seriousness of official culture as grotesque and blasphemous bodies displace reverence and dogmatism. Contemporary political protests, self-described "Carnivals against Capitalism," seek to reenact a type of this "carnivalesque" with similar gestures toward overthrow and upheaval. Richard Schechner (1993) even posits that "revolutions in their incipient period are carnivalesque" (p. 47). Certainly in the twentieth century, the importance of dramaturgy has been recognized by most revolutionary groups, who often envision some public, ritualized enactment in addition to their programmatic elements.

To draw people into the streets—into revolutionary activity and consciousness—was certainly a fundamental goal of much of the protest theatre of the sixties. Such theatrics often were crafted carefully, encoded with ideology and artistry. In the words of Yippie Abbie Hoffman, "We would hurl ourselves across the canvas of society like streaks of splattered paint" (Durland, 1998, p. 68). Protest performances allow activists to enact their liberatory politics, to promote their cause, and to even encourage audience participation. As Baz Kershaw (1997) argues, performance has become central to the sociopolitics of late twentieth-century capitalism. "In such a society the performative becomes a powerful weapon of political conflict, and therefore the aesthetics of performance are relevant to the analysis of political—especially politically conflictual—events" (p. 257). In other words, a great deal of symbolic power is wielded by activists in street theatre and public demonstrations.

Les événements de mai in Paris 1968 usually are seen as the high point of countercultural protest "combining ambitions of political revolution with a desire for totally free expression" (Kershaw, 1997, p. 261). Indeed, one of the first buildings seized by the protesters in Paris was the Odéon Theatre. Occupied for the duration, it became the focus for the whole revolt; in effect, the whole revolt became theatre. The costume department was raided, and people held the barricades dressed as centurions, pirates, knights, and queens. The American radical theatre troupe Bread and Puppet Theatre, as well as other groups, performed "the news" as skits. According to Jean-Jacques Lebel (1969), who organized the takeover of the Odéon, "The May uprising was theatrical in that it was a gigantic fiesta, a revelatory and sensuous explosion outside the 'normal' pattern of politics" (p. 112). Although Kershaw (1997) suggests that the blend of art and politics occurred more in theory than in practice, the legend of May 1968 continues to inspire contemporary activists in the anti-globalization and anti-capitalism movements. Groups like Ya Basta maintain this particular mixture of theatre, celebration, and revolt.

THE ARMOR

The attire of Ya Basta echoes the playfulness of May 1968, but Ya Basta are prepared for more than just symbolic confrontation. Group members are clear that the creation of this armor has not only theatrical and political meaning, but tactical and utilitarian purpose as well. As one activist explains, "We invented, rummaging through ancient history, systems of protective apparel, like plexiglas shields used tortoise-style,[2] foam rubber armor and inner-tube cordons to ward off police batons" (Wright, 2000, p. 3). Using a motley combination of foam padding, cardboard, tarpaulins, inner tubes, life jackets, duct tape, and garbage can lids, Ya Basta's costumes both deflect the police's blows and attract the media's attention.

The preparation of costumes and weaponry is usually a group project, and sometimes equipment and formation "training sessions" are offered. "Hold a 'regalia' making party," suggests one website devoted to "Organizing Tips." "Invite friends over for beverages, conversation, and put together some interesting outfits. Design a helmet with a stuffed animal glued to the top. Get a hold of those 'pool waders,' the ducky ones" (*Yellow Overalls Organizing Tips*, n.d., p. 1). Frequently armor is assembled onsite at the convergence centers where activists gather prior to a protest. Oftentimes objects need to be scavenged upon arrival since it can prove difficult traveling and crossing borders while carrying "weapons" like gas masks and garbage can lids. Using found or "dumpster-dived" objects is important, practically and ideologically, for the movement's larger goals involve trying to exist outside the market economy.

The transformation of these objects of mass culture is a central aspect of Ya Basta's presentation style. In this way, group members demonstrate their symbolic refusal of mass culture itself through the appropriation of the items they have salvaged and assembled. By making objects into armor, Ya Basta reshape their meanings and functions. In other words, the playful use of tires and tarps alters these items' connection to industrialization, harnessing them for the resistance to its globalization. Ya Basta have fashioned their own battalion from recycling, rows and rows of cardboard and tarpaulin shields that seem a flamboyant mimicry of police riot gear. As Kay Turner (1996) observes in an essay in *Recycled Re-Seen: Folk Art from the Global Scrap Heap*, "recycled materials lend themselves to artful parody because they represent the shift of one material use to another; they bring associative meaning with them" (p. 67). Indeed, Ya Basta's recycled attire contains such multiple significations.

Allen Roberts (1996) describes recycling as a type of *détournement*. "As a *détournement*," he writes, "recycling is a subversive diversion, a devious turning away from an invention of what is expected" (Roberts, 1996, p. 84). Although Roberts' essay actually documents recycled art in Senegal, his analytical tools hearken back to late-sixties France. *Détournement* is a concept of the Situationist International, a group of mostly French intellectuals who contributed much of the theoretical inspiration for les événements de mai. The situationists argued that détournement could disrupt the power of dominant culture, creating "situations" that liberated people from capitalism and constraint (Debord & Wolman, 1981). Détournement involves the "theft" of preexisting artistic productions and their integration into a new construction, one that serves the situationists' radical political agenda: "the revolution of everyday life" (Vaneigem, 1994). Images, texts, and objects are decontextualized, détourned, and then recontextualized; the displacement of cultural artifacts reverberates into both the old and the new contexts, destabilizing the primacy and stasis of the originals. Détournement, the situationists argued, provides an opportunity for empowerment as one enacts this subversive misappropriation of images and objects.

Ya Basta's use of discarded objects—of trash—to make protest costumes exemplifies this détournement. By transforming trash into armor, *Ya Basta détourne* the "detritus" of global capitalism, drawing attention to their opposition to it, while protecting themselves from the police response to their actions. In doing so, Ya Basta not only locate themselves amidst the refuse, but also demonstrate that this place of marginality can be regenerated, refashioned, and détourned to counter the very forces responsible for its creation.

The symbolic opposition offered by Ya Basta's apparel is evident not only in their incorporation of recycled objects, but in their use of color. In Prague, as in many other demonstrations, most Ya Basta members wore matching white jumpsuits. Indeed, *Tute Bianche* or "white overalls" are another Italian group affiliated with Ya Basta and with the Social Centres. The color white plays a central role in the ideology of Tute Bianche. The idea of demonstrating in white dates back to 1994 when the mayor of Milan described the people associated with the Social Centre at Via Leoncavallo as "ghosts" after the site had been razed. He incorrectly believed that the destruction of the center would mean the disappearance of the counterculture. His attempt at "exorcism" failed; the movement only grew. Today white is worn as a symbolic marker of marginality and invisibility. "We have always been the invisible in society," says one activist. "The white suit expresses the fact that the state ignores us" (Vidal, 2001, p. F17).[3] Twisting this conception of the hidden and the powerless, a thousand some-odd activists marching in white "strive to make the invisible visible" (*NYC Declaration*, 2000, p. 1).

THE BODY AND BIOPOLITICS

Much of Ya Basta's own justifications about their costume revolve around notions of the body. As with the color white, use of the body as a political symbol counteracts the invisibility of the masses. As global capital has ascended, reads the NYC Ya Basta Collective website, "the majority of . . . citizens have been made to vanish: their dreams, labors, passions, aspirations, communities, their very bodies disappear" (*NYC Declaration*, 2000, p. 1). To resist this, Ya Basta's performances emphasize activists' bodies, the presence—and the dissent—of the people.

In his article "Unruly Arguments: The Body Rhetoric of Earth First!, ACT UP, and Queer Nation," Kevin DeLuca (1999) asserts that the nonverbal—the body—can provide activists with a powerful argumentative force. He contends that the physical acts of Earth First!, ACT UP, and Queer Nation—and by extension, Ya Basta—create a visual performance or "body rhetoric" whereby activists can communicate their messages in a manner that extends beyond "reason" and "words." DeLuca (1999) argues, for example, that treesitters, perched 100 feet or more up in trees in danger of being logged, demonstrate their "utter vulnerability . . . as they intervene on behalf of nature. Quite clearly, the Earth First!ers, human beings, are putting at risk their bodies, their lives, for wilderness, for trees. This is an almost incomprehensible act in a modern, humanist, secular culture" (p. 12). In a similarly "irrational performance," Ya Basta activists put their bodies on the line, prepared to receive the blows of the state; their theatre highlights police brutality and demonstrates the group's resistance to the violence enacted by institutionalized power. These activists choose to prioritize lived, bodily experience over "rationality" and traditional political argumentation, both of which are used as justifications for the exclusion of individuals from the exercise of power.

Recognizing a failure in conventional political channels, Ya Basta encourage political participation on the street level, with the body repeatedly cited as both a symbol and a weapon of resistance. "With our bodies we have come to defend the rights of millions, dignity and justice," announced one Italian activist in Prague. "In the face of total control of the world which owners of money are exercising, we have only our bodies for protesting and rebelling against injustice" (Vidal, 2001, p. F17). Another organizer echoes this: "We trained ourselves to resist the police. We built shields, we collected old masks, tires to use as barriers, and we designed protection for the body. We use the body as a weapon of political struggle" (Cuevas, 2000, p. 3). A Ya Basta member from Milan says,

Our aim is complete determination, dignity, and disregard for the self. Our bodies are our weapons. We will throw them at the state, just as it rains its weaponry at us. We wear the suits and the padding because we have witnessed the extreme brutality that the police and the authorities unleash on dissent, despite non-violence, and the complete disregard for human dignity and suffering. (Vidal, 2001, p. F17)

This repeated emphasis on the meaning and function of bodies appears often in Ya Basta discourse, as they extol the body as a protest tactic, as expression or as armament. For Ya Basta, bodies are symbolic and communicative; bodies are targets of control and violence; they are theatrical, tactical, and resistant.

As these activists indicate, Ya Basta's use of armored bodies goes "beyond the purely practical aspect and is symptomatic of what we call 'biopolitics,' the new form of opposition to power" (Wright, 2000, p. 3). This concept of biopolitics stems from Michel Foucault's (1978) notion of "bio-power," the exercise of power and authority, no longer by sovereign decrees of life or death, but by "the administration of bodies and the calculated management of life" (p. 140). A range of disciplinary institutions—factories, families, universities, armies, and prisons, for example—monitor and control the productive and reproductive capacities of the population. According to Foucault (1978), "this bio-power was without question an indispensable element in the development of capitalism; the latter would not have been possible without the controlled insertion of bodies into the machinery of production and the adjustment of the phenomena of population to economic processes" (pp. 140–141). The discipline of bodies then is fundamental to the state and the market's exercise of power.

If this "bio-power" is the power over life itself, Ya Basta respond with the opposite principle: "bio-power as life, rising up against the state, on its own behalf" (Moose, 2001, p. 5). Ya Basta seek to unleash bodies from disciplinary structures of everyday life with a theatrical and political insurgence in public space. Demonstrably disobedient and undisciplined, Ya Basta have called for a "rebellion of bodies against world power" (Cuevas, 2000, p. 2). The costumes, the armor, and the theatrics of Ya Basta enact this rebellion not just for police and local onlookers, but for the international media that attend these events.

SPREADING YA BASTA

Clearly the performance of political protest relies to a great degree on the media. As the chant from the 1968 Democratic Convention in Chicago proclaimed, "The whole world is watching." Activists recognize the media's utility for broadcasting their image and their issues to millions of viewers, and thanks in large part to both mainstream and alternative media, the tactics of Ya Basta have spread beyond Italy. The New York City Ya Basta Collective, for example, formed shortly after stories and pictures were transmitted from Prague. A Ya Basta group exists in England, calling themselves WOMBLES (White Overalls Movement Building Libertarian Effective Struggles), a name taken from a popular children's television show;[4] the Spanish and South American groups are known as *Monos Blancos* or "white monkeys." With articles in a number of major newspapers and magazines, the media has provided Ya Basta with an opportunity to vocalize their grievances and promote their causes to an international audience (Kingsworth, 2001; Klein, 2001; La Rosa, 2001; Vidal, 2001).

Nevertheless activists are quite wary of mainstream media coverage, for the conflict is often skewed in favor of government and corporate interests and in support of police crackdown. Although activists utilize a variety of tactics in their street demonstrations, even labeling them separately as they did in Prague, the media often lump all dissenters together. Even when police charge peaceful demonstrations, reports are quick to denounce protesters as "terrorists," blaming them, and not police, for violence in the streets. In response, many activists have sought to *détourne* protest, creating public events that are difficult to characterize as violent. Ya Basta hope their armor and tactics subvert some of the negative portrayals of the anti-globalization and anti-capitalism movements. As one Ya Basta member notes,

People can see images on the TV news that can't be manipulated: a mountain of bodies that advances, seeking the least possible harm to itself, against the violent defenders of an order that produces war and misery. And the results are visible, people understand this, the journalists can't invent lies that contradict the images; last but not least, the batons bounce off the padding. (Wright, 2000, p. 3)

Indeed the images broadcast from Prague and from other protests are filled with "mountains of bodies" that send an undeniable message of opposition and refusal to the forces of global capitalism.

Even when the media focus on window smashing that allegedly "prompts" police response, Ya Basta's tactics complicate the justification of police force. After years of demonstrations in Europe, the police's reaction is predictable. Cobblestones or no cobblestones, there will be tear gas and truncheons. Therefore Ya Basta members come prepared to be gassed and beaten. Their apparel protects them—somewhat—from this inevitability, while at the same time drawing news media attention to the clash. Makeshift shields and colorful armaments, cleverly refashioned inner tubes and cardboard, visibly contrast with the police, completely identical in their uniforms, menacingly anonymous in their riot gear. The portrayal of this visual juxtaposition is a crucial part of Ya Basta's performance. As DeLuca (1999) argues, "Although designed to flag media attention and generate publicity, . . . [protests] are more than just a means of getting on television. They are crystallized argumentative shards, mind bombs that shred the existing screens of perception and work to expand 'the universe of thinkable thoughts'" (p. 12).

It appears, however, that the Ya Basta "mind bomb" is beginning to fizzle. With the spread of Ya Basta's tactics has also come the demonization of the group, not only by authorities, but by others within the global justice movement. Although the protests in Prague generated much publicity for Ya Basta, rumors circulated shortly afterwards that the group were actually about "authoritarian communists" ("Ya Basta(rds)!", n.d., p. 1). Some activists criticized the escalation in "weaponry" as a dangerous form of "street fighting bravado" (Jovanovich, 2002, p. 1). Others complained about the group's attempts to dominate the organization of the protests against the G8 Summit in Genoa in July of 2001, particularly when Ya Basta issued their "Declaration of War" against the meeting. With the shooting death of Italian anarchist Carlo Giuliani at the hands of the Genoa *carabinieri*, the "war" between protesters and police exceeded any semblance of a merely symbolic confrontation.

After both the tragedies of Genoa and of September 11, Ya Basta tactics seem to have waned. The New York City Ya Basta Collective have disbanded, and the Italian movement has largely taken off the white overalls and metamorphosed into a group called the Disobedients. According to Tute Bianche spokesperson Luca Casarini, "the phase of civil disobedience has been exhausted" ("Interview," 2001, p. 2). The future of Ya Basta appears uncertain.

Like many radical groups, Ya Basta struggle to maintain their oppositionality against the hegemonic forces that strip the performance of its subversiveness. Nevertheless, Ya Basta have engaged in their public demonstrations, fully aware that any tactic has only a short duration of insurgence before being recuperated by the status quo. As one New York Ya Basta member noted, the group "never meant a creative tactic alone. To think of it as a fashion of practicality, of how to be more successful in 'getting away with it,' is to misrepresent such a complex political project" (Jovanovich, 2002, p. 3). The less glamorous work of community building associated with the Social Centres, for example, remains one of the group's primary foci.

Despite criticisms, Ya Basta's tactics have invigorated the carnival-like atmosphere of anti-globalization protests. Like older forms of carnival, Ya Basta have filled the streets with bodies enacting inversions of social power. Group members insist that the humor and carnivalesque of their costumes and armaments are a powerful force of resistance to the humorlessness and constraint of global capitalism. Indeed, even in the midst of tear gas, it is hard not to laugh as hundreds of "Michelin Man" figures waddle toward the police line. Their cardboard shields and duct-taped armor contrast with the power and money involved in staging these international meetings, highlighting the disparities between those "inside" and those on the streets. With their playful, handmade costumes, Ya Basta enact their ideological, symbolic, and utilitarian performance, a refusal of the politics of global capitalism. Even if only providing a temporary rupture in the dominant paradigm, Ya Basta visibly announce "Enough!"

NOTES

1. The Social Centres grew out of Italy's "creeping May" of mass strikes and university occupations that began in 1968 and continued for over a decade. In the mid-seventies, an increasing number of working-class people began to occupy or "squat" abandoned factories and warehouses, transforming them into autonomous living spaces. "Squatting" involves the occupation of uninhabited buildings without

asking permission or paying rent. While some squats are removed almost immediately, others have remained for months, even years. In Italy, as in other countries, squatting has become a way to organize political and cultural alternatives free from the control of the market and the state. The Social Centres provide a range of services, including cheap concerts, movies, and classes. There are approximately 150 Social Centres in Italy today, and although they often struggle with authorities, some local governments have formally conceded to their presence.

2. "Tortoise-style" is a marching formation used by the Romans in which the front row of an advancing column holds its shields vertically while those behind hold them over their heads, in an attempt to stave off arrows or tear gas cannisters as the case may be.

3. It is interesting to note that as Ya Basta-type actions have spread to other countries, the color signification has changed. In the United States, it is perhaps no surprise that activists choose not to don white because the color is easily associated with white supremacy and the Ku Klux Klan. Nevertheless, the New York City Ya Basta Collective echo the Italian group in their justification for using the color yellow. "It offers the certainty of noticeability or an undeniable presence, like a traffic sign that says 'danger ahead'" (Moose, 2001, p. 10). The NYC Ya Basta members link their yellow and orange jumpsuits to the uniforms worn by chemical cleanup crews, as a symbol of the contamination of contemporary culture, and to the clothing worn by prisoners, in a gesture of solidarity with those incarcerated.

4. Wombles are little rodents who live outside Wimbledon and pick up trash for a living. This moniker reinforces the associations with garbage and with nature and demonstrates the ability of activists to playfully incorporate popular culture and parody into their presentations.

REFERENCES

(2000, November). NYC Declaration. Retrieved February 28, 2002, from http://free.freespeech.org/yabasta/dec.html.

(2001). Mobilization against the G8, Genoa Italy. Retrieved February 28, 2002, from http://free.freespeech.org/yabasta/genoa.html.

(2001, August). Interview with Luca Casarini [Electronic version]. Il Manifesto. Retrieved March 3, 2002, from http://free.freespeech.org/yabasta/lucac.html.

Bakhtin, M. (1984). *Problems of Dostoevsky's poetics*. Manchester: Manchester University Press.

Cuevas, J. R. (2000, October 15). The body as a weapon for civil disobedience [Electronic version). La Jornada. Retrieved November 11, 2000 from http://www.ainfos.ca.

Debord, G., & Wolman, G. (1981). Methods of *détournement*. In K. Knabb (Ed.), *Situationist international anthology* (pp. 8–14). Berkeley: Bureau of Public Secrets.

DeLuca, K. (1999, Summer). Unruly arguments: The body rhetoric of Earth First!, ACT UP, and Queer Nation. *Argumentation and Advocacy, 36*, 9–21.

Durland, S. (1998). Witness: the guerilla theater of Greenpeace. In J. Cohen Cruz (Ed.), *Radical street performance: An international anthology* (pp. 67–73). New York: Routledge.

Foucault, M. (1978). *The history of sexuality* (Vol. 1). New York: Vintage Books.

Jovanovich, M. (2002, January 3). Interview with Yellow Overall TFG Casper. Retrieved on March 13, 2002, from http://slalsh.autonomedia.org.

Kershaw, B. (1997). Fighting in the streets: Dramaturgies of popular protest, 1968–1989. *New Theatre Quarterly, 13*, 255–266.

Kingsworth, P. (2001, September). It's the democracy, stupid. *The Ecologist, 31*, 40–44.

La Rosa, L. (2001, September). *Tute Bianche*—an army of dreamers? *The Ecologist, 31*, 44.

Lebel, J. (1969). Notes on political street theatre, Paris: 1968, 1969. *The Drama Review, 13*(4), 111–118.

Klein, N. (2001, June 8). Squatters in white overalls. *The Guardian*, 23.

Moose. (2001, February 13). [S-26 Global] NYC Ya Basta! Collective Website. Message posted to a-infos-d@ainfos.ca.

Roberts, A. (1996). The ironies of System D. In C. Cerny & S. Seriff (Eds.), *Recycled re-Seen: Folk art from the global scrap heap* (pp. 82–101). New York: Harry N. Abrams, Inc.

Schechner, R. (1993). *The future of ritual: Writings on culture and performance.* London: Routledge.

Turner, K. (1996). *Hacer cosas*: recycled arts and the making of identity in Texas-Mexican culture. In C. Cerny & S. Seriff (Eds.), *Recycled re-seen: Folk art from the global scrap heap* (pp. 60–71). New York: Harry N. Abrams, Inc.

Vaneigem, R. (1994). *The revolution of everyday life.* Seattle: Left Bank Books.

Vidal, J. (2001, July 19). White knights say "Enough" to G8. *The Guardian*, F17.

Wright, S. (2000, October 28). Changing the world (one bridge at a time)? Ya Basta after Prague. Retrieved February 18, 2002, from http://www.geocities.com/swervedc/www.yabasta.it.

"Ya Basta(rds)!" [Electronic version]. Willful disobedience, 2. Retrieved July 1, 2002, from http://www.geocities.com/kk_abacus/vb/wd8yabasta/html.

Yellow Overalls Organizing Tips. Retrieved February 28, 2002, from http://free.freespeech.org/yabasta/orgtips.html.

3

Like Moths to a Flame— Culture Jamming and the Global Spectacle

Åsa Wettergren

INTRODUCTION

The globalization of economic discourse has triggered a contentious response in the form of the globalization of collective action (Ayres, 2001; Castells, 1997; Cohen & Rai, 2000; Smith, 2001; Thörn, 1999; Williams & Ford, 1999). The massive protests concerning global free trade are impressive and may indicate a new era of social movement mobilization (Tarrow, 1994). However, it is unclear what effects these protests will have on the process of economic globalization.

The importance of the mass media as an arena for political struggle is continually emphasized by both researchers and activists (Carroll & Ratner, 1999; Gitlin, 1980; Oskarsson & Peterson, 2001; Williams & Ford, 1999). In the 1950s, even when the phenomenon of television and the mass media was in its youth, the Situationists developed strategies of protesting to attract media attention. From the Situationists' deployment of strategic media-oriented activism, it is possible to follow a number of developing activist strategies, among them the contemporary phenomenon of culture jamming. Other lines of development include a variety of creative street happenings such as installations, street theatre, street parties, and university sit-ins (Thörn, 1997b).

The manifestations and demonstrations of the Global Justice Movement (GJM) tend to involve all kinds of spectacular events. However, so far mass media attention largely has concentrated on the violent protests that usually accompany the peaceful demonstrations. The alternative discourses forwarded by the movement organizations if referred to at all, tend to be fragmented and transmitted in crippled versions by the media. Meanwhile, as seen during the G8 top meeting in Geneva 2001, states respond to the protests by proclaiming a temporary state of emergency during these events, directly violating democratic rights by use of force and repression (Smith, 2001). Through the subtle workings of the mass media and the less subtle workings of the state violence apparatus, serious critics of a hegemonic neoliberal economic discourse are kept excluded and marginalized. Culture jamming appears to be a promising resistance strategy, particularly its specialization in the manipulation of mainstream media and its deconstruction of hegemonic discourses.

In this chapter, I analyze key texts of culture jamming and give examples of the inner tensions, conflicts, and ambivalences displayed within these texts. I argue that these tensions represent the dynamics of a movement in formation, as well as conflicts, tensions, and ambivalences of our time. (While I do not discuss whether culture jamming really *is* a movement, the notion of jamming as a "movement" is an expressed intent of one of the editors.) Finally I explore briefly the relationship between the Global Justice Movement and culture jamming, and the possibility that culture jamming may become a renewed and complimentary resource in the action repertoire of GJM activists.

Important to note, I associate the concept of "postmodernity" with "contemporary society." I refer to the concept of "postmodernity" in two ways. First, postmodernity is a Western cultural experience originating in consumer culture (see, for instance, Bauman, 1992, 1997; Best & Kellner, 1997; Featherstone, 1998; Tetzlaff, 1992). As will be discussed later, consumer culture and postmodernity are closely interrelated. Second, I use the concept of postmodernity in terms of Torfing (1999, p. 60) as a "movement which at once *splits, radicalizes* and *weakens* modernity" (see, too, Seidman, 1994). In this latter sense, postmodernity interferes with modernity while still continually interwoven in it. It is not about a radical break but rather a radicalization of *some* inherent traits of modernity (e.g., individualization, fragmentation, distrust of grand narratives) rather than others (order, progress, unity). "Postmodernity" comprises a range of both subjective experiences and objective structural changes that other social theorists prefer to cover by concepts such as "late modernity" (Giddens, 1995), "network society" (Castells, 1998), and "information age" (Melucci, 1996).

THE ORIGINS OF CULTURE JAMMING

Culture jamming is a symbolic form of protest in the sense that it targets central symbols of dominant discourses, deconstructs the discourses, and reintroduces the symbols in alternative contexts. Culture jamming includes practices such as urban graffiti and changing the message of a billboard. It also comprises the creation of an independent media and highly professional media products with a critical message, and computer hacking, transmission jamming, and pirate broadcasting (Dery, 1993a, p. 6). A range of groups, organizations, and single individuals may claim to be culture jammers but the exact means and ends vary. Most culture jammers tend to be activists involved with the mass media and mass communication in the broadest sense of those words, though one may find culture jammers who prefer face-to-face interaction with the audience through creative happenings in the street.

Various sources agree on the origin of the term "culture jamming." The coining of the term is said to come from the San Fransisco audio-collage band, Negativland, in 1984 (Dery, 1993a; Klein, 1999, p. 281; Lasn, 1999, p. 217). However, the practice of culture jamming dates back to the Situationist strategy of *détournement*, which literally means "turning around" or "turning upside down." The emergence of the Situationists in the 1950s has been interpreted as an attempt to update Marxist theory to the specific conditions of consumer society (Best & Kellner, 1997).[1] Anticipating the French postmodern turn, the Situationists argued that an expanding consumer culture and the emergence of the mass media had turned society into a seductive "spectacle." The working class had raised its living standards but lost its critical awareness, its needs and demands being shaped by consumer culture. With the strategy of détournement and the creation of *situations*—visions of another world possible beyond the false illusions of consumer society—the Situationists declared a cultural war against the spectacle (Thörn, 1997b).

The historical connection to the Situationists is apparently well acknowledged among culture jammers (Klein, 1999, pp. 282–283). Kalle Lasn, the leader of The Media Foundation Adbusters, located in Canada, positions culture jammers as the heirs of the Situationists. In Lasn's (1999, p. 100) account, the Situationists were "the first postmodern revolutionaries." The critical theory of consumer culture and the mass media developed by the Situationists obviously fits well into the social context of contemporary culture jammers. For the culture jammers today, perhaps more than ever before, the hold of consumer culture and the mass mediated illusion of democratic freedoms conceal a reality of conformist resignation under hegemonic neoliberal ideology.

The Media Foundation Adbusters (MFA) was founded in 1989. It publishes and distributes worldwide the culture jammer magazine *Adbusters*, runs the website Culture Jammers Headquarters (www.adbusters.org), and organizes the Powershift Advocacy Advertising Agency, the latter of which produces social campaigns, subvertisements, spoof-ads, and TV uncommercials. The Media Foundation also sponsors the annual events of Buy Nothing Day (November 29, 2002) and Turn off TV Week (April 22–28, 2002).

Though culture jammers have adopted the practice of détournement as well as parts of the social critique developed by the Situationists, they seem to carefully avoid any reference to the Marxist concepts still put forth by the Situationists. This may be explained by the fact that culture jammers do not want to be associated with the old Left movement. Given that the autonomous individual being is central to culture jammers, there is even a tendency to dissociate from the very idea of a "mass movement." MFA is one of the few—and probably the most persistent—culture jamming organizations that actually attempts to forward a single coherent narrative for "the culture jammers movement." However, the role of the MFA is disputed and has been criticized by other culture jammers.

EFFORTS TO HEGEMONIZE THE MEANING OF CULTURE JAMMING

Culture jammers connect explicitly or implictly to a large spectrum of theoretical discourses about consumer society, postmodernism, and the mass media. The adoption of a Situationist discourse appears to be much stronger and more important to the MFA than to other culture jammers, a choice which can be described as both the reason and the consequence of the hegemonizing ambitions of Kalle Lasn.

In Klein's (1999) account of culture jamming, cultural critic Mark Dery stands out as the author of the original culture jammers manifesto in 1993. Dery (1993b) describes America as a virtual society, and "a TV democracy" characterized by widespread ignorance and "aliteracy."[2] The public mind is "colonized by corporate phantasms." In contrast, culture jammers are "visually literate ghostbusters." Culture jamming is "engaged politics . . . in an empire of signs" and it is "semiological guerrilla warfare" targeting "an ever more intrusive, instrumental technoculture whose operant mode is the manufacture of consent through the manipulation of symbols" (p. 5).

Dery (1993b) describes the practice of culture jamming as one based on a shared experience of repression and manipulation by both the mass media and the commercial industry. Though being widely inclusive in his account of culture jamming, Dery does, however, draw a line that prevents the use of the concept of culture jamming in a struggle for a nondemocratic society. Culture jamming can be identified within the limits of a shared struggle, the deconstruction of hegemony in favor of a radically pluralistic society. Central to this is the *true* freedom of expression where "the univocal world view promulgated by corporate media yields to a multivocal, polyvalent one" (p. 12). The means and the end of the struggle coincide as the culture jammer fights for her right for expression by expressing herself in illegal or semi-illegal ways, and in places and contexts allocated for commercial interests only.

The centrality of the freedom of expression may be partly explained by the shared experience of culture jammers suggested by Dery. While the goal of expression is awarded more importance than other democratic rights, it must also be understood against the backdrop of the emergence of the Internet and cyberspace. Jordan (2000) argues that it is characteristic of the cybernetic universe of the Internet that the main issues for power struggles are connected with the freedom of expression. Analyzing cyberpower at the levels of the individual, the social and the imaginary, Jordan concludes that cyberpolitics departs from the assumption that everything—including subjectivity—is or can be turned into codes of information. To fight for the freedom of information/expression becomes the similar fight for the freedom of the individual.

The freedom of expression/information is one of central importance to the MFA as well. The so called "Media Carta" of the MFA holds that "Every human being has the 'right to communicate'—to receive and impart information through any media" (Lasn, 1999, p. 124). However, Media Carta is only *one among several* central ambitions of the movement Lasn tries to "launch." The overall goal of the MFA is to ignite a revolution and build a new society. Unlike the inclusive and vague formulation of a movement identity in Dery's account, Lasn is quite explicit. Culture jamming, Lasn asserts, is an emerging global anticorporate social movement. It is equivalent in importance and impact with the movements of past decades, such as civil rights, feminism, and environmentalism (p. xi). Consequently, in his use of the concept, Lasn repeatedly tries to construct culture jamming as a movement, a strategy, and a lifestyle.

Lasn's (1999) book, *Culture Jam,* functions as an awareness-raising and a "do-it-yourself" type of manual. It implies that the structural preconditions for becoming a culture jammer are objective. What becomes necessary is the push to see the new consciousness. The awareness-raising of the culture jammer in Lasn's account is described as a sudden insight rather than a slow process, and as a personal experience rather than a product of collective action. Lasn writes, "We weren't looking for it necessarily, but each one of us in our own way has had a political awakening; a series of very personal 'moments of truth' about ourselves and how the world works" (p. xii). While the final insight to be reached by the moments of truth is pretty much the same as the aforementioned grievances of the Situationists, or the culture jammers in Dery's account, Lasn's language is considerably more emotional and popular, and addresses primarily an American audience. He continually contrasts the American self-image—a people characterized by "rugged individualism and heroic personal sacrifice in the pursuit of a dream" with "the truth" (p. 77). The truth is that the American "revolutionary spirit" is suppressed and the "once proud people [are] reduced to servitude" (p. 77). In this account, the oppressors are identified as the large corporations, the mass media, and the advertising industry.

Thus, the American spirit must be liberated and people must realize that the American corporate dream runs contrary to the American peoples' dream.

In *Culture Jam*, Lasn (1999) takes the reader through six steps that will "spark a dramatic personal mind-shift that will change the way you relate to corporations" (p. 146). These steps teach the reader to reject ready-made commercial culture and frames of discourse, to reframe the grounds of communication, and to confront injustice in interactions with large corporations.

Lasn emphasizes "the revolutionary impulse" all through his book, and the liberation of the American people is very closely related to a liberation of suppressed emotions, specifically anger or rage. "Rage," he writes, "drives revolutions" (p. 139). Thus, becoming aware of the truth about our present illusionary existence will liberate rage and spark the revolution. Unlike the "moments of truth," the revolution is a collective experience and a collective action, perhaps implying that once the truth is clear to everyone, a collective will can emerge, allowing the American people to throw off their chains and tear down the oppressors. The task of the culture jammers is to act as "the advance shock troups" (p. xi).

Nevertheless, Lasn (1999) seems to draw indirectly from a conventional revolutionary movement discourse when he emphasizes the "newness" of his movement. Although Lasn, like Dery, underlines the heterogeneity of the people calling themselves culture jammers, he makes an effort to formulate a unifying collective narrative. Whereas Dery seems content to settle for a loosely organized network of culture jammers more or less unified through shared experience and democratic values, the "we" of Lasn is more exacting. According to Lasn, culture jammers "share . . . an overwhelming rage against consumer capitalism, and a vague sense that our time has come to act as a collective force" (p. 112). Lasn's culture jammer, it appears, does not seek to attain heterogeneity and plurality, rather unity and truth.

It thus seems that the MFA shelter a tension between their wish to realize, on the one hand, a society of freedom of information, and, on the other hand, the belief that they are the carriers of objective truth. Furthermore, Lasn's tension between the individual characteristics of a strategy like culture jamming, skillfully used in his book, and the unifying collective ambition is bound to cause problems. Lasn both promotes and supports the culture jammer as an individualist, and tries to incorporate him or her into the collective agenda of his movement.

Increased individualization in contemporary society poses a problem to traditional forms of collective mobilization. Culture jamming is interesting because it emerges in the contemporary as a pluralistic and ambivalent field of activists who are ambitious in their efforts to invent new, individualized, and creative forms of collective action. It is possible that the vague unity articulated by Dery could actually be enough to create a sense of solidarity between individuals. Collective action in an individualized society must succeed to build on "social individuals" rather than traditional collectives, as argued by McRobbie (2001). Individualization then must be looked upon as a process distinct from the development of neoliberal values (Beck, 1997; McRobbie, 2001). Lasn's movement discourse indicates that he struggles to account for contemporary individualism and the need to reinterpret collective action, while simultaneously rejecting the contemporary as a neoliberal ideological illusion altogether.

For Dery, a culture jammer struggles for radical democracy. For Lasn, a culture jammer is the holder of truth, a revolutionary leading the people. Besides an expression of a contemporary dilemma of the collective versus the individual, perhaps what we see is the well-known conflict between revolutionary and reformative strategies in the construction of a movement identity (Tarrow, 1994; Thörn, 1997a, 1997b). In the case of culture jamming, the extremes of this spectre would consist of, on the one hand, "the merry prankster" and, on the other hand, "the hard-core revolutionary" (Klein, 1999). This dialectic points to the culture jammer's paradoxical position in postmodernity.

BETWEEN POSTMODERN PLAY AND CULTURAL CONSERVATISM, OR BETWEEN IRONY AND BLOODY REVOLUTION

Although Lasn (1999) and the MFA promote the idea that anyone can become a culture jammer, the most sophisticated culture jams seem to demand a considerable amount of symbolic and cultural capital, with regards both to production and consumption. As frequently mentioned by Lasn, the practice of culture jamming attracts people from academic, art, and media professions, and design and marketing. Dery (1993b) also asserts that culture jammers are "visually literate" implying their capacity to see through the spectacle (p. 5).

Lasn (1999) has a background in marketing, so it is no coincidence that the MFA are involved in the renewal of the First Things First Manifesto. The original version was written by British designer Ken Garland in 1964 and was signed by twenty-two "graphic designers, photographers, and students." The document holds that the purpose of selling trivial products is a waste of the advertiser's talents and skills, and "contribute[s] little or nothing to our national prosperity." Instead, advertisements should be used for information, education, and awareness-raising. An interesting passage maintains, "We do not advocate the abolition of high-pressure consumer advertising: this is not feasible. Nor do we want to take any of the fun out of life" (http://adbusters.org/campaigns/first/toolbox/1964.html).

The renewed 2000 document, written by British graphic designer Jonathan Barnbrook in cooperation with the MFA, is signed by thirty-two "graphic designers, art directors, and visual communicators." The content is largely similar, while more emphasis is put on the negative aspects of consumer culture and on the necessity of the communicative skills of the undersigned to be used in "the exploration and production of a new kind of meaning." It further states that the "scope of debate is shrinking . . . [c]onsumerism is running uncontested." This state of affairs must be challenged "by other perspectives expressed, in part, through the visual languages and resources of design" (http://adbusters.org/campaigns/first/tour/2.html). In an additional text, Lasn further underlines the importance of the "designers," asserting that whether they know it or not "their profession is one of the key sites of struggle over the production and distribution of meaning" (http://adbusters.org/campaigns/first/toolbox/designanarchy/1.html).

Missing from the renewed manifesto is the reservation against "taking the fun out of life," nor is there any reference to "national prosperity" as the new document is composed with an eye to "global commercial culture" and breathes a post–nation-state spirit. The exclusion of "fun" is, I suggest, a response to the ambivalent position held by the culture jammer/converted advertiser.

The connection between postmodernism and consumer culture is widely theorized (Bauman, 1992; Featherstone, 1998; Tetzlaff, 1992). With the concept of *cultural intermediaries* (Bourdieu, 1999), it is possible to outline this complex interaction of social positioning, consumer culture, and post-modernism. A fraction of the middle classes, cultural intermediaries, Bourdieu argues, emerge in the wake between traditional upper class and traditional middle class. The new middle classes try to position themselves in the social field by creating a need for their own skills and services. They are attracted to high-risk/high-profit/open career-possibility occupations, particularly those *intermediary* positions involving "presentation and rep-resentation (sales, marketing, advertising, public relations, fashion, decora-tion, and so forth) and in all the institutions providing symbolic goods and services" (p. 359). As cultural intermediaries, they position themselves as vanguards in the struggles over the art of living, consumption, and culture, and they successfully disseminate their values to the larger population.[3] They embrace a "fun ethic," or values of joy and fun as opposed to tradi-tional modern bourgeois values of asceticism and duty, that is, to the degree that pleasure almost becomes a duty.

Cultural intermediaries, then, are products and producers of consumer culture who are deeply involved in consumer culture and the development of a consumer attitude, or a consumer morality (Bauman, 1990; Bourdieu, 1999). In this sense, they are the carriers of postmodernity, the dissolution of categories, and the erasing of traditional social and cultural boundaries. The question is whether the "fun ethic" can be a source of resistance to the spectacle and consumer culture.

To Lasn (1999), the answer is to suppress the whole idea of fun emerg-ing from consumer culture. He manifestly contests the idea of joyful post-modernity and describes it instead as a degenerated condition to be overcome. A postmodern attitude to Lasn is an attitude of resignation or cynicism, thus counterproductive to the very idea of resistance. "Postmodern cynicism," he writes, ". . . is powerlessness, disconnection and shame" (p. 141).

Consequently, the MFA, as expected, can be categorized under the more hard-core revolutionary end of the spectrum. This latter stance leads the MFA to sometimes adopt a moralistic finger-pointing tone in its visuals and texts. Klein (1999) writes that the MFA is often criticized by other culture jammers of engaging in moralizing. I also argue that the unease and some-times careful dissociation of culture jammers from the MFA may have to do directly with the organization's attempt to hegemonize the meaning of culture jamming.

Although asserting that human beings are free, creative, and wild, and that life should be lived fully without dead time—values that could easily be assimilated in a consumer morality—Lasn (1999) seems determined to suppress any ambiguity and raise a distinction. Culture jamming can be fun, not because it allows us to play with consumer products and use our skills in the techniques of persuasion in a subversive way, but because it releases our authentic human nature and its revolutionary potential. In contrast, Dery's (1993b) open attitude toward ambiguity accentuates the fun in using the tools of consumer culture and mass media as the primus motor of cul-ture jamming *for its own sake* as much as for the purpose of social change. According to Dery, culture jammers are "ever mindful of the fun to be had in the joyful demolition of oppressive ideologies" (p. 6). He further quotes, Jello Biafra, who asks, "What better way to survive our anthill society than by abusing the very mass media that sedates the public? . . . A prank a day keeps the dog leash away!"(p. 6).

Such a tolerance of ambiguity is also expressed by Jonah Peretti, a former MIT graduate student and current director of Research and Development at Eyebeam in New York City. Peretti (2001) writes that "culture jamming is a . . . movement that celebrates the possibility of ironic, humorous and contradictory political actions" (p. 2).

Though not all culture jams are directly related to advertising and mar-keting, it is highly likely that most practitioners have a background in aca-demia, art, marketing, or media. I suggest that, in the culture jammers, we may observe the fun ethic born out of affluent consumer culture and then turned against itself, making culture jamming a strongly ambiguous and ambivalent practice. Practitioners, as I have given examples of, may deal with the ambivalence either through suppression or tolerance.

Part of the tolerant attitude is the culture jammer's characteristic use of irony. As observed by Wahl, Holgersson, and Höök (1998) in a study of female leadership, irony can be used as a strategy to effect structural changes. Even in cases where irony has no external impact, it serves as a way to release the pressure of ambivalent positions, such as the position of female leaders in a gendered power structure that subordinates women. Wahl, Holgersson, and Höök also conclude that the understanding of irony rests on shared experiences and knowledge. Both the person producing the irony and the receiver must know the context and be able to interpret it with similar frames. Analogous to these findings, culture jammers' use of irony can be seen as both a strategy to reveal contingency in hegemonic discourse, and as a way to transcend the paradoxical dependency of the consumer culture they wish to change. As a mobilizing strategy, however, the effectiveness of irony is uncertain. In the consumption of culture jamming, the ironic message can be hard to detect or appreciate by people who are not familiar with the originally intended message, or simply do not recognize the need for or value of the critique. This would suggest that the culture jams merely mobilize the already mobilized, and that they mobilize primarily from the fractions of the upper and middle classes. It seems the MFA have drawn the consequences of this in parts of their production. For example, some of their uncommercials (directed at a mass audience via television) are less ironic and more overtly moralizing, playing on emotions of fear and shock.[4]

In this section, I argue that culture jammers are recruited from the cultural intermediaries imbued by postmodernity and consumer culture, and that culture jamming can be interpreted as fun ethics "turned around." I also suggest that the ambiguity of this move can be seen as characteristic of "postmodern politics" (Best & Kellner, 2001; Burbach, 2001). Postmodern politics further can be fruitfully linked to Jordan's (2000) analysis of "cyberpolitics." Arguing that libertarian discourse is characteristic of cyberpolitics, Jordan asserts that cyberspace emerges as an ideal free marketplace of ideas. Through this discourse, cyber-elites and grassroots alike legitimize their privileged positions as a result of "individual liberty as played out in the free market of goods and ideas" (p. 8). Individual liberty and free markets, notably part of the postmodern utopias (Bauman, 1995, p. 136), are also core issues of cyberpolitics. This is worth mentioning as we now proceed to the *meme concept* used in cyberpolitics. The use of the concept by culture jammers then should come as no surprise.

INFORMATION, ADVERTISEMENT, OR PROPAGANDA? THE MEME CONCEPT

In January 2001 Jonah Peretti ordered a pair of customized Nike shoes with the word "sweatshop" printed on them. Peretti (2001) writes that this prank was an act of culture jamming, intended to "redirect Nike's publicity machine against the company it is supposed to promote" (p. 1).

The request resulted in an e-mail correspondence with representatives of Nike, in which Peretti upholds an ironic but polite tone, whereas the representatives carefully avoid to enter the topic of sweatshops. First they explain that they can not print the word, "sweatshop," because it is "inappropriate slang." When Peretti shows that the word and its explanation exists in *Webster's Dictionary* and belongs to standard English, Nike responds by referring to a clause in which they reserve the right to turn down "material that we consider inappropriate or simply do not want to place on our products."[5] This could have been the end of story, if Peretti had not mailed the correspondence to a hand full of friends where "immediately it began racing around the world like a virus" (p. 2).

To explain the rapid dispersion of his "Nike Adventure," Peretti makes use of the concept of memes. This concept was coined by biologist Richard Dawkins in the last chapter of his book *The Selfish Gene*, first published in 1976. Memes are "tunes, ideas, catch-phrases, clothes fashions, [and] ways of making pots or building arches" (Dawkins, 1989, p. 4). Memes spread "by leaping from brain to brain via a process which, in the broad sense, can be called imitation" (p. 4). Arguing that memes are analogous to genes, Dawkins separates human ideas from human agency. Memes are self-replicating entities living in the human brain and human culture is the product of meme replication.

In 1976, Dawkins argued that memes had an advantage to genes in that they can spread quicker via the emerging mass media, and thus do not need human generations to reproduce. Consequently—to its advocators—the development of computers and the Internet seems to reinforce the relevance of the meme concept.[6]

The connection between memes and electronic media is discussed by Peretti (2001) who attempts to understand how his "Nike-meme" jumped from micromedia to middle media and eventually reached mainstream mass media. Peretti defines micromedia as all personal communications technologies, including face-to-face conversation. Middle media is described as "emerging publishing technologies that help communities filter and aggregate the messy jumble of content produced by micromedia," primarily websites run by private persons (p. 6). Peretti argues that the structure of the mass media leads journalists to look for news stories among the middle media sites, and this is how they picked up his "Nike Sweatshop meme."

This example shows how culture jammers may experiment with funny and inventive ways to access the mass media. Using their knowledge about the structural conditions shaping the methods and interests of the mass media, culture jammers may succeed in "advertising" critical messages that normally would have been selected out.

The existence and workings of memes is also a basic assumption in the MFA narrative. Lasn (1999) speaks about "meme warfare" and asserts that "potent memes can change minds, alter behaviour, catalyze collective mind-shifts and transform cultures" (p. 123). He suggests five core "meta-memes" that culture jammers should help to spread, among them the aforementioned Media Carta.[7]

The use of the meme concept elucidates some inconsistencies in Lasn's (1999) texts. First, embracing the Situationist idea that humans are "born creative, free, and wild," and capable of creating their own authentic culture is not necessarily contradicted by Lasn's adoption of the meme concept.[8] He actually argues that it is the indoctrination of the mass media and advertising industry that makes people passive receivers of the "wrong" memes. Yet, there is an obvious difference between those who produce their own memes and can identify the bad ones, and those who are presumed to be more or less passive receivers of any meme appearing on their TV screens. Thus, secondly, the use of the meme concept provides Lasn with an alternative to traditional mobilization, and helps explain the very central role he ascribes to designers and advertisers. Lasn's "culture jamming movement" is not necessarily contingent upon successful awareness-raising, but upon successful dissemination, or the marketing of the "right" memes. From this angle, the glossy magazines and spoof-ads are quite consistent with the hard-core revolutionary goal of the MFA.

I also suggest that the way the meme concept is adopted by the MFA represents a contemporary dissolution of the categories of information, advertisement, and propaganda. We live in a society in which the increased circulation of information and the increased academic and popular awareness of the contingency of discourse have undermined the objective status of information. In a sense, all information including propaganda or advertisements therefore depends to some extent on mechanisms of persuasion, not on any discourse's undisputed link to objective conditions.

It is a common feature of culture jammers that they struggle for the freedom of expression in any media and the public space. To the MFA, however, the goal of the freedom of information is a stepping-stone toward an entirely new social order. In spite of the critique mentioned earlier, the MFA seems to coexist with a vast amount of other culture jamming groups and individuals, who unlike the MFA tend to deliberately stay away from any formulation of a movement narrative. If the hegemonizing ambitions of Lasn become "too successful," however, some groups most likely will dissociate more clearly from the MFA.

I proceed to briefly discuss culture jamming as a resource in the Global Justice Movement. My argument here remains tentative as, at the time of writing, I am continuing to collect data on culture jamming in the global arena.

CULTURE JAMMING AND THE GLOBAL JUSTICE MOVEMENT

The preliminary results of my interviews[9] conducted with culture jammers confirm the picture of culture jamming as a strongly individualized form of resistance, engaging people who would avoid mass demonstrations or large manifestations. If culture jammers are recruited from the "cultural intermediaries," or the carriers of postmodernity, as I have suggested, it is probably because of the way culture jamming is constructed. Jamming remains tolerant of ambiguity and allows fun rather than dogma to fuel protest.

There are signs of interaction and exchange between culture jamming and street activism. During the 2002 World Economic Forum in New York, I was told that culture jammers would cooperate with activists involved in the Global Justice Movement to protest events and supply demonstrators with communication technology. The invention of the "white overalls" was pointed out as influenced by culture jamming because of its creative and funny, and ironic components. Further, during the World Economic Forum some demonstrators were using shields covered with large pictures of babies. In a riot situation, the police would be facing an innocent child. These examples may indicate that culture jamming—meaning a creative, ironic and funny protest strategy—is being appropriated by street activists, and that the line between street activism and culture jamming is diffuse.

The relationship between culture jamming and the GJM can also be observed in the activities of the MFA. Whereas their Powershift Advocacy Advertising Agency helps produce professional media campaigns for any person or organization with "the right cause," culture jammers' website spreads activist stories and testimonies from the streets of top meeting demonstrations, for instance, Seattle 1999. The MFA has also produced a series of short videos promoting their memes, and around the time of important top meetings they seem to spend a lot of effort and resources to buy space for the anti-ads and airtime for their videos. These activities can be followed at the website (www.adbusters.org). In this sense, the MFA site works a little bit like an independent media site, such as Indy Media, but, unlike the latter, transmitting alternative news from all over the world is not the main purpose of the MFA.

However speculative the previous examples are, culture jamming as a creative way to reinvent protesting may no doubt be employed by street activists, whereas on the other hand the struggle for freedom of expression is also embraced by and enhanced by independent news media sites. Culture jamming as a vaguely defined identity further shares its features with some of the organizations involved in the GJM. One example is the identification of global corporations/neoliberal economic globalization as the core enemy. As culture jammers are most likely "media literate," knowing how to create and manipulate signs, symbols, and frames, their knowledge of and belief in the power of discourse and the mechanisms of persuasion may be quite fruitful in the use of the GJM's goals and issues.

CONCLUDING REMARKS

In this chapter I have analyzed some central culture jamming texts to identify inner conflicts in the construction of the meaning of culture jamming. Through the examples of collectivism-individualism, the meme concept, consumer culture dependency, and the fun ethics, I have demonstrated how culture jamming discourses are connected to and represent central tensions of postmodernity. I argue that the culture jammer most likely is a product and carrier of postmodernity, making culture jamming a profoundly ambivalent form of protest.

As we have seen, within the culture jamming discourse, there are differences in the way these tensions are handled. Lasn and the MFA tend to suppress ambivalence and reject postmodernity, making them vulnerable to accusations of moralizing. Other culture jammers, however, seem to celebrate the capacity of culture jamming to shelter and tolerate ambivalence.

Culture jamming discourses are largely contingent upon the development of the mass media and the information technology, particularly the Internet and the idea of cyberspace. I have demonstrated this with the example of the meme concept and the central culture jamming struggle for the freedom of expression/information.

As we have seen there are connections between the activists involved in the GJM and culture jamming. Further data collection and analysis is needed to understand how they are connected, and how culture jamming as a strategy might be used by other activists. We also need to know if and in what sense the culture jammer's identity makes her different from more "collectively oriented" activists.

This being said, I believe that the tensions and core issues of culture jamming may be found also in a majority of the activist groups involved in the GJM. The construction of a movement in postmodernity has to deal with the challenges of increased individualization; with the problem of representation/hegemonization in the construction of a movement discourse; with the expansion of the Internet and increased flows of information, while the mainstream mass media become increasingly exclusive and hard to access; and finally, with the troublesome dependency on affluent consumer culture and its fun ethics. However, I believe that culture jamming lends itself particularly well to the study of these tensions, because it is still largely tolerated, sometimes even celebrated here. Ambivalence seems to be at the very heart of culture jamming. The question is if this will be subject to change as—provided that the MFA mobilizing strategy is successful—the MFA markets the idea of the "culture jamming movement."

NOTES

1. The Situationist International was constituted in Paris 1957 by a group of European avant-garde artists, influenced by Dadaism and Surrealism, Anarchism and Marxism. Its central intellectual Guy Debord published *The Society of the Spectacle* in 1967 (Debord, 1994). See further Best and Kellner, 1997 and Thörn, 1997b.

2. Roger Cohen, "The rejection of books by children and young adults who know how to read but choose not to" (quoted by Dery in Dery, 1993, p. 2).

3. According to Bourdieu, one distinguishing feature of the new petite bourgeoisie is "its sense of legitimacy in teaching others the legitimate life-style . . .

that of the dominant class, or, more precisely, of the fractions which constitute its ethical avant-garde" (Bourdieu, 1999, p. 365). The new petite bourgeoise thus collaborate with the new bourgeoise in developing norms and values necessary for "the new logic of the economy" (p. 366).

4. The attempt to lift culture jamming from a disparate and mainly individual underground practice to a more organized level might have caused the MFA to direct more efforts into systematic mobilization. Coupled with a moralistic attitude and a tendency to transgress the balance between irony and the pathetic or the highflown, what is sometimes left in the Adbuster's media products is a rather propaganda-like way of marketing the idea of demarketing. I will carry out this analysis in a future article.

5. The full correspondence can be seen on urbanlegends.about.com/library/blnike.htm.

6. Thus Swedish-English professor of Economy, Claes Gustafsson (1994) argues that thanks to computers—the idea and development of which in itself is a meme—"the fungus" (i.e., the meme parasite) has "started to think independently [of humans], it has exported pieces of itself outside its traditional medium" (p. 146).

7. MFA forward five so-called meta-memes—"the core ideas without which a sustainable future is unthinkable" (Lasn, 1999, p. 124): **True Cost:** In the global marketplace of the future, the price of every product will tell the ecological truth. **Demarketing:** The marketing enterprise has now come full circle. The time has come to *unsell* the product and turn the incredible power of marketing against itself. **The Doomsday Meme:** The global economy is a doomsday machine that must be stopped and reprogrammed. **No Corporate "I":** Corporations are not legal "persons" with constitutional rights and freedoms of their own, but legal fictions that we ourselves created and must therefore control. **Media Carta:** Every human being has the "right to communicate"—to receive and impart information through any media.

8. Dawkins (1989) does not dismiss human agency. On the contrary he writes that "we have the power to defy the selfish genes of our birth and, if necessary, the selfish memes of our indoctrination" (Dawkins, 1989, p. 8).

9. Five tape-recorded in-depth interviews with representatives from four different culture jamming organizations in NYC, collected in March 2002.

REFERENCES

Ayres, J. M. (2001). Transnational political processes and contention against the global economy. *Mobilization, 6*(1), 55–68.

Bauman, Z. (1990). *Att tänka sociologiskt*. Göteborg: Korpen.

———. (1992). *Intimations of postmodernity*. London: Routledge.

———. (1995). *Life in fragments*. London: Blackwell.

———. (1997). *Postmodernity and its discontents*. Cambridge: Polity Press.

Beck, U. (1997). *The Reinvention of politics* (Mark Ritter, Trans.). Cambridge: Polity Press.

Best, S., & Kellner, D. (1997). *The postmodern turn*. New York: The Guilford Press.

———. (2001). *The postmodern adventure—Science, technology, and cultural studies at the Third Millennium*. London: Routledge.

Bourdieu, P. (1999). *Distinction—A social critique of the judgement of taste*. London: Routledge.

Burbach, R. (2001). *Globalization and postmodern politics—From Zapatistas to high tech robber barons*. London: Pluto Press.

Carroll, W. K., & Ratner, R. S. (1999). Media strategies and political projects: A comparative study of social movements. *Canadian Journal of Sociology*, 24(1), 1–34.

Castells, M. (1997). *The power of identity* (Vol. 2). London: Blackwell.

———. (1998). *Nätverkssamhällets framväxt* (Gunnar Sandin, Trans.) (Vol. 1). Göteborg: Daidalos.

Cohen, R., & Rai, S. M. (2000). Global social movements—Towards a cosmopolitan politics. In R. Cohen & S. M. Rai (Eds.), *Global Social Movements*. London: Athlone Press.

Dawkins, R. (1989). *The Selfish Gene*. Oxford: Oxford University Press.

Debord, G. (1994). *The Society of the spectacle*. New York: Zone Books.

Dery, M. (1993a). *Culture jaming: Hacking, slashing and sniping in the empire of signs*: Open Magazine Pamphlet Series.

———. (1993b). Culture jamming: Hacking, slashing and sniping in the empire of signs. [Internet]. gopher://gopher.well.sf.ca.us/00/cyberpunk/cultjam.txt [2001, June 29].

Featherstone, M. (1998). *Consumer culture and postmodernism*. London: SAGE.

Giddens, A. (1995). *The Consequences of modernity*. Cambridge: Polity Press.

Gitlin, T. (1980). *The whole world is watching*. Los Angeles: University of California.

Gustafsson, C. (1994). *Production av allvar—om dete konomiska for nuffets metafysik*. Stockholm. Nerenius & Santerus.

Jordan, T. (2000). *Cyberpower and the meaning of online activism* (Issue 5), [Internet]. Cybersociology: www.socio.demon.co.uk [2000, November 10, 2000].

Klein, N. (1999). *No logo—Taking aim at the brand bullies*. New York: Picador.

Lasn, K. (1999). *Culture jam—The uncooling of America*. New York: Eagle Brook.

McRobbie, A. (2001). *"Everyone is creative": Artists as new economy pioneers?* [Electronic Journal]. openDemocracy [2001, September 14].

Melucci, A. (1996). *Challenging codes—Collective action in the information age*. Cambridge: Cambridge University Press.

Oskarsson, M., & Peterson, A. (2001, August 28–September 1). *"Policing political protest"—A study of the police handling of political protest events in conjunction with the EU Summit Meeting in Göteborg, June 2001*. Paper presented at the Vision and Divisions—the 5th Congress of the European Sociological Association, Helsinki.

Peretti, J. (2001). *Culture jamming, memes, social networks, and the emerging media ecology*. Paper presented at the International Seminar on Political Consumerism, Stockholm University.

Seidman, S. (Ed.). (1994). *The postmodern turn—New perspectives on social theory*. Cambridge: Cambridge University Press.

Smith, J. (2001). Globalizing resistance: The battle of Seattle and the future of social movements. *Mobilization*, 6(1), 1–19.

Tarrow, S. (1994). *Power in movement—Social movements, collective action and politics*. Cambridge: Cambridge University Press.

Tetzlaff, D. (1992). Popular culture and social control in late capitalism. In P. Scannell, P. Schlesinger, & C. Sparks (Eds.), *Culture and power*. London: SAGE.

Thörn, H. (1997a). *Modernitet, sociologi och sociala rörelser*. Unpublished Monograph, Göteborg University, Göteborg.

———. (1997b). *Rörelser i det moderna—politik, modernitet och kollektiv identitet i Europa 1789–1989*. Stockholm: Tiden Athena.

———. Nya sociala rörelser och politikens globalisering—Demokrati utanför parlamentet, *Civilsamhället* (Vol. 8, pp. 425–468). Stockholm: Statens offentliga utredningar SOU 1999:84.

Torfing, J. (1999). *New Theories of discourse*. Oxford: Blackwell.

Wahl, A., Holgersson, C., & Höök, P. (1998). *Ironi & sexualitet—om ledarskap och kön*. Stockholm: Carlsson.

Williams, M., & Ford, L. (1999). The World Trade Organisation, Social Movements and Global Environmental Management. *Environment Politics, 8*(1), 268–289.

4

Punishment Before Prosecution: Pepper Spray as Postmodern Repression

Andy Opel

In October 1997, videotape of police officers holding the heads of environmental protesters and swabbing pepper spray in their eyes aired on national television in the United States. Although this was the first time this had been done to nonviolent protesters and the incident drew criticism from Amnesty International as well as public outcry nationwide, no officers were charged in the case and the images quickly faded from public consciousness. Unlike the 1991 videotape of Los Angeles police brutally beating Rodney King, which began a series of events that led to riots and the eventual imprisonment of three police officers, the pepper spray videos failed to galvanize a coherent response to any of the issues involved: police brutality, the rights of nonviolent protesters, or the larger environmental policy questions. This chapter will examine the media coverage of this case, the power of pepper spray as a less-lethal[1] police tool, and the connections of this precedent setting case to the continued police response to civil disobedience practiced by the global justice movement.

Although the Rodney King case and the pepper spray cases differ markedly, the disparity in the response by the public and public officials yields a series of questions. Why was there so much support for a victim of police brutality on a California highway and so little support for nonviolent environmental protesters exercising their First Amendment rights? Why was the use of night sticks to subdue a man called brutality while the illegal application of pepper spray was supported by the attorney general of the state of California? How does the pepper spray video and the public response to it fit into the larger context of environmental politics and the tradition of nonviolent civil disobedience in the United States in the late 1990s? How does the police use of pepper spray alter the terrain for public demonstrations? These are the questions that guide this inquiry into a particular incident of police brutality and the connections of that incident to the current conditions for public displays of political speech.

One place to look for part of the answer to these questions is the media. After all, it was the widespread distribution of the King video that elicited national outrage. The pepper spray video also received national television coverage. While both images were widely circulated on television, the print media played an ongoing role in contextualizing these images. Beyond any comparison to other events, the pepper spray video can be seen as part of a larger cultural discourse about the environment.

The politics of nature discourse embodies a historical tension between the forces of industrialization and the voices for preservation, conservation, and protection of the natural world. By examining the print coverage of the pepper spray cases of 1997 by major newspapers,[2] and placing that coverage within the politics of nature, I hope to uncover one piece of a complex web that can turn a single event into a cultural watershed or make it just another news story.

This chapter examines the media coverage of the 1997 pepper spray cases through a broad comparison with the media coverage of the Rodney King case aided by recent communication theory regarding the environmental movement and audience response to crisis coverage. I conclude with some theorizing about the relationship of this video event to the larger questions about representation and authenticity raised by postmodernism and the implications of this case on the recurring street protests of the Global Justice Movement.

BACKGROUND: GLOBALIZATION, REDWOODS, AND ENVIRONMENTAL PROTEST

The reasons these environmental protesters took the extreme actions of locking themselves together in a U.S. congressman's office are intimately connected to globalization. Charles Hurwitz, CEO of Maxxam Corporation, purchased Pacific Lumber Co. in a hostile takeover in 1986 and with that purchase, became the owner of over 200,000 acres of forest—half of the remaining stands of ancient redwood trees in the United States (Reinhold, 1991; Martin, 2001). Hurwitz is said to have orchestrated the purchase of Pacific Lumber with the help of Michael Milken, the convicted "junk bond" trader of the 1980s (Mills, 1998). Under Hurwitz' ownership, Pacific Lumber doubled the cut rate of the trees (Reinhold, 1991) while "raiding employee pension funds" to "pay off bonds" (Mills, 1998).

Beginning with the "Redwood Summer" protests of 1990, and continuing to this day, environmentalists have been pressuring state and federal
officials to protect the ancient trees from the saw. These protests have
included celebrity appearances such as Bonnie Raitt and Woody Harrelson
and even created a new celebrity in Julia "Butterfly" Hill, a tree sitter who
spent 738 days living atop a redwood (Hill, 2000). A tentative agreement
was reached in 1998 with the state of California and the federal government agreeing to pay Hurwitz $380 million for a 7,500-acres parcel of the
total 60,000-acre stand known as the "Headwaters Grove." Critics, including Green Party presidential candidate Ralph Nader, have attempted to link
Hurwitz' $1.6 billion savings and loan failure to a "debt for nature"
swap where Maxxam Corp. would be held responsible for their taxpayer-
sponsored bailout in the 1980s (Golden, 1996). Despite over twelve years
of political maneuvering, the ancient redwoods in the Headwaters Grove
continue to attract controversy, enacting the struggle between economic
development and environmental protection—a struggle that is being
repeated around the globe.

The protesters who were swabbed with pepper spray in 1997 were engaging this debate over the fate of the Headwaters Grove. In their direct action,
they were engaging the forces of globalization through the particulars of
this one issue.

COMMUNICATION THEORY 2002: AUDIENCE
AND THE ENVIRONMENT

As a way of situating the media coverage of the pepper spray cases in a
larger cultural context, this study draws on the ideas of "image politics"
and "compassion fatigue." In his book, *Image Politics: The New Rhetoric
of Environmental Activism,* Kevin DeLuca (1999) argues that the power of
extreme images (e.g., Greenpeace activists confronting whaling ships) has
driven a number of successful environmental campaigns. "Image events"
are said to be the new form of environmental persuasion, capitalizing on the
power of television to convey complex ideas in a few minutes of videotape.
I argue that the pepper spray cases represent a failed image event where
both the public and the media response were diminished by a cultural saturation of extreme environmental protesting and imagery. The proliferation
of environmental images is part of a larger pattern of image saturation in the
Western world, fueled by the expansion of television (cable and satellite) and
the Internet.

In her book, *Compassion Fatigue,* Susan Moeller (1999) describes the
process whereby the media turn international issues of war, famine, and
disease into "crisis coverage." Audience attention span is said to be calculated to determine how much coverage a given event will receive. Moeller
(1999) argues that the way the news media cover crisis "helps us to feel

overstimulated and bored all at once" (p. 9). Audience "fatigue," characterized by boredom and lack of interest in the news, appears when an issue recurs in the news, yet there is little opportunity for people to help address the issue. Thus, "famine" and "war" in foreign lands become familiar labels for crisis, labels that can be contained and avoided.

Most news generates images that remain anchored in a specific time and place. . . . But on occasion an epiphany occurs in an ongoing news story, a decisive moment is identified, and the essence of that story is crystallized into a compelling news icon. Many times that icon is a visual or a photographic one, for example: the training of the fire hoses on civil rights demonstrators in Birmingham. (Moeller, 1999, p. 48)

Clearly the Rodney King video became another "compelling news icon" with enduring significant social implications. The pepper spray videos, on the other hand, failed to achieve icon status.

RODNEY KING VERSUS PEPPER SPRAY: RACE AND GENDER DIFFERENCES

The King video and the pepper spray video differ in many ways. Examining intrinsic differences, and differences in news media portrayal of these events, provides a useful way to understand the disparity in how these two events were made to mean. Although the comparison between the King incident and the pepper spray case is problematic in many ways, the two incidents share the characteristic of videotaped police brutality that was aired nationwide. In attempting to compare these two incidents of videotaped police brutality, issues of race and gender come into play, in addition to the type of brutality and how it was inflicted.

On March 7, 1991, the *Los Angeles Times* ran three articles and an editorial about the Rodney King beating. In the 1,900-word lead article of the Metro section Home Edition, the *Times* made no mention of King's race, though the videotape made that evident to all who had seen it. The *Times* also published an edited transcript of King's account of the beating, which contained no reference to race. The third article was an overview piece about the history of police misconduct in LA. This piece ended with speculation about the influence of race. "Some of (LA Police Chief) Gate's famous remarks—that African-Americans are more susceptible to chokeholds, for example—suggest an endemic strain of racism in the LAPD" (Skolnick, 1991, p. B7). Similarly, the *Times* editorial focused on the issue of race. "Because the victim was black, the incident inevitably raises questions about police and race relations in LA. . . . The frightening images, captured by amateur cameraman George Holliday, are a grim reminder of a time and a place when all black people were fair game for cops" ("The Investigation," 1991). A *USA Today* story from the same day began: "Rodney King, the black victim of a brutal police beating . . ." (Stewart, 1991). Thus, the news text reinforced the visuals, establishing race as a motivation for the police behavior in the King beating.

Three incidents over the course of a six-week period in the fall of 1997 came to be known as the Pepper Spray Cases. In a front-page story, the *San Francisco Chronicle* outlined the series of events that took place at the Pacific Lumber Company office in the town of Scotia in Humboldt County. The first incident, on September 25, involved seven protesters locked together with metal sleeves preventing access to the handcuffs that linked them. The *Chronicle* reported that they were "repeatedly told to unlock the sleeves or the chemical agent would be used on them" (Van Derbeken, 1997a). When the protesters refused to unlock themselves, police "applied the chemicals." A second incident occurred on October 3, 1997. The *Chronicle* reported two protesters had locked themselves to a Pacific Lumber bulldozer in the Bear Creek watershed near Stafford in Humboldt County and sheriff's deputies were alleged to have said, "We're gonna do to you like we did to your friends in Scotia" (Van Derbeken, 1997a). Pepper spray was then swabbed in the eyes of the activists. A third incident cited in this *Chronicle* article involved four protesters who occupied the office of U.S. Congressional Republican Representative Frank Riggs. These four activists brought a tree stump into the congressman's office and locked themselves together using the same metal sleeve technique used in the September incident. These four protesters were also swabbed in the eyes with pepper spray.

The pepper spray news story was not initiated by these events, but rather by a federal civil rights lawsuit brought against the Humboldt deputies by the protesters. Through the lawsuit, the protesters gained access to the *police* videotape of two of the three incidents. These tapes show young white protesters engaged in nonviolent actions, who then are tortured with pepper spray until they comply with police demands. Of the articles appearing on October 31, 1997, in three major U.S. papers (*SF Chronicle, LA Times,* and the *Washington Post*), none mentioned the ethnicity of either the protesters or the officers. Clearly, this was not framed as a race issue for the print media.

Among the October 31 articles, all three used quotes from the protesters, and only the *LA Times* piece clearly identified the gender of the protesters. "The second taped protest was a sit-in by four women in the Eureka office of Rep. Frank Riggs (R-Windsor). In this instance, two women had liquid swabbed in their eyes while a third was sprayed in the eyes at close range" (La Ganga, 1997). Again the video clearly identifies the gender of the protesters and both the *Times* and the *Chronicle* confirm this by quoting Vernell "Spring" Lundberg and noting her age: 17. The image of young women locked together on the floor of a congressman's office, being swabbed in the eyes by a group of large, older male policemen did not elicit any gendered response from the press other than these passing notations.

Similarly, in the King case, the fact that he was a man was in no way emphasized, though if a woman had suffered similar blows, one can only speculate about the intensity of public reaction.

One of the ways the coverage of the pepper spray cases can be seen as gendered is in the use of the word "hysteria." With its linguistic connections to women, this word can turn the cries of pain into a stereotypical woman's response. The *Chronicle* reported on legal papers filed in defense of the police officers, stating: "Neither mischaracterization of the technique, nor hysteria—'staged or otherwise'—by demonstrators who actively thwart law enforcement efforts 'render unconstitutional the measured and appropriate response' of authorities" (Van Derbeken, 1997b). This idea of "staged hysteria" is repeated in a number of articles, articulated by the defense team as a way to gender the incident, question the emotions expressed on the videotape, and nullify its importance.

A second, more subtle aspect of the gendered aspects of the pepper spray cases comes from pepper spray itself. Small canisters of pepper spray are widely sold to women as a defense tool used against (male) attackers. Pepper spray's dominant, popular association is a defensive one, protecting the innocent from harm. Police officials' offensive (sic) use of pepper spray turns this popular idea on its head, given that the pepper spray is in the hands of men, who use it against women who are literally defenseless. The more widespread conception of pepper spray, as a defensive tool used by women, becomes contested with this new application, asking the audience to reconsider the meaning of pepper spray *or* to see the police as defending themselves against the civil disobedience threats. This inversion was embodied in the graphic used to introduce the story on KRON-TV News, a San Francisco TV station.[3] The graphic showed a canister of pepper spray and the silhouette of a man fleeing. With no precedent for this type of police action, news producers used the available icons to introduce the story, icons that obscured the boundaries between victim and assailant.

HIT ME WITH YOUR RHYTHM STICK

In part, the difference in both the representation of and the public response to these cases can be attributed to the different actions used to inflict pain and attain compliance. In the King case, most people recognize the power of a baton repeatedly beaten against a body. The wood is no match for flesh and bones, and the circle of police in the video conjures images of hyenas tearing and lunging at their prey. These big body movements are contrasted with the meticulous application of one drop of liquid into the eye of a protester. In the October 31 coverage of the pepper spray cases, the *LA Times* and the *Washington Post* both used the same description of the videotape: "The 90 minutes of videotape—striking for an overall sense of calm, not drama—paint a picture of polite police officers carrying out a well planned strategy against protesters posing no threat of physical harm during two separate sit-ins" (La Ganga, 1997, p. A3). The calm was broken only by the cries of the protesters once the chemical was applied. The officers "politely" put the protesters in a headlock and peeled back the eyelid for maximum effectiveness. These are not familiar tactics and as such, could leave many questioning the level of pain. Many people do not have personal experience with pepper spray and it is rarely depicted in popular culture. Were the protesters overreacting? Was this another staged "image event" to advance the environmental cause? The severity of pain is not readily apparent to the viewer and the text coverage does little to advance this understanding.

The coverage of the King case, on the other hand, consistently focused on the intensity of the police brutality and the injuries King sustained. On the first day of coverage, the *LA Times* included an edited transcript of Rodney King's account of his beating.

They continued to pound on me and beat on me, all over my body, all over my body. My ankles, they beat where it hurt my ankles. They beat my whole body where it hurt. You know how it feels when you get your ankles and your knees hurt in foot-ball? It hurts. It hurts real bad, cause it was hit with a stick. And the same with my face, my jaw. ("Victim's Account," 1991, p. A21)

This initial account is followed by a series of references to the injuries King sustained—a fractured cheekbone, eleven broken bones at the base of his skull, and a broken leg. The words "police brutality" appeared consistently in newspapers covering this national story. By the second day of coverage, the *LA Times* reported that the FBI had begun investigating the case for possible civil rights abuses.

This cursory overview of the King case outlines a pattern of coverage emphasizing race, physical harm, and police misconduct. The severity of these injuries far exceeds anything in the pepper spray cases. The usefulness of the comparison lies in the portrayal of the way police attained compliance. The media reinforce and help to define images by adding context, and in the King case, the pain is reinforced through strong language (brutality, brutalized) and by providing details of the injuries suffered. The portrayal of the use of pepper spray differed in a number of significant ways.

I *DON'T* FEEL YOUR PAIN

The use of pepper spray on the environmental protesters occurred within a larger debate in California about the merits of more traditional uses of pepper spray by police. Ten days before the pepper spray story broke, the *San Francisco Chronicle* reported that a man had died in police custody after being pepper sprayed. This incident occurred on the eve of a Berkeley

City Council meeting where a ban on police use of pepper spray was to be considered. Backers of the ban cited thirty-three deaths of pepper spray victims in California and seventy nationwide as evidence of the dangers of this "untested chemical weapon." The *Chronicle* story included information about the pepper spray manufacturer's recommendations for use of the agent as well as details about police policies for the use of nonlethal force. This background then was included in the articles about the environmental protesters, adding detail to an established debate.[4] Like the King case, testimony of the victims was included in many of the initial stories. A 17-year-old girl from the Pacific Lumber Protest is quoted, saying:

Three officers wrenched my head back and applied the pepper spray to my eyes. Then they came to me again, and pinned my head back and did it again, with my tear ducts wide open. People are not expecting law enforcement to act like this. Pepper spray is for assailants. (Van Derbeken, 1997a, p. A1)

This same article cited a 1992 California Department of Justice bulletin saying "pepper spray should be used only in a defensive mode against violent or hostile subjects" (Van Derbeken, 1997a, p. A1). As with the King case, an FBI investigation was initiated the day after the story broke, though this investigation turned out to be an extension of a larger ongoing investigation of the environmentalists' protest actions. The FBI investigation of civil rights violations was cited throughout the subsequent coverage, adding to the portrayal of the severity of the incident.

Unlike the King case, the press coverage of the pepper spray cases largely avoided the subjective word "brutality," opting instead for a more objective, clinical tone. The police actions consistently were described with phrases like "swabbed their eyes," "lifting their eyelids," and "rubbing concentrate in." The words "police brutality" were limited to editorials. In describing the effects of pepper spray, *USA Today* wrote: "Pepper spray is widely used by law enforcement agencies and considered safe in most circumstances. Its stinging, burning sensation on the eyes is temporary" (Ritter, 1997, p. 3A). This statement would carry very different connotations if "baton" were substituted for "pepper spray" and was made six years earlier. The comparison of spray to batons was not lost in a *New York Times* editorial from November 4, 1997:

The anti-logging protesters were not resisting aggressively nor did they pose a threat to the officers' safety. In fact, they were unable to defend themselves against the spray because they were chained and immobile. A beating of passive subjects would not have been acceptable in such circumstances. Neither is the use of pepper spray. ("An Assault," 1997, p. A26)

Parallels between spray and batons such as the *NY Times* articulated were the exception in the overall coverage, which focused instead on the

accusations from both sides about who committed the greater crime—the
protesters or the police.

Analysis of the pepper spray coverage reveals a mixture of objective language with detailed accounts of individual pain and suffering. The coverage
did not overwhelmingly support a conclusion of police brutality, though it
did provide graphic detail about the effects of a contested police tactic.
Pitting the testimony of the protesters against the assertions of proper police
behavior can be seen as undermining the power of the video images.
Without the reference to sports injuries or the ubiquitous understanding of
the pain when wooden sticks hit flesh, pepper spray becomes contested suffering, lacking a popular reference point. The actual pain is nowhere to be
seen, only heard in the cries of the victims. This lack of a popular understanding of the pain induced by pepper spray, combined with press coverage that
pits victim against aggressor, could be one of the reasons this incident failed
to attain the larger status of a cultural icon.

OUTCOMES AND UPDATES: THE TRIAL
AGAINST PEPPER SPRAY

The initial trial brought by protesters, which charged the Humboldt
County Sheriff's Deputies with "sadistic and excessive" use of force, dead-
locked a San Francisco jury. The appeal was brought before U.S. District
Judge—Vaughn Walker. One year after the incidents, the *Chronicle*
reported: "A federal judge threw out a lawsuit yesterday brought by anti-
logging protesters, saying officers 'acted reasonably' when they swabbed
pepper spray in the eyes of the demonstrators" (Barnum & Van Derbeken,
1998, p. A11). The judge made a unilateral decision, granting the arresting
officers qualified immunity, thus preventing the case from being heard by a
jury. Tony Serra, attorney for the protesters, is quoted saying, "It's a green
light for torture. Anyone who has seen the video . . . knows it's torture"
(Barnum & Van Derbeken, 1998, p. A11). Eureka police chief Arnie Milsap
is quoted saying:

It's (pepper spray) not used against peaceful protesters or just passive protesters. It's
used against people who are violating the law or trespassing. Our policy is to facilitate peaceful dissent. (Barnum & Van Derbeken, 1998, p. A11)

This is contradictory given that civil disobedience by definition violates the
law. Four women locked together in an office appear both peaceful and passive to many, though the police consistently framed this incident as violent.
Given that the congressman's office was a public space, provided by public
dollars, this was a logical place to make a peaceful political statement. Little
did these women know that they would be part of a watershed in "pain
compliance techniques" that would significantly alter the landscape of civil

disobedience. The protesters have appealed Judge Walker's decision and the case was heard by the U.S. 9th Circuit Court of Appeals.

The 9th Circuit Court overturned the lower court's ruling and remanded the case for a new trial. In his concurring opinion, Judge Myron Bright wrote: "Now that the court has established that the use of pepper spray in the eyes and on the faces of nonviolent, passive protestors may amount to an unreasonable use of force in violation of the Fourth Amendment of the United States Constitution, the most important issue in the case has been resolved" (*Headwaters Forest v. Humboldt County*, 2000, p. 26). This decision allowed the defendants to continue to pursue their case against the Humboldt County sheriffs though no further legal action has occurred. Nevertheless, the operative word in Bright's concurring opinion was "may," leaving open the possibility that this type of police behavior *may* be reasonable. Individual cities such as Boston have taken the step to limit police use of pepper spray to "self defense against a violent physical assault" (Allen, 2000, p. 3), but as of 2002, no new national laws have appeared to affirm the 9th Circuit Court decision.

SIT-IN, LOCK DOWN: A FAILED IMAGE EVENT

In the early 1970s, Greenpeace developed a strategy for "launching a 'mind bomb,' an image event that explodes in the public's consciousness to transform the way people view the world" (DeLuca, 1999, p. 1). According to DeLuca (1999), a historian of environmental rhetoric, the technique of staging powerful image events played a significant role in "the banning of commercial whaling, harvesting baby harp seals, and ocean dumping of nuclear waste" and many other influential measures to protect the environment (DeLuca, 1999, p. 3). As recently as 1990, Paul Watson, original member of Greenpeace and founder of the Sea Shepard Society, described the process whereby dramatic images are created through protest and the media take that message and "fire it into the brains of millions of people" (DeLuca, 1999, p. 5). This tactic repeatedly has been used by activists across a host of issues to the point where the image "mind bomb" may now be turning into a dud.

As communication research over the last half-century has demonstrated, there is no such thing as a magic bullet. Audiences are known to be active agents in the decoding process, making their own diverse, polysemic meaning out of the daily barrage of information. Though the image event tactic of environmental groups has continued for almost thirty years, the response to the pepper spray cases indicate this technique may be on the verge of breaking down. The environmental groups appears to have been lost, transformed into a struggle between protesters and law and order. Similarly, the theory of agenda setting (Shaw & McCombs, 1977) has demonstrated the ability of news media to shape not what the public thinks, but rather what the public thinks about. In this case, the emphasis has been a focus on the struggle between the protesters and the police as opposed to an emphasis on *why* the activists are protesting in the first place.

From the extreme images of the pepper spray videos to the substantive and sustained reporting of these events in the press, the pepper spray cases had all the makings of an image event with the potential to "explode in the public's consciousness to transform the way people view the world." Instead of a transformation, responses ranged from charges of police abuse to condemnations of the protesters, to a collective yawn from the American public. U.S. Congressman Frank Riggs, whose office was occupied in the third sit-in, defended the police actions on the floor of the House of Representatives, calling the protesters "eco-terrorists" and "belligerent and extreme outsiders." He added, "The videotape does not show what went on in my office on October 16. . . . The victims in this incident were my employees" (Van Derbeken, 1997b).

As was the case in the trial of the officers who beat Rodney King, there was an attempt to recontextualize the images on the videotape by trying to describe what went on before and after the camera was running. CBS Evening News countered this charge on November 5, 1997, when it reported that the office surveillance videotape showed the protesters entering the office peacefully without threats or violence. However, Riggs had charged that the activists were hostile and "belligerent." While the videotape showed the demonstrators to have acted in a peaceful manner and this information was brought to light by a major television news organization, it failed to initiate a larger public debate about appropriate police response to civil disobedience or the environmental issue of protection of old growth redwood forests.

The idea of "compassion fatigue" is one possible explanation for the lack of response to these events. Moeller argues that when a political issue (such as environmental protection) becomes an ongoing intractable problem, public action is inhibited. "If the politicians can't sort it out, or don't have the will to sort it out, then what can the public do?" (Moeller, 1999, p. 52). This social passivity is often reinforced by the agenda setting habits of news media organizations who too often present decontextualized, crisis coverage of social issues. As environmentalists have sought to seize media attention through the skillful use of image events, over time these extreme images have become enmeshed in a widening gyre of extreme "reality TV" where images of car crashes, animal attacks, and *Jackass* stunts have turned "pain TV" into popular entertainment. This steady stream of powerful images may be building up a cultural tolerance to shock value. Moeller (1999) argues that "when we see fairly horrendous pictures that upset us emotionally, we have some sort of mechanism which prevents us getting quite so upset the next time we see something. . . . The ability to stun an audience by delivering real-time pictures of events as they happen is ebbing" (p. 53).

The thirty-year tradition of image events that has been so successful for the environmental community is now part of a larger cultural trend of "shock jocks," "porn stars" and reality TV shows such as *COPS* that has tapped an audience for extreme TV, potentially turning activism into yet another entertainment product.

THEORIZING PEPPER SPRAY: POSTMODERN REPRESSION

Beyond a cultural saturation of extreme, "reality" images and attention getting devices, these pepper spray cases and their (lack of) public attention point to a larger crisis of representation often associated with postmodernism. The postmodern condition can be summarized in part as a plurality of voices, perspectives, and positions that allow for a multiplicity of "truths" to be constructed out of these various subjectivities. Thus, feminists read events one way; environmentalists, another; race, gender, class, sexual orientation, and countless other subjective positions create a diverse pool of perspectives that make any one "truth" increasingly difficult to agree upon. Another aspect of postmodernity concerns changes in the global economic system and the cultural implications of those changes. Harvey (1990) argues that the postmodern condition is characterized as a volatile economic system based on the mobility of capital. Postmodernism also is applied to language, where the meaning of individual words is said to be largely a product of one's subject position, rather than any direct relationship with the thing to which the word refers. Beyond simple polysemy, the symbol of the word is said to be increasingly detached from its referent, opening up a space for social struggle to play out on the contested terrain of language. This postmodern condition has been summarized as a "complex interplay of various mechanisms of social control that include discipline, spectacle, surveillance, the classic overt violence of the state, and the global restructuring of capitalism, along with good old sexism, racism and class domination" (Best & Kellner, 1997). Add to that environmental domination and one can see how pepper spray plays into this postmodern crisis of representation in many significant ways: through its invisible scars, through the intangible and unfamiliar nature of the pain it induces, and through its ubiquitous application during public demonstrations against the architects of global capitalism.

Pepper spray can be seen as a postmodern form of repression because it does not leave any welts, broken bones, or bruises to be displayed after the fact. The invisible nature of the coercion allows for the referent (pain) to become detached from the object (pepper spray). There are no direct markings, no inscription of the pain, so the pain becomes subjective, open to dispute and manipulation for whoever is representing the story. Nancy Delaney, attorney defending the police actions, demonstrated this dispute when she said: "Pepper spray poses no significant risk" and charged the protesters with "staged hysteria" (Van Derbeken, 1997c, p. A23). Pain becomes risk, and the once useful tactic of image events becomes a site of contested suffering, faux-pain with no medical reports to confirm the suffering.

The second major way that pepper spray lends itself to analysis as a postmodern police tool is the lack of widespread exposure to this chemical agent. For centuries, people have understood the effect of wooden sticks used to hit flesh. Thus the batons in the King incident are modernist tools of repression, widely understood and universally condemned. Pepper spray, on the other hand, is a relatively new instrument of repression and as such lacks a common understanding of its effects. In a depoliticized society where few people vote much less march in the streets where they may experience pepper spray or tear gas firsthand, most Americans have no reference to the effects of pepper spray. This lack of exposure opens up the possibility for debate about the effects of pepper spray and disputes about how much this thing "really" hurts. The most common reference probably comes from the local Mexican restaurant where "hot" food leaves your mouth tingling for a few minutes. (Maybe if a burrito were rubbed in the protesters' eyes, a more coherent public reaction would have emerged.) Without physical traces of the pain and without a broad understanding of the effects of pepper spray, punishment before prosecution will continue, collapsing judge, jury, and jailer into a bottle of mace and undermining the Constitution with every application to disperse civil disobedience.

Third, pepper spray inverts the linear narrative of our criminal justice system. In a truly postmodern sense, where linear narrative structure is disrupted, leaving scenes, moments, and pastiche where beginning, middle, and end once stood, pepper spray rearranges the process of law enforcement. Innocent until proven guilty is replaced by guilty by association, guilty of standing on a public street when the leaders of globalization need to get through. The application of pepper spray applies the punishment before any determination of guilt or innocence is established, before a judge or jury determines the proper punishment. Thus we have punishment before prosecution, pain before conviction. Police become the arbiters of pain, embodying judge, jury, and jailer with a single squirt of the latest pain compliance technology. Along with stun guns, TASRs, and rubber bullets, pepper spray falls along a continuum of increasingly "less-lethal" postmodern police tools.

Finally, pepper spray is intimately connected to globalization—a central component of the postmodern condition. In the Headwaters protest in particular and the ongoing global justice movement protests in general, pepper spray is being used in defense of privatization and the global marketplace. The people who gather to contest the closed door decision making, be it by Maxxam Corporation or the WTO, are now subject to pepper spray for the very act of contesting economic policies and practices. The price of free speech has risen to a corporeal level, with the state taking active measures to ensure a population of "docile bodies" (Foucault, 1977). Thus the practices of micro-fascism, applied one drop at a time, discipline activist populations and redirect the bodily confrontations in the streets into other, potentially less visible arenas. Taken together, these "postmodern" qualities suggest an evolving terrain for those hoping to use public demonstrations as a tool for mobilization.

CONCLUSION

The pepper spray videos and the public reaction to them embodies a complex set of contradictions about the perception of "reality TV," environmental activism, civil disobedience, and audience response to news and news production. Given the visual power of these videos and the lack of a coherent response by the public or the judicial system, no one answer appears to account for the widespread acceptance of this new police response to political dissent.

While the comparison to the Rodney King case offers a starting place to examine the news coverage, the differences in the events make any in-depth comparison problematic. The King case involved a long history of racism by the LAPD. As a motorist stopped by police, people from all walks of life could identify with his situation. The environmental protesters on the other hand were engaged in a form of political speech unfamiliar to many. Their issue, saving redwood trees, combined with their tactics, made them stand out from the vast majority of the American public. While environmental protection remains ever present in local, national, and global policy debates, civil disobedience in a public official's office is not widely practiced or condoned by the general public. What the comparison with the King case does show us is that the media *did* do a decent job of representing the pepper spray events. While more coverage, or more strongly worded coverage, may have prompted a stronger public reaction, the coverage that did take place appears sufficient to have elicited a public and a legal response. Given the coverage of these cases, the news media cannot be blamed for the lack of a public reaction. Clearly, something more complex is involved in this intersection of protest, the environment, police actions, and the press.

The protester's strategies put them in an uncommon position, subject to audience critique. Because the protesters were engaged in a political act, their position can be contested, disagreed with, or dismissed as radicalism. Unlike King who appeared as an average, black male motorist, these logging protesters may have been seen as bringing the police actions on themselves. Even if a majority of the population believes in environmental protection, a smaller percentage supports this type of protest and a smaller group still

would subject themselves to this police torture after being given fair warn-
ings. These protesters held to their issue in the face of physical coercion.
The full tape shows one of the girls in Congressman Riggs' office, after having been swabbed once, clearly and calmly stating her reasons for being
there. This segment was not aired on television,[5] but it reflects the depth of
conviction of the protesters and their willingness to endure these new strategies for compliance.

The response from the judicial system and the state of California set a
precedent that has encouraged pepper spray to be the preferred method
for ending nonviolent civil disobedience. This raises the possibility of a
chilling effect on this popular and powerful form of American political
expression. From the lunch counter sit-ins to the antiwar protests of the
60s to the more recent abortion clinic blocking of the pro-life movement,
nonviolent civil disobedience has a long history in this country and around
the world. This form of political speech has proven to be an effective tool
in mobilizing media coverage and political support around a host of issues.
With the sanctioning of pepper spray as an acceptable method for responding to this speech, a once useful tool for mobilizing support has become
compromised.

The events in Seattle, Washington, during the World Trade Organization
(WTO) Meetings from November 30 to December 4, 1999, and the public
demonstrations at subsequent gatherings of the WTO and World Bank,
offer more recent examples of pepper spray use that altered and silenced
political speech. Television news footage, newspaper stories, and first-person
accounts detail the police application of pepper spray on nonviolent protesters as a way to get people to end a sit-in. This initial violence was followed by many incidents where nonviolent protesters were indiscriminately
sprayed, to the extent that the Seattle police force had to order "three emergency shipments of pepper spray and tear gas from a Wyoming manufacturer to replenish their supplies" (Hodson & Sorenson, 1999). These police
actions, combined with widespread police violence, prompted the Seattle
police chief to resign one week after the events.

Whether this tool is a "postmodern" form of repression or a new name
for older agents (mace), pepper spray is now a significant tool to shape and
direct political speech. In the years since the first applications of pepper
spray on violent protesters in the fall of 1997, pepper spray has moved from
a disputed form of coercion to a ubiquitous response to political protest.
Like Rosa Parks, these environmental protesters were activists trained in
nonviolent civil disobedience. One only can imagine what our world would
look like if Rosa Parks had been pepper sprayed as a way to get her to give
up her bus seat. From the redwoods to the streets of Seattle and beyond,
one also must wonder how many modern Rosa Parks have been pepper
sprayed, silenced, and diverted from speaking truth to power.

NOTES

1. This term is used as opposed to "nonlethal" because of the number of deaths that have occurred from the use of pepper spray.

2. This chapter is based on the coverage of the pepper spray cases by the dominant U.S. newspapers, with particular attention to the *San Francisco Chronicle*, as this was the largest paper offering the most thorough and consistent coverage, with the best proximity to the incidents. The King case was examined through the major newspaper coverage, with particular attention to the *Los Angeles Times* for the same reasons.

3. This story aired October 31, 1997, and was archived at http://www.kron.com/av/rm/1997/10/31-pepper_kronv.ram but has since been taken down. Contact KRON-TV for file tape. Summary of the news segment can be found at http://www.headwatersforest.org/news/library/11-06-97_pepper_ MAIN.html.

4. Pepper spray has been associated with a number of long-term effects, including respiratory problems, pulmonary edema and acute elevations in blood pressure, and permanent eye damage (Allen, 2000).

5. The police video was available in compressed format on-line at www.headwaters.org, though the pepper spray web page has since been taken down.

REFERENCES

Allen, T. J. (2000, April 3). Chemical cops. *In These Times* [online] Available at: http://www.inthesetimes.com/issue/24/09/allen2409.html.

An assault with pepper spray (1997, November 4). *New York Times*, A26.

Barnum, A., & Van Derbeken, J. (1998, October 27). Logging foes lose challenge to pepper spray tactic. *San Francisco Chronicle*, A11.

Best, S., & Kellner, D. (1997). *The postmodern turn*. New York: Guilford Press.

DeLuca, K. (1999). *Image politics: The new rhetoric of environmental activism*. New York: The Guilford Press.

Foucault, M. (1977). *Discipline and punish: The birth of the prison*. New York: Pantheon Books.

Golden, T. (1996, August 27). Talks on saving redwoods may be near decisive point. *New York Times*, A9.

Harvey, D. (1990). *The condition of postmodernity*. Oxford: Blackwell Publishers.

Headwaters Forest v. Humboldt County, 240 F.3d 1185. (U.S. App., 2000). LEXIS 35215.

Hill, J. (2000). *The legacy of luna: The story of a tree, a woman and the struggle to save the redwoods*. San Francisco: Harper.

Hodson, J., & Sorenson, E. (1999, December 2). Police restocking tear gas supplies. *Seattle Times*, A24.

The investigation of a videotaped beating. (1991, March 7). *Los Angeles Times*, B6.

La Ganga, M. L. (1997). Police sued over use of pepper spray on protestors. *Los Angeles Times*, A3.

Martin, G. (2001, June 18). A different breed of protester, *San Francisco Chronicle*, A3.

Mills, A. C. (1998, May 26). Headwaters, what's the deal? *Motherjones*. [online] http://www.motherjones.com/news_wire/mills.html, accessed 9/15/02.

Moeller, S. (1999). *Compassion fatigue: How the media sell disease, famine, war and death*. New York: Routledge.

Reinhold, R. (1991, March 27). Failure of S. & L. in California could save a redwood forest. *New York Times*, A1.

Ritter, J. (1997, November 3). Deputies' methods at protest stir outcry: Pepper spray was applied to protesters' eyes. *USA Today*, 3A.

Shaw, D. L., & McCombs, M. E. (1977). *The emergence of American political issues: The agenda-setting function of the press*. St. Paul: West Pub. Co.

Skolnick, J. H. (1991, March 7). It's not just a few rotten apples. *Los Angeles Times*, B7.

Stewart, S. A. (1991, March 7). L.A. police beating victim 'glad I'm not dead.' *USA Today*, 3A.

Van Derbeken, J. (1997a, October 31). Pepper spray in the eyes—protestors sue police. *San Francisco Chronicle*, A1.

———. (1997b, November 1). FBI probes pepper spray 'swabbing': Furor over video of cops smearing protestors' eyes. *San Francisco Chronicle*, A1.

———. (1997c, November 15). Pepper spray ban rejected by judge. *San Francisco Chronicle*, A23.

Victim's account of the police beating (1991, March 7). *Los Angeles Times*, A21.

5

Irony in Protest and Policing: The World Trade Organization in Seattle[1]

Patrick F. Gillham and Gary T. Marx

INTRODUCTION

During a large demonstration against the World Trade Organization (WTO) in Seattle, tear gas fired by police affected many WTO delegates, shoppers, and city officials but was relatively ineffective against protesters who had brought their own gas masks. As a result, police escalated their use of force, including the use of rubber bullets to disperse crowds. When police initially pushed against the lines of demonstrators, the nonviolent activists closed ranks and locked arms tightly. The more police pushed, the more resilient the line became. However, the demonstrators' success in blocking police and WTO delegates also had the effect of inhibiting other activists from moving to new locations and blocked their own street medics from reaching the injured.

This chapter suggests that a neglected perspective involving irony is needed to understand the complexity of these events. Updating and drawing from a more detailed account,[2] we summarize police and demonstrator activities on the first day of the WTO meetings, noting organizational, planning, and tactical efforts. We then identify a number of different forms of irony inherent in the structure of contentious episodes or that may emerge out of interaction. These factors bring a significant degree of indeterminacy and trade-offs, no matter what decisions are made. We conclude with some suggestions to limit violations of Constitutional rights and police and demonstrator violence. Our method involves direct observation and interviews, reliance on mainstream media news reports, e-mail discussion lists, Independent Media Center and police video accounts, and police after-incident reports. By relying on a breadth of sources we hope to provide a clearer empirical picture of the events and ironies that unfolded.

THE BATTLE IN SEATTLE

Protests against the WTO that occurred in Seattle during the week of November 29–December 3, 1999, provide a case study for better understanding the ironies that emerge during mass demonstrations. Together, protesters and police paralyzed the business district for three days, shut down the WTO ministerials, and called international news media attention to the issues raised by the WTO meetings.

Two major protest events helped paralyze Seattle on November 30. The first was the downtown "direct action" where thousands of well-trained activists engaged in nonviolent civil disobedience that effectively closed the core of the city and prevented delegates from attending the WTO meetings. The other major event was an AFL-CIO-sponsored march in which tens-of-thousands of union, environmental, and religious group members walked from a nearby stadium to the city center where they partially converged with the first event.

The troubles began around daybreak on a cold and drizzly Tuesday when thousands of nonviolent protesters filled the streets surrounding the Seattle Convention Center and effectively blocked downtown streets, sidewalks, and hotel doors, making it impossible for most WTO delegates to enter the opening rounds of discussions. The WTO, an international organization whose purpose "is to insure that trade flows as smoothly, predictably and freely as possible" between member nations through the use of multilateral trade agreements (World Trade Organization, 2002), had come to Seattle to start a new round of trade talks. Over six thousand delegates from 135 member nations planned to attend the meetings ("Seattle Police Charge," 1999). Protesters, on the other hand, represented a wide variety of interests and hundreds of advocacy organizations like Greenpeace, Rainforest Action Network, Global Exchange, Jubilee 2000, and the AFL-CIO. They had come to Seattle to express concerns that the WTO lacked transparency; favored corporate power; and made binding trade decisions that violated U.S. and international laws, destroyed the environment, and undermined labor and human rights standards (Beck & Danaher, 2000; Rosset, 2000; Thomas, 2000). Many of the more mainstream organizations planned only to participate in less contentious activities, such as the AFL-CIO permitted march. In the weeks leading up to the WTO Ministerial, however, more radical protest organizers had publicly stated on websites, during large teach-ins, and in nonviolence trainings, that the primary goal of the demonstrations was to "Shut Down the WTO!"

Activists interested in more radical protests organized a few hundred affinity groups. These groups were trained and loosely coordinated through the Direct

Action Network (DAN), a "coalition of community organizations and international sponsors who worked together to mobilize the direct action . . ." (Guilloud, 2000, p. 94). Direct Action Network organizers had divided the area surrounding the Seattle Convention Center into thirteen "wedges" or "pieces of pie" to be filled by ten to twenty affinity groups each (Crass, 2000, p. 49; Lojowsky, 2000, p. 13). Each affinity group consisted of five to twenty people with some commonality such as sharing a common workplace or lifestyle, being involved in other protest events, or attending the same university (Guilloud, 2000, p. 95). To participate in the direct action, affinity groups were asked to refrain from using physical or verbal violence; to carry no weapons, illegal drugs, or alcohol; and to respect private property. Consensus-based decision making was used by each affinity group, and in the larger Direct Action Network. The latter relied on "spokes-council" meetings in which spokespersons from each affinity group came together to make strategic decisions and to share general information (Starhawk, 2000).

This loose network of associations proved very effective on the opening day of the WTO Ministerial. Sometime between 9 and 10 A.M., affinity groups clustered outside the Sheraton Hotel, preventing delegates inside, including U.S. Secretary of State Madeleine Albright, from leaving (Carter & Postman, 1999; History Link, 2002). Police in full body armor and gas masks, overwhelmed and frightened by the number and preparedness of protesters (Cabrera, 2000), tried to clear an escape route for Albright and company. They did so by jabbing and pushing the sitting and prone activists with long batons and by spraying them with pepper gas (Seattle Police, 1999; Independent Media Center [IMC], 1999). Some demonstrators put on goggles to protect their eyes and wrapped bandanas soaked in vinegar around their mouths to neutralize the chemicals. A smaller number of protesters quickly donned gas masks. Activists sitting at the front of police lines pulled themselves into tighter formation by wrapping arms and legs together, and put their heads down. While police tactics proved largely ineffective, especially at disbanding those near the police line, officers were able to make a path allowing some vehicles to leave the parking garage. "Street medics" wearing hand-painted red crosses and protective gloves quickly treated protesters and bystanders who had been sprayed with chemical irritants.

News about the violence erupting outside the Sheraton quickly spread to activists blocking other sectors of the city who communicated by rollerblade, bicycle, two-way radios, and cell phones. This information then was disseminated by word of mouth and over bullhorns. "Flying squads" responded by moving to the street outside the Sheraton. The squads included members of the Black Bloc, a loose affiliation of anarchist affinity groups and individuals (Swart, 2000, p. 53). The Sheraton assault was not atypical as police tried the same tactics to clear protesters from other Seattle sites (History Link, 2002; Hough, 2000, p. 39; Lojowsky, 2000, pp. 13–15; Quenzer, 2000). In almost all cases, police were unsuccessful in pushing the crowds more than a few blocks from their original lines.

As confrontations intensified around the city, the number of vandalism incidents seemed to increase in proportion to police use of force (Gillham & Marx, 2000). Just before police slowed their attack around 11 A.M., small groups of youth, many of them dressed in black and some claiming membership in the Black Bloc, began smashing store windows with both hammers and crowbars that had been concealed inside backpacks, and with newspaper boxes sitting on nearby sidewalks. Targeted were multinational corporations believed by protesters to be responsible for human and animal rights abuses and global environmental degradation, such as Nike, McDonalds, and the Gap. With little success, some demonstrators opposed to the vandalism tried policing their own. Such efforts at control were met with shouts and cursing from those engaged in the "property transformation" (Field notes 11/30/99; Swart, 2000, p. 53). To the dismay of many, groups of officers often stood by and watched, claiming they were unable to make arrests because they were understaffed, told to hold skirmish lines, and inhibited by the human barricades and massive number of people in the streets (Egan, 1999; IMC, 1999; McCarthy & Associates, 2000; McCarthy, Louden, & Kolman, 2000; Seattle Police, 1999). By noon, police estimated that 25,000–50,000 demonstrators, delegates, and bystanders filled a fifteen-block perimeter around the Convention Center (Cabrera, 2000; Gillham & Marx, 2000; Verhovek, 1999).

Those WTO delegates able to exit their hotels were prevented from entering the meetings because of the human barricades set up at intersections immediately outside the Convention Center. Independent Media Center video footage (1999) shows that delegates looked surprised at first or even amused by the blockades. As the day continued, however, some delegates became frightened, angry, and frustrated. A few tried breaking through the human barricades. One delegate (or possibly a body guard, it is unclear which) brandished a handgun in plain view of police and tried to bust through the protesters' line. Fortunately, protesters tackled the gunman before shots were fired. But instead of disarming the man, police quickly doused the protesters with pepper spray, allowing him to slip through the line of frightened and now incapacitated activists (IMC, 1999; McCarthy & Associates, 2000, p. 137).[3]

During these challenging hours, Seattle officials not only struggled with securing delegates access to the Convention Center. They also had to decide what to do with approximately 20,000–50,000 additional demonstrators participating in the AFL-CIO permitted march scheduled to pass by the city center in the early afternoon ("Seattle Police Charge," 1999; Carter & Postman, 1999). For obvious reasons, officials were concerned about doubling the number of people downtown, which was already chocked by throngs of protesters, bystanders, delegates, international media personnel, and police.

In the end, authorities let the march proceed as scheduled, with the hope that the more moderate marchers would stay out of the blockaded area and might actually attract some of the bystanders and exhausted activists away from the contested area (Carter & Postman, 1999; McCarthy & Associates, 2000). As the large crowd marched past the zone of contention, union marshals appeared divided over whether to direct people away from the blockades, or back to the stadium. How many marchers continued back to the stadium or joined the downtown blockades and whether weary bystanders and demonstrators actually left because of the march is unclear, though it appears that some thinning of the downtown crowd had begun after the noon hour (Gillham & Marx, 2000).

In response to the protests and a demand from the White House to clear the streets or risk having the WTO Ministerial cancelled, Seattle Mayor Paul Schell imposed a state of emergency at 3:32 P.M., placing a fifty-block section of the city under curfew from 7 P.M. to 7:30 A.M. ("Countdown to Chaos" 1999; Quenzer, 2000).

For the next several hours, Seattle police and other state and local law enforcement agencies pushed demonstrators and bystanders away from the city center. This task was made easier by an abundant supply of chemical irritants and other less than lethal weapons that had arrived from other municipalities in the early afternoon (Gillham & Marx, 2000). Many in the exiting crowd were directed onto Capitol Hill, an upscale neighborhood overlooking the city center, though several hundred activists and bystanders remained in the curfew zone throughout the night. Looters also entered this zone probably after hearing local news reports about the "chaos" encasing Seattle. The night proved no less exciting than the day as police and protesters played cat and mouse on Capitol Hill and in the downtown curfew zone until early morning.

The IMC, located on 2nd Avenue in the heart of downtown Seattle, was the site of some of the more contentious engagements that evening. Activist video footage shows protesters and bystanders under a pale yellow light and in a fog of smoke and gas seeking asylum from police in the IMC (IMC, 1999). King County Sheriff officers are shown trying to enter the IMC through the front door, perhaps in pursuit of fleeing protesters. Volunteers in the building locked the door and refused police access. Shortly afterwards, police surrounded the building and prohibited anyone from exiting. While activists report serious concern that police would storm the building, the police eventually left (IMC, 1999), perhaps in pursuit of looters.

IRONY IN PROTEST AND POLICING

Social scientists long have examined the unintended consequences of social action (e.g., Merton, 1957; Sieber, 1981; Stone, 1989, 1997). Ironic outcomes are an especially interesting consequence in which a result contradicts the intent of the action. Marx (1981) has argued that ironic consequences are linked to social trends of increased complexity involving ever more differentiated and specialized, loosely connected systems and increased efforts at intervention. In some systems the complexity is so great as to almost guarantee what Perrow (1984) terms "normal accidents." These may be inherent in the structure of the situation or emerge out of the choices actors make and their interactions, or they may flow from uncontrollable (and often unthought of, or unexpected) influences outside of the local system. Our analysis of the Seattle demonstrations suggests a number of structural and interaction-related ironies, which are briefly discussed next.

The *spillover* or *flypaper effect* is an action on the part of either police or demonstrators that affects people outside the target group. An obvious case in policing is the inability of police to keep their tactics from impacting nonparticipants. In Seattle, for example, police not only gassed demonstrators, but also residents on Capitol Hill, downtown employees and small business owners, news reporters, delegates unable to pass through the crowds, and law enforcement personnel lacking gas masks. Given shifting wind patterns, the instability of tear gas often presents blowback problems, as does protesters throwing canisters back at police.

This ironic effect occurs with protesters too. In Seattle, many affinity groups were so effective at blockading intersections that they prevented friendly media, organizers, and other activists from moving to other strategic locations. Their blockades also inhibited street medics and other medical personnel from reaching the injured.

Reciprocal and neutralizing effects are caused when moves by one opponent lead to similar moves on the other side (whether offensively, defensively, or both). They are after all joined together, however unwillingly, in a kind of hostile dance. Georg Simmel (1985) noted this more broadly in his observation that parties to conflict interactions come to resemble each other. In a free market economy with civil liberties, challengers have enormous room to maneuver. As police pushed against demonstrator lines, nonviolent activists held each other's arms tighter, or closed ranks. Rather than causing demonstrators to disperse, police actions strengthened the lines. Anticipation that police might use tear gas prompted many protesters to bring gas masks and bandanas soaked in vinegar to neutralize the effects of pepper spray and tear gas.

The old adage "tit-for-tat" seldom lessens tensions. Reciprocity can lead to *escalation* where the level of confrontation increases rather than decreases. Outside the Sheraton Hotel thousands of demonstrators blocked intersections as well as all the exits from the building, preventing the Secretary of State from attending the opening talks. In response, police used pepper spray and batons to clear the street. Demonstrators reacted by rushing in flying squads to bolster the human blockades, while self-styled anarchists took the lead in creating barricades with trash dumpsters and newspaper boxes. Police then escalated the situation further by firing rubber bullets into the crowd. At that point some in the streets began breaking windows.

After the curfew was declared, police chased groups of people through the streets indiscriminately firing tear gas and pepper spray. And the spiral continued into the next day. As news of police behavior spread, many demonstrators felt an increased sense of solidarity and the need now to stand up to the police, an action far beyond the original goal of protesting against the WTO. At a large march the next day, a steelworker expressed the consequences of the escalation, "we knew that there was a good possibility that this nonviolent action [the march] would be met with violence again. I believe everyone was aware that we had no choice; we had to stand up for our First Amendment rights no matter what the cost, even if the cost was our life" (Goodman, 2000, p. 17).

Even in the absence of aggressive actions mere police presence may unintentionally heighten a sense of resistance in some demonstrators and bystanders. Thus for some, the very presence of police dressed in heavy body armor and riot helmets, and carrying visible weapons, suggested a symbolism inconsistent with a democratic society. Interpreting the situation in that way may have led some to participate more aggressively than would have been the case with a lessened or less threatening police presence.

Looked at from another perspective, demonstrators may have unintentionally contributed to the escalation in police tactics and the curtailing of civil liberties. Many protesters effectively neutralized the use of chemical irritants by bringing their own masks. Stymied police then resorted to weapons such as concussion grenades, rubber bullets, and batons fired from guns. Well-trained protesters intent on closing down the meeting had the strategic advantage against the underprepared and small number of police. (On the first day there were only 400 Seattle officers in the streets [Quenzer, 2000].) Protesters on the perimeter of the pie were able to keep police away from other activists effectively blockading the doors, sidewalks, and streets closer to the center. When the ranks of demonstrators swelled in the early afternoon after the arrival of thousands of marchers from the AFL-CIO rally, city and state officials declared a curfew and no-protest zone, called in the National Guard, and made it a felony for non-police to possess a gas mask. In these ways, what started as individual efforts to protect against the effects of tear gas contributed to a spiraling (with each police response) that fortunately did not end in the death of any protesters or police.

A subset of escalation is the *non-enforcement effect* (Marx, 1981). Aware of the possibility of unwanted escalation, police may have allowed some laws to be broken by more moderate demonstrators, hoping they would then exercise control over more serious violations. Out of similar concerns demonstrators may have ignored their own self-policing standards or been unable to control those bent on destruction, communicating the idea that such behavior was temporarily acceptable—what collective behavior students call an *emergent norm* appeared (Turner & Killian, 1987). While non-enforcement may at times have the desired effect, these examples suggest that the line between too little and too much control is dynamic and hard to determine in advance.

Dramatic action by one or both sides may attract opponents, allies, and bystanders interested in identifying "What's going on?" This *excitement effect*, or the sense that something out of the ordinary is happening, may be seductive. Scenes associated with protests may operate like magnets. Helicopters and searchlights, the reverberation of concussion grenades, the wail of sirens, and the sight and smell of gas-filled streets may draw people toward rather than away from an event. Demonstrators, on the other hand, dressed in turtle costumes or wearing medic badges, parading with banners and colorful puppets, and blocking traffic may attract spectators as planned, or may unintentionally attract police reprisal. And persons with a variety of motives consistent, inconsistent, and irrelevant to police and demonstrator goals may be drawn in. This appears to be the case when looters entered the city after viewing local television portrayals of "chaos in the streets."

Sometimes actors engage in activities completely opposite their prescribed roles. In this *role reversal effect* demonstrators may police themselves while police do nothing or are themselves disorderly (Marx, 1970; Stark, 1972). In Seattle, protesters protected the Nike store from those trying to break the windows, while security guards hid injured demonstrators from police at Pike Place Market. Such actions likely are related to a strong violation of the actor's sense of justice and appropriateness of the behavior, or in the case of non-enforcement, its absence.

The complexity of issues being struggled over may lead to unexpected alliances as well. With the *strange bedfellow effect*, groups typically at odds may find common ground, or at least set aside differences long enough to join in opposition against a common opponent (Coser, 1964). Consider, for example, the female union worker who in reference to a joint union/ environmentalist march exuberantly proclaimed, "Steelworkers and Turtles united at last" (Guilloud, 2000, p. 77). Or the IMC (1999) portrayal of an Earth First!er at a union gathering arguing that the dichotomy made between good jobs and protection of the environment is a false one.

The *secrecy effect* is another ironic form associated with contentious events. Because of the need to prevent infiltration or revelation of sensitive information, protesters and police work to hide certain information from each other. But secrecy can prevent the flow of information from and to members and allies, just as easily as it inhibits information flowing to opponents. This creates a particular tension for demonstrators who are especially vulnerable to this effect, because they must be more suspicious of unknown people who may be working for police or for rival groups. At the same time, their commitment to democracy and need for resources makes them very vulnerable to infiltration (Marx, 1974). Direct Action Network organizers were partially successful at avoiding this effect by relying on the affinity and spokes organizational model. This structure worked to the protesters' advantage because it was impossible for police to infiltrate all affinity groups and discover the full extent of their plans. Police or informants who attended DAN spokes-meetings would only be able to ascertain who the informal leaders and trainers were, as well as gain very general ideas about the numbers of groups represented, the areas to be blocked, and the time of events. They could not learn about the creative and disruptive tactics planned by each group, or the total numbers of participants involved in the actions.

While police were able to hide many of their strategic plans up to the day of the demonstrations, once the actions began, well-organized protesters were able to identify and inform each other about much of what police were doing. Cell phones, police scanners, bicycles, rollerblades, and bullhorns became effective means to reveal police plans.

Previous legal decisions can themselves have lasting ironic consequences. Such *prior reform effects* occur as a result of changes in the legal and normative systems. In response to police infiltration of protest groups in the 1960s, Seattle adopted some of the nation's most stringent restrictions against police intelligence gathering, including a civilian audit (Quenzer, 2000). While the city ordinance protected organizers' expression of assembly, it also made it more difficult for Seattle police to gather intelligence on the planning of legal and illegal activities. Fortunately for the Seattle PD, other agencies, such as the FBI did not face the same restraints and probably were relied upon for some pre-protest surveillance.

Local reforms are not the only source of legal ironies. The very structure of a democratic society legitimates conflicting values, which when exercised may result in ironic consequences. Thus in Seattle, those asserting their freedom to demonstrate on behalf of protecting the environment, public health, and working conditions interfered with the rights of delegates, downtown employers and employees, and holiday shoppers. One affinity group blocking an intersection justified this in chanting, "We don't have a voice, so they won't either" (IMC, 1999). Likewise, in an effort to protect the rights of nonprotesters, the Mayor established a curfew and no-protest zone, denying demonstrators the right to be directly heard by those they most wanted to reach. No matter what the goal, training, or sufficiency of resources these conflicts remain.

CONCLUSION—LIMITING CONSTITUTIONAL VIOLATIONS AND VIOLENCE

While some ironic outcomes seem inherent in complex police-protest situations, this is not to argue that demonstrations must end in violence and denial of basic rights. There is much room for discretion and variation in outcomes. Thus, in retrospect a number of actions could have been taken to reduce the level of violence and Constitutional violations in Seattle.

To minimize injury and property damage, police could have first been better prepared in terms of organization, training, and cooperation with other agencies. This is one of the central critiques of the Seattle Police cited in two after-incident reports (McCarthy & Associates, 2000; Quenzer, 2000). Both reports stressed that a more developed task-force approach involving multiple local law enforcement agencies, as well as a comprehensive contingency plan would have been most desirable.

Authorities could also have established clearly defined protest and no-protest zones before the event. This buffer strategy is a way of partially sat-isfying potentially conflicting goals. The protest established at the 1968 Democratic National Convention and used for the 2000 Republican and Democratic Conventions offer examples. Such zones allow demonstrators to voice discontent, while allowing freedom of expression and movement for their targets, minimizing the need for conflictual police interaction. The failure of Seattle authorities initially to do this resulted in limitations on both the right to protest (as police became more aggressive) and on delegates' freedom of movement. When this solution was tried the next day it was too late since demonstrators had already "claimed" what was eventually declared a no-protest zone.

Similarly, officials could have engaged in more preemptive measures such as eliminating resources that might be misused. Thus newspaper boxes later used as battering rams to smash windows and dumpsters used to block intersections could have been removed until the protests were over.

Moreover, city officials could have implicitly conceded victory to the demonstrators on the first day, even at the cost of some cancelled meetings, instead of using force to try and clear the area. As shown, it takes two to escalate. Police of course would have been concerned with appearing weak and creating a precedent that might invite subsequent trouble and later challenges to their authority. However it is far from clear that a more lim-ited initial police presence would have led to even more disorder. Instead, there are indications that DAN demonstrators would have been satisfied with a one-day blockade of the WTO meeting followed by a mass arrest (Hyde, 2000; Plante & Dornin, 1999; Postman & Carter, 1999). Escalation, therefore, may have resulted more from inconsistent police use of force and its overall increase than it did from capitulation to protesters.

Violence and Constitutional violations could also have been minimized by moving the meetings elsewhere. After realizing that demonstrators were intent on, and capable of, closing the WTO meetings that day, an alterna-tive plan would have permitted city officials to relocate all or some of the meetings. Of course, similar concerns regarding authority and capitulation would have made such a decision unlikely.

While some efforts were made by local authorities and universities to promote public debate about the WTO, a much greater effort was in order. This is especially the case given the breadth of critics (unions, mainstream environmentalists, religious groups, international development and aid groups, and even member nations) and extensive criticisms levied against the WTO noted earlier. Doing so would have acknowledged that there are multiple sides to the complex issues and might have provided a legitimate outlet for protesters besides taking to the streets.

In contrast to Seattle authorities, demonstrators could have taken greater responsibility for the actions of other protesters. While there was a debate between organizers about the use of nonviolent marshals to help control more disruptive protest actions, it was finally decided that demonstrators would be accountable to each other through affinity groups, and that affinity groups would be responsible to the larger DAN collective by agreeing to the four guidelines noted earlier. While this might not have prevented all property damage and violence against police, it could have helped minimize such actions. By emphasizing anarchistic individualism at the expense of collective responsibility, some activists unwittingly alienated many sympathizers and contradicted values of tolerance and respect for the ideas of others— values seemingly essential for building the kind of world promoted by many in the global justice movement.

Together, police and protesters could have minimized the conflict by following the previously agreed upon script. Demonstrators were expecting to be arrested en masse the first day, whereas police were assured that activists would engage in predictable civil disobedience. But this script never unfolded. Even if police were not able logistically to process all the people who were willing to be arrested, arrests would have removed some persons from the zone of contention, and may have prevented others from feelings that an agreement had been violated. Similarly, had protesters not so effectively shut down the city and created high levels of uncertainty for police, the violence and civil liberty violations associated with the protests may have lessened.

These observations reflect our larger analysis, that the violence to people, Constitutional rights, and property might have been lessened had police and organizers more diligently imagined and prepared for a broader variety of possible consequences of their actions.

IRONY DOESN'T PRECLUDE DISCRETION

Relying on IMC and other accounts, we have sought documentation for our description of events but our basic point is not to offer a history as such. Rather we view the Seattle WTO protests as a window into broader phenomena. We seek to go beyond simplistic blaming (of which there is plenty—whether involving inappropriate police behavior or irresponsible protest behavior), to noting how the conditions of such protest situations and the choices actors make may have multiple, conflicting, and unintended consequences. The search for heroes and villains may be emotionally gratifying, but all too often it is self-serving and ideological, rather than reflective of careful empirical evidence.

This is not to justify or excuse unprofessional police behavior, or seriously disruptive protest that interferes with the rights of others, particularly when the latter does not involve civil disobedience, with its tenant to willingly accept punishment as a matter of conscience. At times criticism is morally, legally, and administratively appropriate and even necessary. An understanding of the complexity of such events and of seemingly inherent conflicts can help us know when this is the case. It can also help in planning for the protection of future demonstrations.

By noting the limitations on rational planning we are not calling for its abolition. Instead, we call attention to the need for a nuanced and empirically grounded approach and for dialogue among contending parties of good will.[4] The inherent conflicts noted here call for balanced solutions rather than maximizing one value such as absolute order or freedom of expression at a cost to others. Authoritarian societies are defined by order without liberty. But democratic societies can only exist with *both* liberty and order. Thus, in situations where rights conflict, compromise is usually the best approach.

NOTES

1. Special thanks go to Stanley Yntema for his invaluable field assistance and collection of post-WTO documentation. Anonymous reviewers also provided insightful comments to earlier chapter drafts. Please direct comments to Patrick Gillham, at gillham@colorado.edu.

2. The original article (Gillham & Marx, 2000) contains additional narrative detail, references, and extensive footnotes (available online at www.garymarx.net).

3. The IMC video captures a much different perspective on this incident than that portrayed in the police report. In the latter, police are commended for spraying the protesters and there is no mention as to why police did not detain the gunman. The video on the other hand shows protesters obstructing the gunman's path, hardly a justification for drawing a weapon, and the man slipping through the line after police gassed the demonstrators.

4. Some protesters might ask whether dialog is even possible with the WTO, which monopolizes world power and is guided by assumptions of neoliberal economists that tend to confound GDP with quality of life and that sidestep questions about ecological thresholds and human rights. Conversely, WTO authorities might ask whether constructive talks can occur with opponents that simply do not understand economic theory or the complexities of our globalizing world.

REFERENCES

Beck, J., & Danaher, K. (2000). Ten reasons to oppose the WTO. In K. Danaher & R. Burbach (Eds.), *Globalize this! The battle against the World Trade*

Organization and corporate rule (pp. 98–102). Monroe, ME: Common Courage Press.

Cabrera, L. (2000, February 24). WTO tapes show extent of police fears. *Seattle Post Intelligencer.* Retrieved August 30, 2002, from http://www.seattlepi.nwsource.com.

Carter, M., & Postman, D. (1999, December 16). There was unrest even at the top during the WTO riots. *Seattle Times.* Retrieved August 30, 2002, from http://www.seattletimes.com.

Coser, L. (1964). *The functions of social conflict.* New York: Free Press.

Countdown to Chaos. (1999, December 5). Countdown to chaos in Seattle. *Seattle Times.* Retrieved August 30, 2002, from http://www.seattletimes.com.

Crass, C. (2000). Shutting down the WTO and opening up a world of possibilities. In S. Guilloud (Ed.), *Voices from the WTO* (pp. 49–50). Olympia, WA: Evergreen State College Bookstore.

Egan, T. (1999, December 2). Blame: Clenched fists in Seattle lead to pointed fingers. *New York Times.* Retrieved August 30, 2002, from http://www.nytimes.com/library/world/ global/ 120299wto-protest.html.

Gillham, P. F., & Marx, G. T. (2000). Complexity and irony in policing and protesting: The World Trade Organization in Seattle. *Social Justice, 27*(2), 212–236.

Goodman, J. F. (2000). Standing up for democracy. In S. Guilloud (Ed.), *Voices from the WTO* (p. 17). Olympia, WA: Evergreen State College Bookstore.

Guilloud, S. (Ed.). (2000). *Voices from the WTO: An anthology of writings from the people who shut down the World Trade Organization.* Olympia, WA: Evergreen State College Bookstore.

History Link. (2002). Ministerial week time line. *WTO History Project.* Retrieved August 30, 2002, from http://depts.washington.edu/wtohist/Protests/timeline.htm#ministerial.

Hough, S. (2000). Dumpster dancing. In S. Guilloud (Ed.), *Voices from the WTO* (pp. 39–40). Olympia, WA: Evergreen State College Bookstore.

Hyde, D. (2000). Tribulations of a John WTO. In S. Guilloud (Ed.), *Voices from the WTO* (pp. 60–61). Olympia, WA: Evergreen State College Bookstore.

Independent Media Center. (1999). Showdown in Seattle [videotape]. Seattle Independent Media Center. Seattle, WA.

Lojowsky, M. (2000). Comes a time. In S. Guilloud (Ed.), *Voices from the WTO* (pp. 12–16). Olympia, WA: Evergreen State College Bookstore.

Marx, G. T. (1970). Civil disorder and the agents of social control. *Journal of Social Issues, 26,* 19–57.

———. (1974). Thoughts on a neglected category of social movement participation: The agent provocateur and the informant. *American Journal of Sociology, 80,* 402–442.

———. (1981). Ironies of social control: Authorities as contributors to deviance through escalation, nonenforcement and covert facilitation. *Social Problems, 28,* 221–246.

McCarthy, R. M., & Associates. (2000, July). *An independent review of the World Trade Organization Conference disruptions in Seattle, Washington November 29–December 3, 1999: Final report.* San Clemente, CA.

———. Louden, R. J., & Kolman, J. (2000, April). *An independent review of the 1999 World Trade Organization Conference disruptions in Seattle,*

Washington: A preliminary report for the city of Seattle focusing on planning and preparation. San Clemente, CA.

Merton, R. (1957). *Social theory and social structure.* Glencoe, IL: Free Press.

Perrow, C. (1984). *Normal accidents: Living with high risk technologies.* New York: Basic Books.

Plante, C., & Dornin, R. (1999, December 2). Troops sent to Seattle as part of terrorism contingency plan. *CNN.* Retrieved August 30, 2002, from http://www.cnn.com/1999/ US/12/02/wto.05/index.html.

Postman, D., & Carter, M. (1999, December 1). Police switch to new strategy. *Seattle Times.* Retrieved August 30, 2002, from http://www.seattletimes.com.

Quenzer, T. (2000, April 4). After action report: Nov 29–Dec 3, 1999 World Trade Organization Ministerial Conference. *Seattle Police Department.* Seattle, WA.

Rosset, P. (2000). A new food movement comes of age in Seattle. In K. Danaher & R. Burbach (Eds.), *Globalize this! The battle against the World Trade Organization and corporate rule* (pp. 135–140). Monroe, ME: Common Courage Press.

Seattle Police. (1999). WTO combination 1 [videotape]. *Seattle Police Department.* Seattle, WA.

Seattle Police Charge. (1999, December 1). Seattle police charge as protesters challenge curfew. *CNN.* Retrieved August 30, 2002, from http://www.cnn.com/ US/9911/30/wto.05/index. html

Sieber, S. D. (1981). *Fatal remedies: The ironies of social intervention.* New York: Plenum Press.

Simmel, G. (1985). *The sociology of Georg Simmel.* K. Wolff (Ed.). New York: The Free Press.

Starhawk. (2000). How we really shut down the WTO. In S. Guilloud (Ed.), *Voices from the WTO* (pp. 47–48). Olympia, WA: Evergreen State College Bookstore.

Stark, R. (1972). *Police riots.* Belmont, CA: Focus Books.

Stone, D. A. (1989). Causal stories and the formation of policy agendas. *Political Science Quarterly, 104,* 281–300.

———. (1997). *Policy paradox: The art of political decision making.* New York: W. W. Norton & Company, Inc.

Swart, S. (2000). From the black block. In S. Guilloud (Ed.), *Voices from the WTO* (pp. 53–54). Olympia, WA: Evergreen State College Bookstore.

Thomas, J. (2000). *The battle in Seattle: The story behind and beyond the WTO demonstrations.* Golden, CO: Fulcrum Press.

Turner, R., & Killian, L. (1987). *Collective behavior.* Englewood Cliffs, NJ: Prentice Hall.

Verhovek, S. H. (1999, December 2). Talks and turmoil: The hosts; Seattle is stung, angry and embarrassed as opportunity turns to chaos. *New York Times.* Retrieved August 30, 2002, from http://www.nytimes.com.

World Trade Organization. (2002). *The World Trade Organization.* Retrieved August 30, 2002, from http://www.wto.org/english/res_e/doload_e/ inbr_e.pdf.

Part Two

Representing Resistance: The U.S. Media and the Global Justice Movement

6

Mapping the Emerging Global Order in News Discourse: The Meanings of Globalization in News Magazines in the Early 1990s

Ilia Rodríguez

INTRODUCTION

During the 1990s the "global village" emerged as a common referent in media discourses about supranational processes of social change. From advertising messages to corporate publicity, from popular fiction to news reports and features, media texts became instrumental in mapping the changing international order by providing audiences with definitions and interpretations of globalization as a process of economic, cultural, and geopolitical change in the late twentieth century. The purpose of this research was to explore the role of mass communication in the production of knowledge about "globalization" at a time when this construct began to enter the imagination of larger segments of the public. In particular, this chapter focuses on news media content to explore how the theme of globalization was framed in journalistic texts. On the basis of a textual analysis of articles, columns, and visual representations published between 1992 and 1994 in two U.S. news magazines (*Time* and *Newsweek*) and one Latin American regional news magazine (*Visión*), this study sought to identify specific issues associated with globalization in news coverage, outline the framing devices suggesting what was at stake in processes of global change, and discuss the repertoire of visual representations of the global order constructed in mainstream news magazines. The analysis also aimed to illuminate the core values and ideological underpinnings of a seemingly fragmented and contradictory popular discourse on globalization.

GLOBALIZATION AND THE MASS MEDIA

Globalization has been defined by Robertson (1990) as a "particular series of developments concerning the concrete structuration of the world as a whole" (p. 20). For Giddens (1990), the concept refers to the "intensification of worldwide social relations which link distant localities in such a way that local happenings are shaped by events occurring many miles away and vice versa" (p. 64). Among the developments most often discussed in scholarly literature as driving forces of this process of change are the internationalization of capital led by a transnational business elite, the rise of neoliberalism as a hegemonic discourse, the practices of a growing number of transnational social movements and networks, diffusion of common patterns of material and cultural consumption, awareness of the global ecological degradation, massive migratory movements across borders, and development of communication technologies and global media systems facilitating data flows and people's growing awareness of the interaction between cultures across the world (e.g., Arnason, 1990; Bennett, 1987; Hannerz, 1990; Rosenau, 1990). Most sociological approaches to globalization thus tend to emphasize the movement toward economic integration, cultural homogeneity, the formation of institutions for global governance, and the weakening of the nation state as key features. Critical of this conceptualization, Featherstone (1990) has argued that globalization operates simultaneously along various forms of stratification, producing "third cultures" that do not necessarily undermine national sovereignties or lead to centralization or homogenization of culture. Globalization, he posits, needs to be understood also in terms of diversity, disintegration, and heterogeneity of social and cultural forms. Similarly, Rosenau (1990) has approached globalization as a dynamic process characterized by conflicting trends toward both centralization and decentralization, interdependency and localism, and state-centered and multi-centric patterns of organization changing the rules in world politics. According to Appadurai (2000), the multiple and disjunctive flows of people, artifacts, discourses, and images are not "coeval, convergent, isomorphic, or spatially consistent"; and it is precisely the simultaneity and intricate global and local configurations of these flows that demand attention in theoretical work and empirical research (p. 5). For the purpose of this research, I was interested in exploring how media discourses represent these conflictive trends to construct definitions of globalization for the general public.

A common theme in much theoretical work on globalization is the role of media organizations and communication technologies as relevant or active agents in the process of globalization. In the particular case of multimedia conglomerates, media industries are positioned to play a distinctive role in their double capacity as transnational corporations operating in international financial markets, and as cultural institutions engaged in the symbolic construction of the global order. For instance, Time Warner, a corporation that promoted itself as a "vertically integrated global entity," launched in 1990 a marketing strategy with a new motto: "The World Is Our Audience." Likewise, Sony Corporation—the Japanese giant that acquired Columbia Pictures, Tri-Star, and Columbia Records during the 1980s—appropriated the slogan "Think Globally, Act Locally" to sell their corporate "commitment" to "global localization" (Sreberny-Mohammadi, 1991, pp. 123–126). In this respect, the selling of globalization to the market becomes a part of the phenomenon of globalization itself.

In the field of mass communication studies, early critical research on the dynamics of globalization was conducted primarily at the level of political-economic analyses of transnational media organizations. Since the 1970s, scholars have been documenting trends toward transnationalization of communication industries; concentration of media ownership; vertical integration; and global expansion of American, Japanese, and European multimedia conglomerates (e.g., Mattelart 1979; Nordenstreng & Schiller, 1994; Schiller, 1976). Researchers have maintained that such economic trends lead to growing corporate control of information and culture with detrimental effects on diversity of content, expression of political dissent, and local and indigenous cultural production. The net result of this media environment is, as it has been argued, the celebration of global consumerism and homogenization of imagery that legitimizes existing power relations at the national and international levels (e.g., Boyd-Barrett, 1977; Dorfman & Mattelart, 1979; Hamelink, 1994; Herman & McChesney, 1997; Mattelart, 1979; Schiller, 1989).

Influenced by theses on media imperialism and cultural dependency, content analyses and other text-centered approaches to global media production during the 1970s and 1980s attempted to expose the one-way flow of information from developed to underdeveloped countries, and how the values in U.S. media products naturalized Western imperialism (e.g., Beltrán & Cardona, 1977; Dorfman & Mattelart, 1979; Golding, 1977). During the 1980s and 1990s, this approach became a focus of criticism and reassessment for its economic determinism, epistemological ambiguity, and inattention to the dynamics of cultural consumption in late capitalism (e.g., Boyd-Barrett, 1998; Fejes, 1981; Lee, 1980; Martín-Barbero, 1993; Mattelart & Mattelart, 1992; Reeves, 1993). As John Tomlinson (1991) wrote, changes in the configuration of global power posed the need to rethink the notion of cultural imperialism—often conceptualized as imposition of Western values and the intended spread of the cultural values of U.S. capitalism—in terms of globalization as a "far less coherent or culturally directed process" that involves interconnection, interdependency, and interplay between local and global cultural practices (p. 175).

While theoretical work on globalization and the expansion of a global consumer culture has attracted the attention of researchers in the past decade, few textual studies have been conducted to examine popular discourses on the global condition. Ferguson (1992) provided a starting point for the study of the meanings and images of the "world as a whole" in the media in her discussion of seven "myths" about globalization constructed in public discourses: "Big Is Better," "More Is Better," "Time and Space Have Disappeared," "Global Cultural Homogeneity," "Saving the Planet Earth," "Democracy for Export via American TV," and "The New World Order." The overall effect of these myths, states the author, is to reinforce the "gospel of the global market" in a discourse whose "ideological overtones are heavy with normative, determinist implications of historical inevitability" (p. 87). The ideology of globalization, Ferguson maintains, has become a "teleological doctrine that promotes, explains, and justifies an interlocking system of world trade" dominated by Western powers (p. 89). Such proposition, although illuminating, called for close textual analyses of media texts to specify the contexts in which such meanings of globalization are deployed, and how they are articulated in popular culture. Recent contributions to this topic include the work of Parameswaran (2002) and Kraidy (2002), whose research draws on postcolonial theories to explore the construction of narratives of globalization in mainstream media. The goal of this chapter is to contribute to the understanding of this problem by focusing on mainstream news magazines as a particular type of text in which to explore the process of signification.

METHODOLOGY: MEDIA FRAMES AND THE SOCIAL CONSTRUCTION OF MEANING

The methodology selected for this research was frame analysis. Pan and Kosicki (1993) have defined frames as central organizing themes or macropropositions that connect different semantic elements of a news story (headlines, quotes, leads, visual representations, and narrative structure) into a coherent whole to suggest what is at issue. Framing involves selecting some aspects of a perceived reality and making them more salient in a text, in ways that promote a particular problem definition, causal interpretation, moral evaluation, or treatment recommendation (Entman, 1993). According to Gamson, Croteau, Hoynes, and Sasson (1992), the concept of framing implies at least three levels of abstraction. One level is the framing of particular events; another level is that of issue-frames such as nuclear power or abortion, in which particular events appear in an unfolding story; and a third level is that of larger frames that transcend a single event or issue (for example, the "cost-benefit" frame, which could be applied to a variety of problems) (pp. 384–386). The third level of abstraction, or larger frames, is the focus of analysis here. This method was chosen because it allowed for the examination of how relationships among story elements suggest patterns of interpretation of concrete events or issues, as well as for the contextualization of such narrative structures within broader political and cultural discourses that transcend specific events or issues reported.

Verbal and visual representations were approached as interrelated symbolic systems that combine to construct meaning in news texts. As Hall (1973) has observed in his writings about photojournalism, the selection of photographs is not based solely on conventional news values—such as drama, impact, conflict, or novelty—but also is linked to interpretations that seek to exploit the connotative value of visual images. Thus, the display of the photo within a set of thematic interpretations "permits the sign (photo) to serve as the index of an ideological theme" (p. 184). According to Hall (1982), the role of the news media in this process of signification becomes crucial in situations when events are remote to the reader or break the conventional frame of expectations, when powerful interests are at stake, or opposite views are debated. The framing of the globalization exemplifies one of the situations in which mass media may become particularly influential. Since global changes are the product of complex and often remote developments that audiences are only beginning to grasp, the mediation of news reporting can be expected to play a more prominent role in shaping the public's understanding of current trends.

Three main research questions guided this investigation: (1) What are the issues associated with the theme of globalization in mainstream news magazine articles? (2) What are the frames constructed in news articles to suggest what is at issue in processes of globalization? (3) What images of the world are constructed by the visual representations of a changing world order?

To answer these questions, a textual analysis of articles, columns, and visual representations in three mainstream news magazines was conducted. News magazines were selected for analysis taking into account their emphasis on providing context and interpretation, and their prominent display of visual imagery. More specifically, two U.S. magazines (*Time* and *Newsweek*) and a Latin American regional magazine (*Visión*) were chosen for comparative study given the interest in exploring differences and similarities in discourse produced for regional and international audiences. These particular publications were selected based on the following criteria. First, they are large-circulation commercial publications producing news and commentary on current events considered of general interest. Second, as indicated by readership data, these magazines appeal to white-collar, professional middle classes, which tend to be more interested in international affairs. Third, all magazines have international audiences. In the case of *Time*, the magazine had become a multinational medium for a multinational audience of over 6 million readers; likewise, *Newsweek*—with a foreign readership of over 870,000 out of a total circulation of 3,059,410 by 1986—also had been expanding its global reach. Both *Time* and *Newsweek* have special editions reaching the "international information elite" around the globe (Hachten, 1987, p. 74). *Visión*, a regional magazine owned by a Mexican firm and published in Buenos Aires, Argentina, was a Spanish-language, bi-weekly publication with some 800,000 readers and correspondents in thirteen Latin American countries, London, Washington, Los Angeles, and Paris in the early 1990s.

A search for articles with the terms "global" and "globalization" in headings and abstracts was used as a strategy to identify items in which the theme of globalization was likely to be present. Using the online databases ArticleFirst and Academic Index to locate materials in *Time* and *Newsweek*, and a search in the content pages of *Visión*, a selection of fifty-nine articles and ninety-four visual images published between January 1992 and November 1994 was identified. The analysis of written texts sought common frames or organizing ideas that suggested meanings for an array of diverse symbols and viewpoints on globalization. Particular attention was given to those framing devices that suggest how to think about the issue: metaphors, catch phrases, depictions, and historical examples from which lessons were drawn. By charting the salience and repetition of certain viewpoints in headings, leads, transitions, and closing paragraphs, a core position was coded for each article. The analysis of visual images (seventy-one photographs and twenty-three illustrations) focused on the examination of codes of denotation and connotation to explore the visual representations of the world order and to relate these to the frames constructed in written texts. The following section presents a description of frames and core positions identified taking selected examples from content, followed by discussion of the inventory of visual images and relationships to the dominant frames in written texts.

FRAMING THE GLOBAL ORDER

Issue Areas Associated with Globalization in News Coverage

In the selection of fifty-nine articles and columns identified for analysis, the theme of globalization was articulated through coverage of four issue areas or general topics. The expansion of the global economy was the area most often associated with globalization, with 32 percent of the items focusing on such issues as global market expansion, free trade, regional integration, or economic competition in the marketplace. A second issue area identified was foreign relations and international security, with 30 percent of the items covering the restructuration of the post–Cold War international order. A third issue was environmental degradation, with 20 percent of the items focusing on global warming and other ecological threats or hopes for the survival of humankind. Cultural homogenization was another area identified, with 17 percent of the items addressing the diffusion of American popular culture as the new global culture, and the technological developments compressing time and space in the global society. This tendency to discuss globalization through coverage of distinct issue areas not only reflected the fragmentary nature of the media's discourse on globalization, but also, as summary descriptions and subsequent discussion will illustrate, provided some clues on how conflicting global trends were interpreted in public discourse.

Dominant Frames in News Discourse

Within coverage of the four issue areas outlined previously, six salient frames suggested general patterns of interpretation for the issues and problems associated with globalization. Taking into consideration core positions emphasized in articles and columns, these frames were labeled as follows by the researcher: (1) Systemic Interdependence, (2) International (In)Security: United States as Global Cop, (3) The Free Trade Gospel, (4) Cultural Homogenization: U.S. Hegemony in the Global Village, (5) Global Warming: Doomsday or Hope?, and (6) The North-South Divide.

Systemic Interdependence

One way of framing globalization was as a condition in which domestic economic growth was becoming more and more dependent on external trends in the international community. This frame was found to be most salient in articles focusing on trade and commerce, where global interdependence was framed along these lines: If the present national economy was "sluggish," it was "not primarily a domestic problem" for if "European and Japanese economies" were "stumbling," that was "bad for them, and for us." The United States was acting as a "big engine of growth in the world economy," but recovery "could be a lot easier in the United States if Japan and Europe were expanding more rapidly" (*Newsweek*, August 3, 1992, p. 43). Thus, whether or not the president of the United States would be able to "fix" the national economy depended on the global order; yet "leaders around the world—who know it will take a strong U.S. recovery to help their own foundering economies—anxiously watched the Clinton transition" in 1992 (*Time*, November 23, 1992, p. 24). A columnist for *Visión* defined this global condition as a "prisoner's dilemma" where self-interest could no longer be the basis of economic policy, because a negative reaction of others in the economic world would end up harming national interests (April 1–15, 1993, p. 11). This idea of systemic interdependence was found also in some environmental stories. Even when the focus of the report was a local environmental crisis like a flood or drought, references were made to the effects of global weather patterns affecting various regions of the world (e.g., *Time*, July 19, 1993, p. 22; May 3, 1993, p. 59). Nonetheless, be it in stories about the economy or the environment, this notion of systemic interdependence was built on the national or local angle as the departing and ultimate point of reference in news coverage.

International (In)Security: United States as Global Cop

In contrast to the systemic interdependence that was seen as a characteristic of the global economy and ecology, fragmentation and chaos were constructed as dominant features of a global political arena where "disorder"
roamed "untamed" (*Newsweek*, July 26, 1994, p. 36). The rise of ethnic
nationalism, movements for local self-determination, and global mafias
were discussed as serious threats in the post–Cold War global society. While
in the economic arena "jealous sovereignties" were "grouping" in "economic blocs with political ties," in the political world there was an "explosive chaos" producing fragmentation. Consequently, the need to establish
new rules for military intervention was perceived as necessary to "ensure
that the quilt of ethnic ambition is not forced into service as a shroud"
(*Time*, July 6, 1992, p. 36).

The global commons also witnessed the emergence of "new mafias" posing
the "most serious criminal threat in history." Even though no "single-world
conspiracy" had "crystallized," it was argued that crime and "inter-gang
alliance" were growing due to the availability of computer technology, the
collapse of communism, the demand for narcotics, increased migration of
peoples, and the declining significance of national borders (*Newsweek*,
December 13, 1993, p. 22).

Therefore, some columnists considered the role of the U.S. government as
"global cop" a matter of "responsibility," since the events after the Cold War
dictated changes in U.S. interests. The "overriding national interest" was to
maintain "an open world in which America can thrive." "Constant engagement" rather than "isolationism" should direct foreign policy, working "with
the United Nations, not under it" (*Time*, November 8, 1994, p. 98). The
United States had become a "neurotic lion," but "America's skittishness" had
to be overcome because in a "one-superpower world" only the United States
could lead a multinational force able to intervene in "failed nations" like
Somalia or Yugoslavia (*Newsweek*, July 26, 1994, p. 37). While "global
anarchy," "internecine conflicts," and "primal bloodlust" proliferated in
"emerging nations," the intervention of the "lonely superpower" seemed
a "likely growth industry in the emerging global society." The U.S. president
"called the shots," for "no leader in history has ever been so powerful"
(*Newsweek*, December 14, 1992, p. 42). Writers for *Visión* also saw disorien-
tation and insecurity in the global political order, and framed ethno-localism
as a threat to the future of democracy (e.g., October 1–15, 1993, p. 11;
November 16–30, 1994, p. 16). While an isolationist tendency in the United
States reflected a weakened domestic economy and internal problems, the
world needed the U.S. "military and moral leadership" (August 1–15, 1993,
p. 22). But rather than recommending more rules for military intervention,
a columnist called for a new "planetary ethic" because "capitalist democracy"
was only a "form" in need of "content" (June 16–30, 1993, p. 18).

Free Trade Gospel: Global Opportunity and America First

If chaos, uncertainty, and genocide prevailed in the political arena, the economic sphere constructed in the texts analyzed presented a dramatically different scenario. Where the global economy was at issue, globalization often was discussed in terms of the "benefits" of free trade in an open market economy. A common issue of concern in *Time* and *Newsweek* was whether U.S. openness to the international economy helped the world, but hurt the nation. The articles nonetheless reinforced the position that globalization opened new opportunities abroad for local businesses, and in the long term made U.S. corporations more competitive.

The world, according to one writer, was experiencing a "truly global expansion for the first time since World War II." Although unemployment remained a problem, "for an unschooled worker like Buaban Wanmoon [a female factory worker in Indonesia], a robust world economy offers the best job security there is . . . never have so many people around the world been getting better off so fast" and "GATT will help sustain the trend" (*Newsweek*, October 10, 1994, p. 47). Even the "disappearance" of jobs in the United States was "not a bad thing, since the same economic changes that erase old jobs are creating new ones by the millions." The "real benefit" of international trade and investment came from the "less visible ways in which they make for a healthier economy" (*Newsweek*, July 12, 1993, p. 42). A more cautious approach to free trade was observed in *Visión*, where a concern with the "phantom" of global competition ("el fantasma de la competitividad global") was said to be reducing employment opportunities. But even from this perspective, the problem was not the "theory" of competition and free trade, but the "abuses" and lack of "responsibility" of firms in both the private and public sectors (May 1–15, 1994, p. 16).

Cultural Homogenization: U.S. Hegemony in the Global Village

The notion that the world looks more and more like the United States was a recurrent theme in articles about globalization as cultural change. In the words of a *Time*'s columnist, the "global village is defined by an international youth culture that takes its cues from American pop culture," and even though the "world will not become America," America "may still, if only symbolically, be a model for the world" (Fall, 1993, p. 86). Other writers predicted that distinctions between a technologically advanced "fast world" and a "slow world" would become more evident, as the world became a "grid of 30 or so highly advanced city regions or techno-poles, all plugged into the same international circuit" and "linked by the lingua franca of English and the global marketplace" (*Time*, Fall, 1993, p. 85). A columnist saw the confirmation of this trend in the "global warming for

U.S. basketball," a game that would "pass soccer as the number one game on the face of the earth" (*Newsweek*, January 13, 1992, p. 29).

Prominent figures in the emerging global society were, not surprisingly, moguls in the communications industry: Ted Turner was not only declared "Man of the Year" in 1992 by *Time*, but the "prince of the global village" (January 6, 1992, p. 20). Two other members of the global village profiled were Bill Gates, whose plans for expanding his businesses in China and Japan were discussed in a news article, and Rupert Murdoch, owner of a growing global media empire (*Time*, July 11, 1994, p. 67; September 20, 1993, p. 64). Likewise, in *Visión* the star of the "Hispanic global village" ("aldea global hispana") was Mexican entrepreneur Emilio Azcárraga, owner of the television empire Televisa and whose business deals in Mexico, Brazil, Chile, Argentina, Venezuela, and the United States were profiled (May 6, 1992, p. 14).

Global Warming: Doomsday or Hope?

Most of the stories with a focus on the environment made global warming the focus of coverage and debate. The two alternative core positions emphasized in coverage were: (1) global warming was the cause of imminent devastation, and (2) global warming was a pattern that could be reversed by human action or by natural processes. In the articulation of the first position, speculation and "doomsday science" often were part of the discourse. For example, as reported in *Time*, in the summer of 1993, floods, heat, and snow produced a "season in hell." Changing weather patterns served as a "warning that depletion of the ozone layer might have an effect on global climate" (July 19, 1993, p. 22). Further, rising temperatures had led scientists to "predict" that a new "ice age" would begin within the next 2,000 years, or even sooner, as a result of the greenhouse effect: "Many of the world's great cities will be crushed to rubble . . . the Earth ecuatorial regions will remain habitable, but consider what might happen when northern latitude peoples, who hold most of the world's weapons and wealth, attempt to move in with their southern cousins" (*Newsweek*, November 23, 1992, p. 62).

Regarding the second core position, sources claimed that recent developments were suggesting more encouraging scenarios. For example, in *Visión*, the agreement among eight South American government officials to protect the Amazon forest, the "big lung of the world" ("el gran pulmón del mundo"), was seen as a reason to be hopeful (March 3, 1992, p. 20). Likewise, Clinton's action plan to curb gas emission was deemed a positive sign, even if it had "no teeth" (*Time*, November 1, 1993, p. 71). Other articles emphasized the view that "what harm man can do, nature can undo." For instance, it was reported that since the eruption of Mt. Pinatubo in the Philippines, scientists were finding that "mother nature" was applying "her own highly efficient methods" to cool down the earth (*Time*, July 20,

1992, p. 19). If that was not enough, *Newsweek* reported that atmospheric researchers in seven universities, "tired of playing Cassandra," were finding that air pollutants may negate the greenhouse effect, and environmental control "might be doing more harm than good" (February 3, 1992, p. 54). Global warming, as sub-text in the narrative about global trends, was the only discursive arena where opposite views on a specific issue were reported and a space for debate was opened in reporting. For all other issue areas, the salience of a core position made alternative or oppositional views seem irrelevant or nonexistent.

The North-South Divide

The only noticeable difference in the narratives constructed in the magazines selected was *Visión's* framing of globalization as the continuation of a pattern of uneven economic development in the underdeveloped societies that created a North-South divide. For instance, one writer observed that as globalization advanced, the gap between rich and poor nations increased and new "walls" were being erected in the North to keep out the millions of migrants in search of economic survival. The coverage of the United Nations Conference on Trade and Development in 1992 highlighted how poverty was growing as fast as global trade was expanding, and suggested that money allocated for weapons during the Cold War should be used to provide economic development aid to poor countries (November 1–15, 1993, p. 28). Emphasis on the gap between the North and the South was visible also in coverage of global environmental degradation. In contrast to *Time* and *Newsweek*, the framing of the issue of ecological degradation in *Visión* stressed how underdevelopment and poverty were the root cause of current ecological threats. From this point of view, industrial societies, with high levels of energy consumption and wasteful habits, had to assume the responsibility for cleaning up the planet. As stated by some columnists, yesterday's "nuclear threat" was "today's ecological degradation"; but the world powers responsible for the current degradation were not willing to pay the high cost of cleaning up the environment (June 1–15, 1992, p. 6; July 16–31, 1992, p. 22). In *Time* magazine, this logic was inverted by a writer who argued that as "more people in developing countries begin to enjoy the energy-consuming pleasures of cars, air conditioners, and central heating, U.S. efforts to control greenhouse gasses will be more difficult" (May 3, 1993, p. 59).

Despite this difference in perspective, *Visión* shared with *Time* and *Newsweek* the underlying assumption that globalization was an irreversible historical process set in motion by economic competition. Therefore, resistance to globalization through delinking or protectionism was ruled unrealistic, even when Latin America continued to be "marginalized" in the new world order (March 11, 1992, p. 20). Market integration, free trade agreements, and the consolidation of a hemispheric economic bloc were thus considered logical consequences of the new trend (March 11, 1992, p. 18). As one columnist put it, globalization would not be "peaceful nor moderate" for it demanded "increased efficiency" from national firms in developing countries; however, the redefinition of the role of government and businesses as "partners" and "protagonists" within the world system was preferred to the alternatives of protectionism or isolationism (May 6, 1992, p. 6). In other words, in the few instances where the "free trade gospel" was questioned, the dominant orientation of the debate did not open space for the consideration of a third alternative in economic policy or political action. In the following section, the discussion will highlight how these framing patterns were reinforced by the visual representations included in coverage.

THE VISUAL REPERTOIRE: MOVERS AND SHAKERS AND TROUBLEMAKERS IN THE GLOBAL STAGE

Images reproduced in these magazines were drawn from a repertoire of familiar symbols and icons, and most of them referred to distinctive features of American society and culture. Most salient in the inventory of images analyzed was the association of globalization with American popular culture, modern technologies of communication, expansion of trade and industry, and the reassertion of U.S. political leadership. Images where individuals were the subject of attention constituted the largest category in the inventory of images (twenty-seven out of ninety-four items). With the exception of a picture of an Asian American female business owner, these were images of men in positions of leadership and influence, particularly in politics, business, and the military. Photos of U.S. President Bill Clinton were the most common in all magazines, along with pictures of past and present leaders such as Russian President Boris Yelstin, British Prime Minister John Major, French Minister François Mitterrand, Japanese Minister Morihiro Hosokawa, U.S. army generals, Iraqi President Saddam Hussein, German leaders Konrad Adenauer and Helmut Kohl, and South Korean leader Kim Young Sam. Photographs of business leaders included Ted Turner, Bill Gates, and Rupert Murdoch. Whereas the connotation with power and influence in decision making in global affairs was evident in the representation of leaders, another set of actors was placed on the stage as "troublemakers" who threatened international order.

In the category of "troublemakers," twenty-one pictures of unidentified individuals and groups were used to depict events associated with disorder and global insecurity. One distinct set of actors were ethnic groups and separatist movements such as the pro-independence Quebecois in Canada, Slovak separatists in Bratsilava, separatists in Moldova, and Bosnian Muslims and Serbs in Sarajevo. Another set of "unruly" elements threatening the global village were organized criminals in drug trade and illegal traffic of undocumented workers. Those pictured in these articles included a suspected member of the Lithuanian mafia, a Czech drug user, a "reputed member" of Colombia's Cali drug cartel, a member of a Russian mafia, and Chinese traffickers arrested by the U.S. Coast Guard.

Where humans were not the center of attention in visual representations, modern communication technologies and Western cultural icons (twenty out of ninety-four items), and urban industrial sites (twenty-six out of ninety-four) were the most visible subjects. Computers, television sets, satellites, airplanes, and telephones were common referents. Other familiar cultural icons were the Statue of Liberty, the image of the U.S. dollar, the logos of television networks Univision (U.S.) and Televisa (Mexico), and the picture of basketball player Magic Johnson in front of the Eiffel Tower in Paris. In terms of stages or sites of human action, only three illustrations of Earth re-created the world "as a whole" for audiences. Most of the photographs and illustrations identified sites in Western and urban industrial environments: garment factories, steel plants, a tire manufacturing plant, high tech electronic plants, a harbor, cargo ships, airports, highways, slums, and skyscrapers. The few images of natural landscapes found were included in coverage of environmental disasters. When placed in the context of issues covered and core positions emphasized in articles, this repertoire of visual images indeed supported and reproduced the dominant frames identified in written texts to re-create a fractured global society.

PICTURES IN CONTEXT: SPLIT IMAGES OF THE WORLD ORDER

The fragmentation of news discourse on globalization, with a focus on economic, political, ecological, or cultural angles rather than on the interrelated trends driving global change, produced three distinct and conflictive images of the global village: an economic world characterized by free flows and increasing integration, the political world of conflict and division, and the world of cultural homogenization.

Within the general topic of economic expansion, where free trade and systemic interdependence frames were common, the visual imagery reinforced notions of flow and movement of goods and services, hard and disciplined work, financial success, industrialization, and technological innovation. Pictures of factory and industrial workplaces, export goods, means of transportation, technologies of communication, factory workers, and successful entrepreneurs were most common in articles about the global economy. In general, no visual signs of chaos, protest, failure, unemployment, ecological impact of capitalist expansion, antagonism, or instability were present in economic stories.

In contrast, in articles about foreign relations and international security, the images of conflict, "disorder," and diversity were commonplace. Ethnic differences and conflict, criminals, political demonstrators, troops, and military and police personnel accompanied the reporting of political issues.

It was among these visual and written texts that representations of ethnic diversity and national identities were found, as well as references to differences between rich and poor, and developing and developed countries.

On the other hand, when the subject was global culture, visual images focused on technologies of communication and American goods and popular media culture in a one-way flow to the rest of the globe. With the exception of one article (*Time*, December 20, 1992, p. 70), the influence of foreign cultures on American life did not receive attention in visual or written texts. Here, again, the view of globalization as the unilateral diffusion of American popular and business cultures across the world was reinforced in all magazines.

DISCUSSION

As Arnason (1990) has noted, one of the effects of globalization is the activation of national identities and projections. Framing patterns in journalistic texts analyzed for this chapter suggest that national and regional interests prevailed as the preferred framework from which to define and evaluate globalization. The "global" order represented in the magazines examined acquired different geographical configurations according to the issue and angle covered (i.e., economy, international security, ecology, or cultural homogenization) but it never added up to a "whole" in news coverage. For *Time* and *Newsweek*, Europe, Japan, and the United States were the central geographical referent in coverage of "global" processes and leaders. And as expected, *Visión* added a Latin American perspective to its coverage, although this angle did not alter the dominant tendency to frame globalization as a U.S.-led phenomenon. In all magazines, U.S. and European relations were emphasized, while the interests and experiences of other nations and international actors were ignored. With the exception of some environmental stories, where the fate of the entire planet was assumed to be at issue, national issues or regional concerns remained the starting point for the definition of the global situation.

Along these lines, globalization was defined primarily as one-way flows of material and cultural goods and services from the United States to the rest of the world, with emphasis on the advantages of such flows (and/or disadvantages as addressed in some articles in *Visión*) for the national (or regional) interest. Even in stories where globalization was framed as systemic interdependence, attention was given to the comparative advantages that ensured the continuing leadership of the United States. In fact, in the three publications analyzed, writers associated globalization with the restructuration of U.S. political, military, and economic hegemony in the post–Cold War era. As mentioned earlier, the only salient difference in content was *Visión's* references to the gap between rich and poor nations and the continuing economic and technological dependency of Latin America. But as noted before, attention to this angle was characterized by a tone of resignation to the status quo that did not challenge current economic policies adopted in Latin America or explore alternatives. In *Time* and *Newsweek*, the lack of any specific references to developing societies in stories about global economic and cultural affairs was remarkable. References to third world societies in the U.S. magazines were found, however, in reports where political instability, environmental disasters, and ethnic conflicts were underscored. Interestingly, it was in connection with instability, deviance, and threat that ethnic diversity, popular struggles for local empowerment and self-government, and ideological difference came to the forefront in news coverage.

When all frames and angles emphasized are taken into consideration, one could argue that news discourses on globalization in the early 1990s reflected some of the conflictive and contradictory processes of integration/disintegration and homogenization/differentiation that scholars like Rosenau (1990), Featherstone (1990), and Appadurai (2000) have discussed as defining features of the new world order. But the fragments of this split image of the global order constructed in news texts make up only a narrow representation of global processes of change. First, news reporting characterized by an emphasis on distinct and disconnected issue areas tended to obscure the interconnections, synergy, and cause-effect relations among economic, political, cultural, and environmental trends. Thus, the understanding of the relationships between capitalist expansion and ecological degradation, or between geopolitical interests and technological developments and cultural trends, was kept outside the limits of news discourse on globalization. Second, the frames and images selected for emphasis shared a common ideological overtone that closed the possibility of imagining a different kind of global village. Globalization was assumed to be an irreversible historical process accelerated by the conclusion of the Cold War and the expansion of capitalism and trade. Although subtle differences in perspective were observed in *Visión*, *Time*, and *Newsweek*, all magazines declared "unrealistic" any opposition or resistance to the globalization of capital. Policies to promote market integration, free trade, and foreign investment were favored as logical, adaptive strategies in a competitive global village. In the political realm, emphasis on the moral and military leadership of the United States, and the need to redraft rules for American intervention around the globe overshadowed any debate over development of policies of multilateral negotiation and cooperation in world governance. In the cultural sphere, the focus on the popularity of American popular culture as a global culture of choice also tended to reinforce the notion of globalization as a U.S.-led process of cultural homogenization. Across issue areas and frames, the echoes of economic determinism shaped the rationale behind these core positions and hindered further discussion of alternative political options, economic strategies, and cultural projects available to local and global actors.

Although exploratory and limited in scope, this comparative analysis suggests how underlying the fragmented and polysemic surface of news discourses on globalization, a particular set of core values and perspectives on globalization had acquired currency in both U.S. and Latin American popular discourse by the early 1990s. This brand of globalism, as Hamelink (1993) has argued, promotes a mode of integration in which a preferred, autocentric value system is imposed on a global scale, disregarding the reality of a polycentric cultural space and treating difference and resistance as a threat to global stability. In the context of the neoliberal policies adopted around the globe since the 1980s, this seemingly disconnected and contradictory set of images and frames penetrated the public realm with a set of assumptions that provided support to the hegemonic interests of corporate capitalism and the geopolitical agenda of the United States in the post–Cold War era.

REFERENCES

Appadurai, A. (2000). Grassroots, globalization and the research imagination. *Public Culture, 12,* 1–19.

Arnason, J. (1990). Nationalism, globalization and modernity. *Theory, Culture and Society, 7*(2/3), 207–236.

Beltrán, L. R., & Cardona, E. F. (1977). Latin America and the United States: Flaws in the free flow of information. In K. Nordenstreng & H. Schiller (Eds.), *National sovereignty and international communication* (pp. 33–64). Norwood, NJ: Ablex.

Bennett, J. (1987). Anthropology and the emerging world order: The paradigm of culture in an age of interdependence. In K. Moore (Ed.), *Waymarks: The Notre Dame Inaugural Lectures in Anthropology.* Notre Dame, IN: University of Notre Dame Press.

Boyd-Barrett, O. (1977). Media imperialism: Toward an international framework for the analysis of media systems. In J. Curran, M. Gurevitch, & J. Woollacott (Eds.), *Mass communication and society.* London: Edward Arnold.

———. (1998). Media imperialism reformulated. In D. K. Thusu (Ed.), *Electronic empires: Global media and local resistance* (pp. 157–176). London: Arnold.

Carragee, K. M. (1991). News and ideology. *Journalism Monographs, 128,* 1–31.

Dijk, T. Van. (1991). The interdisciplinary study of news as discourse. In K. B. Jensen & N. W. Jankowski (Eds.), *A handbook of qualitative methodologies for mass communication research* (pp. 108–120). London: Routledge.

Dorfman, A., & Mattelart, A. (1979). *Para leer al Pato Donald.* (19th ed.). Mexico: Siglo Veintiuno.

Entman, R. M. (1991). Framing U.S. coverage of international news: Contrasts in narratives of the KAL and Iran air incidents. *Journal of Communication, 41*(4), 6–27.

———. (1993). Framing: Toward clarification of a fractured paradigm. *Journal of Communication, 43*(4), 51–58.

Featherstone, M. (Ed.). (1990). Global culture, nationalism, globalization and modernity. *Theory, Culture and Society 7*(2/3), 1–14.

Fejes, F. (1981). Media imperialism: An assessment. *Media, Culture and Society, 3*, 281–289.

Ferguson, M. (1992). The mythology about globalization. *European Journal of Communication, 7*, 69–93.

Gamson, W., Croteau D., Hoynes, W., & Sasson, T. (1992). Media images and the social construction of reality. *Annual Review of Sociology, 18*, 373–393.

Gamson, W., & Modigliani, A. (1989). Media discourse and public opinion on nuclear power. *American Journal of Sociology, 5*(1), 1–37.

Giddens, A. (1990). *The consequences of modernity*. Stanford: Stanford University Press.

Golding, P. (1977). Media professionalism in the third world. In J. Curran et al. (Eds.), *Mass communication and society* (pp. 191–308). London: Edward Arnold.

Gurevitch, M. (1991). Globalization of electronic journalism. In J. Curran & M. Gurevitch (Eds.), *Mass media and society* (pp. 178–93). London: Edward Arnold.

Hall, S. (1982). The rediscovery of 'ideology': Return of the repressed in media studies. In M. Gurevitch, T. Bennett, J. Curran, & J. Woollacott (Eds.), *Culture, society and the media* (pp. 56–90). London: Routledge.

——— . (1973). The determinations of news photographs. In S. Cohen & M. Young (Eds.), *The manufacture of news*. Beverly Hills: Sage.

Hamelink, C. (1983). *Cultural autonomy in global communications*. New York: Longman.

———. (1993). Globalism and national sovereignty. In K. Nordenstreng & H. Schiller (Eds.), *Beyond national sovereignty: International communication in the 1990s* (pp. 371–393). Norwood, NJ: Ablex.

———. (1994). *Trends in world communication*. Penang, Malaysia: Southbound.

Hannerz, U. (1990). Cosmopolitans and locals in world culture. *Theory, Culture and Society, 7*, 237–251.

Herman, E., & McChesney, R. (1997). *Global media*. London: Cassell.

Kraidy, M. M. (2002). Hybridity in cultural globalization. *Communication Theory* 12(3), 316–339.

Lee, C. C. (1980). *Media imperialism reconsidered*. Beverly Hills: Sage.

Martín-Barbero, J. (1993). *Communication, culture and hegemony*. London: Sage.

Mattelart, A. (1979). *Multinational corporations and the control of culture*. New Jersey: Humanities Press.

Mattelart, A., & Mattelart, M. (1992). *Rethinking media theory*. Minneapolis: University of Minnesota Press.

Nordenstreng, K., & Schiller, H. (Eds.) (1994). *Beyond national sovereignty: International communication in the 1990s*. Norwood, NJ: Ablex.

Pan, Z., & Kosicki, G. M. (1993). Framing analysis: An approach to news discourse. *Political Communication, 10*, 55–75.

Parameswaran, R. (2002). Local culture in global media: Excavating colonial and material discourses in National Geographic. *Communication Theory, 12*(3), 316–339.

Reeves, G. (1993). *Communication and the 'Third World'*. London: Routledge.

Robertson, R. (1990). Mapping the global condition: Globalization as the central concept. *Theory, Culture and Society, 7*, 15–30.

————. (1992). *Globalization: Social theory and global culture.* London: Sage.

Rosenau, J. (1990). *Turbulence in world politics.* Princeton: Princeton University Press.

Schiller, H. I. (1976). *Communication and cultural domination.* White Plains: International Arts and Sciences Press.

————. (1989). *Culture, Inc.* New York: Oxford University Press.

Sklair, L. (1991). *Sociology of the global system.* Baltimore: Johns Hopkins University Press.

Sreberny-Mohammadi, A. (1991). The global and the local in international communication. In J. Curran & M. Gurevitch (Eds.), *Mass media and society* (pp. 118–137). London: Edward Arnold.

Straubhaar, J. (1991). Beyond media imperialism: Asymmetrical interdependence and cultural proximity. *Critical Studies in Mass Communication, 8,* 29–38.

Thrift, N. (1992). Muddling through: World orders and globalization. *Professional Geographer, 44*(1), 3–7.

Tomlinson, J. (1991). *Cultural imperialism.* Baltimore: Johns Hopkins.

Wolfsfeld, G. (1991). Media, protest, and political violence. *Journalism Monographs, 127,* 1–55.

7

Whose Public Sphere?
The Party and the Protests
of *America 2000*

Anne Marie Todd

The Democratic National Convention (DNC), August 14–17, 2000, is an exemplar historical moment for the study of protests and demonstrations for social change. While the events inside the walls of Los Angeles' premier sports arena, Staples Center, were indicative of American politics as usual, the protests outside the convention and the subsequent media coverage of these demonstrations reveal provocative power relationships of American politics. An examination of the protests illustrates that the global justice movement is a collection of diverse groups including labor, environmental, fair trade, feminist, and anarchist contingents. The vivid images of confrontation between anti-globalization activists and Los Angeles police established the DNC as a media spectacle, revealing the richness of the convention protests as sites of cultural and political representation. Dubbed *America 2000,* the convention itself is an "official" symbol of participation in American democracy, and when confronted with the activist rhetoric of social change, the event speaks to the meaning of protest in the contemporary public discourse—and the meaning of the public sphere itself. This chapter is organized in three parts. First, I describe the DNC as a powerful media event with great political and cultural influence. Next, I contextualize the DNC in current discussions of Habermas' ideal public sphere. Finally, I examine media representations of the clash of police and protesters, and the implications for social and political activism. This media analysis explicates the news discourse of the *Los Angeles Times,* other national newspapers, and the subaltern discourse of the protests themselves—through pamphlets

and publications collected throughout the marches and demonstrations outside the area of the DNC proceedings.

THE DEMOCRATIC MEDIA CONVENTION: A POLITICAL SPECTACLE

Los Angeles is the quintessential media town. Traveling through this city,
one is constantly bombarded with media images—billboards the size of skyscrapers, gigantic video screens, and a Hollywood attitude all contribute to
the town's media saturation. This multifarious media network is double-
edged. On the one hand, media publicity is essential to a social movement's
ability to raise public awareness of a specific issue, or set of issues. In this
way, the Los Angeles mobilization "is a pivotal moment in the new global
justice movement. . . . The protests and events will shine a bright spotlight
on issues of particular urgency to California, such as the criminalization of
youth, and the prison-industrial complex" (Zoll, 2000). On the other hand,
the intense commercialization of Los Angeles' mass media belies the issues
of the protests themselves. Indeed, the several days of marches and demonstrations during the DNC in downtown Los Angeles are in striking juxtaposition to the official convention business housed in Staples Center. A concert
Monday night, August 13, featuring "Rage Against the Machine" witnessed
the most visible confrontation between protesters and police, but bouts of
arrests and minor skirmishes marked the duration of the convention.

America 2000 certainly is a media-saturated event, with both mainstream
and subaltern coverage. Events inside the convention largely were covered
by network news, which enjoyed a viewership of nearly 18 million
(*New York Times* 2000, August 20). The events outside received both mainstream and alternative media coverage. The protests were thoroughly and
extensively documented. Independent Media Center issued its own press cre-
dentials to all comers. The affordability of video cameras and the ease of
posting on the Web means that activists are newly able to record their struggles and communicate their message (Ehrenreich, 2000, August 25–31).

As a media event, the DNC is the "perfect venue for activists to educate
a mass audience about the party's rightward, pro-corporate agenda and to
connect concerns about globalization, the death penalty, and poverty with
the party's advancement of these problems" (Zoll, 2000). The mediation of
this event is particularly important in studying the contemporary public
sphere because the DNC is literally part of a campaign to persuade the
American public to vote for the Democratic Party, in particular for the presidential candidate, Al Gore. The mass media are a powerful force in the
manipulation of public opinion and policy decisions. The economic concentration of media and the increasing efficiency of news production create
a new situation for movements seeking social change (Gitlin, 1980).
Corporate media frame the Democratic Convention to create a sense of

government control, while also maintaining an element of hysteria, even danger to pique their audiences' interest, and keep the ratings up. The media portrayals of the protests reveal establishments' strategies of containment and control. *America 2000* illustrates how images mediate social relations through spectacle, which separates the official, political realm from the elements of society represented on the streets (see Debord, 1967, 1970; Kellner, 2001).

Media events exhibit characteristics of contest, conquest, or coronation (Dayan & Katz, 1992). *America 2000* is a contest because it represents a stage in the national contest for the chief executive of the United States. "Contests pit evenly matched individuals or teams against each other and bid them to compete according to strict rules" (Dayan & Katz, 1992, p. 33). The national Democratic and Republican conventions are ritual steps in the competition for the White House Oval Office, and follow strict historical standards that govern the convention proceedings and facilitate the exclusion of dissident voices. *America 2000* signifies a conquest as an event celebrating Gore's triumph in the primaries and symbolic of a Democratic Party win in November (Dayan & Katz, 1992, p. 35). The convention is the forum where the presidential and vice-presidential candidates establish their platforms, and initiate campaign strategies for the rest of the election season. Furthermore, the attitude of the DNC's message conveys political prowess; the power of the Democratic Party to bring positive change to America.

The DNC is the coronation of the Democratic candidate for the presidency. "Coronations, more than other events, keep their distance from reality, since time and place and ceremonial symbols must all be kept unpolluted" (Dayan & Katz, 1992, pp. 34–35). An official protest area was established to ensure the security of the convention and maintain a pristine image of democracy, specifically the Democratic political party. The high security surrounding the convention establishes the event as a coronation. Strategies of control and containment are necessary to maintain the sanctity of the convention proceedings, hence the designation of a protest zone, and the high level of police force throughout the convention. In this way, the media spectacle of the DNC justifies the existing political system's conditions and goals (see Debord 1967, 1970). The news media produce discursive and visual images of control that reify ideological notions of control and authority.

AMERICA 2000: PROTECTING THE "OFFICIAL" PUBLIC SPHERE

America 2000 exemplifies Habermas' notion of the public sphere wherein the delegates are representatives of a public capable of making rational decisions. Elected representatives literally convened to discuss the future of the nation. Delegates constructed campaign strategies based on public opinion of national issues, intending to represent common interests.

However, the situation was complicated by the expressions of dissent out-side the convention itself. These protests directly challenged the legitimacy and accountability of the official business of the Democratic Party. Habermas (1989) describes his concept of the public sphere as "a domain of our social life in which a thing as public opinion can be formed" (p. 398). He characterizes the public as a bourgeois public sphere of private persons assembled to form a public, to discuss issues of the common interest. In the tradition of salons of eighteenth century Europe, the DNC is conceived as an intellectual gathering for an enlightened discussion of public affairs—in this case, party strategy for the upcoming November election.

Habermas (1989) introduces implicit eligibility requirements that condition participation in the public sphere on property ownership and education. The delegates of the DNC must meet such eligibility requirements—while not explicitly based on wealth, the delegates are chosen as representatives of public opinion, based on conventional qualifications. The liberal ideal of public discussion requires rational adults who are enlightened enough to make reasoned decisions concerning matters of society and the state. In this way, the convention is a forum for the formation of public opinion, legiti-mate because it comes from rational, enlightened adults—namely the polit-ical delegates of the Democratic Party.

Countless theorists have commented on the applicability of the notion of a public sphere in a globalized world. The traditional public sphere of policy decision makers has exploded in the proliferation of information dissemi-nated via new technology (see Asen & Brouwer, 2001; Mater, 2001). Fraser (1993) notes several weaknesses of Habermas' bourgeois public sphere, which are relevant to an analysis of the Democratic National Convention. First, Habermas' masculine public sphere fails to provide open access, par-ticipatory parity, and social equality, because protocol and décor govern discursive interactions of the public sphere as indicative markers of status. Not only is this evident in the exclusive access to official convention events, but also in the government's treatment of the protesters outside Staples Center. The status quo values of order and control (in the name of security) were privileged over the social concerns of the demonstrators and arguably, the Constitutional values of free speech and the right to assembly.

According to Fraser, the public sphere is *the* place for idea building and deliberation over community issues. The public sphere remains exclusive because sociocultural norms are never questioned. "In stratified societies, arrangements that accommodate contestation among a plurality of com-peting publics better promote the ideal of participatory parity than does a single, comprehensive, overarching public sphere" (Fraser, 1993, p. 14). Marginalized groups have no venues to express their views that are not con-trolled or mediated by dominant groups. *Subaltern counterpublics* represent a rhetorical response to the official public sphere as "parallel discursive arenas where members of subordinated social groups invent and circulate counter discourses, so as to formulate oppositional interpretations of their identities, interests, and needs" (Fraser, 1993, p. 14). It is this manifestation of the public sphere that concerns the present analysis—the rhetorical strategy of social movements constitutes oppositional public spheres.

In this way, the scene of the DNC represents a stratified society that suppresses contestation and promotes one overarching, comprehensive public sphere rather than an ideal of participatory parity. The exercise of state force over dissident demonstrators exemplifies government strategy for protecting the sanctioned public discussion by excluding any undesirable elements of the American public. The democratic public sphere features the bourgeois public as a normative ideal, and (brings into question) what it means to be public. The anti-globalization protests at the DNC critique how decision making and opinion formation occur within the American democratic public sphere.

The DNC necessarily decides what constitutes official public business, through the selection of issues for discussion. Through the categorization of public and private interests, convention planners determine what is appropriate for the public domain. Calhoun (1998) argues that states and their representatives—in this case the convention delegates who represent the electorate—influence national agenda-setting, mass media, and the formation and maintenance of public discourse (p. 382). Economic privatization allows certain practices and groups to be shielded from public deliberation, and thus exempt from legal recourse. Indeed, this is one of the overarching themes of the protest agenda—that corporate interests affect political policymaking, by keeping certain issues outside the jurisdiction of public legislation. This bourgeois suppression of alternative public fora is inherently antidemocratic, so a universal public sphere remains unaccountable to contemporary cultural and social diversity. Both the administration of the Democratic Party and the convention planners have their hands deep in the pockets of corporate giants. This condition is exacerbated by corporate media channels, which determine what is important to include in the representation of the convention, and the protests (see Chomsky, 1999; Chomsky & Herman, 1988, 2002).

Administrative strategies for containing the demonstrations work with media representations to undercut the protesters' message. Police cordoned off blocks around the convention, and confined protesters gathered near Staples Center to a small parking lot. The designation of an official protest area outside the convention itself is a tangible symbol of how the public sphere is kept exclusive by convention planners and law enforcement. An anarchist protester explains: "We don't have a voice, we're totally shut out. The fence around the Staples Center is a metaphor for the way we're caged out of the entire system" (Ehrenreich, 17 August, 2000). Tom Morello of the punk band "Rage Against the Machine," who performed at one of the protest rallies, notes the symbolic function of the protest zone:

The glaring metaphor of the 20-foot-tall barbed-wire fence and the storm-trooper police on the other side of it with tear gas, guns and riot helmets protecting the Democratic convention from the people of Los Angeles. . . . There was a balcony outside the Staples Center where people were drinking fine wines and champagne and eating shrimp cocktails, looking down at the "rabble." The real people's convention was being held on the streets outside. (Morello, 2000)

Vividly reminiscent of eighteenth-century salons, which were intellectual gatherings of the public sphere, the DNC is a dramatic enactment of the contemporary public sphere. The rhetorical confrontation evident in this dialectical engagement of political delegates and the people they represent reveals the cultural and political politics of representation as protesters and police battle for legitimacy outside of the convention itself.

THE PLAYERS OF THE PUBLIC SPHERE: THE PROTESTERS VERSUS THE LAPD

The status of *America 2000* as a media event reveals the powerful influence of contemporary news media in shaping American perceptions or reality—in this case, an understanding of the magnanimity of the protests. Media orchestrate everyday consciousness through their pervasiveness and symbolic capacity. In many ways, mass media define reality through their interpretations of events, which also limit opposition, and in this way have become central to the distribution of ideology (Gitlin, 1980, p. 2). Media frames are composed of tacit theories about "what matters" through interpretation, presentation, selection, emphasis, and exclusion" (Gitlin, 1980, p. 7).

In this way, because protests are expressions of opposition to the established proceedings of the DNC, media representations of the demonstrations determine their significance. That is, news coverage limits the effectiveness of the protests, by describing them as disorderly, but contained by the LAPD. As a media-produced symbol of democracy, the DNC is a rhetorical appeal to ideologies of authority and control. The newspapers, television, and other media representations of the events surrounding the convention take on certain media frames or selective emphasis of the goings on of the DNC. This analysis focuses on how the media frame the players in the protest drama, particularly the protesters and the police, and asks how the discourse of *America 2000* influences the rhetoric of protest.

Examination of local and national newspaper coverage before and during the election reveals police and media tactics of containment in both the predictions and descriptions of the demonstrations during the DNC. First, the media predictions of the protest crowd were grossly overestimated. "The original estimates of protesters—70,000 and up—were wildly exaggerated. Crowds never exceeded the 15,000 on hand for the "Rage Against the Machine" concert Monday night, and most of those were revelers" (Scheer, 2000). Furthermore, LAPD intelligence predicted nearly 50,000 protesters would converge at the DNC, but that figure proved wildly inflated. LAPD projected that 40 percent (20,000 activists) would be veterans of Seattle, and 20 percent were expected to cause property damage (Rappleye, 2000). Thus, the initial perceptions of the protesters certainly shaped media portrayals of the actual protests in two ways. First, the exaggerated projections of numbers served to undermine the numbers of protesters that did show up, dwarfing them in comparison to what could have been. This seems to imply that the protests were a failure in the sense that they didn't meet their goal of attracting the projected number of protesters.

Second, the "fearsome numbers were matched by intelligence that profiled dissident activists as violent subversives bent on wrecking havoc." Anarchists were described as wielding tiki torches as "Molotov cocktails-on-a-stick" and employing "Campbell's Soup cans as incendiary devices" to express their hatred for that company (Rappleye, 2000). In this way, the exaggerated reports of protesters make the actual demonstrations seem tame by comparison, but the heightened expectations of the planned demonstrations helped to paint the protesters as irrational and dangerous.

The *New York Times* noted the real fears of police that demonstrators could "create disruptions in widely spread out areas of this widely spread out city" (Purdum, 2000, August 13). For this reason, "the department is spread throughout the city, advertising its strength or bravado not only to those near the convention but to the rest of the area as well" (Shuster & Newton, 2000). The anticorporate theme of the protests is mentioned here in a way that incites fear of the potential damage caused by volatile protesters. It is the unpredictability of the protests that is most threatening to the police and event planners who fear their potential failure to contain the demonstrations.

A second media strategy in containing the protests is the description of the protests and protesters in media accounts of the convention. Mass media certainly color public perception of the demonstrations and constitute an impressive ideological influence on shaping audience opinion of the convention events. Media create ideology by defining public situations through selective coverage, emphasis, and tone (Gitlin, 1980, p. 9). Media treatment of the protesters reveals discrepant interpretations of the demonstrations and police reactions to them. For example, protesters and police have different accounts of Monday night's concerts. Protesters claim they tried to shut down the concert and were preparing to ask the crowd to leave peacefully, but police claim that "protest organizers had lost control of the event, leaving police with the responsibility to clear the area" (Shuster & Newton, 2000). Police officials report reality through interviews with the media, and in their reports, they minimize the effect of the protests by depicting them as out of control and disorderly, thus warranting police action. The protest coordinators are represented as helpless in the face of mob fury.

It is useful to examine media depiction of both sides of this drama to determine how these media representations affect social activism. That is, it is important for social movements that are trying to garner public support or change public perception in some way to effectively convey an image of success to the media audience. The power of the media can influence social activism positively or negatively, but regardless, media representations are inherently affected by the economic motives governing mainstream media production. Network executives of news programs covering the protests outside the convention are interested in attracting the most sizable audience, and so will resort to dramatic headlines to attract viewers (Hertz, 2002). Mainstream media show images, but are often unwilling to tell the whole story, or even criticize police containment efforts (see FAIR, 2000; Solomon & Cohen, 1997). Examination of this type of news coverage seems to present a dual image of the protest events—a wild, unpredictable crowd, but a stable situation thanks to police presence and skill. God bless America and so forth.

As proponents of social change, anti-globalization protesters desire media coverage to draw attention to their cause(s), so the ample media exposure of the DNC protests helps to strengthen the movement by increasing public awareness. Opposition movements use the media spotlight to recruit members and public sympathy for their causes, as well as placing issues on national political agendas by broadcasting images of resistance (Gitlin, 1980, p. 242). Publicity is central to social movement strategy. Visible confrontation helps increase awareness of issues and the movement itself (see Cathcart, 1978).

Conversely, negative media portrayals can hinder efforts toward social change by threatening the stability of the status quo in the eyes of the public. Maintaining a sense of stability by making the demonstrations seem insignificant may limit the impact of the protests by precluding serious consideration of their challenge. Describing the protests on the eve of the convention, J. R. Hicks, executive director of the LA Human Relations Commission said "we expect it to be peaceful, but the death penalty is a highly volatile issue" (Terry, 2000). This is one of many descriptions of the volatility of the protesters, indicating the negative slant of media portrayals of the protests in general, and the activists themselves. One *Los Angeles Times* report claimed "there were so many marches that demonstrators could scarcely keep from running into each other" (Martelle & Riccardi, 2000). This exemplifies media attempts to contain the impacts of the protests by depicting the demonstrations as an entirely disorganized affair. The same article quoted delegates who claimed the protesters are not effectively communicating their message (Martelle & Riccardi, 2000). News media work to undermine the effectiveness of the demonstrations in the eyes of the American public by painting protesters and their causes as volatile and impossible to take seriously.

The mediation of the demonstrations reveals efforts to discredit the activists themselves, who are characterized as misguided social misfits. "Self-policing, especially for anti-authoritarian protesters, is an awkward task. Trying to control the behavior of their own runs counter to the individualistic and laissez-faire spirit of the resurgent protest movement, some demonstrators said" (Martelle & Riccardi, 2000). In this way, the agents of social change are seen as incapable of affecting social and political conditions, and are judged unworthy of serious consideration. A *Los Angeles Times* profile of a protest organizer concludes that an activist's life is a luxury (Texeira, 2000). This characterization undermines the seriousness of protester goals, and thus discourages public support of their activities. A *Los Angeles Times* report that the demonstrations on the second day of the convention were "free of the sort of disorder that broke out Monday night after a Rage Against the Machine concert" (Martelle & Riccardi, 2000). This characterizes the protests as both disorderly and contained by the police. "Mass media define the public significance of movement events or, by blanking them out, actively deprive them of larger significance" (Gitlin, 1980, p. 3). This is indeed the case at the DNC.

The planning and organization of the LAPD were well broadcast before and during the convention. The department planned for this event with a six-inch-thick security plan "to deter demonstrations and to offer a 'calming effect' on city residents and visitors" (Shuster & Newton, 2000). The protests are described as potentially volatile, invoking the possibility of severe impacts on the maintenance of social order. Media descriptions of police capability are aimed at reassuring the American public that the protests are under control. The LAPD "confronting" DNC demonstrators is "bigger, better-equipped and technologically improved over the force that failed in the 1992 riots" (Shuster & Newton, 2000). Media coverage of the technological virility of the LAPD seems gratuitous and obviously aimed at instilling confidence in the force's ability to contain a potentially volatile situation. And it is the potential volatility that makes the mediation of the department's prowess particularly important in the shaping of public opinion.

Representing the strength of American government, the LAPD symbolizes the stability of the established social and political order. The rhetoric of the police is indicative of administrative strategies of control and civility. In response to accusations of excessive and arbitrary force, LAPD officials defend their tactics as necessary to end a violent situation. However, this contradicts some media accounts that characterize police action as excessive. Police raced through downtown even when there were no serious demonstrations underway (Shuster & Newton, 2000). The police and convention officials desired a media image of political order, it seems at any cost. To this end, the LAPD was "determined to maintain control of the streets. . . . The idea is to control crowds through intimidation. Lethal force is eschewed, but force of any other kind is maximized" (Rappleye, 2000). Here the rhetorical strategies of stability, authority, and control are quite evident. In this way, the antics of the police illustrate how administrative strategies of control worked to contain the image and thus the impact of the protests.

Administrators transform issues of protest into issues of authority, make protesters seem like a minority, attribute base motives to the protesters, and present the establishment as a defender of civil liberties (Windt, 1982). These strategies are evident in the media representation of the police control of the situation. Coverage of the police ability to contain the situation was mediated as issues of authority, rather than protest, as did media lack of focus on the protesters' message. The predictions of the protests made the protests seem like a minority, and both the predictions and the accounts of the volatile situation predicted dire and terrible consequences, like property damage if the protesters were not contained.

Furthermore, the tactical actions of the police explicitly comment on social power relationships. Witness to physical and verbal skirmishes in the streets of Los Angeles, the media audience interprets the interaction of police and protesters as a contest of power. More than a few critics claim the LAPD was itching for a fight (Scheer, 2000). "The most intense use of force—and the most striking television images—involved the liberal use of riot guns that spat glowing sparks as they fired stinging rubber pellets" (Rappleye, 2000). In this way, the police treated these demonstrations as riots, which helped to incite the minds of the American public. Whether incendiary or not, the vivid media images of police engagement of the protesters ensured a rapt audience, much to the delight of media executives.

According to the watchdog group, Fairness and Accuracy in Reporting (FAIR), in its July 25 report on convention coverage, "what emerges from this coverage is an image of activists as a paramilitary mob preparing to take to the streets to frustrate and discredit the police" (Zoll, 2000). This contradicts the protesters' view of their efforts as described in personal accounts of their activities, and in pamphlets distributed by demonstrators. One protester recounts the feeling of solidarity enjoyed by the activists:

Though we were to have been a misinformed mass of bodies with no unifying issue, it felt like just the opposite to the people gathered in the street. Everyone had some cause they were supporting, but everyone was there to support everyone else's cause, in solidarity, as people. There were marchers on many different topics, and people showed up regardless of their personal stake to let it be known that they recognized that something was not right, in contrast to the general rosy glow that we are supposed to accept in America. (Newell, 2000)

The central issue at stake for the protesters was the pervasive allegiance to establishment ideals, and unquestioning acceptance of mediated visions of reality. The demonstrations are fundamentally about issues of power in American conceptions of democracy.

At the bottom of it all, though, is that there is too much money being concentrated in the hands of too few. We are protesting police racism. We are protesting unmitigated corporate greed and control. We are protesting that a mere 7 corporations control the country's media outlets. We are protesting the stringent two party system. We are protesting the use of genetic modification of our food. We are protesting the mere lip service being given to the use of soft money in elections. And we are gathering a youth movement that will not be classified and it will not be pacified. (Newell, 2000)

An examination of police accounts of the DNC protests offers a strikingly different view of activist efforts. Media portrayals of police efforts depict the police presence as effective in controlling the demonstrations. The media frames of the DNC reveal an administrative strategy to convey a sense of police control over the protests to establish public confidence in establishment and institutional authority.

CONCLUSIONS: IMPLICATIONS FOR SOCIAL MOVEMENTS

This analysis tells us a lot about the way that the pervasive media affects efforts toward social change and anti-globalization protests in particular. Gitlin argues that in a society floodlit by media coverage, it is nearly impossible for an opposition movement "to define itself and its world view, to build up an infrastructure of self-generated cultural institutions, outside the dominant culture. . . . The social meanings of intentional action have been deformed beyond recognition" (Gitlin, 1980, p. 3). Indeed the convention delegates only saw the events on television, as though they would not even look out the windows of the Staples Center to see the reality outside the convention (Tobar, 2000).

Media renditions of the DNC protests define the reality of the situation. "People find themselves relying on the media for images of their heroes . . . for a recognition of public values, for symbols in general, even for language" (Gitlin, 1980, p. 1). The confrontation of the protests reveals the many ways in which the media determine the heroic players of this social drama, and defines our social values. This happens in several ways. First, the designation of an Official Protest Area discloses the underlying emphasis on government control of the demonstrations and the assertion of state authority in the containment of protesters. Second, the juxtaposition of the televised images of the "chosen" political elite against the visual oppression of protesters is a literal manifestation of the official public sphere actively marginalizing subaltern counterpublics. Third, the media spectacle created through various media channels, most notably televised coverage of the convention protests, is symbolized in the image of protester as radical and irrational, even dangerous, effectively subdued by dominating government force. The Democratic National Convention represents the ideological construction of media events, and implications for cultural and political advocacy and social change. Throughout all of these elements run themes of authoritarianism and oppression, which parallel the substantive issues of the demonstrations at the Democratic National Convention. While it is impossible to survey to what extent attitudes were changed, or consciousness altered, this type of discourse is necessary to challenge administrative efforts to contain and squelch protest movements. The recurring themes of environmental exploitation, police brutality, corporate greed, and political corruption in the anti-globalization protest rhetoric offer a counteradvocacy to the official narrative of the Convention propaganda and media spectacle.

The DNC exemplifies how challenges to "official" public fora are contests for media spin and public perception and involve issues of authority and control. Indeed as DeLuca and Peeples (2002) note, media *produce* the public sphere. *America 2000* demonstrates how the media and administrative authorities work to establish and maintain the authority of the "official" public sphere by containing the impact of the demonstrations on public perceptions of the convention and the Democratic Party.

The anti-globalization protests themselves are a critique of the ideological construction of the convention, and democracy itself as the disintegration of pure democratic values of truly public advocacy and social change. In light of the power of media representation in the social construction of our national identity, the administrative strategy succeeded in presenting an image of a stable situation under police control and authority, but failed in consideration of the grander plan of activists to attract national media coverage. Through pervasive media coverage, the protests question the legitimacy and accountability of the official convention proceedings. This activism serves to expand the public sphere by publicizing the discourse of subaltern counterpublics. The protests of *America 2000* were significant as a primetime critique of government authority, and the American public sphere.

REFERENCES

Asen, R., & Brouwer, D. (2001). Introduction: Reconfigurations of the public sphere. In R. Asen & D. C. Brouwer (Eds.), *Counterpublics and the state* (pp. 1–32). Albany, New York: State University of New York Press.

Calhoun, C. (1998). Community without propinquity revisited: Communications technology and the transformation of the urban public sphere. *Sociological Inquiry 68*, 373–397.

Cathcart, R. (Spring 1978). Movements: Confrontation as rhetorical form. *Southern Speech Communication Journal, 43*, 233–247.

Chomsky, N. (1999). *Profit over people: Neoliberalism and the global order.* New York: Seven Stories Press.

Chomsky, N., & Herman, E. (1988/2002). *Manufacturing consent: The political economy of the mass media.* New York: Pantheon Books.

Dayan, D., & Katz, E. (1992). *Media events: The live broadcasting of history.* Cambridge: Harvard University Press.

Debord, G. (1967/1970). *The society of the spectacle.* Paris: Editions Buchet—Chastel. English translation: Black and Red.

DeLuca, K., & Peeples, J. (June 2002). From public sphere to public screen: Democracy, activism and the "violence" of Seattle. *Critical Studies in Media Communication, 19*(2), 125–151.

Ehrenreich, B. (2000, August 17). Truth is out: LAPD takes on protesters in prime time. *LA Weekly Daily,* 10.

———. (2000, August 25–31). A street-side view of the Democratic Convention. *LA Weekly,* 24.

Fairness and Accuracy in Reporting (FAIR). (2000). Media unconcerned as LAPD attacks peaceful crowd, harasses IMC, [online]. Available: www.fair.org/activism/democratic-convention.html.

Fraser, N. (1993). Rethinking the public sphere: A contribution to the critique of actually existing democracy. In B. Robbins (Ed.), *The phantom public sphere* (pp. 1–32). Minneapolis, MN: University of Minnesota Press.

Gitlin, T. (1980). *The whole world is watching: Mass media in the making and unmaking of the new left.* Berkeley: University of California Free Press.

Habermas, J. (1989). *The structural transformation of the public sphere: An inquiry into a category of bourgeois society* (T. Burger & F. Lawrence, Trans.). Cambridge, MA: MIT Press.

Hertz, N. (2002, July 5). Interview on "Now with Bill Moyers," [online]. Available: www.pbs.org.

Kellner, D. (2001). *Grand theft 2000: Media spectacle and a stolen election.* Lanham, Maryland: Roman & Littlefield.

Martelle, S., & Riccardi, N. (2000, August 16). 95 arrested as protesters and police make a day of it. *Los Angeles Times,* A24.

Mater, M. (2001). A structural transformation for a global public sphere? In R. Asen & D. C. Brouwer (Eds.), *Counterpublics and the state* (pp. 211–234). Albany, New York: State University of New York Press.

Morello, T. (2000, August 28). Doing battle in Los Angeles. Interview in *Newsweek,* 4.

Newell, M. (2000, September). Fear and disillusionment in Los Angeles. *Trojan Horse, 3*(1), 1.

Purdum, T. (2000, August 17). Protesters shift their attention to the Los Angeles police. *New York Times,* A18.

———. (2000, August 13). Police and protesters ready; Politicians hope for the best. *New York Times,* A20.

Rappleye, C. (2000, August 17). Fear itself: Keeping democracy safe from the streets. *L.A. Weekly,* 11.

Scheer, R. (2000, August 18). Dream city comes off like "Blade Runner." *Los Angeles Times,* B9.

Shuster, B., & Newton, J. (2000, August 16). LAPD's response to protests shows its strength and, critics say, its faults. *Los Angeles Times,* A1.

Solomon, N., & Cohen, J. (1997). *Wizards of media Oz: Behind the curtain of mainstream news.* Monroe, Maine: Common Courage Press.

Terry, D. (2000, August 14). 3,500 rally to condemn death penalty. *New York Times*, A15.

Texeira, E. (2000, August 16). Activism in motion. *Los Angeles Times*, U11.

Tobar, H. (2000, August 16). Protests are just a TV show for delegates. *Los Angeles Times*, A1.

Windt, T. (1982). Administrative rhetoric: An undemocratic response to protest. *Communication Quarterly, 30*(3), Summer, 245–249.

Zoll, D. (2000, August 9). Crashing the party (Or: Y2GO2K2KLA). *San Francisco Bay Guardian*, 22.

8

Framing Globalization and Media Strategies for Social Change

Nancy Snow

In the summer of 2001, I was contacted by an editor from the staff of New York *Newsday*, a mainstream corporate media publication with a circulation of well over 650,000, one of the top ten newspapers in the United States. She was looking for any story line that was both lively and provocative. I immediately jumped at the chance to analyze how the corporate media frames the globalization debate and I knew such a piece would spark some discussion since it was running in a corporate media publication. To my surprise, she loved the idea, even though in conversation I explained that I was decidedly pro-globalization protests and thought the mainstream media didn't do a very effective job of explaining the underlying legitimate grievances of the movement. When I completed my essay, I provided a title to go along with the overall theme: "Sticks and Stones Can Break Our Bones but Frames Can Really Hurt Us," which was a warning to all resistance people and social change advocates to be vigilant about how the corporate media control the tone, content, and pictures of their messages.

The title was also a condemnation of how the global media unfairly "framed" the protesters in Genoa, Italy. I knew the headline choice was a futile attempt to set the tone of the editorial, because standard journalistic practice requires that the newspaper editorial staff provides its own headline. On the date of publication, not only did the piece run in *Newsday*, but it also got picked up by Media Channel and Common Dreams, two progressive media sites that chose to use it for a debate about the press coverage of globalization protests. Very quickly I received dozens of e-mails from globalization

protesters around the world who attacked me as everything from a corporate shill to a cushy academic who wouldn't know a protest march if it
appeared outside her ivory tower. I knew the reason why. They didn't read
beyond the headline, and unfortunately the headline *Newsday* chose to
frame my essay was, "Genoa Protesters: Your Image Needs Work." It was
a tough media lesson for me, as it is for any freelance writer who is at the
mercy of how the mainstream media choose to frame their subjects. The
experience underscored how often the media choose titles that intentionally
provoke in order to draw an audience. How ironic that I was framed
(wrongly accused) by the title of the editorial. I figured that the editorial
staff would edit the piece because I was so critical of how often the mainstream media are wrong about the social movement picture. The editorial
staff didn't edit a word of my actual critical essay, but the headline change
did the readers a great disservice. The experience of those who "flamed" me
in their e-mails, that of not reading much beyond the headline, is a common
one. We all are time constrained and media headlines serve as our eye
candy. I chose to respond to each person who wrote me, whether negative
or not, and promised that I would use this "framing experience" as an opportunity to write about media strategies for social change advocates. Here are
some lessons I've learned about the mainstream, corporate media system that
dominates our mental landscape. Anyone who chooses to work within this
system, needs to understand how most media staff are conditioned to
approach resistance stories.

CONFRONTING THE MEDIA CLUTTER AND NOISE

We live in a media world cluttered with noise. Persuasive messages compete
for the attention of a public that is increasingly inattentive and otherwise
distracted by the day-to-day responsibilities of life. The vast majority of
messages delivered are in the form of advertising from private companies to
get an individual consumer to buy a product. Resistance organizations are
in the message-delivery business as well, but their task is more complex
than selling a loaf of bread or a piece of jewelry. Community-based organizations and activists must convince citizens, local decision makers, and
public policymakers that there are broader social problems that need attention and action. They need people—not to buy products—but to "buy into"
ideas for social change. Media advocacy is a method to overcome clutter
and noise through the strategic use of communications for advancing a
social or policy solution to a problem.

Traditional media advocacy tends to approach media campaigns in good
versus evil "We're right, They're wrong" terms, which can inflame or turn
off an already tuned out public. Likewise, we are well aware of the tendency
on television talk shows to frame debate in "us versus them" drama. This may
be the result of what author Deborah Tannen calls the "argument culture"
in America, "a pervasive warlike atmosphere that makes us approach public

dialogue, and just about anything we need to accomplish, as if it were a fight." This polarizing and warlike approach in media and toward media leaves us without the tools to make the sound policy and social decisions we are advocating.

Strategic media advocacy includes broadening the frame of public debate from solutions at an individual level to an environmental or policy level. Community groups that use media advocacy strategically can reframe news media coverage from the individual to the collective, from the person, to the community. It takes both competence and engagement. Here are some strategies.

All Media Matters

The social movement sector is full of experts on their issues, but not often full of experts who either value strategic use of *all* media or know how to use it effectively. For many progressive organizations, it's still vogue to hate the mainstream media for its sensationalized news format, focus on the bottom line, and community news coverage that is either inadequate or incomplete. If you feel that strongly about the mainstream media, then utilize the press you know and love. Some resistance groups view social change groups that try to engage media strategically as "selling out" to the corporate media. For many, the only acceptable media is noncommercial or independent media, or Internet chat rooms that reinforce the "down with CNN" mantra. Commercial-driven, mainstream media is seen as the enemy that never gets it right. If you want to truly challenge and try to change the system overall, you will need to understand and work with all media.

Like Any Good Speaker, Know Your Audience

If the mainstream corporate media is not seen as the enemy, then more often than not, resistance groups use media advocacy ineffectively. Because community groups are so often strapped for resources, they often don't plan out a strategy or think through their target audience. They rely on Jane Q. Public campaigns or general efforts to "change public opinion," rather than develop media campaigns that resonate with an audience they are most likely to reach. A "Save the World" campaign against a backdrop of clutter and noise is a wasted use of limited resources. Think through what your message is and how you are going to make your way through the clutter. Is your audience a middle-class housewife in Des Moines or a Green Party member in Germany? The audience will determine your message and which media outlet you'll choose.

Papa, Don't Preach

Resistance groups need to pay closer attention to their audience and how it perceives a problem. Preaching is for church, not media campaigns. Many social change organizations adopt a condescending approach in their media strategies. Because they *know* they're right, they try to convince their audience that it is ignorant or irresponsible on some particular issue. The audience ends up feeling bad about what it doesn't know or isn't doing. Result: It tunes out. As media guru Tony Schwartz wrote in *The Responsive Chord*, good media campaigns reinforce what people already believe about themselves; they don't tell people anything new. That "chord" must emotionally connect with people's existing belief systems because people are naturally resistant to change.

Media Advocacy: For Better Health!

Finally, strategic media advocacy must avoid the "literal sclerosis" so often at play in consensus-driven organizations. Advertisers are famous for making big, bold claims that undergo little scrutiny. Consider the coffee commercial jingle, "The best part of waking up is Folger's in your cup." Some social change groups would tackle that claim for weeks, hold a town hall meeting to investigate, and call for further study. What results is language that is often complex, boring, or lacking in any emotional connection to the audience. As Michael Shellenberger of Communication Works says, "A lot of nonprofits want to speak the whole truth to power. Once the whole truth is known then everyone will follow—so the thinking goes. Advocates need to identify wedge issues and specific messages that capture the public's attention if they are to succeed." Strategic media advocacy leads by the heart, then mind.

Know What's Newsworthy

Charlotte Ryan, author of *Prime Time Activism* (1991), reports this from ABC News Correspondent Sam Donaldson about how he goes about choosing sources for news stories:

To sit down while you're facing a deadline and say, "Gee, there must be some other experts we haven't thought of. Let's beat the bushes and launch a search of the city or country for them." Well that takes a lot more time than flipping a card on a Rolodex . . . we know these guys [on the Golden Rolodex] provide a succinct response. You can't come to me and say, "Sam, I know you're on deadline, you need a comment on such and such, go out and take a chance on Mr. X. No, I'm sorry folks. I don't have the time to take a chance with Mr. X.

Why do so many good resistance sources for news remain anonymous "Mr. X"? News production is a bit like a beauty contest under an extremely tight deadline. The competition is stiff for visibility. Mr. X may be in the crowd of competitors but goes unnoticed and never makes the cut to the Rolodex. The making of news is generally routine and predictable. Mr. X (or Ms. X) is not.

Reporters reach for routine sources for information because so many work under the pressure of daily deadlines and don't have time to cultivate new sources. Further, there is *no incentive* for reporters to seek out a Ms. or Mr. X for news. Editors and producers are always up against the clock and need the story. The standard operating procedure for reporters is to turn to their trusted and highly recycled sources so that they can meet deadlines and keep their bosses happy. Their Golden Rolodexes are heavily stacked with names of government officials and industry insiders who pop up regularly in news reports.

When we think about the news, it's easy to assume that so much of it is "breaking," "eyewitness," or "action" oriented. We picture reporters at the ready or at the mercy of unpredictable and chaotic day-to-day events. If all news were made this way, our Mr. X might pop up in a news story as an eyewitness to late-breaking news. The typical news frame in mainstream news is done in an exciting and unpredictable angle in order to increase an audience that is quick on the draw with the remote control. The reality of social change is quite different.

Most news reports are about prescheduled and prearranged events that are promoted by regularly used sources. News making is more mainstream than against the stream. News reporting and what is considered newsworthy tilts in favor of those considered powerful or important. Those powerful and important are located in institutions that are perceived as consistent, nonproblematic, and credible news sources. These include major government institutions like City Hall, Police Departments, the Court system, state legislatures, school districts, and major corporations and industries. If our Mr. X lies outside these institutional sources for news, he's probably not going to make the Golden Rolodex once again.

If you want reporters to know you, you better first know your reporters. Before you send out that next press release, keep in mind that reporting is generally routine and sources are predictable and consistent. It's not a conspiracy but "just the way we've always done it." Stories about the everyday goings on in the world, particularly poverty and human rights abuses, are not going to be considered newsworthy unless there is a breaking news event such as a violent unrest that has some dramatic appeal or may affect other communities. Reporters are probably not going to cover these subjects routinely. Reporters are certainly aware of and many are even sensitive to the fact that resource-rich neighborhoods receive more coverage—but that's where the bulk of their sources live and work. If you want to change that reality, you've got to identify the reporters who cover subjects similar to your organization's concerns so that you can help to fill in the news gaps.

It's easy to point fingers at the media for all our social ills and blame reporters for not doing their jobs. If Mr. X wants to have more influence with the media, he'll have to recognize and acknowledge the enormous economic pressures and time deadlines that reporters work under every day.

Reporters are interested in good stories but they are also interested in work-ing with sources who are open to their presence. If Mr. X thinks that the news media don't care about his issue or cover his organization only when something negative occurs, he'll be sure to be a one-hit wonder with the press. Reporters are no different from you and me. They are sensitive to public opinion that holds the media responsible for much of our common problems. If sources are not cooperative or reactive, then reporters will move on to more predictable sources that value their relationship with the news media.

As you identify reporters and their sources, target a few reporters that cover topics of related interest to your organization and think of ways that you might be useful to that reporter. What can you or your organization do to help that reporter do his job better? Reporters love sources who know other sources. If you are seen as a repository of information and contacts, you'll make your way to the Golden Rolodex and to a first-name basis with a reporter. Are you listening, Mr. X?

REFERENCES

Ryan, C. (1991). *Prime time activism: Media strategies for grassroots organizing.* Boston: South End Press.
Schwartz, T. (1973). *The responsive chord.* Garden City, NY: Anchor Press.

9

Representing the South

Emma Miller

The postwar General Agreement on Tariffs and Trade evolved into the World Trade Organization (WTO) in 1994, determining the global rules of trade. The two other institutions that have had direct impact on the global South[1] are the International Monetary Fund (IMF) and the World Bank, which oversee the global economy and lend money to developing countries. Under the auspices of these three institutions, which are primarily controlled by developed countries, many developing countries have experienced harsh austerity measures, resulting in increased hardship for the poorest. The 1970s and1980s involved a critical deterioration in trade terms for primary commodity producers in developing countries of Africa and Latin America. It was also during this period that huge loans were made available to poor countries, largely by the IMF. By the early 1980s many countries were borrowing money just to pay the interest on debts. This situation has continued for the past twenty years. During this period, trade, investment, and finance have all been increasingly "liberalized"; that is, government regulation and control of these activities has been eroded. While the institutions described here have been demonised by critics of neoliberal economic policies, it is important to note that it is the most powerful of the rich country governments who really make the decisions. Through these institutions, rich nations have insisted that developing countries open their markets to goods from the North, while the European Union and the United States have sustained or increased subsidies to their domestic sectors, particularly in agriculture. Transnational companies, which lobby hard for liberalization, have benefited greatly from the increased profits that result. Meanwhile, citizens of the South have been locked into poverty by policies that favor the already rich and the transnationals. As well as increasing inequality within and between nations, the policies of these institutions have demonstrated little regard for the environmental consequences of globalization, or for the increase in corruption and crime resulting from diminished regulation.

Western media corporations have been subject to many of the same forces as other businesses in the last two decades. They have experienced mergers and corporate growth, assisted by reduced government regulation and diminished public service obligations. Ironically, therefore, the era of globalization has coincided with an increasingly parochial focus by the Western media, which will be discussed under the heading of double standards. As individuals are increasingly defined by their economic activity and corporations move into every area of life, consumerism is the dominant ideological force in the North. Consumer issues have become central to Western media output. Meanwhile coverage of the South, where it existed at all, has diminished, allowing a limited and distorted view of the developing world. I will begin here by briefly outlining the concerns surrounding international debt. The debt issue is central here because people have tended to take to the streets most in countries where the impact of neoliberal policies in relation to debt can be felt most acutely. The impact of the policies of the Bretton Woods institutions—the IMF and the World Bank—is critical for the so-called heavily indebted countries of the South. I will outline some of the protests that have taken place in the South over the last decade and examine the news coverage they have had relative to protests in the North. Western media coverage of neoliberal resistance in the North focuses on minority violent elements at some demonstrations, while often dismissing the majority as middle-class do-gooders. The UK International Development Secretary, Clare Short, described protesters at the G8 summit in Genoa in July 2001 as "white do-gooders" (Roberts, 2001, p. 7). While protesters in the South are campaigning against the same neoliberalism as those in the North, the fact that southern protests are largely ignored by Western media sustains this marginalized representation of northern resistance. This chapter will include examples of acts of resistance in the South, and refer to media responses to these. The impact on audience understanding of global events will then be discussed.

INTERNATIONAL DEBT

"There can be little dispute that Third World debt was the greatest economic, cultural and humanitarian disaster of the twentieth century. Not even the horror of two world wars and numerous lesser conflicts can stand comparison with the scale and depth of the unrelenting tragedy that has swept through the developing nations over the last four decades" (Rowbotham, 2000, p. 10).

Ellwood (2001) has documented how World Bank president Robert McNamara contracted huge loans to the South in the 1970s, ostensibly for "development" though also providing a bulwark against the perceived worldwide communist threat. During the 1970s and early 1980s, as prices for commodities plummeted, interest rates on the debts of poor countries soared. By the early 1980s, many countries were borrowing money just to pay the interest on debts. By 1982, Mexico could not pay its debts and "the debt crisis was born."

The Bretton Woods institutions agreed only to lend more money if the relevant country implemented rigorous controls over public spending—under Structural Adjustment Programs. Rowbotham (2000) has argued that legal conditions accompanying loans since the start of structural adjustment have amounted to international economists virtually taking control of these nations. In advancing loans, they demanded that the developing nations adhere strictly to an economic program that is deliberately and avowedly corporate-friendly. The group of seven most powerful countries, known as the G7, has a key role. The seven relevant countries are: UK, United States, Canada, France, Germany, Italy, and Japan. The leaders of these countries hold an annual summit and have significant control over the Bretton Woods institutions. The G7 controls nearly half of the votes on the IMF's board, while the poor countries that are the fund's main clients control less than 2 percent of the votes. The United States dominates the IMF, with 17 percent of the votes—enough to block key policy decisions.

Several high-profile former staff members of the Bretton Woods institutions have resigned over the years. Economist Susan George left the World Bank and is now a key contributor to the critique against the Bretton Woods institutions. The resignation from the World Bank by Joseph Stiglitz, its ex-chief economist and vice-president, in January 2000, provided an important boost to critics of the Bretton Woods institutions. He became an outspoken critic of World Bank policy, arguing that it was undemocratic and unrepresentative. Within months of Stiglitz's resignation, a senior development economist, Professor Ravi Kanbur, left the Bank in protest. In February 2001, the retiring head of the IMF, Michael Camdessus, made a speech including the following comment: "Widening gaps between rich and poor within nations, and the gulf between the affluent and the most impoverished nations, are morally outrageous, economically wasteful, and potentially socially explosive" (Simms, 2002, p. 2).

Mindful of the criticisms leveled at them by campaigning organizations, anti-capitalist protesters, and former staff like Stiglitz, the IMF and World Bank embarked on a public relations campaign in 1999–2000. The World Bank website's homepage is now headed, "The World Bank Group: Our Dream Is a World Free of Poverty." At its annual meeting in September 1999, it claimed poverty reduction as its core strategy. It was at this point that the discredited structural adjustment policies (SAPs) became poverty reduction strategy papers (PRSPs). These are papers that poor country governments now have to produce before receiving debt relief. Critics of the IMF's new strategy argue that PRSPs impose a new layer of conditions. The extent to which these reforms signify serious attempts to alleviate poverty in the South can be judged by more recent events in Argentina. The fund had pushed Argentina into implementing austerity measures in the middle of a recession, with devastating effects. The ensuing riots and deaths on the streets of Argentina illustrated the human consequences of such unsustainable policies (Gill, 2002; Goni, 2002).

The popular conception of international debt, fostered by Western media, is that poorer countries are indebted to wealthier countries. In fact, national and international economies now rely almost entirely upon the creation of money by a process that automatically involves the creation of debt. The wealthier the nation—the more advanced its economy—the larger its debt.

For example, the American national debt is fast approaching $6 trillion, outstanding U.S. mortgages are in excess of $4.5 trillion, and commercial debts exceed $4 trillion. The United Kingdom, Germany, Japan, and all the G8 countries carry similarly staggering national private and commercial debts. No one even pretends that these can ever be repaid (Rowbotham, 2000, p. 150).

While "debtor" nations must beg for debt deferment from the Paris Club and World Bank/IMF, wealthy nations constantly defer their escalating unmanageable debts. There is an irony underlying discussions of "third world debt" by the key decision-making institutions. All of the countries holding sway in the G7 and the Bretton Woods institutions have considerable international debts of their own. Among these, the country with most influence on decisions about the debts of developing countries is the most indebted of "developed" countries, the United States. While rich countries accumulate massive debts with impunity, they simultaneously impose stringent economic conditions on the so-called "debtor" countries

Despite the failure of Bretton Woods policies in assisting development in the poorest countries through the second half of the twentieth century, similar conditions are still attached to their loans up to the present. As Rowbotham (2000) argues, more recent policies continue to serve the purposes of globalization. In recent years, there has been growing demand from within developing countries, supported more recently by Western campaign groups, for the cancellation of their international debts. The lending institutions have become key targets of protesters concerned about global poverty in recent years. In the following section, I give an account of some of these resistance movements.

RESISTANCE

Because my focus is resistance in the global South, I do not intend to discuss protest in the North in any detail. However, a brief outline of the key institutions and rallying points will provide background reference for common issues with the South. The defeat of the Multilateral Agreement on Investment (MAI) in 1998 was the first major rallying point for the Northern resistance. The MAI had been negotiated in secret at the Organization for Economic Co-operation and Development (OECD), a club of twenty-nine of the world's richest countries. The MAI was deserted in 1998 following its veto by France and supported by a massive activist campaign revealing its corporate agenda. This was an important moment for the resistance movement in successfully blocking a neoliberal flagstone. From the late 1990s, the northern anti-globalization movement has protested at meetings of the key bodies behind the global economy: the WTO, the IMF, the World Bank, the OECD, the G7, and the EU Summits. The North American Free Trade Agreement (NAFTA) has become a focus of concern over recent years, as now has its extension, the Free Trade Area of the Americas (FTAA). These bodies constitute an unelected international governance that has assumed phenomenal power. Just as IMF and WB policies in the South have demanded that economies be increasingly privatized, there is a massive push toward privatization in the west. Protesters in the North are concerned about the policies of these bodies, and the influence of corporations in shaping the policies in their own interests.

Seattle was the wake-up call for the Western media in terms of covering global resistance to neoliberalism. However, coverage of this movement has remained limited mainly to those protests that take place at the rallying points of the Western decision-making bodies. These meetings have become increasingly remote precisely to avoid protesters, as was the case in Doha and Okinawa. When the WTO met in 2001 in the desert City of Doha, Qatar, apart from the official NGO contingent, there was little protest in the militarized streets. However, diverse and colorful protests took place in over thirty countries from Australia to Bulgaria, Bangladesh to Honduras (Joy & Ellis-Jones, 2002). Even in Seattle, the role of poor country delegates to the WTO has been marginalized in the media. Drewry, Macmullan, and Bentall (2002) argue that contrary to popular belief, it was not really the riots that forced the collapse of talks but a highly courageous stance by poor country delegates, using the consensus model to block what was a rich country agenda.

In general terms, while protests in the South have become increasingly widespread, they remain largely unnoticed by the international community. The World Development Movement (WDM), a UK antipoverty NGO, released its first "States of Unrest" report in September 2000, to restore some balance to the debate around the so-called anti-globalization protests. The report charts protests in developing countries in the period between the Seattle protests in November 1999 and the Annual Meetings of the IMF and World Bank in Prague in September 2000. In these months, a total of 1 million civilians had protested on more than fifty separate occasions across thirteen poor countries. All these protests called for an end to economic reforms prescribed by IMF in their country. In April 2002, the WDM produced its second "States of Unrest" report, documenting protest in the South during 2001. This account included protests in twenty-three countries, charting seventy-seven incidents of civil unrest involving millions of people. Of the twenty-three countries documented, nearly three-quarters have IMF-sponsored privatization programs. Half had protests by public sector workers, including teachers, doctors, and the police, aimed at policies that cut or freeze wages or lead to redundancies. Over a third of the countries had demonstrations against the rising prices of basic goods and services because public subsidies have been removed. The following examples are just a small selection from a range of sources, to illustrate the variety of actions that have taken place in the South in recent years. They have been selected to represent a wide geographical range as well as to illustrate how different sectors of society have taken to the streets to protest against neoliberal programs.

In 1996 the Asian Pacific Economic Community (APEC) meeting in Manila, the Philippines, was wreathed in tear gas and a ring of steel around the summit center as thousands of sweatshop workers converged on the city. (Ainger, 2001)

In April 1996, some 1,500 families of landless peasants gathered near the town of Eldorado dos Carajas in Brazil. Part of the Movement of the Landless Worker (MST),[2] they were demanding land reform. Military police opened fire on the demonstrators. Nineteen dead men were left beside the highway and sixty-nine people were wounded. Survivors believe there is a mass grave containing women and children nearby. (Baron Cohen, 2001)

On May 2, 1998, hundreds of thousands of peasants, agricultural laborers, tribal people and industrial workers from all regions of India took the streets of Hyderabad to reject the WTO and neoliberal policies, and to demand the withdrawal of India from the WTO. This demonstration followed a three-day convention, hosted by the All-India People's Resistance Forum (AIPRF), with representatives from more than 50 organizations present. The convention preceding the protest, attended by more than 900 representatives of peoples' movements, produced the "Declaration of Indian People against the WTO" which states that "We, the people of India, hereby declare that we consider the WTO our brutal enemy. This unaccountable and notoriously undemocratic body called the WTO has the potential not only to suck the sweat and blood of the masses of two-thirds of the world, but has also started destroying our natural habitats and traditional agricultural and other knowledge systems . . . converting us into objects of Transnational Corporations' economy of consumerism. . . . The WTO will kill us unless we kill it" (Nadir.org, 1998). Early in 2000, protestors in Cochabamba, Bolivia took to the streets, staging a general strike that shut down much of the nation. Under orders from the World Bank, the Bolivian Government privatized Cochabamba's public water system. It was handed over to a subsidiary of the American Bechtel corporation, which had been formed for that purpose. Within weeks, the Aguas del Tunari company had doubled or trebled water bills for some of the city's poorest families, with some families paying a quarter of their income for water. During the mass demonstration, one teenager was shot dead and over 100 protestors were seriously wounded. In April 2000, the company quit the city. (Shultz, 2002)[3]

On August 29, 2001, the confederation of South African Trade Unions (COSATU) reported that at least 65 percent of workers stayed away from work in a planned protest against privatization. Although commercial centers were said to be less affected, in part because employers brought in casual workers, many industrial areas were virtually shut down. COSATU estimated that over 5.5 million workers heeded the strike call, and that more than 3 million other workers joined the protest action. COSATU reported that in some areas, workers had been victimized and intimidated. Babelegi outside Pretoria was effectively sealed off by a heavy police presence. The police also put roadblocks around Bizana in an attempt to disrupt the protest. (Craven & Mothapo, 2001)

In September 2001, roads in Mexico City were brought to a standstill as thousands protested in the streets in response to plans to impose taxes on some foods and medicines. Protesters complained the taxes will have a disproportionate effect on the poor. (Ellis-Jones, 2002)

Argentina hit the headlines worldwide at the end of 2001, as civil unrest spread throughout the country in response to austerity programs demanded by the IMF. The government announced it would default on its debt repayments to the IMF, declaring national bankruptcy. Most media give the impression that the crisis emerged from the blue. WDM has documented that civil unrest in response to economic hardship has been a common feature in Argentina since December 1999. For over two years people had called on their government to release them from harsh economic policies imposed by the IMF. (Joy & Ellis-Jones, 2002)

On 18 December, 2001, Malawi University was closed because of disturbances by students and citizens. The demonstrations were against the increasing cost of living, including soaring maize prices and unemployment. Police, who used live ammunition, rubber bullets and tear gas, broke up the demonstrations. One student was killed. The Malawi government had already implemented economic reforms required by the IMF, which was urging the country to accelerate the pace of privatization by making the public sector "more attractive" to potential buyers. (Ellis-Jones, 2002)

The eight examples received various levels of attention in Western mass media. In order to obtain a comparison of Western media coverage of anti-globalization protests in the North and South, I selected a limited sample of three news stories and quantified their occurrence across the print media in the United States and Britain, using the Lexis-Nexis database. This database stores a wide range of international print media, including local and national newspapers. I compared coverage of three events between 1998 and 2001, searching each story separately in British and U.S. prints news outlets. I selected a two-week period for each of the events, when coverage was at its peak. The search was conducted using the terms "protest and/or demonstration" with the location and dates. The results strongly support the view that coverage is heavily weighted toward events in the North. The sample of three stories included the major news story arising from the protests at the 1999 meeting of the WTO in Seattle. The search for Seattle covered the period November 24 through December 7, 1999. The results for this period were a total of 324 stories in the UK print media. During the same period in the United States media, there were 2,067 news items covering the protests in Seattle. The results of coverage of stories from the South vary markedly from these figures, based on two of the events listed under the previous section on resistance. The first event was selected as a protest that paralleled Seattle in its focus against the WTO. This took place in Hyderabad, India, in May 1998, and provides a stark contrast between coverage of the North as compared to the South. Although hundreds of thousands of protesters participated, there was no coverage in either the British or American media archived in Lexis-Nexis. The second example from the South was selected because of its location in Africa. It was a deliberate choice to focus on Africa, which tends to attract more stereotypical coverage in Western news media, as discussed subsequently. This story was also selected because it took place sometime after Seattle, when, it is argued, the Western media "woke up" to the protests against globalization. The story was the general strike in South Africa, which took place toward the end of August 2001, and involved millions of individuals. This sample included a two-week period from August 16. Despite the millions of people involved in the general strike, there were only seventy-four stories across the UK media and 155 in the United States. The results of this limited sample indicate that protests in the South are still excluded from coverage in the Western news media.

WHY THE DOUBLE STANDARD?

The connections between diverse economies and cultures have been growing for centuries. In that sense globalization is not a new story. What has changed in the last quarter century or so is the rapid rate of technological change, which has allowed more rapid exchange of information and trade. The period of globalization has involved the meteoric rise of the transnational corporation as ruler of global trade. The news media on the whole are a business like any other, and have been similarly exposed to an unprecedented rise in mergers and corporate growth, expanding their global reach. Mass media ownership and government policies are key issues in influencing media behavior and content. The ironic outcome of the increased concentration of ownership resulting from globalization is that it has coincided with an increasingly parochial focus by the Western media. McChesney (2000) describes this media revolution as "a poison pill for democracy." Two of the consequences of these processes are marginalization of documentaries and increasing parochialism of the news in both American and British broadcasting. As profit remains the core motive of broadcasting corporations, so costs are cut by laying off journalists and by concentrating on stories that are inexpensive and easy to cover.

Such "lightweight" stories also minimize what Herman and Chomsky (1988) describe as the risk of "flak" such as the threat of legal action from corporations. In the United States, McChesney (2000) points to the decline of international news in the United States, from 45 percent of the network TV news total in the early 1970s to 13.5 percent in 1995.

While British television output has retained some commitment to public service broadcasting, recent research indicates that this is also in decline. Research commissioned by the Campaign for Quality Television (CQT) was conducted by Barnett and Seymour (1999) at the University of Westminster. It traced the decline in "foreign affairs" coverage on British TV over twenty years. While consumer affairs had not existed in Britain in the 1970s, it had become the fourth most covered subject across all channels by 1997–1998. The Third World and Environment Broadcasting Trust (3WE) regularly monitors output on British television from developing countries. Most recently, Stone (2000) calculated a dramatic decline on all channels.

Research on broadcasting, commissioned by the Department for International Development (DID) (2000), was conducted by Glasgow Media Group. This study, focused on broadcasting on developing countries in the first three months of 1999. The most critical conclusion drawn from that study about television coverage of developing countries in the new millennium is that—as a window on the world—British television is rapidly narrowing its audience's view. The television news profile indicated that the attention of British television news is skewed toward the richer and more economically powerful developing countries. Most of the poorest and least developed African countries in the Sahel and across central sub-Saharan Africa were not mentioned. The exceptions to this related most noticeably to dramatic events such as political conflict and natural disasters. Explanations and context given in most news accounts were limited. Many of the countries covered were mentioned only in the context of visits by westerners, sports or disaster/exotic stories. There were exceptions to this, with Channel 4 News and BBC2's Newsnight offering the most in-depth coverage of issues such as elections and trade in the South. The programs that covered developing countries most were consumer oriented—mainly holiday and exotic cooking programs. The agenda of many of the holiday programs was dominated by an emphasis on bargain hunting and consumer concerns. Local people most frequently were referred to as service providers, or in relation to "ethnic" entertainment. The Travel Show on BBC2 was exceptional in its attention to consideration of the ethics of tourism and genuine attempts to engage with local people. Wildlife programs also featured heavily.

Thus, innovation and investigation are curbed increasingly in the field of reporting the world among American and British broadcasters. As there is less programming on the developing world, the emphasis is also changing as consumerism predominates on our television screens. The conclusions of the three separate UK research studies published in 1999 and 2000 indicate that commercial values are pervasive throughout program formats, and that reduced output on developing countries is attributable to consumerism.

Corresponding with this is the increasing narcissism of British and American news coverage. As referred to in the British DID study, stories from developing countries often center on the involvement by British or U.S. citizens or celebrities. Moeller (1999) comments that the Americanization of crises has become prevalent. She argues that Americans want the world to subscribe to American cultural icons. As residents of other countries know this, they produce the icons to ensure coverage. The student democracy movement in Tiananmen Square made sure to carry their Statue of Liberty in front of the cameras. Placards are written in English across the world.

As the DID study indicated, coverage of the South tends to focus on crises, with repetitive imagery of famine, war, disease, and death—what Moeller (1999) and others refer to as the "Four Horsemen of the Apocalypse." Because of this emphasis, most of the images we see of the inhabitants of developing countries are those of the victims of crises: restricted essentially to passive roles. Such representations are further simplified because the stories are about the victims, not by them. At the same time, formulaic coverage of similar types of international crises makes us feel that we have seen this story before. Coverage of the Ethiopian famine of 1984–1985 demonstrated the limited range of explanations offered in news reports on the origins and nature of such crises, as demonstrated in research by Philo (1993). Pilger (1992) similarly questioned the simplistic nature of the coverage: How many of us were aware during 1985—the year of the Ethiopian famine and of "Live Aid"—that the hungriest countries in Africa gave twice as much money to us in the West as we gave to them.

While images of the developing world are largely restricted to scenes of chaos and suffering, the role of the West in these contexts is not included. The fact that poverty, famine, and, increasingly, extreme climate conditions have political causes rooted in the West barely achieves a mention. The tendency to refer instead to some biological conception of social difference does not assist understanding of global events. Allen and Seaton (1999) reject what they describe as primordialism, arguing that wars are not the product of natural difference, but of social processes. Primordialism enables governments of rich states to absolve themselves of responsibility for events, allowing them to adopt increasingly oppressive measures against refugees and immigrants. Events that are taking place in the South that do not conform to passive roles tend to be ignored. Thus, coverage of the pro-democracy movement focuses very much on Western-led demonstrations at the meeting points of global decision makers.

Writing about events in Bolivia, following the killing of five protestors, Gregory Palast (2000) commented on the lack of coverage of the story in the American media. At the center of the story were huge American and British multinationals, including Bechtel of San Francisco and Britain's United Utilities. Networks could have obtained high-quality video footage of the military gunning down civilians. Most importantly, this general strike in South America offered a dramatic parallel to protests in Washington against the International Monetary Fund and World Bank, which were occurring that very week. However, illustrating the priorities of the Western news agenda, the story was published in the *Washington Post* . . . in paragraph 10 of the story, on page 13 of the Style section, mentioned in passing in a story on the lifestyle of some local anti-WTO protesters.

In summary, Western mass media coverage of the South is in decline. As McChesney (2000) reports, this decline has been dramatic in the United States. While the reduction in media coverage of developing countries has occurred later and less markedly in Britain, the research quoted here indicates there is no room for complacency. Processes associated with globalization— the mergers and acquisitions resulting in huge and powerful transnational corporations—have influenced the mass media at least as much as any other business sector.

CONCLUSION

Resistance to neoliberal economic policies has been increasingly active in the global South over the past decade. Resistance in the poorer countries of the South began earlier and is more widespread than in the North because people there have suffered directly from economic policies imposed by the global financial institutions. They have also been forced to endure long-standing unfair trade conditions with the North. The links between international trade and debt are central to understanding the position of poor countries. As farmers in the South have received consistently low prices for the commodities they produce, their countries have been forced to borrow funds from the Bretton Woods institutions. These bodies have in turn required them to impose harsh austerity measures on their populations while introducing trade reforms that further favor governments and corporations based in the North. Meanwhile, contrary to the popular perception encouraged by Western media news frames, the most indebted countries globally are in the North.

Supporters of neoliberalism argue that developing countries would be even more vulnerable without the Bretton Woods institutions and the WTO. However, these institutions clearly are inadequate in promoting justice or equality. The consumerism that has driven Western economies since

World War II has resulted not only in environmental degradation, but in mass exploitation and increasing revulsion in poor and particularly Islamic countries. Systematic exploitation of former colonies by transnational corporations has inspired huge movements of resistance. The increasing emphasis on consumerism has been accompanied by the significant growth in power of these corporations, whose power in influencing the global economic institutions has made the latter a target of protesters internationally. A new form of international coalition is required. Christie and Warburton (2001) are among those arguing for sustainable development, where the goal is economic development that brings a higher quality of life for all, without doing so at the expense of future generations, the poor, and the environment. George (1999) warns of the necessity of having replacement policies that restore power to communities and institute democracy as well as fair distribution on an international level. The threat is transnational. So must be the response.

It is difficult for voices proposing alternatives to be heard. An increasingly narrow range of interests is being represented in the news media, which are owned by a small group of companies—what Monbiot (2000) describes as a "great corporate blob coalescing." As the previous evidence indicates, the resistance to neoliberalism in the global South has been sidelined by Western media. It is in the best interests of the major corporations to focus only on the protests in the North, where they argue, the protesters consist of middle-class do-gooders or violent anarchists at the other extreme. Further, the tired range of stereotypical roles allocated to inhabitants of developing countries for Western audiences precludes those millions who have taken to the streets, in many cases risking their lives, as indicated in the section on southern protest. The risks to the lives of those protesters can be reduced by media attention. To take one example as documented by Castells (1997), the Internet enabled the creation of a network of international groups that supported the Zapatista uprising on January 1, 1994. This was the first day of NAFTA, when about 3,000 lightly armed men and women took control of the main municipalities adjacent to the Lacandon forest, in the impoverished Mexican state of Chiapas. Although several dozen Zapatistas died in conflict with the Mexican Army, it is probably the case, as Castells suggests, that the Mexican government was inhibited from large-scale repression by the Internet campaign. Following negotiations with President Carlos Salinas a ceasefire was agreed on January 27.

As McQuillan (2000) rightly posits, when the OECD abandoned the MAI in October 1998, the pressure mounted to accelerate the General Agreement on Trade in Services (GATS)—a WTO initiative currently under negotiation in Geneva. Susan George (1999) commented that the MAI would have given all rights to corporations, all obligations to governments, and no rights at all to citizens. The same is true of GATS, which seeks to undermine the role of local and national governments in regulating their economies—North and South. The links and shared interests are increasingly entwined.

NOTES

1. "The South" is meant to refer to what would previously be described as third world countries, in Africa, Latin America, Asia and the Pacific. This is an imprecise geographical term, particularly as the countries of the formerly Soviet led "Eastern bloc" have been subjected to the same neoliberal policies and have experienced increased austerity and poverty as a result.

2. The MST organizes landless families to occupy idle land belonging to absentee landlords, taking advantage of a clause in the Brazilian constitution which makes such land expropriable. In Brazil 1 percent of the population owns 50 percent of the arable land. Since the MST's founding in 1985, more than 250,000 families have won title to more than 6 million hectares of land in a veritable "'land reform from below." The new farmers created by this process earn on average 3.7 times the minimum wage, while still-landless rural workers get only 0.7 of the minimum wage. Infant mortality among the new farming families has dropped to half the national average (Rosset, 2002).

3. The company which quit Bolivia following protests against its subsidiary's control of water provision, Riley Bechtel, has filed a $25 million legal demand against Bolivia under the arbitration arm of the World Bank. The demand is for the profits they expected to make, despite the fact that Bechtel Enterprises already has revenues of more than $14,000 million annually, and has reportedly completed 19,000 projects in 140 countries (Shultz, 2002).

REFERENCES

Ainger, K. (2001, September). To open a crack in history. *New Internationalist*, 338, 9–13.

Allen, T., & Seaton, J. (1999). Introduction. In T. Allen & J. Seaton (Eds.), *The Media of Conflict* (pp. 1–7). London: Zed Books.

Barnett, S., & Seymour, E. (1999). *A shrinking iceberg travelling south*. London. Campaign for Quality Television.

Baron Cohen, D. (2001, September). Beyond the Barricade. *New Internationalist*, 338, 26–27.

Castells, M. (1997). *The power of identity. The information age: Economy, society, culture*, Vol. II. Oxford: Blackwell.

Christie, I., & Warburton, D. (2001). *From here to sustainability*. London & Sterling, VA: Earthscan.

Craven, P., & Mothapo, M. (2001). First day of anti-privatization strike in S. Africa. Retrieved June 2002 from HYPERLINK http://lists.lights.com/pipermail/ gpn-announcements/2001-August/ 000025.html

Department for International Development. (2000). *Viewing the world: A study of British television coverage of developing countries.* London: DID.

Drewry, M., Macmullan, J., & Bentall, J. (2002). *Trade justice.* London: Trade Justice Movement.

Ellis-Jones, M. (2002, April). *States of unrest II.* London: WDM.

Ellwood, W. (2001). *The no-nonsense guide to globalization.* Oxford: New Internationalist Publications Ltd.

George, S. (1999). A short history of neo-liberalism. Retrieved June 2000, from http://www.globalexchange.org/economy/econ101/neoliberalism.

Gill, T. (2002, January 15). The IMF's delinquent pupil. *The Guardian,* 16.

Goni, U. (2002, January 8). Argentines ray for recovery. *The Guardian,* 20.

Herman, E., & Chomsky, N. (1988). *Manufacturing consent.* New York: Pantheon Books.

Joy, C., & Ellis-Jones, M. (2002, Spring). States of unrest. *WDM in Action,* 12–13.

Kemp, K. (2000, May 7). Stock Exchange chief backs anti-capitalists. *Sunday Herald,* 1.

McChesney, R. W. (2000). *Rich media, poor democracy.* New York: The New Press.

McQuillan, R. (2000, Autumn). It's back. *WDM in Action,* 12.

Moeller, S. (1999). *Compassion fatigue.* New York and London: Routledge.

Monbiot, G. (2000, January 20). The corporate great blob coalesces. *The Guardian,* 22.

Nadir.org. (1998, June 2). Peoples' Global Action against "Free" Trade and the WTO. Issue number 2. Retrieved June 2000, from PGA Bulletin: http://www.nadir.org/nadir/initiativ/agp/en/PGAInfos/bulletin2/m16asia.htm.

Palast, G. (2000, July). Bolivia vanishes: See style section. Retrieved June 2002, from http://www.oneworld.net/anydoc_mc.cgi?url=http://www.mediachannel.org/views/oped/palast.shtml

Philo, G. (1993). From Buerk to Bank Aid: The media and the 1984 Ethiopian famine. In J. Eldridge (Ed.), *Getting the message, news, truth and power.* London and New York: Routledge.

Pilger, J. (1992). *Distant Voices.* London: Vintage.

Ransom, D. (2001). *The no nonsense guide to fair trade.* Oxford: New Internationalist Publications Ltd.

Roberts, B. (2001, July 1). Short in blast at the rich. *The Mirror,* 7.

Rosset, P. (2002, Jan/Feb). The end of the styrofoam strawberry. *New Internationalist, 342,* 32.

Rowbotham, M. (2000). *Goodbye America: Globalisation, debt and the dollar empire.* Oxfordshire: Jon Carpenter.

Rowling, N. (1987). *Commodities: How the world was taken to market.* London: Free Association Books.

Shultz, J. (2002, April). Riley Bechtel. *New Internationalist, 344,* 29.

Simms, A. (2002, Jan/Feb). Going down in history. *New Internationalist, 342,* 20–21.

Stone, J. (2000). *Losing perspective: Global affairs on British terrestrial television 1989–1999.* London: 3WE.

Wainwright, H. (2002, March). Globalise the Left. *Red Pepper,* 5.

World Bank Website: http://www.worldbank.org.

World Development Movement. (2000). Report on resistance to IMF policies on poor countries. Retrieved September 2000, from: http://www.wdm.org.uk/cambriefs/DEBT/unrest.

10

Speaking Out Against the Incitement to Silence: The British Press and the 2001 May Day Protests

Karin Wahl-Jorgensen

> Be warned. If given to a delicate disposition, do not read the papers or watch the TV tomorrow. London will be overrun by anarchists with frankly silly haircuts who are but one brick-throw from achieving the end of western civilisation.
>
> —*Bell, 2001, p. 12*

In this chapter, I tap into discourses about the global justice movement in the British daily press, based on an analysis of 277 news reports, opinion pieces, leading articles, columns, and letters to the editor about the 2001 May Day protests published between January 1, 2001, and January 1, 2002. I look at mainstream daily newspapers because I view them as discursive battlefields. Newspapers are the sites through which societies imagine themselves (Anderson, 1983). They are the places that articulate rationalities, defining what constitutes "common sense" (Allan, 1999, pp. 87–94). Britain has the second-highest newspaper readership in the world (Bairstow, 1985), and although readership figures are in decline, the majority of the population still regularly picks up a paper. Thus, "newspapers are a main source of news for significant numbers of the population" (Billig, 1995, p. 110), and they provide a lens through which readers/citizens interpret their place in the world.

I draw on Foucault's (1990, 1991, 2002) work on the relationship between rationality and power to make sense of how the global justice movement is covered. I suggest that the dominant discourses on protests against the globalization of capital treat the protesters as irrational threats to the social order. The chapter shows that *most* press coverage of the global justice movement is framed in terms of three distinct themes. These include discourses of law and order, which construct the protests as a problem of policing; discourses of the economy, which bemoan the negative impact of the protests on the national economy; and discourses of spectacle, focusing on the irrational and spectacular aspects of global justice activism. Together, these discourses constitute an "incitement to silence" about the effects of globalization. Nevertheless, it is not difficult to find a set of resistant discourses. Discourses of recognition, which are sympathetic to the protesters, represent a distinct and regular contribution to the public debate about the global justice movement.

Coverage of the 2001 May Day Protests shows that hegemony is never complete, but that the resistance offered by the global justice movement has real consequences for the discourses circulating in the public sphere: The global justice movement has fought its way into a position where its claims are taken seriously within the mainstream of public debate.

WRITING ABOUT GLOBAL JUSTICE

Other work done on the global justice movement has demonstrated the difficulties protesters face in seeking to communicate their message, and also calls our attention to the depoliticized ways media construct the movement. As Hills (2000) points out, media coverage reduces protests to the status of "exotic carnivealesque chaos," and mocks participants for their ignorance, constructing them "as improper or deviant occupants of a rational public sphere" (p. 9). Also, the dominance of law and order discourses in media coverage of anti-globalization protests has been widely discussed (Hills, 2000; Lawless, 2001; Luckman & Redden, 2001). Luckman and Redden (2001), in studying the strategies of protesters at the World Economic Forum meeting in Melbourne in September 2000, suggest that the protesters, even if demonized in the news media, "achieved a remarkable agenda-grab at what should have been a slick celebration of globalization's ability to 'lift all boats'. . . . As long as the movement receives media attention, it puts the onus uncomfortably on the corporations and international economic organizations it targets" (p. 28). This observation shows why the alliance between social movements and news media is both a dangerous and crucial one (Gamson & Wolfsfeld, 1993). Though the constraints of journalism limit ways of writing about protest, the social movements desperately need the oxygen of publicity (DeLuca & Peeples, 2002).

UNDERSTANDING MAY DAY COVERAGE: THE USES
OF RESISTANCE

The 2001 May Day protests were a key moment in understanding the trajectory of discourses about the British global justice movement. As a

European labor day, May 1 historically has been a day of peaceful protests and meetings for progressive groups in Britain. The discourses surrounding the 2001 protests should be understood in relation to the preceding year's events. Following the 1999 Seattle protests, the global justice movement gained strength in Britain, and members planned to mark their presence by organizing large-scale protests in London as part of the May Day 2000 events. The media coverage of these protests focused on the disruption caused by a small fraction of the protesters, who, among other things, adorned a statue of Winston Churchill with a Mohican hairstyle, smashed shop windows, and fought with police (Boggan, 2001, p. 4).

From the beginning, May Day 2001 was understood as an attempt to disrupt the daily life of the capital. A diverse set of activist groups planned activities under the heading of "Mayday Monopoly," inviting "protesters to converge on streets, utilities, train stations and prisons named in the game" (Boggan, 2001, p. 4). In response to these plans, the London authorities organized a major police operation involving 6,000 officers to contain the protesters.

Theoretical Approach

I am particularly interested in coverage of the 2001 May Day protests because it ultimately challenged, even if in a limited way, dominant ways of talking about globalization. If we, as Foucault has suggested,[1] should study the discontinuities of history, it is worthwhile looking at moments of substantial challenge to dominant discourses.

I use the moment of May Day 2001 to explore the possibilities to "transform the political situation and produce a real alternative" available to marginalized social movements (Gills, 2000, p. 4). In analyzing the media coverage, I operate from the assumption that language works to construct and reinforce dominant relations of power. It is a tool in the service of hegemony that allows the state to maintain dominance without the use of coercion (Gramsci, 1971, p. 271). I would agree with Flyvbjerg's (1998) suggestion that the dominant rationality is the rationality of power. Flyvbjerg (1998) argues that "power is knowledge. Power determines what counts as knowledge, what kind of interpretation attains authority as the dominant interpretation. . . . Defining reality by defining rationality is a principal means by which power exerts itself" (pp. 226–227). By taking an interest in the rationality of power, my method is aligned with discourse analysis, which points to "socially and institutionally originating ideology, encoded in language" (Fowler, 1991, p. 42).

I am interested in media coverage because it allows us to look at "how public domain communicative events are transformed as they move along the chain" of social practices, in particular those of mass communication (Fairclough, 1995, p. 41). In other words, we cannot grasp the consequences of May Day protests by looking just at the *acts* of protest; we must also examine how these acts were molded into a set of media discourses. I use the term "discourse" to denote "a type of language associated with a particular representation, from a specific point of view, of some social practice" (Fairclough, 1995, p. 41). We should look at discourse as "a form of power that circulates in the social field and can attach to strategies of domination as well as those of resistance" (Sawicki, 1988, p. 185).

Key to understanding the challenges of creating debate about globalization is what we might call "the incitement to silence" about topics uncomfortable to dominant forces in society. In *History of Sexuality,* Foucault (1990) suggests that our era is marked not by sexual repression, but rather by a confessional culture that produces an "incitement to speak" about sex (pp. 32–33). To Foucault, the "incitement to speak" creates knowledge about sex that helps to control populations. I suggest that today, the rationality of power is well served by an "incitement to silence" about the effects of globalization, and that the discourses identified here are among the chief mechanisms for hushing up resistance to globalization, placing it outside the "sphere of legitimate controversy" (Hallin, 1989, pp. 116–117). These discourses, through their incitement to silence, construct subjects of the state as depoliticized consumers who worry about shopping and safety, rather than as citizens who worry about politics. They consolidate the media's claim to serving the needs of a free-market liberal democratic society, but also further a process of evacuating citizens from the realm of politics.

Method

To investigate the mechanisms of the "incitement to silence" and their relation to the rationality of power, this chapter takes up Foucault's challenge to [M]ove toward a new economy of power relations, a way that is more empirical, more directly related to our present situation, and one that implies more relations between theory and practice. It consists in taking the forms of resistance against different forms of power as a starting point. . . . Rather than analyzing power from the point of view of its internal rationality, it consists of analyzing power relations through the antagonism of strategies. (Foucault, 2002, p. 329)

How do we locate the specific strategies of power by looking at newspaper articles? If we understand newspaper articles as a way to access the discourses circulating in society, we can view them as encapsulating strategies of power, or strategies for defining the rational and the common-sensical.

The vast majority of the 277 articles I read about the 2001 May Day Protests easily could be placed within one of four categories. They discussed the protests in terms of (1) law and order, (2) consequences for the economy, (3) spectacle, or (4) recognition of the protesters' substantive concerns.[2]

On occasion, the discourses analyzed here co-habit single news articles.[3] Nevertheless, for the purposes of this analysis, I have divided the stories into four distinct categories, based on the set of discourses dominating each story.[4]

In reducing the discourses surrounding the 2001 May Day Protests to these four categories, I do not mean to imply that discourse—and, by extension, power—operates in simple or quantifiable ways. Foucault has called our attention to the "tactical polyvalence" of discourse, or the fact that discourse ought to be viewed "as a series of discontinuous segments whose tactical function is neither uniform nor stable" (Foucault, 1990, p. 100; see also Flyvbjerg, 1991, p. 121). We can get at the specific nature of discourses and their relationship to the rationality of power by asking some key questions of the texts. We can look at who is speaking, the position they are speaking from, and the context in which they are placed (Foucault, 1990, p. 100). We can seek to understand how silence and secrecy serve as "a shelter for power, anchoring its prohibitions" (Foucault, 1990, p. 101). And we can examine how silence and secrecy are resisted through discourse.

Perhaps it goes without saying that by looking only at newspaper articles, we severely limit our understanding of how power works. We have access only to a particular set of "official" and public representations. If "power relations are rooted in the whole network of the social" (Foucault, 2002, p. 345) and its workings often take place in dynamic, informal, micro-political settings (Flyvbjerg, 1998), we are missing out on understanding what we ought to know about how decisions are made and contested. An examination such as this one can only scrape at the surface of complex discursive practices. What we *can* do with such a method is to search for and locate resistance where we might least expect to find it.

DISCOURSES OF LAW AND ORDER AND THE ECONOMY

Discourses of Law and Order

The most common way of talking about the global justice protests came in the form of discourses of law and order—that is, discourses preoccupied with the consequences of the protests for the security of citizens and institutions. These stories dominated the accounts of the protests, making up a total of 164 out of the 277 articles about the protests (59 percent).

The earliest article of the year about May Day 2001 set the tone. Appearing in the moderate *Times* newspaper on February 13, it warned that "extremist groups are plotting to paralyse London with violent May Day protests 48 hours before the expected general election polling day" (Tendler & McGrory, 2001, Home News Section). The language of this article gave a taste of the tone that came to dominate the coverage, by describing the protesters as unruly mobs whose sole aim is destruction, and who should be contained at all costs.

The articles that followed cemented metaphors of war, invasion, and terrorism. Some debated in earnest whether companies suffering economic losses as a result of the protests would be able to claim on their insurance, given recent initiatives to classify the global justice movement as a form of terrorism (Mac attack, 2001, p. 12). An *Evening Standard* article was not alone in whipping up the moral panic when it reported that the intelligence services "fear protesters may try to use a network of ventilation shafts in a bid to disable the Tube as well as move around the capital" (cited in Steel, 2001, p. 6).

These stories operate from the assumption that all that is interesting about the protests is how they might interfere with the lives of decent, law-abiding citizens. Such discourses discipline the population by, on the one hand, excluding the unruly elements that refuse normalization and, on the other hand, setting out clear rules for how to behave to avoid exclusion. Discourses of law and order also legitimate the police as the apparatus of surveillance and coercion that will guarantee a citizenry of "docile bodies" (Foucault, 1991, p. 135) safe from violence.

The articles that speak of law and order constitute a set of meta-discourses, striving to define the context in which the protests should be understood, and the language that should be used to talk about them. Thus, an article published on May 1 in the conservative quality paper the *Daily Telegraph* covered a speech given by Prime Minister Tony Blair on the evening before the protests, in which he strongly endorsed heavy policing. This piece was remarkably similar to a series of articles on the same speech in other papers. It opened with a quote from Blair making a last-ditch effort at fixing the discursive field: "Tony Blair warned May Day demonstrators yesterday that damaging property, defacing statues and bringing fear to a city centre is not political protest but crime, 'pure and simple'" (McSmith, 2001, p. 1).

In a speech where Blair also suggested that the protests support a "spurious cause," he staked out his claims for excluding the protests from the realm of legitimate political concern. As such, he imposed the rationality of power on interpretations of the event. He painted a picture of the protesters as being beyond the realm of rationality and politics—as criminals who must be excluded from society through heavy policing. The populist tabloid newspaper *The Sun* went even further than Blair in its ideological construction of the events of May 1; its special section on the protests came under the heading "May Day Riots."

To further elaborate on the distinction between deviant protesters and law-abiding citizens, newspapers gave advice to readers on how to avoid being troubled by the May Day events. Thus, most major dailies carried an article that warned "reasonable people" to stay away from London on May 1 (e.g., Williams, 2001, p. 15). Other articles passed on specific instructions about how to dress to avoid the violence of the protesters:

Thousands of London workers have been told to dress casually today to avoid being abused or attacked by anti-capitalists during the May Day protests.

The "dress down" advice, which has also been given to civil servants, is part of a huge security operation, which will seek to protect City staff and West End shops on a day when parts of London are likely to come under siege. (Norfolk, 2001)

This article made no pretensions to take any notice of why the protesters are protesting. Instead, it focused entirely on the anticipated battle through which the capital may "come under siege," and the threats it might constitute to the health of the body politic likely to be "abused" and "attacked"—but ultimately "protected" by police. One journalist participating in the protests suggested that the warning "was an excuse to treat those of us who did turn up as dangerous marauders, in dramatic defiance of the evidence before their very eyes" (Williams, 2001, p. 15).

Articles dominated by law and order discourses were written mainly on the basis of official news releases, news conferences, and speeches. Each of the stories was peopled by the same small cast of high-powered dignitaries who spoke as one in their call for extensive police involvement in the protests. This cast usually included—and often exclusively consisted of—Sir John Stevens, the metropolitan police commissioner; Jack Straw, the home secretary; Geoff Hoon, the defense secretary; and Tony Blair. The reliance on such official sources is a key element of what Gaye Tuchman (1972) has called the "strategic ritual" of objective news reporting. In their effort to produce a journalism free of subjective opinion and led only by the search for the "truth," journalists write their stories by juxtaposing quotes from authoritative sources. Those who are quoted determine what kinds of narratives dominate the news and, thus, what is considered reasonable and what is considered deviant. If they speak in one voice, they carve out in stone the rationality of power.

Most reports on the actual protests focused on the (limited) extent of disruption, and ignored the large peaceful crowds. As one participant wrote in a letter to the editor, "You will have seen footage of a rough-looking guy dismantling a traffic light—you will not have seen footage of 1,000-plus people below him calling him a wanker" (Williams, 2001, p. 15). Many of the articles that expressed sympathy toward the protesters did so partly on the basis of a sense that (1) police use of force was excessive, and (2) the media were complicit in creating the moral panic that justified the police presence in the first place. A commentary in the *Evening Standard* forcefully made this point:

The policing and reporting of yesterday's May Day protests was so excessive as to seem like gross provocation. In their gleaming cockroach ranks, the 6,000 officers looked as if they were there to pick a fight, not stop one. An excitable reporter on News 24 actually described a group of baffled herbivores in sweatshirts as "rioters." She wished. (Pearson, 2001, p. 15)

A number of such articles, while accepting that the debate was about law and order, thus questioned the extent of the policing. Although these articles were by no means radical—after all, they did not challenge the rationality stipulating the *need* for policing, but only its excesses—they did highlight the absurdity of the fact that 6,000 officers were required for the surveillance of 5,000 civilians demonstrating for what was ostensibly a democratic cause.

A couple of articles allowed for responses by the protesters, even if they devoted most of their column inches to the voices of authority. Thus, a *Guardian* report on Tony Blair's speech denouncing the protests cited spokespersons for a range of activist groups:

Some protesters immediately responded that many thousands of people wanted to demonstrate against the effects of the monetary system and free trade, but were being discouraged by the fear of thousands of riot police in central London with orders not to tolerate any disturbances.

"The point about a democracy is to allow freedom of expression," said a spokeswoman for a genetics protest group. (Vidal, 2001, p. 1)

This *Guardian* article heeded one of the cardinal rules of journalism; that of fairness, which requires journalists to "try to find every viewpoint on a story" (Brooks, Kennedy, Moen, & Ranly, 1992, p. 12). Finding sources among activists is more difficult than getting a quote from a government spin doctor, but not impossible. Nevertheless, the constraints of daily news production—what the American journalist Buzz Merritt (1995) has called the "tyranny of space and time" (p. 15) means that journalists will tend to write the story that is easiest to come by. In this case, the easy story is the one that explains the May Day protest as a problem of policing, not as a political event. Thus, the rationality of power wins out in part as a result of newsroom practices.

Discourses of the Economy

If the aim of the law and order discourses was to depoliticize the protests and construct them as "spurious," a set of functionally similar, but much less frequent, discourses were ones predicting the extent to which the protests would affect the financial well-being of the country. The economy was a central theme of 25 of 277 stories, or 9 percent of the total. It was only rarely a concern *before* the protests, but made the news in the months following them and, again, in the weeks following September 11. These discourses removed the protests entirely from the realm of the political, turning them into an event that could be quantified as a variable of economic disruption, but had no meaning apart from that. The law and order discourses ensured readers of the efforts made to protect a fragile social order from the violence of protesters. Discourses on the economy assessed how the events had hit a nation of consumers where it hurt the most: In the economy. The following *Birmingham Post* article illustrates these discourses:

Central London businesses lost around pounds 20 million through missed trade and property damage, Westminster Council said, while hundreds of thousands of pounds were spent on the massive police operation and the clean-up process. (May Day protests: Final cost, 2001, p. 7)

After September 11, these concerns quite suddenly resurfaced in a climate of heightened concern about the economy. A spate of stories published in late September and October detailed the loss of income suffered by the upscale department store Selfridges. A typical story reads as follows:

Selfridges is estimated to have lost up to GBP 700,000 in takings because of the May Day protest outside its flagship Oxford Street.
    Strikes on London Underground and fewer foreign tourists are also expected to hurt half-year figures out on Thursday. (Flanagan, 2001, p. 19)

Through the discourse of the economy, the May Day protests are equated with other events damaging to the nation and inconvenient to its population—the London Underground strike and the decline in U.S. tourism linked to the events of September 11. Good citizenship, these stories imply, consists of consuming to get the economy back on an even keel, rather than in directly participating in politics.

More than anything, discourses on law and order and on the economy assume that the political ideas underpinning the protests are not in the "public interest." As such, they not merely reduce the protests to a problem of damage limitation. They reduce citizens to consumers, who want to go about their daily lives without any inconvenience, and have no need to know about political events.

Discourses of Spectacle

The conception of the citizen as consumer entails a slew of assumptions about why people read newspapers. Notwithstanding the high-minded ideals of a liberal democratic press as a central institution of the public sphere (e.g., Habermas, 1989; Wheeler, 1997)—the ideals to which journalists themselves subscribe (Wahl-Jorgensen, 2002b)—newspaper traditions are built on the need and desire to "tickle the public" (Engel, 1996).[5] Although liberal democratic theorists have happily assumed that newspapers are around to provide political information and conversation, journalistic practices work differently. To sell newspapers, the news must be made into an exciting spectacle that can bring a smile to weary faces.[6]

The May Day protests, and the global justice movement in general, offer a rich repository of spectacle and jokes for this purpose. The discourses of spectacle, accounting for 19 out of 277 stories, or 7 percent of the total, are primarily concerned with having a laugh at the expense of protesters, portraying them—both individually and as a group—as ridiculous, naive, and dangerous. By joking about others, we show them as unworthy of serious attention, as an irrational "Other" who can be safely disregarded (Eliasoph, 1998, chapter 6). A story headlined "Yellow Submarine singer is sent down to the cells," published in the *Evening Standard,* is typical of how these discourses work:

An alleged rioter from the May Day protests who walked into court today singing an antifascist song to the tune of the Beatles' Yellow Submarine will be held in custody until the end of the month. Unemployed and homeless Keith Spence, 24, who is accused of throwing sticks and bottles at police and punching an officer in Regent Street, arrived humming "We all live in a fascist regime, a fascist regime, a fascist regime." (Yellow Submarine singer, 2001, p. 4)

This account celebrates how the bizarre and destructive behavior of the protester is contained by the law. However, in the discourses of spectacle, most protesters are not portrayed as being dangerous, but merely amusing and irrational. A common theme is what is seen as the hypocritical nature of the protesters who, as middle-class beneficiaries of capitalist privilege, take on the cause of globalization. A lengthy eye witness column, titled "Mobile in hand hate in his heart" and published in the conservative, mid-market tabloid the *Daily Mail* thus mused:

This capitalism thing may be the greatest evil of all time but it does produce some very nice photographic equipment. I have never seen such a well-equipped demonstration. Half the crowd seem to have cameras. Everyone seems to have a mobile phone. And for every ponytailed anarchist eco-warrior in combat gear and a strange hat, there are ten conventionally-dressed, clean-shaven young people for whom this is not so much a protest as an exciting day out with a mild whiff of danger. (Hardman, 2001, pp. 4–5)

The article articulates a common theme in conservative critiques of the global justice movement in Britain: That it consists of spoiled middle-class youth who have no direct experience of the evils of global capitalism, and therefore have no reason to protest against it. This theme provides a particular variation on the incitement to silence. It suggests that only individuals who directly are affected by events can speak up about it in public. Using citizens as sources for news only on the basis of their personal experience is a widely documented journalistic practice (Eliasoph, 1998,

Wahl-Jorgensen, 2001), but one that has fatal consequences for democracy because it represents the "evaporation of politics in the public sphere" by depoliticizing citizenship (Eliasoph, 1998, p. 230).

Another strategy of the discourses of spectacle is to belittle the protests themselves, demonstrating that it was not necessary to take them seriously in the first place. Thus, an article in the *Times*, reporting on the minute scuffles between police and protesters, arrived at the following conclusion:

After months of planning by anarchists, Trotskyists, eco warriors, members of the Turkish Communist Party, militant cyclists and animal-lovers who simply wanted to feed the pigeons in Trafalgar Square, this was all that came of the Monopoly demonstration that so many had predicted would end in bloodshed and mayhem. (Cobain, 2001, Home News section)

This example does not necessarily offer us much hope for the transformative nature of news coverage. The protesters appear to be a silly and disjointed bunch bereft of real ideals and incapable of staging a political event, despite their best efforts. At this level, the article reproduces the rationality of power, which dismisses global justice as a "spurious" cause. Yet, it also illustrates the polyvalent nature of discourse, and shows that the boundaries between the hegemonic and the counter-hegemonic are porous if, indeed, they exist at all. The article pokes fun of the protesters, but also has a laugh at the expense of the police and politicians for their exaggerated preoccupation with May Day. Mark Steel, a left-wing journalist and social movements veteran, wrote a series of humorous and spectacular articles for *The Independent* which were more explicit in their condemnation of the authorities' stance on the protests:

Then came Tony Blair, who declared the violence had to be condemned. It is bad enough, after a demonstration, when politicians condemn violence that hasn't happened. But he went one further and condemned it when it hadn't yet not happened. But it shows he is prepared to show zero tolerance to any violence that takes place in his own imagination. (Steel, 2001, p. 6)

These spectacular discourses, then, occasionally laugh *with* the protesters, and against authority. It seems that opening up a space for spectacle and joking also lets subversion in through the door.

Discourses of spectacle dramatize the bind in which any social movement is caught. On the one hand, it must court the attention of mass media to get coverage for its cause, and making a spectacle out of a good cause is a sure-fire winner (DeLuca & Peeples, 2002). But on the other hand, the spectacular nature of the protests becomes the proof of the movement's irrationality and thus its illegitimacy. Of course, media institutions are ultimately responsible for constructing the spectacle for mass consumption. In an *Independent* article published on May 2, one demonstrator identified only as "Stefan" justified the violent militancy of small groups of protesters: "We are not stupid. We know breaking windows will not bring corporations to their knees. But it gets our cause noticed, and the more chaos the better" (Milmo, 2001, p. 6). Stefan might be just the kind of protester who haunts the dreams of police chiefs, and gives the global justice movement a bad name. But his actions are much more likely to get media coverage than a peaceful protest against the exploitation of child labor in Asia. As DeLuca and Peeples (2002) put it:

Yes, violence is disturbing. But for people excluded by governmental structures and corporate power, symbolic protest violence is an effective way to make it onto the public screen and speak to that power. (p. 144)

Given the narrow range of protest coverage documented in this chapter, it is perhaps not surprising that the global justice movement has appropriated spectacle and carnival into its repertoire of strategies. Indeed, one of the groups of activists most successful at capturing the attention of the media has been the pie-throwing activists, whose "pie-litical" targets include heads of large corporations, such as Bill Gates and Lord Sainsbury, and major politicians, such as Willie Brown and Jesse Ventura. One member of the "Cherry Pie Three" militant bakers cooperative thus states that "to catch people's attention, it's got to be something bigger and different. Which is the curse and the blessing of pie" (Vanderford, 2001, p. 15).

Perhaps needless to say, the discourses of joking and spectacle are rarely part of the sanctioned or "official" account of the events that appears in the "hard news" and ostensibly objective sections of the newspaper. They come in the shape of columns and eyewitness reports and are designed to be read as interpretive discourse, rather than as a representation of "truth"—an epistemological distinction that works against their legitimation. This problem of legitimation is not unique to discourses of spectacle, but should also be seen as the context for discourses of recognition.

Discourses of Recognition

Despite the overwhelming force of the discourses that provide an incitement to silence, the 2001 May Day coverage also provides evidence of a set of discourses resistant to authority and supportive of the global justice movement. Out of 277 items analyzed, 50 (18 percent of the total) engaged substantively with the claims of the protesters, and most of these were sympathetic to the cause of the protesters. They were written by activists, participants in the protests, academics, concerned citizens, and left-wing journalists.

Perhaps the most important aspect of discourses of recognition is that they communicated the substance of protesters' concerns. One letter from a

Bristol activist to the *Western Daily Press* was typical in conveying this information, otherwise entirely absent from accounts of the protests:

So, what motivates the peaceful demonstrators? One aim is to bring about the cancellation of debt to poor countries, and the abolition of the International Monetary Fund (IMF), the World Economic Forum (WEF) and the World Trade Organisation (WTO). (Harvey, 2001, p. 9)

Writers celebrating the protests reinterpreted them as success for democracy, and thus reclaimed a *political* way of interpreting the events of May 1. A leading article in the left-leaning tabloid *The Mirror* polemically opined: "Democracy survived. Not in the hands of baton-wielding police, but in the hearts of kids in anoraks taking on the system" (Routledge, 2001, p. 6).

Despite their sympathy for the protesters' concerns, many of the supportive writers were quick to distance themselves from what was seen as the overly confrontational methods of the protesters, to speak from a position of respectable bourgeois rationality. One letter to the editor typically stated: "Whatever the rights and wrongs of the May Day protests it is clear that the protesters have got a lot to protest about. This is because none of our conventional, political and business leaders are willing to stand up and speak out against the failures of capitalism" (Smith, May 18, p. 10).

Discourses of recognition often also problematized the media coverage of the protests, calling attention to how the ideas of the protesters had been lost in the obsession with policing: "As usual it was the protest itself which made the news rather than what the protest was about . . . The debate about globalization is a serious one and it will go by default if what grabs the headlines are the activities of a few barmy and destructive anarchists bent on their own agenda" (Dawson, May 7, 2001, p. 13).

This commentary underscores the mechanisms that provide the incitement to silence. More specifically, it points to a blind spot in journalism. Because conflict and violence are hot news topics, and earnest activists are not (e.g., Allan, 1999, p. 62), and because of the fact that elite and government sources set the news agenda, the debate on globalization is silenced in the crush of news practices. Guy Taylor, the outspoken and media-friendly leader of the major British global justice group "Globalise Resistance," elaborated on the incitement to silence. In an opinion he railed out against London Mayor Ken Livingstone, suggesting that when he "appeals to peaceful protesters to stay at home, he is making a political intervention. The establishment, which Ken has joined, has a policy to deter those who want to protest against globalization" (Taylor, 2001, p. 4). Similarly, John Peacock (2001), writing in *The Independent,* explained that what "seems to have provoked such ire [among politicians] was the attack, not on shop premises, but on some of the great mythologies of the Western world— namely that increased economic wealth leads to happiness and that economic determinism is clearly common sense" (p. 7).

These writers provide a sophisticated analysis of how the power of rationality has kept globalization off the agenda because talking about it would threaten the hegemony of global capitalism. In doing so, they introduce a distinct rationality into the public discourse; one that resists the overdetermined interpretation imposed by the authorities. It is the rationality of the underdog, which both needs and feeds on substance and logic, rather than the coercion characterizing the rationality of power. One letter writer commented:

> In an era of stupefying political blandness, peaceful protest is one of the few ways in which ordinary citizens can try to exert influence on events. Given that neither the Conservative nor New Labour parties even begin to express public concern about the environment and the destructive effects of unregulated global markets, it is also one of the few ways in which these issues can be brought into the mainstream of political debate. (Willmore, 2001, p. 2)

Indeed, some discourses of recognition suggested that the global justice movement could solve the problem of citizen alienation from politics—a topic that was central to the public debate in May 2001, as Britain prepared for a general election, correctly predicted to have the lowest turnouts since 1918. A leading article in *The Scotsman* argued that "in their peaceful incarnations, these activists have a playful approach to public life that conventional politicians could learn from. But their concerns go largely unrepresented in mainstream politics, which caters for parties with positive programmes rather than protest groups" (The May Day protest phenomenon, 2001, p. 13).

The wealth of positive discourses on the May Day protests should be seen in the light of a systematic problem in the representation of protesters. The protester's claims hardly ever appeared on the covers of the mainstream press, or even in the "hard news" sections. On the contrary, with a few notable exceptions,[7] discourses of recognition appeared either in the editorial page columns, leaders, or letters to the editor. As mentioned earlier, these genres have much less epistemic authority than "straight" reports. In particular, letters to the editor are often ridiculed in the newsroom as the ramblings of the insane (Wahl-Jorgensen, 2002a). The entrance of globalization onto the news agenda as a serious issue was consequently inauspicious, but it is nevertheless clear that the concerted efforts of activists, writers, and regular citizens to counteract the incitement to silence have begun to chip away at the edges of hegemony.

CONCLUSIONS: SKETCHING OUT A FRAMEWORK FOR UNDERSTANDING PROTESTS, RATIONALITY, AND POWER

This chapter has demonstrated that there is a narrow range of meanings associated with the global justice movement, determined by the rationality of power, and helped along by newsroom practices. Discussion of the 2001 May Day protests took place in a context that provided an incitement to silence about globalization. It did this by speaking of the protests in terms of their damaging effects on law and order and on the economy, and by making a spectacle out of the protesters' incompetence. Nevertheless, these silencing discourses contained moments of resistance and counterhegemony. And a substantial amount of coverage of the protests recognized the seriousness of protesters' concerns. This coverage gradually seeped into the mainstream, even if it mostly appeared outside "hard news" sections. As such, the chapter has shown us that it pays to speak out against the incitement to silence. So what can we learn from this accomplishment?

Bent Flyvbjerg (1998), in his study of the power relations that shaped a major Danish city-planning project, suggests that "the free play of antagonistic relations" (Foucault, 2002, pp. 346–347) between parties engaged in a power struggle is likely to benefit those already dominant. Flyvbjerg discovered that the most powerful groups involved in the project often won disputes not on the force of the best argument (Habermas, 1987, pp. 297–298), but through intimidation, coercion, and rationalization. He suggests that when the antagonism is out in the open, rationality has no force, and the most powerful party, who is by definition most capable of coercing others to accept their positions, wins out.

This study has shown that when parties in a power struggle are so marginalized that their concerns have no place in decision-making, the free play of antagonistic relations, in the form of protest, is the only way for them to compel the media to notice their cause. It is a curious fact that engaging in what is seen as spectacular, irrational, coercive, violent, and antisocial behavior is the most reliable way to introduce new rationalities that may have transformative consequences, in a context of incitement to silence. As a sympathetic *Guardian* opinion piece put it, "Even by simply making the slogan of anti-capitalism common currency, the movement has raised the possibility of a systemic alternative, derided as a nonsense for most of the past decade" (cited in Monitor, 2001, p. 6).

The fact that we maintain a debate about the globalization of capital bespeaks a great political accomplishment: That of bringing a set of powerful undemocratic institutions and processes, whose progress toward global hegemony has been mostly unhindered by resistance and scrutiny, onto the agenda of the public sphere. We are reminded that globalization is best understood as a "partial, incomplete, and contradictory process" (Chin & Mittelman, 2000, p. 30), always already open and vulnerable to challenge.

NOTES

1. See Foucault, 2002, p. 113.
2. Out of the 277 articles analyzed nineteen did not fit into one of the four categories discussed here, but fell into three distinct, if small, subcategories. Four articles

provided information about the protests, six focused on civil liberties issues, and the remaining nine dealt with celebrity involvement in the anti-globalization movement.

3. For instance, as I will discuss later in more detail, some of the articles that framed the 2001 May Day protests in terms of law and order were sympathetic to protesters. Likewise, such sympathy could be found in discourses of spectacle; stories that mostly poked fun at the protesters, to turn the event into a spectacle for mass consumption.

4. The decision about which discourses dominated each story was based on a reading of how the story was "framed"—what discourses dominated the first paragraph. Usually the remainder of the story would not stray from the dominant discourse.

5. See Conboy (2002) for a discussion of the history of the popular press in Britain, which provides a detailed exploration of the role of entertainment.

6. See Holland (1998) for a compelling analysis of how "the politics of the smile," or the emphasis on livening up the reader's day, has brought about the sexualization of the popular press.

7. There were two exceptions to this rule: First, a report in the conservative tabloid *The Daily Mail* interviewed participants in the Glasgow May 1 parade, citing participants:

Part-time student John McArthur, 25, from Paisley, one of the leaders of the parade, said he was rebelling against "an unequal society." He said: "We are here to celebrate freedom which is being restricted by this rightwing Government. The protesters here are just some of the people who have grown sick and tired of being repressed by this unfair economic system." He added: "This is just the beginning. We will no longer sit back and take it" (Dawson, 2001, p. 5).

A special section in the left-wing quality paper *The Guardian* (Brooks, 2001, p. 5) devoted most of a page to vox pop interviews with protesters explaining why they were attending the protest, and why it was for a worthwhile cause.

REFERENCES

Allan, S. (1999). *News culture*. Buckingham: Open University Press.

Anderson, B. (1983). *Imagined communities: Reflections on the origin and spread of nationalism*. London: Verso Books.

Bairstow, T. (1985). *Fourth-rate estate*. London: Comedia.

Bell, A. (2001, April 30). Mayday call from a sinking civilisation. *The Herald*, 12.

Billig, M. (1995). *Banal nationalism*. London: Sage.

Boggan, S. (2001, May 1). May Day: The targets: Gap, McDonald's, and a hairdresser. *The Independent*, 4.

Brooks, B. S., Kennedy, G., Moen, D. R., & Ranly, D. (1992). *News reporting and writing*. New York: St. Martin's Press.

Brooks, L. (2001, May 2). May day protests: Why I was there . . . *The Guardian*, 5.

Chin, C., & Mittelman, J. (2000). Conceptualizing resistance to globalization. In B. K. Gills (Ed.), *Globalization and the politics of resistance* (pp. 29–46). Houndmills: Palgrave.

Cobain, I. (2001, May 2). Rain rescues capitalism from spike-haired horde. *The Times*, Home News section.

Conboy, M. (2002). *The press and popular culture*. London: Sage.

Dawson, A. (2001, May 7). BBC Radio Leicester presenter John Florance with thoughts on last week's May Day events. *Leicester Mercury,* 13.

Dawson, T. (2001, May 2). Carnival atmosphere at protest in Scotland. *The Daily Mail,* 5.

DeLuca, K., & Peeples, J. (2002). From public sphere to public screen: Democracy, activism, and the "violence" of Seattle. *Critical Studies in Media Communication 19*(2), 125–151.

Eliasoph, N. (1998). *Avoiding politics: How Americans produce apathy in everyday life.* New York: Cambridge University Press.

Engel, M. (1996). *Tickle the public: One hundred years of the popular press.* London: Gollancz.

Fairclough, N. (1995). *Media discourse.* London: Edward Arnold.

Flanagan, M. (2001, September 17). Markets braced for Wall St. reopening. *The Scotsman,* 19.

Flyvbjerg, B. (1991). *Rationalitet og magt, bind I: Det konkretes videnskab.* Århus: Akademisk Forlag.

———. (1998). *Rationality and power: Democracy in practice.* Chicago: University of Chicago Press.

Foucault, M. (1990). *The history of sexuality: An introduction—volume I.* London: Penguin.

———. (1991). *Discipline and punish: The birth of the prison.* London: Penguin.

———. (2002). *Power.* London: Penguin.

Fowler, R. (1991). *Language in the news: Discourse and ideology in the press.* London and New York: Routledge.

Gamson, W., &. Wolfsfeld, G. (1993). Movements and media as interacting systems. *Annals of the American Academy of Political and Social Science 528,* 114–125.

Gills, B. K. (2000). Introduction: Globalization and the politics of resistance. In B. K. Gills (Ed.), *Globalization and the politics of resistance* (pp. 3–12). Houndmills: Palgrave.

Gramsci, A. (1971). *Selections from prison notebooks.* London: Lawrence & Wishart.

Habermas, J. (1987). *The philosophical discourse of modernity.* Cambridge, MA: MIT Press.

———. (1989). *The structural transformation of the public sphere* (Thomas Burger with the assistance of Frederick Lawrence, Trans.). Cambridge, Mass.: MIT Press.

Hallin, D. (1989). *The "Uncensored War": The media and Vietnam.* Berkeley, CA: University of California Press.

Hardman, R. (2001, May 2). Mobile in hand hate in his heart. *Daily Mail,* 4–5.

Harvey, DJ J. (2001, May 1). Message behind the May Day protests [Letter to the editor]. *Western Daily Press,* 9.

Hills, M. (2000). Conceptualising the Fourth World: Four approaches to poverty and communication. *Media Development 1,* 3–8.

Holland, P. (1998). The politics of the smile: 'Soft news' and the sexualisation of the popular press. In C. Carter, G. Branston, & S. Allan (Eds.), *News, gender and power* (pp. 17–32). London: Routledge.

Lawless, J. (2001). Black masks/black skin? KCOP's "exclusive investigative report." *To the Quick, 4,* 35–49.

Luckman, S., & Redden, G. (2001). The sense of translocal community: Mediating S11. *To the Quick, 4,* 21–34.

Mac attack: Riot police walk past a restaurant damaged in last year's riots in central London. (2001, May 1). *Insurance Day,* 12.

The May Day protest phenomenon. (2001, May 2). *The Scotsman,* 13.

May Day protests: Final cost to businesses put at pounds 20 m. (2001, May 2). *Birmingham Post,* 7.

McSmith, A. (2001, May 1). May Day "vandals" warned by Blair. *The Daily Telegraph,* 1.

Merritt, D. (1995). *Public journalism and public life: Why telling the news is not enough.* Hillsdale: Lawrence Erlbaum Associates.

Milmo, C. (2001, May 2). May Day protests: The headquarters—spikies' hq open to anyone but "pigs and journos." *The Independent,* 6.

Monitor: All the news of the world—the anarchists failed to deliver. (2001, May 5). *The Independent,* 6.

Norfolk, A. (2001, May 1). London braced for May Day trouble. *The Times,* Home News section.

Peacock, J. (2001, May 5). Faith and reason: A message from Buddha on the May Day protest. *The Independent,* 7.

Pearson, A. (2001, May 2). You're just not the right kind, m'Lord. *The Evening Standard,* 15.

Routledge, P. (2001, May 2). A defeat for liberty. *The Mirror,* 6.

Sawicki, J. (1988). Identity politics and sexual freedom: Foucault and feminism. In I. Diamond & L. Quinby (Eds.), *Feminism and Foucault: Reflections on resistance* (pp. 177–193). Boston: Northeastern University Press.

Smith, B. (2001, May 18). Stand up and see a greener view of the world [Letter to the editor]. *Birmingham Post,* 10.

Steel, M. (2001, May 2). Yellow submarine, again? Those sick, sick anarchists. *The Independent,* 6.

Taylor, G. (2001, May 1). This hysteria shows we are winning the arguments against globalisation. *The Independent,* 4.

Tendler, S., & McGrory, D. (2001, February 13). Anarchists plot May protests to disrupt election. *The Times,* Home News section.

Tuchman, G. (1972). Objectivity as strategic ritual: An examination of newsmen's notions of objectivity. *American Journal of Sociology, 77,* 660–679.

Vanderford, A. (2001). "We can lick the upper crust": Pies as political pranks. *To the Quick, 4,* 7–20.

Vidal, J. (2001, May 1). Blair attacks "spurious" May Day protests. *The Guardian,* 1.

Wahl-Jorgensen, K. (2001). Letters to the editor as a forum for public deliberation: Modes of publicity and democratic debate. *Critical Studies in Media Communication 18*(3), 303–320.

———. (2002a). The construction of the public in letters to the editor: Deliberative democracy and the idiom of insanity. *Journalism 3*(2), 183–204.

———. (2002b). The normative-economic justification for public discourse: Letters to the editor as a "wide open" public forum. *Journalism & Mass Communication Quarterly, 79*(1), 121–133.

Wheeler, M. (1997). *Politics and the mass media.* Oxford: Blackwell.

Williams, Z. (2001, May 4). You can't keep a good protest down. *The Evening Standard*, 15.

Willmore, I. (2001, May 3). Policing of May Day [Letter to the editor]. *The Independent*, 2.

Yellow Submarine singer is sent down to the cells. (2001, May 10). *The Evening Standard*, 4.

11

Probing Symbiotic Relationships: Celebrities, Mass Media, and Global Justice

Donnalyn Pompper

Social science researchers from diverse traditions have probed the phenomena of entertainment-celebrity logic, news as a social construction, and hegemonic institutions' marginalization of dissent. Alone, these literatures do much to advance our understanding of power distribution and sociopolitical change. Combined, however, they offer mass communication a potent theoretical framework for examining the implications of symbiotic relationships linked by seemingly disparate ideologies. Using the globalization paradigm as a lens, I analyze the development of mutually beneficial liaisons among global justice activists, popular culture celebrities, and newsworkers. This chapter attempts to fill gaps in our literature by contributing to theory about the roles celebrities play in the global justice movement and how activists can work within the traditional, hegemonic mass media apparatus.

I suggest that competition for resources and the struggle to manipulate public opinion in the current mass-consumption phase of late capitalism inspire this dynamic. More specifically, social movement organizations rely on news media to spread their messages—even though protesters seldom are successful in amplifying their voices above the din of elite authorities (Gamson, 1991; Pompper, 2000; Shoemaker & Reese, 1996). In recent years, social movement organizers have enlisted popular culture celebrity spokespersons to bolster the perceived newsworthiness of their messages. Furthermore, celebrities seek sociopolitical issues to promote a socially conscious image and enhance their fame (Gamson, 1994; Gitlin, 1980; Ross, 1997). Finally, news media thrive on a constant stream of dramatic events and entertainment news frames to attract audiences and increase ratings (Brill, 2000; Gans, 1979; Postman, 1985; Severin & Tankard, 2001).

Examining these symbiotic relationships against a backdrop of globalization is timely and relevant. Still reeling from an unprecedented number of regional trade agreements ratified during the 1990s, including the North American Free Trade Agreement (NAFTA) (Alphabetti, 1998), policymakers promise the unification of a global economy replete with legislated international trade agreements to benefit all countries and elevate under-developed nations. However, critics charge that a handful of multinational corporations in search of profits destroy the nation-state, promote cultural imperialism, sanction exploitation of poor countries, and victimize citizens. Consequently, it is clear that globalization has affected nearly every aspect of modern life on this planet—from food we eat and clothes we wear, to values that shape our realities.

Among the many social science disciplines, it is perhaps mass communi-cation researchers who devote greatest attention to "reality construction," particularly as it relates to the inner workings of the news media as an apparatus controlled by hegemonic forces. Yet, in search of discovering relationships among messages and society—studied far less are opposition groups' voices of protest. Use of sophisticated communication strategies among society's nonelites demands focused scholarly attention. In particular, very little research has examined popular culture celebrities' increasingly important role in social movements, a gap addressed in this chapter.

Celebrities' affiliation with globalization issues has proven a double-edged sword. Media have focused on celebrity endorsers like Kathie Lee Gifford and Michael Jordan (to some degree) to put a human face on globalization's dark side; representing such celebrities as villains. Yet, using their popular culture celebrity status to promote social issues they care about, luminaries ranging from Susan Sarandon to Robert Redford have garnered favorable media attention for themselves and global justice groups. This dynamic is examined in greater depth throughout this chapter.

Overall, key literature that framed this analysis of the symbiotic relation-ship among global justice activists, popular culture celebrities, and the news media is divided into four subsets: news media and social movements, celebrity culture and mass media, social movements and celebrities, and social justice as beneficiary.

NEWS MEDIA AND SOCIAL MOVEMENTS

Ideologically, news media gatekeepers and social movement activists seem to occupy opposite ends of the spectrum—with newsworkers dedicated to objectively seeking "the facts," and activists subjectively promoting social change. However, both entities may have more in common than is apparent to the eye.

Theorists have posited that U.S. media promote the interests of an elite power structure (Herman & Chomsky, 1988; Molotch & Lester, 1975; Shoemaker & Reese, 1996), thus nullifying journalists' objectivity claims (Glasgow University Media Group, 1976, 1980; Hall, 1979). News, a social construction, does not happen in a vacuum (Berger & Luckmann, 1966; Tuchman, 1978). Indeed, journalism is a practice with a definable milieu that culminates in a manufactured product shaped by a complex, yet artificial or subjective, selection, collection, organization, and dissemination of data (Carey, 1986; Darnton, 1975; Fowler, 1991). Conflict between what is, and what is represented by the news media, raises serious questions about the sociopolitical implications of newsmaking—especially for small constituencies, the powerless, common people in the streets, and those expressing unpopular views.

Since the daily practices and routines of journalism result in news produced by, about, and for elites, mainstream news media marginalize nonelites such as social movement organizations. For instance, authorities' access to journalists is uncomplicated, like "a dance," while doors are closed to nearly everyone else (Gans, 1979, p. 116; Molotch & Lester, 1974). Also, the news media are more likely to cover an issue or event if it involves authorities (Fishman, 1980; Sigal, 1973) which, in turn, satisfies the masses' curiosity about "how the other half lives" (Jamieson & Campbell, 2001, p. 61). Furthermore, Gerbner (1972) suggested that the media can under- or misrepresent people, underscoring their powerlessness through symbolic annihilation. For example, news media marginalize protest groups, particularly those of radical ideologies (McLeod & Detenber, 1999), resulting in news coverage that promotes "official" definitions of protest and focuses on the "legality of actions" rather than the "morality of issues" (McLeod & Hertog, 1992, p. 260).

At the core of the "news as social construction" debate lies the definition of "newsworthiness" and an important clue for groups who seek access to mainstream news media. Early contemporary journalists characterized news as novelty: "When a dog bites a man, that is not news, because it happens so often. But if a man bites a dog, that is news."[1] In journalism schools across the United States, students are trained to define newsworthiness in terms of timeliness, impact/consequence or importance, prominence of the people involved, proximity to audiences, conflict, unusual nature of the event, and currency (people's interest in an ongoing situation) (Mencher, 2000). Furthermore, a sociologist who studied newsroom cultures of CBS, NBC, *Newsweek* and *Time* concluded that "enduring news values" enable journalists to decide what is news: ethnocentrism, altruistic democracy, responsible capitalism, small-town pastoralism, individualism, and moderatism (Gans, 1979, pp. 53–55). Similarly, a study of how daily newspaper editors construct the front page posited that these gatekeepers rely on traditional news values, while finding ways to obscure their own ideological biases (Reisner, 1992).

It has been argued that "social disorder" (Gans, 1979, pp. 42–52) and "deviance" (Gitlin, 1980, p. 152) also constitute core news values, thereby discouraging excess. Hence, "moderatism" has become entrenched as an enduring news value: "[I]insofar as the news has an ideology of its own, it is moderate" (Gans, 1979, p. 52). As morality tales for discouraging socially unacceptable behaviors, for example, media negatively portray atheists and "religious fanatics," as well as college students "who play when they should study" (Gans, 1979, p. 51). Another popular criterion used to determine newsworthiness, "if it bleeds, it leads" (Kerbel, 2000), emphasizes a news media appetite for visual violence that results from norm deviation. Beyond visuals, newsworkers also use language (Fowler, 1991), frames (Entman, 1993), pegs and hooks (Ryan, 1991) consistent with dominant ideology to reinforce the enduring news value of moderatism.

Consequently, social activists' issues rarely are considered newsworthy—*unless* they can be packaged as dramatic, social disorder stories or morality tales that eschew extremism. Herein lies a strategy used by social activists who form symbiotic relationships with newsworkers in order to spread their messages to the masses.

Historically, few social movement groups have successfully used news media to advance their cause like the southern student nonviolent sit-in movement that began early in 1960 in Nashville, Tenn. (Sumner, 1995). Activists saw the television medium as an ally in achieving their goal of ending racial segregation, and cultivated newsworkers who showed violence initiated by those other than student activists. Also successful in overcoming racial barriers and garnering news media attention were civil rights and anti-Vietnam movement leaders of the 1960s, including Huey Newton, Eldridge Cleaver, Stokely Carmichael, Tom Hayden, Jerry Rubin, and Abbie Hoffman (Gitlin, 1980). These charasmatic leaders offered "symbolic imagery" to newsworkers producing stories about emotionally charged issues (Downs, 1972).

Instead of waiting for news opportunities to present themselves, social movement organizations in subsequent decades have found that they can spread their views by creating "pseudo-events" (Boorstin, 1961; Campbell, 1998), "image events" (DeLuca, 1999; Hunter, 1971), and "media events" to subsidize news media coverage (Gandy, 1982). Protesters sometimes directly initiate "a barter arrangement" with newsworkers by providing action that makes for good pictures and soundbites (Gamson, 1989, p. 6). The Greenpeace environmental activists have been heralded as an early example of an interest group manipulating news media conventions and routines—by sailing protesters to the offshore sites of nuclear explosion tests and by featuring volunteers using their bodies as shields to protect nursing baby harp seals from hunters' weapons. According to a former Greenpeace director, staged media events unfold "in the public's consciousness to transform the way people view their world" (Hunter, 1971, p. 22). Thus, the TV screen has been characterized as "the contemporary shape of the public sphere" (DeLuca & Peeples, 2002, p. 126).

Analyses of how news media cover protests are few in number, yet rich in findings. For instance, it is suggested that newsworkers marginalize protest groups (Duemler, 2000; McLeod & Hertog, 1992; Phillips, 2000) and often portray movements and organizers negatively (Chomsky, 1999; Chomsky & Herman, 2002)—perhaps because they are constrained by journalism's routines that limit ways of writing about protest (DeLuca & Peeples, 2000). Importantly, audiences report that their perceptions of activists and social issues are shaped by newsworkers' representations. For example, newspaper stories may affect readers' perceptions of activists' legitimacy (Shoemaker, 1982), and those exposed to a television news story slanted against protesters are more critical of protesters and their issues than those who viewed a balanced story where protesters and authorities were represented equitably (McLeod, 1995). Similarly, McLeod and Detenber (1999) found that viewers are more likely to support the status quo and criticize protesters—including their free speech civil rights.

Beyond maximizing opportunities resulting from traditional news conventions and routines, social movement groups have celebrated a significant shift in news production in recent years—the "softening" of news, replacement of "old news" in favor of "new news"—commonly referred to as "entertainment news." The "new news" concept emerged from the 1992 U.S. presidential election when candidates appeared on *Larry King Live,* the *Arsenio Hall Show,* and on MTV (Severin & Tankard, 2001). More broadly, television's traditional three network evening broadcasts, daily newspapers, and three major newsmagazines have faced unprecedented competition for market share in recent decades. But according to one media critic, audiences stopped seeing the distinction between news and entertainment long ago (Brill, 2000). "New news" is defined as "part Hollywood film and TV movie, part pop music and pop art, mixed with popular culture and celebrity magazines, tabloid telecasts, cable and home video" (Katz, 1992, p. 39)—where younger audiences consider fashion, entertainment, music, and technology to be news. Assignment editors make newsworthiness decisions based on a "famous face" criterion, in effect reducing news production costs because "it is easier to anticipate who will be involved than what is going to happen" (Epstein, 1973, p. 144).

Not all newsworkers and media critics have responded favorably to this hard-to-soft news shift, however. For instance, journalists were enraged when ABC news president sought to make news more appealing for the younger generation and hired popular culture celebrity actor Leonardo DiCaprio to conduct a White House interview with President Bill Clinton as part of the network's Earth Day 2000 celebration. Certainly, it would seem that journalists don't mind covering celebrities. They simply don't want to be replaced by them.

In closely monitoring news conventions, routines, and taking advantage of the "news as entertainment" approach, social movement activists have developed sophisticated media placement strategies and discovered allies in newsworkers—and vice versa. Journalists can depend on activists to provide easy-to-package soundbites and video clips that make news production easier—and more entertaining. As exemplified in the DiCaprio Earth Day incident, what better way to make news entertaining than to involve celebrities?

CELEBRITY CULTURE AND MASS MEDIA

Mass media and celebrities are inherently dependent upon one another. Celebrity is central to the culture apparatus (Gitlin, 1980), wherein culture is defined as "the active process of generating and circulating meanings and pleasures within a social system" (Fiske, 1989, p. 23)—and mass media are vehicles for shaping and distributing meaning (Hall, 1979). Perhaps celebrity culture came of age in 1966 when John Lennon of the Beatles told a London newspaper reporter that the rock-and-roll band was "more popular than Jesus" (Cleave, 1966). The Beatles learned firsthand that fame comes at a price. A highly publicized anti-Beatles moral debate and U.S.-based record album ban cast a Beatles' "dark side" that shadows the band's legacy in spite of its international celebrity status (The Dark Side of Beatlemania, 2002). Celebrity is a phenomenon constructed through the media. Today, the sheer number of celebrities is without precedent (Giles, 2000). Yet, the celebrity-mass media dynamic—relationships among discourse, production, and audiences—and its affect on social values, is underexplored in the scholarly literature (Braudy, 1997; Gamson, 1994). Symbiotic relationships among celebrities and the mass media are the focus of this section, where "celebrity" refers to popular culture entertainment figures.

Long before mass media developed and the word "celebrity" entered our vocabulary, acts of heroism were made famous locally through oral tradition where individuals rarely achieved mass notoriety during their lifetime. With urban growth and the rise of literacy during the Renaissance, modern theatre, portraiture, and engraving began emphasizing "the individual face" (Braudy, 1997, p. 266), facilitating widespread recognition during one's lifetime. Furthermore, the American and French revolutions created a "free market of fame" wherein writing, painting, and engraving became a "lever to power" (Braudy, 1997, p. 393). It has been suggested that the growth of popular mass media has led to a social transition where celebrity is prized over mythic characters, and old heroic figures such as religious, political, and military leaders have been replaced by entertainers in the public mind (Boorstin, 1961; Edelstein, 1996; Loftus, 1995) such as Elvis Presley (Fraser & Brown, 2002).

The rapid expansion of the cinema-television industry in the United States during the twentieth century gave birth to celebrity culture, and now the meanings of celebrity, success, and power are blurred and synonymous (Gamson, 1994; Marshall, 1997). Hollywood sets the standard of both mainstream cinema and stardom (Gledhill, 1991). In particular, television has become the "vehicle for fame" (Giles, 2000, p. 24), since the medium's early content involved bringing celebrities into Americans' living rooms. Furthermore, global communication systems and the proliferation of entertainment media worldwide has given rise to international celebrity, for we easily can share those whom we admire among a global village (Fraser & Brown, 2002). In addition, new industries were spawned to support the celebrity "engine" (Lippman, 1960, p. 121). Building and maintaining celebrity images has created new jobs, such as increased numbers of entertainment reporters (Gamson, 1992), as well as chat talk show hosts (Giles, 2000), newsworkers for magazines created by celebrities (Johnson, 2002), and publicists,[2] press agents, and image managers (Bernays, 1923; Ewen, 1998; Gamson, 1992). Boorstin (1961) contrasted the obsolete private secretary who shielded public people from the masses with the contemporary press secretary who is charged with keeping her/his employer in the public eye.

Beyond media's noncommercial content, social critics have critiqued celebrity endorsements of products and services. Gamson (1992) equates the growth of celebrity culture with the "birth of modern American consumer culture" (p. 4) beginning in the 1950s (Gamson, 1992). Marshall (1997) suggests that the celebrity is "an ideological support for consumer capitalism" (p. 43). By extension, celebrities indirectly benefit mass media operations that rely on financial support from advertising sales. Accordingly, Ewen (1998) argues that the mass media "are able to invest the everyday lives of formerly everyday people with a magical sense of value, a secularized imprint of the *sacred*"[3] (p. 93), and are bestowed with the power to engineer "mass constituencies and popular consent" (p. 94). A celebrity's attractiveness (Giles, 2000), combined with expertise about a product or service being endorsed (Buhr, Simpson, & Pryor, 1987; Ohanian, 1991) shapes consumer behavior (Goldsmith, Lafferty, & Newell, 2000; Marshall, 1997; Mathur, Mathur, & Rangan, 1997; McCraken, 1989; Till & Busler, 2000). Even though the term "celebrity" has come to "embody the ambiguity of the public forms of subjectivity under capitalism," (Marshall, 1997, p. 4), it is doubtful that the public is entirely cognizant of celebrities' hegemonic role (Parenti, 1978). Furthermore, the public projects onto the celebrity an "interpersonal reality" (Fraser & Brown, 2002, p. 185). For example, American newsmagazines' ritualized narrative used in covering celebrity deaths positions the celebrity as "one of us"

(Kitch, 2000, p. 171), and "reality" programming and talk shows have fostered an "illusion of intimacy" between celebrities and audiences (Schudson, 1978).

Ironically, newsworkers who make celebrities famous in the first place may end up trashing them later on: "They'll print anything whether it's true or not, nothing personal, that's how it is, they have space to fill, nobody asked you to become famous so don't blame them, what goes up must come down" (Ephron, 1989, p. 104). News media attention to celebrity scandal has attracted significant scholarly attention (e.g., Bird, 1992). Indeed, celebrity-mass media relationships may prove positive or negative for both parties involved. Potential risk runs both ways.

Another subset of scholarly inquiry involving the celebrity-mass media dynamic includes celebrities' influence on people exposed to media messages (Basil, 1996; Brown, Basil, & Bocarnea, 1999). Kornhauser (1968) suggests that decline in political leadership creates a state of anomie among masses who lack direction and therefore, become receptive to "pseudo-authority" (p. 63). More specifically, the uses and gratifications of parasocial relationships literature posits that society continues to fragment as people combat loneliness by watching television (Rubin, Perse, & Powell, 1985; Rubin & Rubin, 2001) instead of socializing with real people. Postman (1985) argues that by absorbing "simplistic, nonsubstantive, nonhistorical and noncontextual" public discourse, we Americans are "amusing ourselves to death" (p. 141). Horkheimer and Adorno (1972) coined the term, "cult of personality" offered by Hollywood to explain the malleability of mass consciousness.

Other media effects researchers support a theory of celebrity identification (Fraser & Brown, 2002) to explain psychological bonds—how mass media audiences engage in a "process of identification" with a celebrity and how the process "leads media consumers to role model a celebrity's perceived values and behavior" (p. 183). The theory of celebrity identification is broadly related to Herbert C. Kelman's (1958) research on identification and Albert Bandura's (1977) social learning theory, the process of adopting behavior by modeling others. Advertisers of the 1920s rationalized using celebrity endorsers for "the spirit of emulation" (Fox, 184, p. 90). Alperstein (1991) characterizes this phenomenon as "pseudo-social interaction," wherein audiences develop imaginary relationships with television commercial actors (p. 43). Similarly, this dynamic emerges when film stars play "an active symbolic role" in the lives of moviegoers (Marshall, 1997, p. 12). All in all, celebrities affect people's clothing styles and health behaviors, such as HIV prevention (Brown & Basil, 1995; Coleman & Meyer, 1990; Hoffner & Cantor, 1991; McGwire, 1974). Children imitate film heroes (Albert, 1957; Noble, 1975). And people of all ages identify with the appearance and behaviors of celebrities whom they admire (Hoffner & Cantor, 1991), perhaps hoping that they, too, might achieve star status (Alberoni, 1972).

Neither are policymakers immune to celebrities' charisma. Hollywood has had a hand in politics since the days when Will Rogers moonlighted as a political columnist in the 1920s. More recently, film actor Richard Dreyfuss dined with President Bill Clinton and traveled to Israel three times to meet with then-Prime Minister Shimon Peres and key Middle East peace negotiators. Also, Charlton Heston met with congressional representatives Newt Gingrich and Phil Gramm to discuss the National Rifle Association's position on gun control (Meyer & Gamson, 1995). Similarly, Ronald Reagan staged photo ops with Michael Jackson; George Bush, Sr. shared the stage with film actor Arnold Schwarzenneger; Mikhail Gorbachev appeared in Wim Wenders' 1993 motion picture, *Far Away, So Close!*; and Nelson Mandela has appeared extensively in *Vogue* magazine. Marshall (1997) characterized such incidents as "slippages in identification and differentiation" steeped in "emotive and irrational, yet culturally deeply embedded sentiments" (p. 19). Collectively, celebrities are an integral part of our culture.

A relatively small cluster of individuals among the public sphere, celebrities possess presence and agency (Marshall, 1997). They are idolized by the public (Boorstin, 1961). Eventually, celebrities can parlay their power to motivate masses into an enhanced image that enables them to compete for greater fame. The celebrity, a "human pseudo-event" (Boorstin, 1961, p. 56), is "the crowning result of a society that makes a fetish of competition" (Mills, 1956, p. 74). In fact, celebrities such as Ronald Reagan, Sonny Bono, Jesse Ventura, and Clint Eastwood have used their celebrity status to win political office—a highly valued, elite social position in our culture.

In sum, the celebrity-mass media dynamic shapes the culture apparatus with a wide range of effects. In particular, popular culture celebrities and the mass media enjoy a special brand of simpatico. Celebrities are obliged to the mass media for creating their star status and perpetuating their image in a competitive arena, while the mass media rely on celebrities for product-service endorsements in advertisements and for news-editorial content. Furthermore, the public's huge "appetite for gossip" (Ephron, 1989, p. 104) must be sated. Next, I examine relationships between celebrities and social movement activists.

SOCIAL MOVEMENTS AND CELEBRITIES

As addressed earlier in this chapter, newsworkers and social activists may seem ideologically opposed. However, forming a symbiotic relationship has enabled social activists to attract coverage like never before since they provide newsworkers with dramatic fodder used to package stories for audiences who prefer the entertainment-news format. It may be posited that celebrities and social activists have even less in common—even though celebrity politics were all the rage during the late 1960s/early 1970s when the media used

Jane Fonda to symbolize and define abnormal gender activity in conjunction with the actress' association with left-wing causes (Perkins, 1991). Hence, strategic alliances among popular culture celebrities and those who organize and embrace social issues have become a regular feature in modern U.S. political and social life (Prindle, 1993).

To help celebrities navigate the political scene with advice on selecting charities and campaigns, as well as providing updates on key players central to issues the stars care about, a unique industry of personal political consultants or "power-channelers" has emerged in Hollywood and Washington, D.C. Many of these political gurus are former insiders who campaigned for high-profile politicians, lobbied for interest groups, and served as staffers for elected officials. These consultants have become "indispensable to the maturing new class of monied Hollywood elite" (O'Connor, 2000, p. B1). According to a *Los Angeles Times* report, liberal, A-list celebrities who retain political advisers include Barbra Streisand, Rob Reiner, Steven Spielberg, Kim Basinger, Robert Redford, Norman Lear, Jimmy Smits, and David Geffen (Fiore, 1997; O'Connor, 2000, p. B1). One Hollywood consultant told *USA Today:* "We mobilize Hollywood; they mobilize the public" (Harris, 1994). Hence, celebrities are tapping into the interacting systems of social movements and mass media (Gamson & Wolfsfeld, 1993).

Indeed, elites of various industries have harnessed celebrity authority-power—in academia, architecture, art, electoral politics, fashion, literature, and medicine. Enlisting a celebrity to serve as a spokesperson enables organizations to capitalize on the celebrity's image, for names have "symbolic currency" (Gitlin, 1980, p. 151). Sociologist Max Weber (1968) invokes the universal phenomenon of "charisma" to explain relationships between leaders and the public (p. 1112). Weber suggests that the masses prefer an individual—a prophet—as opposed to rational forms of government and traditional power structures (p. 1118). Applying this concept in a mass communication context, Gitlin (1980) argues: "Charisma can now be fabricated as a mysterious aura, as 'star quality,' in the relation between celebrities and audiences that is incarnated through the mass media" (pp. 148–149).

On the other hand, non-elite grassroots social movements also have reaped the rewards of associations with celebrities in struggles for legitimacy amidst hegemonic forces (Blyskal & Blyskal, 1985; Gamson, 1994; Sudjic, 1989) by engaging in symbolic politics (Castels, Yazawa & Kiselyova, 1996). Exactly what role do celebrities play in social movements? First, athletes like Michael Jordan, actors like Robert Redford, and musicians like Don Henley possess significant accumulated personal wealth and may offer financial support to causes in which they altruistically believe. Second, celebrities extend the boundaries of a conflict to the public (Schattschneider, 1960) when they engage audiences to support their "pet cause" through fund-raising promotions linked to ticket and CD sales. Also, celebrity activists use their media skills to take social messages to the masses as supporters of various disease telethons and record public service announcements. Third, celebrities use their clout to arrange strategic liaisons and meetings among activists and policymakers with financial and political power, even though elites routinely ignore activists (Gledhill, 1991). However, politicians are captivated by charismatic celebrities who are able to manipulate the publicity machine. Finally, celebrity involvement functions to construct collective identities for social movements, enhance visibility, and lend an air of credibility to causes (Cathcart, 1978; Meyer & Gamson, 1995). Often, celebrities' role is to act as bait for attracting the attention of media (Ryan, 1991) who, otherwise, take little notice of activists (unless drama is involved)—as addressed earlier in this chapter. One grassroots organizer told the *Los Angeles Times* how important celebrity involvement can be to awareness campaigns: "There are so many causes and special interests in the country . . . and there is an awful lot of competition for attention. The right kind of celebrity can set you apart" (Fiore, 1997).

While liaisons with social movements offer celebrities a publicity vehicle for promoting their social conscience and enhancing their image, celebrities who have linked with multinational corporations whom activists oppose become easy publicity targets. As the punk band Rage Against the Machine performed outside the 2000 Democratic National Convention in Los Angeles, a band member told reporters: "The real people's convention was being held on the streets outside" (Scheer, 2000). On the negative side, corporate sponsorship has become "an important lever" for activists (Klein, 1999, p. 359), and celebrities like Kathie Lee Gifford and Wal-Mart have experienced the ire of activists at the controls of the publicity machine. During a now infamous episode of the ABC network's *Live With Regis and Kathie Lee* program, Gifford broke down and cried on the air when accused of endorsing a clothing line manufactured by sweatshop workers. Similarly, human-rights activists picketed concerts of Celine Dion and Hootie and the Blowfish when they learned that tour sponsors had a hand in dealing with a Burmese junta. In an odd twist of fate, Hootie members joined forces with activists by sporting "Suzuki out of Burma" T-shirts on stage.

Seemingly, celebrities elicit a wide range of audience interpretive responses, for a mercurial public scrutinizes celebrities' "legitimacy to speak for a movement" (Gamson, 1992; Gamson, 1994; Meyer & Gamson, 1995, p. 181) and is quick to turn its back on idols who have fallen from grace. Because some celebrities find themselves cornered by "contradictory logics" as they try to serve the media and their constituencies at once (Gitlin, 1980, p. 162), they sometimes seek the most moderate or liberal causes and consensual claims within large social movement groups (Prindle, 1993) or speak on issues in which they are intrinsically involved.

Celebrities have expressed mixed sentiments about aligning with activist movements. Actress Janeane Garofalo speaks out about Hollywood portrayals of women, but is less vocal in other spheres: "I try to avoid it (speaking out about different issues), because . . . I think people are very cynical with *actors*[4] trying to tell them what to believe in, or lobbying for any kind of changing of government policy" (Janeane, 2000, p. 82). On the other hand, actress and former talk show host, Rosie O'Donnell responded to a reporter's question about her activism: "I have a responsibility as well as an opportunity to speak to millions of people on a daily basis. It's sad that celebrities' opinions are given so much weight, but they are, in the culture we live in" (Nordlinger, 2000).

Of course, not all celebrities are taken seriously by the media—or opinion leaders. Bianca Jagger, former wife of the Rolling Stones' Mick Jagger, has become a political and environmental activist in her native Nicaragua: "How much longer do I have to apologize for going to Studio 54 . . . that does not mean I am not a person of substance who is concerned with serious and deeply felt ideas" (Moody, 1992, p. 58). Similarly, when actresses Jessica Lange, Sissy Spacek, and Jane Fonda tried to explain the plight of the American farm wife to a House committee, one congressional representative quipped: "I don't have time to play *Hollywood Squares*" (Fiore, 1997). The event resulted in extensive news media attention, however. And prior to a Hollywood career as a screenwriter/producer/director/executive producer, Nora Ephron-as-journalist wrote cynically about celebrities' selflessness in *Esquire* magazine: "[T]he most effective way for a celebrity to cloak himself in goodness was to buy a lesser disease, preferably one that primarily affected children" (Ephron, 1989, p. 104). Indeed, stakes are high in the image game and celebrities carefully select social issues with which they align themselves.

Not all celebrity-social movement liaisons prove fruitful for activists, either. Overall, a celebrity's aura may overshadow the social issue he or she promotes, leading to news media coverage that focuses on the visuals and ignores the issues behind demonstrations (Gitlin, 1980). Use of a celebrity spokesperson also may foster dissent within social movements because insiders feel better qualified to champion their group's cause (Gitlin, 1980), or fear being labeled as a "sell out." Furthermore, celebrity involvement in social movements tends to "soften," "depoliticize, or deradicalize" the issues as they are tamed and homogenized by the celebrity, in media coverage, or both (Hills, 2000; Meyer & Gamson, 1995, p. 188). For example, Meyer (1990) posits that celebrity involvement in the nuclear freeze movement did little to challenge authorities or clarify the issues, and Meyer and Gamson (1995) observe that very few celebrities link with the anti-abortion movement because it is too controversial and polarizing.

Consequently, the celebrity-social movement liaison is a potent combination for grabbing the media spotlight and using it as a resource for mobilizing mass audiences and influencing policy. The relationship may be volatile, however. Despite the potential for significant image-enhancement rewards, celebrities choose their endorsement partners cautiously—whether they be multinational corporations or social activist groups. Similarly, social activists have much to gain by enlisting the support of a high-profile celebrity in terms of mass media coverage, enhanced public awareness, and policymakers' suppport. However, the spillover effect of losing public support vis-à-vis a celebrity perceived negatively, can severely damage a social movement's already tenuous reputation.

In sum, the literature offers a substantial platform for building theory about symbiotic relationships among social movement groups, popular culture celebrities, and the news media. Next, I examine the implications of this dynamic in a globalization context and offer suggestions for future research.

GLOBAL JUSTICE AS BENEFICIARY

Synergies created by the overlapping spheres of mutual interest among global justice activists, popular culture celebrities, and the news media suggest that there may be more at work than merely a logical coming of age of a 1960–1970s socially active generation. Indeed, I posit that late capitalism has accelerated this dynamic in recent years. Originally, voices of dissent were celebrated as the colonies transitioned to United States. Post–yellow journalism-era newsworkers set objectivity as the highest journalistic standard. And once upon a time, entertainers achieved notoriety simply for best practicing their craft. Yet, as argued in this chapter, voices of dissent have become marginalized, the news media are anything but impartial, and popular culture celebrities have become surrogates for political leadership. A socioeconomic structure that produces illogical interdependencies exemplifies production in "the age of simulation" where "signs of the real" are substituted for "the real itself" (Baudrillard, 1988, p. 167). Yet the ends seem to justify the means for the global justice movement, which advances its agenda by harnessing the power of these postmodern relationships.

In toto, the global justice movement is a loose coalition of seemingly disparate citizens who share a mutual fear and distrust of policymakers and multinational corporations. Diverse views abound regarding what "globalization" refers to. As simplified by Andrew Ross (1997), to some, "globalization" means the rise of supranational institutions with decision-making power to shape and constrain nation-states' policy options. To others, "globalization" is the monumental impact of global economic processes—production, capital flow, trade, consumption, and economic interdependence. Some see it as the emergence of new global cultural forms, media, and communication technologies that shape inter-intra cultural relations of affiliation, identity, and interaction. Many others, quite simply, view "globalization" as

a means used by policymakers to enable "greater forces"[5] to operate unin-
terrupted, leaving the nation-state "no choice but to play by a set of global
rules not of its own making" (Ross, 1997, pp. 9–37). Thus, a collection of
ideologically diverse labor union members, human rights activists, environmentalists, and others have literally linked arms to oppose globalization,
organizing the "global justice movement" in order to ensure that global trade
is regulated fairly, where emerging economies and multinational corporations
share the policymaking table.

In recent years, celebrities have embraced the social movement scene.
News media have extensively covered such liaisons, for a who's who of
entertainers linked with social issues: actor Paul Newman's work with the
environmental lobby; actor Robert Redford's Institute for Resource
Management workshops addressing climate change and cooperation
among nations; singer John Denver's Choices for the Future symposia;
actress Meryl Streep's protest of pesticide spraying; actor Ted Danson's
foundation of the American Oceans Campaign; rock singer Don Henley's
Walden Woods Project, which also involved rock singer Bonnie Raitt and
folk singer Arlo Guthrie; actor Tom Cruise's hosting of Earth Day in 1990;
and actress Linda Evans' Take Pride in America campaign.

Also consider, actor Martin Sheen's arrest for scaling the fence of a toxic
waste facility during a demonstration; entertainers such as Jane Fonda,
Joanne Woodward, Paul Simon, Billy Joel, Jimmy Buffet, Carly Simon, and
David Letterman who have served as Nature Conservancy board members;
actor Ed Asner's involvement with the World Wildlife Fund; actor James
Earl Jones' narration for the Audubon Society; singer Barbra Streisand's
financial support of The Environmental Defense Fund, AIDS research,
reproductive issues, and others; and actor Michael Keaton's support of the
American Rivers Association.

Other celebrity activists include actors Denzel Washington, Angela
Bassett, Alfre Woodard, and Danny Glover, who perform volunteer work in
South Africa; singers Joan Baez, Stevie Wonder, and BeBe Winans who have
hosted benefit concerts in South Africa; boxing champion Oscar De La
Hoya's outreach to the Latin community; supermodel Christy Turlington's
relief work in El Salvador; actor Marlon Brando's support of Native
American causes; entertainers supporting animal rights issues, including
Betty White, Brigitte Bardot, Doris Day, Kevin Nealon, and Shari Belafonte;
actress Elizabeth Taylor's creation of AMFAR for AIDS awareness and
research; actor Jerry Lewis' long-standing support of the Muscular
Dystrophy Association; actors Susan Sarandon and Tim Robbins' human
rights activism; actress Sally Struthers' support of children's issues worldwide; actor Richard Gere's outspokenness on human rights abuses in China;
and singers Sting and Madonna's support of rain forest preservation.

In particular, numerous partnerships between social justice activists
and celebrities have been amplified by the news media. For instance, a 1992

project called NetAid promoted a new activist website, www.netaid.org, a "global portal for social activism" (Hartigan, 1999, p. D1). The project encouraged information sharing on issues ranging from the environment to human rights by combining the global communications power of the Internet with the lure of a celebrity concert series featuring U2 singer Bono, as well as other bands and vocalists: Bush, the Corrs, the Counting Crows, Celine Dion, Jewel, Eurythmics, Wyclef Jean, George Michael, Jimmy Page, Pete Townshend, and Robbie Williams. And as reported in the *Wall Street Journal* in 2001, celebrities including actor Ralph Fiennes and rock singer Annie Lennox backed environmentalists in urging European Parliament members to support environmentalists' boycott of Exxon Mobil (Herrick, 2001).

Another somewhat bizarre celebrity-as-global-justice-activist 2002 media event included U2's Bono and U.S. Treasury Secretary Paul O'Neill spending two weeks traveling together across Africa, visiting Ghana, South Africa, Uganda, and Ethiopia. *Harper's Magazine* reported the trek in the context of the U.S. war on terrorism, suggesting (perhaps sarcasticallly) that global trade will defeat terrorism because "poor nations nurture radicals" (Fishman, 2002, p. 33). Hence, celebrity-social justice activists offer news frames and provide visuals for image-hungry news media who produce entertainment-oriented news that appeals to audiences of celebrity worshipers.

In conclusion, this chapter attempts to fill gaps in our literature by contributing to theory building about the roles that popular culture celebrities play in the global justice movement and how activists can work within the mass media apparatus. Undoubtedly, the global justice movement benefits from symbiotic relationships with celebrities and the news media. Voices of dissent are getting through to mainstream news media gatekeepers and global justice messages are making it onto the news agenda for dissemination to mass audiences. What we are less certain about is whether global justice activists are garnering enough public support. Perhaps most importantly, are policymakers listening? What is being done to modify the globalization paradigm? Furthermore, what new strategies are activists creating to keep the mainstream news media interested? Researchers may consider empirically testing the argument posited here, as well as examining new directions for this arena of inquiry. More specifically, research is needed to understand how social movement groups and celebrities can avoid the downside of their symbiotic relationship—the public's fickle attitudes and potential for negative news media representations.

NOTES

1. Attributed to both John Bogart and Charles A. Dana, later nineteenth, early twentieth century. <http://www.poynter.org/dr_ink/040802.htm>

2. Giles (2000) characterized publicists as the "gatekeepers" of celebrity culture (p. 19).

3. Italics in the original.
4. Italics in the original.
5. "Greater forces" include "global competition, responses to IMF or World Bank demands, obligations to regional alliances, and so on" (Ross, 1997).

REFERENCES

Alberoni, F. (1972). The powerless "elite": Theory and sociological research on the phenomenon of the stars. In D. McQuail (Ed.), *Sociology of mass communications* (pp. 75–89). Harmondsworth, England: Penguin.

Albert, R. S. (1957). The role of mass media and the effect of aggressive film content upon children's aggressive responses and identification choices. *Genetic Psychology Monographs, 55*(2), 221–285.

Alperstein, N. M. (1991). Imaginary social relationships with celebrities appearing in television commercials. *Journal of Broadcasting & Electronic Media, 35*(1), 43–58.

Alphabetti spaghetti: Are regional trade agreements a good idea? (1998, October 3). *The Economist, 348*(8088), 19–21.

Bandura, A. (1977). *Social learning theory.* Englewood Cliffs, NJ: Prentice-Hall.

Basil, M. D. (1996). Identification as a mediator of celebrity effects. *Journal of Broadcasting & Electronic Media, 40*(4), 478–495.

Baudrillard, J. (1988). *Selected writings.* Stanford, CA: Stanford University Press.

Berger, P. L., & Luckmann, T. (1966). *The social construction of reality.* New York: Anchor Books Doubleday.

Bernays, E. L. (1923). *Crystallizing public opinion.* New York: Liveright Publishing Corporation.

Bird, S. E. (1992). *For enquiring minds: A cultural study of supermarket tabloids.* Knoxville, TN: The University of Tennessee Press.

Blyskal J., & Blyskal, M. (1985). *PR: How the public relations industry writes the news.* New York: William Morrow & Co.

Boorstin, D. J. (1961). *The image: A guide to pseudo-events in America.* New York: Harper & Row.

Braudy, L. (1997). *The frenzy of renown: Fame and its history* (2nd ed.). New York: Vintage Books.

Brill, S. (2000, June). Learning from Leo. *Brill's Content, 3*(5), 23–24, 121.

Brown, W. J., & Basil, M. D. (1995). Media celebrities and public health: Responses to "Magic" Johnson's HIV disclosure and its impact on AIDS risk and high-risk behaviors. *Health Communication, 7*, 345–370.

Brown, W. J., Basil, M. D., & Bocarnea, M. C. (1999, May). *Involvement with an American role model: Mark McGwire's influence on public opinion toward two health issues.* Paper presented to the 49th Annual Conference of the International Communication Association, San Francisco.

Buhr, T. A., Simpson, T. L., & Pryor, B. (1987). Celebrity endorsers' expertise and perceptions of attractiveness, likeability, and familiarity. *Psychological Reports, 60*, 1307–1309.

Campbell, R. (1998). *Media and culture.* New York: St. Martin's Press.

Carey, J. W. (1986). Why and how? The dark continent of American journalism. In R. K. Manoff, & M. Schudson (Eds.), *Reading the news* (pp. 146–196). New York: Pantheon Books.

Castels, M., Yazawa, S., & Kiselyova, E. (1996). Insurgents against the global order: A comparative analysis of the Zapastistas in Mexico, the American militia and Japan's AUM Shinrikyo. *Berkeley Journal of Sociology, 40,* 21–59.

Cathcart, R. (1978). Movements: Confrontation as rhetorical form. *Southern Speech Communication Journal, 43*(3), 233–247.

Chomsky, N. (1999). *Profit over people: Neoliberalism and the global order.* New York: Seven Stories Press.

Chomsky, N., & Herman, E. (2002). *Manufacturing consent: The political economy of the mass media.* New York: Pantheon Books.

Cleave, M. (1966, March 4). How does a Beatle live? John Lennon lives like this. Retrieved on September 20, 2002, from http://www.geocities.com/nastymcquickly/articles/standard.html.

Coleman, P. L., & Meyer, R. C. (1990). *Proceedings from the enter-educate conference: Entertainment for social change.* Baltimore, MD: Johns Hopkins University Center for Communication Programs.

The Dark Side of Beatlemania. (2002, September 20). http://www.beatlesagain.com/bapology.html

Darnton, R. (1975). Writing news and telling stories. *Daedalus, 104*(2), 175–194.

DeLuca, K. (1999). *Image politics: The new rhetoric of environmental activism.* New York: The Guilford Press.

DeLuca, K., & Peeples, J. (2002). From public sphere to public screen: Democracy, activism, and the "violence" of Seattle. *Critical Studies in Media Communication, 19*(2), 125–151.

Downs, A. (1972). Up and down with ecology—The "issue-attention cycle." *The Public Interest, 28*(1), 38–50.

Duemler, D. (2000). The right to be heard: Creating a social movement for the 21st century. *Social Policy, 31*(2), 45–51.

Edelstein, A. (1996). *Everybody is sitting on the curb.* Westport, CT: Praeger.

Entman, R. M. (1993). Framing: Toward clarification of a fractured paradigm. *Journal of Communication, 43*(4), 51–58.

Ephron, N. (1989, June). Famous first words. *Esquire,* 104.

Epstein, E. J. (1973). *News from nowhere: Television and the news.* New York: Random House.

Ewen, S. (1988). *All consuming images: The politics of style in contemporary culture.* New York: Basic Books.

Fiore, F. (1997, December 21). Casting celebrities to make them a hit on political stage. *Los Angeles Times,* A1.

Fishman, M. (1980). *Manufacturing the news.* Austin: University of Texas Press.

Fishman, T. (2002, August). Making a killing: The myth of capital's good intentions. *Harper's Magazine, 305*(827), pp. 33–42.

Fiske, J. (1989). *Understanding popular culture.* Boston : Unwin Hyman.

Fowler, R. (1991). *Language in the news: Discourse and ideology in the press.* New York: Routledge.

Fox, S. (1984). *The mirror makers: A history of American advertising and its creators.* New York: Vintage Books.

Fraser, B. P., & Brown, W. J. (2002). Media, celebrities, and social influence: Identification with Elvis Presley. *Mass Communication & Society, 5*(2), 183–206.

Gamson, J. (1992). The assembly line of greatness: Celebrity in twentieth century America. *Critical Studies in Mass Communication, 9*(1), 1–24.

———. (1994). *Claims to fame: Celebrity in contemporary America.* Berkeley: University of California Press.

Gamson, W. A. (1989). Reflections on the strategy of social protest. *Sociological Forum, 4,* 455–467.

———. (1991). Forward. In C. Ryan, *Prime time activism: Media strategies for grassroots organizing* (pp. xi–xiv). Boston, MA: South End Press.

Gamson, W., & Wolfsfeld, G. (1993). Movements and media as interacting systems. *Annals of the American Academy of Political and Social Science, 528,* 114–125.

Gandy, O. (1982). *Beyond agenda setting: Information subsidies and public policy.* Norwood, NJ: Ablex.

Gans, H. (1979). *Deciding what's news: A study of CBS Evening News, NBC Nightly News, Newsweek, and Time.* New York: Pantheon Books.

Gerbner, G. (1972). Violence in television drama: Trends and symbolic functions. In G. A. Comstock & I. A. Rubinstein (Eds.), *Media content and control: Television and social behavior, Vol. 1* (pp. 28–187). Washington, D.C.: U.S. Government Printing Office.

Giles, D. (2000). *Illusions of immortality: A psychology of fame and celebrity.* New York: St. Martin's Press, Inc.

Gitlin, T. (1980). *The whole world is watching.* Berkeley: University of California Press.

Glasgow University Media Group. (1976). *Bad news.* London: Routledge & P. Kegan.

———. (1980). *More bad news.* London: Routledge & P. Kegan.

Gledhill, C. (1991). Introduction. In C. Gledhill (Ed.), *Stardom: Industry of desire* (pp. xiii–xx). London: Routledge.

Goldsmith, R. E., Lafferty, B. A., & Newell, S. J. (2000). The impact of corporate credibility and celebrity credibility on consumer reaction to advertisements and brands. *Journal of Advertising, 29*(3), 43–54.

Hall, S. (1979). Culture, the media and the "ideological effect." In J. Curran, M. Gurevitch, & J. Woollacott (Eds.), *Mass communication and society* (pp. 315–348). Beverly Hills, CA: Sage.

Harris, D. (1994, October 19). Celebrities lend time, money to the cause. *USA Today,* 2A.

Hartigan, P. (1999, August 13). Web site + rock stars + activism = ? *The Boston Globe,* D1.

Herman, E. S., & Chomsky, N. (1988). *Manufacturing consent.* New York: Pantheon Books.

Herrick, T. (2001, August 29). CEO's controversial views lead to tough summer for Exxon Mobil. *Wall Street Journal,* B1.

Hills, M. (2000). Conceptualising the fourth world: Four approaches to poverty and communication. *Media Development 1*, 3–8.

Hoffner, C., & Cantor, J. (1991). Perceiving and responding to mass media characters. In J. Bryant & D. Zillman (Eds.), *Responding to the screen: Reception and reaction process* (pp. 63–102). Hillsdale, NJ: Lawrence Erlbaum Associates, Inc.

Horkheimer, M., & Adorno, T. W. (1972). *The dialectic of enlightenment.* New York: Continuum.

Hunter, R. (1971). *The storming of the mind.* Garden City, NY: Doubleday.

Jamieson, K. H., & Campbell, K. K. (2001). *The interplay of influence: News, advertising, politics, and the mass media.* Stamford, CT: Wadsworth Thomson Learning.

Janeane Garofalo, steal this actress! (2000, September/October). *Mother Jones, 25*(5), 82.

Johnson, S. (2002, Winter). Magazine symbiosis: Celebrities still breeding celebrities. *Magazine Matters,* 6–7.

Katz, J. (1992, March 5). Rock, rap, and movies bring you the news. *Rolling Stone,* 33–40, 78.

Kelman, H. C. (1958). Compliance, identification, and internationalization: Three processes of attitude change. *Journal of Conflict Resolution, 2*(2), 50–60.

Kerbel, M. (2000). *If it bleeds, it leads.* Boulder, CO: Westview.

Kitch, C. (2000). A news of feeling as well as fact: Mourning and memorial in American newsmagazines. *Journalism, 1*(2), 171–195.

Klein, N. (1999). *No logo.* New York: Picador USA.

Kornhauser, W. (1968). Mass society. In *International encyclopedia of the social sciences* (Vol. 10, p. 63). New York: Macmillan and The Free Press.

Lippman, W. (1960). Blazing publicity: Why we know so much about "Peaches" Browning, Valentino, Lindbergh and Queen Marie. In C. Amory & F. Bradlee (Eds.), *Vanity Fair* (pp. 121–122). New York: Viking Press. (Original work published 1927).

Loftus, M. (1995, May). The other side of fame. *Psychology Today, 28*(3), pp. 48–53, 70–80.

Marshall, P. D. (1997). *Celebrity and power: Fame in contemporary culture.* Minneapolis: University of Minnesota Press.

McGwire, W. J. (1974). Psychological motives and communication gratification. In J. Blumler & E. Katz (Eds.), *The uses of mass communications: Current perspectives on gratifications research* (pp. 167–196). Beverly Hills, CA: Sage.

McLeod, D., & Hertog, J. K. (1992). The manufacture of "public opinion" by reporters: Informal cues for public perceptions of protest groups. *Discourse and Society, 3*(3), 259–275.

McLeod, D., McLeod, D. M., & Detenber, B. (1999). Framing effects of television news coverage of social protest. *Journal of Communication, 49*(3), 3–23.

McLeod, D. M. (1995). Communicating deviance: The effects of television news coverage of social protest. *Journal of Broadcasting & Electronic Media, 39*(1), 4–19.

Mencher, M. (2000). *News reporting and writing,* 8th ed. Columbus, OH: McGraw Hill Higher Education.

Meyer, D. S. (1990). Protest cycles and political process: American peace movements in the nuclear age. *Political Research Quarterly, 46*(3) 451–471.

Meyer, D. S., & Gamson, J. (1995). The challenge of cultural elites: Celebrities and social movements. *Sociological Inquiry, 65*(2), 181–206.

Mills, C. W. (1956). *The power elite.* London: Oxford University Press.

Molotch, H., & Lester, M. (1974). News as purposive behaviour: On the strategic use of routine events. *American Sociological Review, 39*(1), 101–112.

———. (1975). Accidental news: The great oilspill as a local occurrence and national event. *American Journal of Sociology, 81*(2), 235–260.

Moody, J. (1992, April 27). Under no one's thumb. *Time, 139*(17), 58–60.

Noble, G. (1975). *Children in front of the small screen.* Beverly Hills, CA: Sage.

Nordlinger, J. (2000, June 19). Rosie O'Donnell, political activist—A celebrity and her platform. *National Review, 52*(11)., 33–36.

O'Connor, A. (2000, November 1). Keeping stars bright politically. *Los Angeles Times*, B-1.

Ohanian, R. (1991). Construction and validation of a scale to measure celebrity endorsers' perceived expertise, trustworthiness, and attractiveness. *Journal of Advertising Rsearch, 19*(3), 39–52.

Parenti, M. (1978). *Power and the powerless.* New York: St. Martin's.

Perkins, T. (1991). The politics of "Jane Fonda." In C. Gledhill (Ed.), *Stardom: Industry of desire* (pp. 237–250). London: Routledge.

Phillips, P. (2000). Mainstream corporate media dismiss democracy. *Social Policy, 31*(2), 43–44.

Pompper, D. (2000). *Framing the public policy issue of environmental risk, 1983–1997.* Unpublished doctoral dissertation, Temple University, Philadelphia.

Postman, N. (1985). *Amusing ourselves to death: Public discourse in the age of show business.* New York: Penguin Books.

Prindle, D. F. (1993). *Risky business: The political economy of Hollywood.* Boulder, CO: Westview.

Reisner, A. E. (1992). The news conference: How daily newspaper editors construct the front page. *Journalism Quarterly, 69*(4), 951–986.

Ross, A. (1997). Introduction. In A. Ross (Ed.), *No sweat: Fashion, free trade, and the rights of garment workers* (pp. 9–37). London: Verso, 1997.

Rubin, A. M., Perse, E. M., & Powell, R. A. (1985). Loneliness, parasocial interaction, and local television news viewing. *Human Communication Research, 12*(2), 155–180.

Rubin, A. M., & Rubin, R. B. (2001). Interface of personal and mediated communication: Fifteen years later. *Electronic Journal of Communication, 11*(1).

Ryan, C. (1991). *Prime time activism: Media strategies for grassroots organizing.* Boston: South End Press.

Schattschneider, E. E. (1960). *The semi-sovereign people.* New York: Holt, Reinhart, & Winston.

Scheer, R. (2000, August 18). Dream city comes off like "Blade Runner." *Los Angeles Times*, B9.

Schudson, M. (1978). *Discovering the news: A social history of American newspapers.* New York: Basic Books.

Severin, W. J., & Tankard, J. W., Jr. (2001). *Communication theories: Origins, methods and uses in the mass media,* 5th ed. Boston, MA: Allyn & Bacon/Longman.

Shoemaker, P. J. (1982). The perceived legitimacy of deviant political groups: Two experiments on media effects. *Communication Research, 9*(2), 249–286.

Shoemaker, P. J., & Reese, S. D. (1996). *Mediating the message: Theories of influence on mass media content,* 2nd ed. Boston, MA: Allyn & Bacon/Longman.

Sigal, L. V. (1973). *Reporters and officials.* Lexington, MA: D. C. Heath.

Sudjic, D. (1989). *Cult heroes.* New York: W. W. Norton and Co.

Sumner, D. (1995). Nashville, nonviolence, and the newspapers: The convergence of social goals with news values. *The Howard Journal of Communications, 6*(1–2), 102–113.

Till, B. D., & Busler, M. (2000). The match-up hypothesis: Physical attractiveness, expertise, and the role of fit on brand attitude, purchase intent and brand beliefs. *Journal of Advertising, 29*(3), 1–13.

Tuchman, G. (1978). *Making news.* New York: Free Press.

Weber, M. (1968). *Economy and society,* Vol. 3. New York: Bedminster.

Part Three

Organizing Online:
The Internet, Technology,
and the Global
Justice Movement

12

Mapping the Repertoire of Electronic Contention[1]

Sasha Costanza-Chock

This chapter defines electronic civil disobedience (ECD) as a specific subset of collective action tactics that lies within what I call, following Tilly (1995), the repertoire of electronic contention. I attempt to avoid here what I see as persistent pitfalls in discussions about electronic activism: on the one hand, the tendency on the part of some activists and scholars to romanticize electronic action, and on the other, the dismissal of contentious electronic tactics as ineffective, as distractions from "real" mobilization, or as a troubling "return of the mob" (e.g., Ayres, 1999; Badaracco & Useem, 1997; National Infrastructure Protection Center, 2001). Either extreme represents a failure to carefully engage with and differentiate the wide range of tools and techniques that make up the electronic action repertoire, or to consider what "effective" might mean in this context.

To focus in on the question of effectiveness, I draw from the work of Staggenborg (1995), who differentiates between three broad types of movement outcomes: political and policy, mobilization, and cultural. In order to begin mapping the terrain of the repertoire of electronic action, I ask: Which electronic tools and tactics have been employed by social movement actors to achieve which kinds of outcomes? How it is that social movement organizations (SMOs) and other movement actors decide to employ, or not to employ, various tactics from this electronic repertoire? To address these questions, I briefly analyze two instances of ECD: the Virtual Sit-In for a Living Wage @ Harvard University and the Netiroteo Pa' Vieques (Netstrike for Vieques). Finally, I offer tentative suggestions about how attention to political opportunity structures might illuminate the process of diffusion of the repertoire of electronic^2 contention.

THE REPERTOIRE

In describing the wide array of strategies, methods, tools, and tactics employed by social movement actors, Tarrow (1998) has built on Tilly's (1995) concept of repertoires of contention to differentiate between three styles or modes of action: conventional, disruptive, and violent. Tarrow recognizes that these categories overlap, and that a given campaign or even single action may involve elements of more than one category, but distinguishes between them for analytical purposes. I argue here that there are forms of electronic contention that can be located within each mode, keeping in mind that the "soft" nature of the boundaries between categories does not suddenly solidify in the realm of the virtual. As with any action, specific styles of electronic contention may operate in several categories simultaneously, but a typology remains a useful tool.

Conventional Electronic Contention

The vast majority of electronic contention by SMOs involves the use of the Internet to amplify and extend "traditional" movement communications efforts. Conventional electronic contention receives the most attention from social movement scholars, and has figured in many recent analyses of transnational movements. For example, much has been said about the effective use of the Internet by the Zapatista movement in Chiapas, Mexico, to draw attention to indigenous land rights claims, gather support from international civil society, and focus the media eye on the conflict in a preemptive "infostrike" that succeeded (for the most part, for a time) in deterring violent state repression. The Zapatistas were able to mobilize enough domestic and international support to raise the costs of violent action above levels acceptable to the Mexican government (Keck & Sikkink, 1998; Kumar, 2000; Schulz, 1998). This illustrates how the Internet has been used by transnational advocacy networks to operate through what Keck & Sikkink (1998) term "information politics," or the ability to quickly move information to the point of maximum effectiveness. In a similar vein, Smith (2001) describes how the transnational network that coalesced in Seattle in 1999 made extensive use of the Internet, both before and during protests against the WTO ministerial meeting, to aid mobilization efforts (http://www.protest.net) and to provide reports from the street that countered mainstream media interpretations of the conflict (http://www.indymedia.org). A wide range of conventional electronic contentious tactics are by now widespread among SMOs and other movement actors. These tactics include:

- *Representation*—I am thinking here primarily of SMO websites. It would be impossible to catalog the hundreds of thousands of sites devoted to social movements, but these generally present organizations in terms of mission, projects, history, membership, and links to affiliated groups, and usually include contact information. One function of such sites is to establish a kind of ongoing presence for organizations and other movement actors. In contexts of extreme repression, websites may be the only way for organizations that operate entirely underground to have a persistent visible presence at all. For example, this is the case for the Revolutionary Association of the Women of Afghanistan, who have spoken of how their website (www.rawa.org) has served as a kind of "virtual base" from which they are able to represent themselves to the world as well as engage in all the other forms of conventional electronic contention described next (Tamina, 2001).

- *Information distribution*—This includes, but is not limited to, the distribution of information about movement goals, campaigns, actions, reports, and so on via website, e-mail, listservs, bulletin boards, chat rooms, ftp, and other channels. Information may be designed for the general public or for specific receivers, for example press releases, academic reports, or radio programes and video segments for rebroadcast. In some cases the same information may be repackaged differently for various intended audiences.

- *Research*—Many SMOs use the Internet as a resource for gathering specific information relevant to their cause, including information about opponents or targets, information produced by other movement actors, case studies of parallel situations, historical background, theory, economic data, environmental data, media analysis, and so on.

- *Cultural production*—Visual art, music, video, poetry, net.art, and other forms of cultural production by artists active in, associated with, or supportive of social movements are often posted, distributed, or sold online. Some forms of art make use of the Internet itself as a medium. This includes online "agitprop"; for example, site parodies or replicas of target sites that subtly alter wording or images to express activist viewpoints and discredit the target have been launched against, most prominently, the WTO (see http://www.gatt.org).

- *Fund-raising*—This includes appeals to membership and donations as well as the online sale of "SMO merchandise" —T-shirts, books, buttons, posters, and so on. This is problematized by certain kinds of companies that might be considered (or consider themselves) SMOs but have a main organizational function that is commercial, for example Fair Trade Federation (http://www.fairtradefederation.com). Fund-raising efforts are also aided by computer-assisted direct mailing campaigns and by member database management.

- *Lobbying*—This includes electronic versions of certain kinds of collective action aimed directly at influencing the political process and legislative outcomes. Online petitions and e-mail campaigns fall into this category. Targets may be elected officials and government bodies, multilateral institutions, transnational nongovernmental organizations (TNGOs) or other SMOs.

- *Tactical communication*—This refers to the use of the Internet or other electronic communications to aid mobilization efforts, both before and during street or "real world" collective actions. This includes calls to action distributed electronically, as well as coordination *during* street actions using Internet, pager, cell phone, WAP, or other electronic communications technologies.

While this last subcategory of tactical communications during street protest might be framed in the popular press or by police as "disruptive" (Wells, 2000), I place it within the domain of conventional electronic action in order to better differentiate those electronic tactics that are *in and of themselves* disruptive, as described next.

Disruptive Electronic Contention

Tactics of disruptive electronic contention are often referred to as hacktivism.[3] However, many disruptive electronic actions do not necessarily involve illegal entry into target systems, and can be accomplished either by individuals with minimal programming skills or very large groups of people with no programming skills engaging in simple online activities, as in the case of e-mail flooding. The range of disruptive techniques, both "hacktivist" and otherwise, includes:

- *E-mail floods*—Target systems can be incapacitated if forced to handle an extremely high volume of e-mail, especially if e-mails contain large attachments (typically image files or very long texts). This can be done by an individual using software that automatically sends repeated messages at high speed, or by groups of hundreds or thousands of people all sending messages simultaneously.
- *Form floods*—Similar to e-mail floods, but uses rapid repeated filling out of online feedback, membership, or purchasing forms to slow or crash the target system.
- *Fax bombs*—Jamming targeted fax machines by sending extremely high volume (for example, one word per page) faxes.
- *Viruses, Worms, and Trojan Horses*—Software designed to take a wide variety of actions, including data destruction, providing access to restricted files, allowing remote control of targeted servers, or simply displaying a message, can be introduced either to specific targeted systems or onto the public Net.
- *Data theft or destruction*—Hacktivists can gain entry to corporate, government, multilateral institution, or other target servers and steal private or classified documents useful to SMOs for drawing media attention or for other tactical purposes. They can also destroy or alter data.
- *Site alteration or redirection*—This involves illegal entry to target sites and alteration of text or images, or rerouting that sends visitors automatically to a different site (often one that expresses an oppositional viewpoint to target policies or actions).
- *Denial of service*—Various strategies, including some of those listed earlier, that result in blockage of public access to the target site are termed Denial of Service

(DOS) attacks. When targets are companies that rely on online sales, such actions can have significant economic as well as symbolic impact.

- *Virtual Sit-ins or Netstrikes*—Technically a form of DOS, this tactic involves large numbers of people sending repeated simultaneous requests to target sites for web pages or other files, with the result that the target site becomes inaccessible to regular users. This can happen because the server is so overloaded that it no longer is able to process requests to view a page, or because server administrators are forced to remove a target site in order to keep the server from becoming overwhelmed.

Out of the range of tactics that could be termed disruptive electronic contention, and in fact out of the whole repertoire of electronic contention, it is only this last tactic of virtual sit-in or netstrike that explicitly requires the collective simultaneous participation of large numbers of people.[4] For that reason, I focus on this tactic in the case studies that follow. First, though, a brief word about the third category of electronic tactics.

Violent Electronic Contention

An increasing amount of government and corporate literature dealing with electronic contention is focused on what is perceived to be the rising threat of violent electronic action, or "cyberterrorism" (e.g., Denning, 2001; National Infrastructure Protection Center, 2001; Paul, 2001). Depending on one's definition of violence, tactics that fall under this rubric might include certain kinds of property destruction such as server wipes or data corruption, but certainly include potential scenarios where hackers are able to cause human injury or death by gaining control over networked computer control systems—for example, air traffic control, electrical power grids, gas mains, and the like. I will return to the ramifications of increased government attention to "cyberterrorism" in the wake of September 11 near the end of this chapter, in the section on repression.

Having briefly outlined the various categories of electronic contention, what can we say about the different kinds of outcomes that might be expected from each? To address this question, I have found it useful to turn to feminist social movement theory.

OUTCOMES OF ELECTRONIC CONTENTION

Staggenborg (1995) has synthesized the work of several theorists (Gamson, Gusfield, Mueller, and others) to propose three broad categories of movement outcomes: political and policy outcomes, mobilization outcomes, and cultural outcomes. *Political outcomes* refers to direct legislative or institutional impacts and includes social movement contributions to policy agenda setting, the passage or blockage of specific legislation, or the implementation of existing policies. *Mobilization outcomes* refers to social movements' ability to bring together groups of people in collective action, while *cultural outcomes* more broadly includes "changes in social norms, behaviors, and ways of thinking among a public that extends beyond movement constituents or beneficiaries" (Staggenborg, 1995, p. 341).[5]

Using these categories for reference, it is useful to ask which kinds of outcomes are likely to be affected by the various strategies of electronic contention. Are certain electronic tactics more effective at promoting certain kinds of outcomes? Keep in mind that electronic contention is not in itself a social movement, but rather a set of tactics that can be employed, ignored, or rejected by a variety of movement organizations and other actors, and that uses of specific tactics by organizations are always situated within specific political opportunity structures (Melucci, 1996; Tarrow, 1998). Having briefly described the various tactics of electronic contention, I tentatively put forth the following matrix of relationships between tactics and outcomes as shown in Figure 12.1. As can be seen in Figure 12.1, the sphere of electronic contention comprises a body of techniques ranging from clearly illegal and "destructive" actions (site defacement, data destruction) to the more conventional (online petitions, e-mail campaigns, fund-raising), with many electronic tactics located somewhere on the shifting boundaries in between (virtual sit-ins, e-mail and fax bombings, form floods). I am suggesting that it is useful to think about the relationships between the electronic tactics employed by SMOs and the various kinds of outcomes they seek. While it is beyond the scope of this chapter to discuss all of these tactics and outcomes in depth, I will attempt to illustrate the usefulness of such an approach by focusing on one subset of the repertoire of electronic contention: electronic civil disobedience (ECD).

ELECTRONIC CIVIL DISOBEDIENCE

Using the categories I have laid out in Figure 12.1, ECD can be thought of as a set of disruptive electronic tactics that are effective primarily at achieving mobilization and cultural outcomes. While several other forms of contentious electronic action also involve mass participation, such as online petitions or e-mail campaigns, these tactics differ from ECD in that they are not based on simultaneous or synchronous participation. In addition, these types of collective electronic action would be classified as conventional rather than disruptive. Meanwhile, disruptive electronic tactics other than ECD typically do not require mass collective action, but can be implemented by an individual or a very small group.

ECD therefore lies in a strange zone both conceptually and legally. At the moment, there is a kind of framing battle taking place around this tactic, with corporate and government actors pressing to cast ECD as a form of "cyberterrorism" (e.g., Denning, 2001; NIPC, 2001; Paul, 2001) and with

FIGURE 12.1   Repertoire of Electronic Contention Tactic/Outcome Matrix

	Political Outcomes	Mobilization Outcomes	Cultural Outcomes
Conventional Tactics	• Electronic lobbying • Online petitions • Non-flooding e-mail and fax campaigns [e.g., cwa-union.org]	• Tactical Internet use • Planning for conventional street mobilizations via Web, e-mail, listserv, BBS calls to action [e.g., www.protest.net] • Coordination during mobilizations	• Information distribution • Alternative news [e.g., www.indymedia.org] • Alternative commentary [e.g., www.zmag.org] • Alternative publishers [e.g., www.autonomedia.org] • Oppositional electronic art [e.g., www.rtmark.com] • Online fund-raising • Online merchandising • Online research • Representation [e.g., www.rawa.org]
Disruptive Tactics	Some proponents of electronic collective action have claimed direct policy outcomes. [e.g., www.etoy.com "toywar" campaign]	• Mass participation in e-mail flood, Form flood, or Fax bomb campaigns [e.g., Netstrike for Vieques: www.freespeech.org/pro vieques] • Virtual Sit-in, mass participatory Distributed Denial of Service [e.g., Electronic Disturbance Theater: www.thing.com/rdom/ecd]	• Site alteration • Site redirection • Data theft • Data destruction • Viruses, Worms, and Trojan Horses • Individual or small group hacktivist actions: Email flood, Form flood, Fax bomb, slave server Denial of Service attack
Violent Tactics	Cyberterrorism (physical harm to humans caused by disruption of power grids, water system, air traffic control, and so on). *While it seems that violent electronic tactics likely would result in outcomes in all three spheres, careful theorization of cyberterrorism is beyond the scope of this chapter.		

some SMOs, activists, intellectuals, and free speech advocates trying to locate ECD as a new form of legitimate protest activity (e.g., Critical Art Ensemble, 1994, 1996; Electronic Disturbance Theater, 2001; Electronic Frontier Foundation, 2001). It is therefore an interesting moment to examine the ways in which activists develop and use these techniques, and to look at how various kinds of SMOs perceive ECD and choose whether or not to use it. To paint a more detailed picture of these processes, I focus here on two instances of ECD. I chose the first example, the Virtual Sit-In for a Living Wage @ Harvard University, in order to highlight ways in which ECD can be linked to actions in the "real world" and to point out the internal debate around tactics that often takes place within and between social movement actors. I include the Netstrike for Vieques to illustrate the dynamics of cross-movement diffusion of the electronic repertoire.

CASE 1: VIRTUAL SIT-IN FOR A LIVING WAGE @ HARVARD UNIVERSITY

Background

In the spring of 2001, approximately thirty students from the Harvard University Progressive Student Labor Movement (PSLM) occupied University administrative offices in an attempt to force the University to comply with a City of Cambridge living wage ordinance that tied minimum salaries to a cost of living formula. Several hundred employees on Harvard's janitorial staff were receiving below the living wage, and the administration was increasingly employing temp workers who not only received below living wage but also received no benefits. To top it all off, Harvard announced that it had just reached an unprecedented $18 billion endowment. PSLM members who were not inside the occupied offices, together with other supportive students, built a tent city outside the occupied building that served as a home base from which rallies, music events, film screenings, and media visits were managed. In the third week of the action, as media attention seemed to reach a plateau and administration officials continued to refuse to negotiate with activists, a group called the Electronic Disturbance Theater (EDT) offered to help the PSLM escalate their tactics by adding a "Virtual Sit-In" to the building occupation.

Actors

The major groups involved were the PSLM, the Harvard administration, the Harvard student and professor supporters, student groups such as Students Against Sweatshops, various local and national media, various local and national unions including Communication Workers of America, nonprofits including Justice for Janitors, and the EDT. Actors did include direct beneficiaries of the proposed policy changes (Harvard employees), but a majority were what McCarthy & Zald (1977) have termed "conscience constituents."

Action

After two meetings during which the EDT explained and demonstrated the virtual sit-in technique to PSLM, both groups came to a consensus decision to use the tactic. Initially, opinions within the PSLM were mixed, with some students immediately excited about using the virtual sit-in as an escalation tool but others voicing either skepticism about the usefulness of such an action or fear about the possible repercussions. Concern was articulated both in terms of whether there might be adverse affects on student and faculty computer systems that would alienate potential supporters of the Living Wage campaign, and in terms of a fear that the media might frame the electronic action in terms of "hacking" or "cyberterrorism," undercutting the legitimacy of the PSLM. In response to these concerns, it was decided that the action should not be targeted at Harvard University servers directly, since that might interrupt student access and decrease support for the campaign. In addition, it was determined that the action would be announced as an EDT operation in support of the Living Wage campaign, not as a PSLM action per se. EDT agreed with this logic and built a virtual sit-in targeting the websites of eight major corporations with board members who were also on the Harvard Board of Trustees, the body ultimately responsible for financial decision making at the University. The virtual sit-in tool automatically sent repeated requests for nonexistent pages called "living_wage@Harvard.now" to the targeted corporate servers for as long as participants kept their browsers open. The theory was that large numbers of participants would flood corporate target servers with requests, slowing access to their sites and filling server logs with "living_wage@ Harvard.now not found" messages. A press release about the action went out to local and national media on the day of the Virtual Sit-In.

Outcomes

The immediately observable outcome was in terms of mobilization. The Virtual Sit-In for a Living Wage attracted around 600 participants during the course of the twelve-hour action. At around 5 P.M. the Communication Workers of America (CWA) national office in Washington, D.C., called the EDT to say that they had received an e-mail about the action and had decided to participate. In terms of political outcomes, it is impossible to quantify the degree to which the action contributed to the Harvard administration's partial capitulation to the PSLM, which took place one week later with the decision to create a review committee that would include administrators, professors, students, and employees. The Virtual Sit-In was not mentioned by any administration officials in any public communications, although it was clear that they were aware the action took place. A story about the action did go out on the AP wire, but there can be no doubt that any direct policy impact the Virtual Sit-In had was dwarfed by the physical sit-in, which received sustained national press attention and had a long-term physical presence in the center of the campus. In addition, from the point of view of the PSLM it could be argued that the Virtual Sit-In had the negative effect of causing some degree of internal disagreement and apprehension, at least initially. This would align with a criticism of Electronic Civil Disobedience as a distraction from "real" action.

Following my proposed tactic-outcomes matrix, the most effective outcome here was in terms of mobilization, especially the participation by Communications Workers of America. This also led to cultural outcomes: for example, a positive report on the virtual action was sent out the next day by the CWA national office to 750,000 telecom workers. This in turn increased the already massive flood of solidarity e-mails and phone calls from around the country, helping to strengthen the resolve of students inside and to build "moral pressure" on the Harvard administration. In addition, CWA became interested in the possibility of incorporating virtual sit-in tactics into their own action repertoire. This was another kind of cultural outcome: diffusion of tactics. To illustrate this last point, I will provide a very brief description of a second ECD action, the Netstrike for Vieques.

Netstrike for Vieques

About three months after the Virtual Sit-In for a Living Wage, in May 2001, Communication Workers of America (CWA) collaborated with Electronic Disturbance Theater (EDT) and the Committee for the Rescue and Development of Vieques (Comite Pro Rescate y Desarollo de Vieques, or CPRDV) to help launch a "netstrike" in support of civil disobedients who were attempting to force a halt to U.S. Navy military exercises on Puerto Rico's "baby sister" island. While about thirty activists broke onto the Navy's target range and forced delays in scheduled bombing practice, over 1,300 participants from around the world used a Web-based tool developed by EDT to flood www.navy.com with protest messages. The Netstrike for Vieques used the Navy's own online enlistment form, filling required "name," "address," and other fields with requests that the Navy cease bombing and honor demands by Viequenses and many other prominent Puerto Ricans (including the Mayor of Vieques, the Mayor of San Juan, and the Governor of Puerto Rico) for a public referendum to decide the fate of the U.S. military presence. Several hours into the action, at around 4 P.M., CWA sent out a call to action to its 750,000 members. Nearly a thousand people joined the action during the next hour. At 5 P.M., EDT received a phone call from the administrator of www.navy.com, who demanded that the action be brought to a halt. According to the administrator, the Netstrike had "completely flooded our enlistment database with thousands of messages, and now our site is starting to crash" (EDT, personal communication, December 4, 2001). The administrator warned EDT that unless the action ended, participants would risk federal prosecution under the Computer Fraud and Abuse Act, potentially facing large fines and up to five years imprisonment. After consulting with CWA and CPRDV, EDT called an end to the action and declared it a victory. An article about the action went out on the AP wire. EDT culled organization names from hundreds of e-mails sent by supporters in over twenty countries and created a list of participants that was published on the Netstrike site and forwarded to the listservs of both CWA and CPRDV. It is worth noting here that several days later, the Navy announced plans to begin phasing out its operations in Vieques over a three-year period.[6]

How do these two ECD actions compare in terms of outcomes? The Netstrike for Vieques had greater effects in the category of mobilization than the Virtual Sit-In for a Living Wage, with more than twice as many people participating in the action. In addition, the actual disruptive effects of the Netstrike were confirmed by Navy Web administrators, while the actual disruptive effects of the Living Wage action on the targeted corporate servers were negligible. In terms of cultural outcomes, the Living Wage action resulted in some degree of press coverage (AP wire) and distribution of an action report by CWA, and also served to pique CWA interest in adopting the tactic for its own campaigns. The Netstrike for Vieques resulted in a greater amount of coverage, with an AP article, two radio interviews, postings to a dozen indymedia.org sites in both Spanish and English, postings to other alternative Web news sites, an article in the Indy Media weekly broadsheet that went out to over a hundred alternative print publications around the world, and several e-mail reports that went out to CWA's 750,000 members and to CPRDV's listserv (C. Biggs-Adams, personal communication, December 4, 2001). Direct policy outcomes could not be claimed by either action, although it could be argued that each added some small degree of pressure on the target to respond to policy demands made by activists. In both cases, it is interesting that the targets did in fact yield policy concessions within days of the action, although no one would claim that these electronic disturbances played more than a very small peripheral role in much larger ongoing campaigns.

Another interesting difference was the degree to which internal debates took place about whether to use the tactic, with some PSLM members raising serious doubts but with CPRDV embracing the action more enthusiastically. Although it is difficult to disentangle the various factors that might influence the diffusion of ECD, or of the repertoire of electronic contention more generally, it might be useful to turn here to a discussion of political opportunity structures.

POLITICAL OPPORTUNITY STRUCTURE AND ELECTRONIC CONTENTION

Estimates of the percent of the world's population with Internet access range from 4 percent to about 8 percent, and this group is highly concentrated in the postindustrial global North, with further concentration along lines of income, gender, ethnicity, and rural/urban residence (Hafkin & Taggart, 2001). These figures should remain visible in the background of any discussion about electronic activism. Who has access to the necessary tools? Who can afford to use them? Who can benefit from which tactics in the repertoire of electronic contention?

At the same time, we should be wary of dismissing the potential of electronic tactics on the grounds that access to the necessary tools is limited to a small global elite.[7] It is certainly the case that even extremely marginalized groups with little to no Internet access have been successful in some ways in using the Internet to gain attention, the Zapatistas being the "classic" example. In addition, it is useful to consider Internet use not only by SMOs articulating their own concerns before a global audience, but also by global elites or "conscience constituents" using the Internet to mobilize support for allied groups that lack access.[8] It is also important to problematize simplistic boundaries between conscience constituents and beneficiaries by recognizing that "elite" movements representing groups from the global South, or disenfranchised groups within wealthy nations, may contain members of beneficiary groups—including diasporic southerners. Yet while even many resource-poor SMOs have linked with other movement actors to engage in "information politics" facilitated by the Internet, most such activity has been through forms of conventional electronic contention. What can attention to political opportunity structures tell us about the likelihood of or need for social movements to adopt disruptive electronic strategies such as ECD?

Why ECD, Why Now?

Some theorists of ECD (Critical Art Ensemble, 1994, 1996; Electronic Disturbance theater, 2001; Wray, 1999) have claimed that the tactic steps into a global political opportunity structure that reflects the increasing power of transnational capital. The argument is that, while transnational corporations (TNCs) have long been powerful actors, some of which command more resources than whole nation-states, they increasingly act through multilateral bodies such as the WTO to overturn national legislation—for example, environmental standards—with the justification under neoliberal economics that all barriers to trade interfere with the optimum functioning of the market. The national laws that attempt to govern markets that are overturned by multilateral institutions were often won in the first place by social movements after years of hard-fought struggle. One political failure that forces the involvement of nonstate actors under these conditions is that TNCs are not accountable to any kind of democratic process. Their accountability is only to investors and to the market. There is in this case no existing political structure that allows input from below into corporate policy.

Add to this context the decoupling of TNCs from physical or national location, in the sense that TNCs increasingly are able (indeed, forced) to relocate production, assembly, and information services to the area of cheapest labor/highest profit, and we see that SMOs and other movement actors cannot remain locally bound if they are attempting to change corporate policy (Klein, 2000). Of course, social movements have never been *only* local, and in fact most of the first movements that fit a useful definition of the term were always transnational—including the movement for the abolition of slavery, the women's suffrage movement, and many others (Florini, 2000; Keck & Sikkink, 1998; Melucci, 1996). However, while movements as well as corporations may have always been transnational, the global mobility of both—in terms of capital, labor, and information flow—has risen steadily since World War II and exploded since the end of the Cold War.

Most recently, the virtualization of capital has meant the simultaneous decoupling of capital flow from material goods and services, and the relocation and in some cases evaporation of physical sites of capital. Just-in-time inventory management allows the elimination of warehouses through the instant transmission of inventory data from point-of-sale to point of production. The point-of-sale itself—the storefront—has also become increasingly virtualized, in the case of Internet-only businesses to the point of disappearance. In this case, the virtualization of capital not only provides positive openings for the application of ECD tactics by SMOs but arguably makes it *necessary* to strike in the virtual sphere, since the virtual storefront or headquarters may be the only publicly accessible target. In fact, actions targeted at physical sites of production may have decreasing effects on policy outcomes, since a strike that shuts down one plant seems more and more likely to be met by the targeted company's relocation of that plant or the outsourcing of all production. In this context—no physical storefront, no warehouse, no company factory—ECD provides a means to strike in the virtual sphere and to strike multiple targets at the same time, as was the case in the Virtual Sit-In for a Living Wage @ Harvard. ECD is also a relatively low-cost form of mobilization for resource-scarce SMOs, since collective actions with global participation can be organized by a few activists with Internet access. The Net has proven to be an effective medium for coordinating actions on a global scale, whether the aim is conventional, disruptive, or even violent activity in either the virtual or "real" sphere. This has been the case in many of the examples already mentioned here, as well as in the coordination of Carnival against Capital and the battle for Seattle (Scott & Street, 2000). The promise of ECD is, then, to take the virtualized site of corporate capital as the pressure point toward which actions can be oriented.[9]

Repression

The emergence of ECD has of course not gone unnoticed by targets. A growing body of corporate and government publications, conferences, grants, and laws are aimed at criminalizing and heavily penalizing all disruptive electronic contention including ECD. Crucial to this process has been the framing of electronic contention as "cyberterrorism," which dele-gitimizes these tactics and consolidates state and corporate control over the flow of information and virtual capital.

Modes of Repression

Koopmanns (1997) distinguishes between *institutional repression,* or codified repression by the state in the form of legislation and prosecution of movement actors, and *situational repression,* or violent police or military action. ECD would appear at first glance to lend itself more to the former than to the latter. From the perspective of SMOs, this is a drawback if Koopmanns is correct in suggesting that situational repression generally functions to amplify movement activity while institutional repression is gen-erally effective at dampening mobilization efforts by sapping the resources of movement actors or organizations over the long run.

The problem here for practitioners of disruptive electronic contention is twofold: first, it seems far more likely that ECD participants will be repressed with institutional means (arrest and prosecution) than with situational means (violent police action). Second, in the case of violent police action against electronic protesters—certainly conceivable in the wake of police forced entry to "Indymedia" warehouses in Seattle, 1999 and Genoa, 2001, where many were beaten and walls were described as "blood-spattered" (Morris & Carroll, 2001)—such action occurs in domestic space, not public space. It then becomes more difficult, although not impossible, for ECD actors to take advantage of the potentially movement-amplifying effects of violent police action. Images and reports of such repression must be recorded and disseminated by the activists under attack. This was done effectively by members of the Seattle Indymedia Center in 2001, who used a live webcam to document FBI agents entering their space to seize computer equipment (http://www.indymedia.org).

Repression, Post-9.11

Within the United States, the political opportunity structure for disruptive (or even conventional) electronic contention has been limited severely by the national climate in the wake of the September 11 attacks. Protest action of all kinds has been muted, first by an environment of shock and mourn-ing, next by the rising tide of nationalism multiplied by the mass media organs, and then by the passage of legislation curtailing civil liberties in the name of the "War on Terrorism." In terms of limiting the electronic action repertoire, the passage of the Patriot Act has further marginalized proponents of ECD tactics by greatly increasing the potential for legal action against organizers or participants. The Patriot Act includes clauses that could mean life imprisonment for individuals who engage in disruptive electronic actions against government or corporate websites (Electronic Frontier Foundation, 2001). It is worth noting that perhaps equally as powerful as the legislation is the mass mediated reframing that shifts any talk of "hacktivism" or "electronic civil disobedience" into a discussion about "cyberterrorism." This last might most productively be thought about in terms of a "terrorism master frame," already central to some right-wing and military discourse prior to September 11, passing into dominance. In any case, the current legislative and media frameworks will obviously have major effects on the willingness of SMOs to incorporate ECD or other disruptive electronic strategies into their repertoire of tactics. The changed political opportunity structure would not seem to favor a high rate of diffusion of disruptive electronic tactics.

Diffusion

We can observe the effects of a contracting political opportunity structure on the diffusion of tactics by looking at the Communications Workers of America (CWA), described earlier as a participant in both the Virtual Sit-In for a Living Wage @ Harvard and the Netstrike for Vieques. When CWA first heard about and participated in the Living Wage action, they were already using multiple conventional electronic tactics. They had a website for representation and news distribution, including calls for support of telecom worker actions around the world. In addition, they had a listserv called "e-activist" that they used to distribute especially urgent calls for action. After participating in the Virtual Sit-In, CWA began to take an even more active role in disruptive electronic tactics by helping the EDT publicize the Netstrike for Vieques before, during, and after the action via their e-activist listserv. Several hundred CWA members joined the Netstrike as a result. Afterwards, CWA national office members asked the EDT to help them develop a similar netstrike to be used in a campaign against Verizon, where CWA was being illegally blocked in their efforts to organize Puerto Rican telecom workers.

EDT worked with CWA to develop a netstrike against Verizon, and the stage was nearly set when the events of September 11 caused CWA to back off from the action and from the entire campaign. In this case, the diffusion of ECD, and the expansion of CWA's electronic repertoire to include tactics of disturbance, was stopped cold by a drastically changed political opportunity structure. Mobilization of any kind was deemed inappropriate, since dissent could so easily be framed by Verizon and by the mass media as a lack of patriotism. Later, passage of the USA Patriot Act pushed CWA even further away from a willingness to use the netstrike tactic due to new potential legal ramifications (i.e., a heightened threat of institutional repression). CWA's problems with Verizon remain, however, and recently CWA has begun to reorganize their campaign. Part of this renegotiation of strategy involves discussion of which electronic tactics will be used at what moment, and includes a debate over whether to push ahead with the netstrike despite the potentially high cost of institutional repression under the Patriot Act. Some CWA organizers see an electronic disruption that violates the new legislation as a potential leverage point for even greater media coverage of their campaign.

Diffusion of Electronic Tactics to Countermovements

Bleiker (2000) and Tarrow (1998) have talked about the dissemination of dissent tactics among movement organizations and between movements, and Ayres (1999) has described the "cyber-diffusion of contention," or the use of the Internet to spread information about specific campaigns and tactics between SMOs within allied social movements. We should also expect the diffusion of tactics to countermovements. On the heels of the appropriation of sit-ins and direct action tactics by Operation Rescue during the 1990s, and in light of Meyer & Staggenborg's (1996) observation that movements and countermovements are forced to shift arenas and tactics in an ongoing dialectic process, we would certainly expect to see any and all elements of the repertoire of electronic contention eventually replicated by counter-movement SMOs.

CONCLUSION

My intent in this chapter has been to sketch the terrain of the electronic repertoire of contention. I have provided case studies in an attempt to show how empirical research on electronic contention might benefit by locating actions within a tactic/outcome matrix, and I have explored how changing political opportunity structures and differing levels of repression affect the diffusion of contentious electronic tactics. I end with an invitation for future work on the use of the Internet by social movements to take account of the differences between conventional, disruptive, and violent electronic contention, and to specify the relationships between tactics, outcomes, political opportunity structure, and diffusion. Of course, I hope that social movement organizations might also find it useful to carefully consider the relationship between the electronic tactics they adopt and the outcomes they aim for. Finally, while I have tried to address questions of what the repertoire of electronic contention looks like, what outcomes it might generate, how it spreads, and how it is constrained, I encourage exploration of related questions that have emerged at the margins: How does electronic contention get framed,[10] and how might various kinds of electronic contention be useful for doing framing work? What is the role of emotions and of the body in electronic collective action? To what degree do issues of access, embodiment, and the criticism that "virtual activism might undermine real activism" encourage us to develop a combined theory and practice of linked, hybrid, mestizo, or cyborg physical/electronic collective action? These and other questions about the repertoire of electronic contention become increasingly important as the Internet expands, capital becomes virtualized, and social movements struggle for points of leverage from which to engage transnational corporations, nation-states, and multilateral bodies.

NOTES

1. I express my great thanks to Dr. Silke Roth for introducing me to the relevant social movement studies literature and for guidance throughout the development of this chapter. In addition, the comments of Drs. Larry Gross and Oscar Gandy, Jr., have been helpful, as have those of the IAMCR Herbert Schiller Prize committee. I thank the Annenberg School of the University of Pennsylvania for supporting my study and research, and the networked activists of Federation of Random Action, Communications Workers of America, and the Comite Pro Rescate y Desarollo de Vieques for inspiration.

2. use the term "electronic" here mostly to describe various kinds of Internet-based contentious activity, although there are many electronic tools and tactics used by social movement actors that do not involve the Internet at all (for example, pirate radio stations, cell phones and pagers, mobile sound systems, and so on). While it could be argued that a term such as "computer-mediated" would be more appropriate, I will remain with the more inclusive "electronic."

3. Hacktivism, Electronic Direct Action, Electronic Civil Disobedience, Electronic Disturbance, or Netstrikes, as well as Hacking, Netwar, Cyberwar, Infowar, and Info-terrorism. Struggles over the naming of disruptive electronic contention are part of broader struggles for control over framing the virtual terrain: The corporatization of the Internet has limited what counts as the public sphere online, while at the same time a rhetoric has emerged that freedom of information should trump dissent—in this case, electronic disruption is not legitimate if it blocks access to information. Most recently, "national security" has been given precedence over disruptive dissent of all kinds, electronic or otherwise.

4. It is possible for an individual programmer to initiate an action that functions technically just like a virtual sit-in. A virtual sit-in could be simulated by a hacker who gained control over hundreds of remote computers and used them as "slaves" to conduct the sit-in, then tried to claim that hundreds of people had participated in the action. This raises interesting questions about the potential meanings of embodiment during a virtual sit-in, and about the ways targets understand and respond to such actions.

5. All three kinds of outcomes involve framing work. Issues often have to be framed one way in the institutional context in order to pass legislation, another way in the mobilization context in order to encourage collective action, and other ways in order to target public opinion or attract media attention.

6. Rescinded as of December 15, 2001.

7. Also see http://www.unesco.org/webworld/com/strength/strength01.shtml for a review of participatory media projects for development, including many innovative Internet projects in poor rural areas in southern countries.

8. Of course, this also raises questions about the boundaries of collective identity. If "everyone is a Zapatista," how does the "Zapatista bandwagon" disperse, distort, and empty the movement of meaning, and how does it strengthen the movement? On the one hand, stretching boundary lines to be as inclusive as possible can increase

the number of movement members and ultimately, collapse binary distinctions on which the exclusion of marginalized groups rests. On the other hand, overbroad inclusivity can potentially mask the continued existence of unequal relations of power behind a facade of "sameness." See Gamson (1995) for a brilliant discussion of this problem.

9. This does not mean I advocate the position that "the streets, as a site of struggle, are dead" (e.g., Critical Art Ensemble, 1996). Rather, I would argue for a *linked* or hybrid physical/virtual movement theory and practice, where electronic action remains grounded in embodied actions and the virtual embedded in the real, as in both cases of ECD described in the chapter.

10. Sandor Vegh (veghs@otal.umd.edu) is currently doing interesting empirical work on mass media framings of hacktivism.

REFERENCES

Ayres, J. M. (1999). From the streets to the Internet: The cyber-diffusion of contention. *Annals of the American Academy of Political and Social Science,* November, 132–143.

Badaracco, J. L., & Useem, J. (1997). The Internet, Intel and the vigilante stakeholder. *Business Ethics,* 6(1), 18–29.

Biggs-Adams, C. Personal communication, December 4, 2001.

Bleiker, R. (2000). *Popular dissent, human agency and global politics.* Cambridge: Cambridge University Press.

Critical Art Ensemble. (1994). *The electronic disturbance.* New York: Autonomedia/ SemioText(e).

———. (1996). *Electronic civil disobedience.* New York: Autonomedia/SemioText(e).

Denning, D. (2001). Activism, hacktivism, and cyberterrorism: The Internet as a tool for influencing foreign policy. Retrieved from the Terrorism Research Center: http://www.terrorism.com/documents/denning-infoterrorism.html.

Electronic Disturbance Theater (2001). *Hacktivism: Network Art Action.* New York: Autonomedia.

———. Personal communication, December 4, 2001.

Electronic Frontier Foundation (2001). EFF Analysis of U.S.A-Patriot Act Surveillance Legislation. Retrieved from http://www.eff.org/Privacy/Surveillance/Terrorism_ militias/20011031_eff_usa_patriot_analysis.html.

Florini, A. M. (Ed.). (2000). *The third force: The rise of transnational civil society.* Tokyo/Washington: Japan Center for International Exchange/Carnegie Endowment for International Peace.

Gamson, J. (1995). Must identity movements self-destruct? A queer dilemma. *Social Problems,* 42(3): 390–407

Hafkin, N., & Taggart, N. (2001). Gender, information technology, and developing countries: An analytic study. U.S. AID Office of Women in Development.

Keck, M. E., & Sikkink, K. (1998). *Activists beyond borders: Advocacy networks in international politics.* Ithaca, New York: Cornell University Press.

Klein, N. (2000). *No logo.* New York: Picador U.S.A.

Koopmanns, R. (1997). Dynamics of repression and mobilization: The German extreme right in the 1990s. *Mobilization,* 2(2), 149–165.

Kumar, C. (2000). Transnational networks and campaigns for democracy. In A. M. Florini (Ed.), *The third force: The rise of transnational civil society.* Tokyo/Washington: Japan Center for International Exchange/Carnegie Endowment for International Peace.

McCarthy, J. D., & Zald, M. (1977). Resource mobilization and social movements: A partial theory. *American Journal of Sociology, 82,* 1212–1241.

Melucci, A. (1996). *Changing codes: Collective action in the information age.* Cambridge: Cambridge University Press.

Meyer, D., & Staggenborg, S. (1996). Movements, countermovements, and the structure of political opportunity. *American Journal of Sociology, 101,* 1628–60.

Morris, S., & Carroll, R. (2001). British protesters claim Genoa police took brutal revenge for summit riots. *Guardian of London,* Friday, July 27, 2001.

National Infrastructure Protection Center. (2001). Cyber protests: The threat to the U.S. information infrastructure. Retrieved from http://www.nipc.gov/publications/nipcpub/cyberprotests.pdf.

Paul, L. (2001). When cyber hacktivism meets cyberterrorism. Sans Institute. Retrieved February 19, 2001, from http://www.sans.org/infosecFAQ/hackers/terrorism.htm.

Schulz, M. S. (1998). Collective action across borders: Opportunity structures, network capacities, and communicative praxis in the age of advanced globalization. *Sociological Perspectives, 41*(3), 587–616.

Scott, A., & Street, J. (2000). From media politics to e-protest: The use of popular culture and new media in parties and social movements. *Information, Communication & Society, 3*(2), 215–240.

Smith, J. (2001). Globalizing resistance: The battle of Seattle and the future of social movements. *Mobilization, 6*(1), 1–19.

Staggenborg, S. (1995). Can feminist organizations be effective? In M. M. Ferree & P. Y. Martin (Eds.), *Feminist Organizations* (pp. 339–355). Philadelphia: Temple University Press.

Tamina (2001). RAWA: Empowering Afghan Women. Lecture/screening at University of Pennsylvania, November 28, 2001.

Tarrow, S. (1998). *Power in movement: Social movements and contentious politics.* Cambridge: Cambridge University Press.

Tilly, C. (1995). *Popular contention in Great Britain, 1758–1834.* Cambridge, MA: Harvard University Press.

Wells, J. (2000). $1 million bail ordered for protesters; Berkeley-based activist allegedly led mayhem. *San Francisco Chronicle,* 5 August 2000, A3.

Wray, S. (1999). On electronic civil disobedience. *Peace Review, 11*(1), 107–113.

13

Alternative Alternatives: Free Media, Dissent, and Emergent Activist Networks

Ted M. Coopman

During the media democracy protests at the National Association of Broadcasters (NAB) 2000 National Radio Convention in San Francisco, CA, several lawyers representing arrested demonstrators were themselves arrested trying to enter the City Court House. Local television news crews missed the colorful scene of one of the lawyers verbally dressing down a police officer. However, it was captured on video by an independent journalist and was published on the San Francisco Independent Media Center (IMC) website. A local TV station saw it there and came to the SF-IMC to get the tape. This is where a conflict arose. The news crew arrived at the IMC and wanted the tape gratis. They were under the impression that the video journalist who shot the footage "worked" for the IMC and, in turn, the IMC was sponsoring the protests. Therefore, as an interested party, the IMC should be willing to give the TV crew a copy of the tape. The fact that the IMC shared office space with the Media Access Project, a protest sponsor, only confused matters more. It took some time to explain to the crew and the TV station's news director (via cell phone), that the journalist worked independently, not for the IMC. Further, the IMC is an open forum and has no reporting staff, and while the IMC was covering the protests, they were not involved with the group that organized it. After thirty minutes of negotiation, the station agreed to purchase the tape for $300. Mass media meets free media.

In this chapter, I explore the idea of free media as a distinct form related to, but separate from, what has been described as alternative media. First,

I present the basic idea of free media and its origins. Next I discuss the general characteristics of alternative media and its relation to free media. Third, I explore the emergence of the free media model. Then, upon this foundation, I investigate the main characteristics of free media. Finally, I conclude with the possible repercussion of free media of dissent and democracy.

FREE MEDIA AND FREE RADIO

The idea behind "free media" comes from the term "free radio." An increasing number of small unlicensed radio stations began to appear in the early 1990s. Originally coined as "micro radio" by Mbanna Kantako, one of its early pioneers, it came to mean a small watt noncommercial, usually leftist, unlicensed FM radio station (Coopman, 2000a). These stations targeted underserved communities and often propagated "counter-knowledge." "Producing such a counter-knowledge involves, among other processes, recovering facts, events, and bits of information the dominant knowledge has repressed or dismissed as insignificant" (Fiske, 1996, p. 191).

As this movement developed, the idea of micro radio was embraced by a wider variety of people including small entrepreneurs frozen out of the quickly consolidating radio market. These individuals approached the Federal Communication Commission (FCC) to legitimize these micro stations. The FCC eventually created a Low Power Radio Service, ironically banning the commercial activity of the original petitioners as well as the pirates who ignited the process in the first place. The U.S. Court of Appeals, in *Ruggiero v. FCC & US,* later vacated the blanket ban on the pirates as overbroad and thus, unconstitutional. As more and more groups got involved in the Micro Radio Movement, a distinction developed between micro radio and what was coming to be known as free radio. Beginning with Free Radio Berkeley, other stations around the nation began to adopt the "free radio" identity, such as Free Radio Austin and Free Radio Twin Cities. These stations tended to be anarchist centered in both organizational structure and political orientation. Of course, not all of these types of stations adopted the free radio title. In fact, Free Radio Berkeley returned to the air after being shut down as Berkeley Liberation Radio. However, the main point for my argument here is their unifying rejection of licensing and the legitimacy of the FCC to prohibit their operation. So, rather than simply being small or micro in size or low power, these stations sought to be "free" of the system that governs the airwaves in the United States.

Soley (1999) attributes the idea of free radio to the rise of resistance radio during the Nazi era. He defines free radio as radio free of government regulation of the spectrum. While I fully agree with his assessment, I will expand on this central idea to include financial and organizational considerations. I will explore this and the evolution of Micro Radio in the United States in more detail later in this chapter.

DEFINING ALTERNATIVES

The consolidation of commercial and noncommercial media in the last decades of the twentieth century, combined with dramatically lower costs of communication technology, especially involving the Internet, has led to an explosion of new media outlets and techniques. Any medium beyond the scope of advertiser-based commercial media tends to fall under the catchall phrase of "alternative media." Alternative media, like alternative lifestyles or alternative music, is an imprecise way to describe something. Everything is an alternative to something else. While vague descriptions can be useful for slippery subjects, I believe that our current media environment has moved to a stage where more precise terminology is called for. Lumping together National Public Radio (NPR) and your local pirate radio station into one big alternative to commercial mass media is ridiculous. Several authors have approached the issue, most notably Atton (2002) and Downing (2001). Usually, terms like "radical," "activist," or "advocacy" media are applied. All are useful, but most fall short of capturing the emerging media that have started to develop during the late twentieth and early twenty-first centuries.

What's the Alternative?

Alternative media is supposed to be the "other," the outside perspective on politics, culture, and society. It is supposedly media that exists or functions outside the established cultural, social, or economic system. More often than not, such media has the appearance of being something different, but when you look beneath the surface, it can be indistinguishable from the mainstream media it purports to be a foil to. While there are multiple reasons for this, the most influential forces are financial, organizational, and regulatory. Before we explore these elements, we should review what makes alternative media "alternative." Atton (2002) exhaustively analyzes multiple theories on alternative media. From this he constructs a typology of alternative and radical media. His analysis breaks down into six elements. The first half deal with products. First are the types of content and news values, usually politically, socially, or culturally radical. Second are the forms and aesthetics used in presenting the content. Third are the reprographic innovations/adaptations, or how the products are physically produced. Atton then moves to processes. The first process would be distribution: how the products are distributed and whether they are transformed during this process. Then there are the transformed social relations, roles, and social responsibilities, including organizational issues. Finally, there are the transformed communication processes, such as horizontal linkages and communication networks (p. 27).

Atton's typology gives us a good general overview of what we are talking about when we discuss alternative media. I find his analysis reflective of much of my own research and experiences. Many of these elements are shared with what I call free media. In fact, free media would be considered alternative media by these criteria. However, most of what is commonly called alternative media would not fall within the boundaries of free media. In the United States, most media that would commonly be considered to be alternative would not conform to all of Atton's elements. Much of this media would be best termed "progressive" or of having alternative elements. Further, this status often falls by the wayside as the operation becomes more entrenched in the dominant cultural, financial, and regulatory environment. An example of this is National Public Radio (NPR). As NPR has become more dominant and institutionalized, it has lost its early reputation as *the* alternative to commercial media. Oddly enough, NPR has an audience and market penetration that far exceeds any mainstream news programming by any of the commercial television or radio networks. NPR's 620 affiliate stations can reach 92 percent of the American public (Kiger, 2002). In many ways, it is as aggressive and dominating as any commercial media network. In its defense, NPR still promotes and produces some truly alternative or even radical programming. This is the reality of most American alternative media. It is actually mainstream media with alternative elements.

The gold standard of alternative media in the United States is the Pacifica Network. Having pioneered the model of listener sponsored radio in the 1940s, it has managed to battle its way into the twenty-first century. After decades of bucking the status quo, it has become progressively mired with bureaucracy and regulatory enforced conformity. Pacifica is on a regular schedule of upheaval and revolt as the rank and file volunteers and staff battle management and each other to define the network and its mission. While still radical and cutting edge in many ways, Pacifica operates under strict rules and conditions that continue to erode its ability to act as the voice of the people. One could point at Pacifica in general, individual Pacifica stations such as KPFA in Berkeley, CA, or programs such as Democracy Now! with Amy Goodman, as personifying dissent. The issue is vulnerability. Pacifica operates at the sufferance of the FCC and the IRS. The networks multiple "near-death experiences" illustrate the pitfalls of dissenting in an institutionalized environment (Downing, 2001; Walker, 2001).

Alternative magazines with corporate advertisers and institutionally supported student radio and TV stations are but a few examples of the potential pitfalls of trying to present alternative ideas and culture in an environment dominated and controlled by mainstream ideas and culture. Alternative media flows from popular culture (Atton, 2002; Downing, 2001). Again, this is not to minimize the struggles of dedicated people or the great service these media organizations have performed. Public broadcasting, Pacifica, independent stations and networks, and corporate broadcasters all form important parts of a media environment that is critical to the maintenance of culture and democracy. However, there are certain things that these types of media cannot do.

In the case of free media, Atton's typology would be extended to encompass operating outside of traditional regulatory, organizational, and financial constraints. It is these three critical elements that set free media apart from alternative media. Atton (2002) combines the ideas of alternative and radical media and Downing (2001) connects radical media with social movements. In the past, I have favored the term radical or guerrilla media. Many in the free radio movement embrace the title of "pirate," while others insist that it is those who monopolize the airwaves for profit that are the true pirates. Such is the confusion of using these charged words. While useful when describing individuals, it can cause problems when trying to describe a phenomenon. A community such as Grovers Beach, CA, put Excellent Radio on the air illegally because it had no local radio station. Promoting local music and broadcasting city council meetings should not be considered radical acts. And while "guerrilla" sounds as flashy as "pirate," it evokes a hit-and-run guerrilla warfare image. Many of these free radio stations operate in a fixed location on a full-time schedule. I find all these terms inadequate in describing the types of media emerging in a climate of cheap global communication and media monopolization in the late twentieth and early twenty-first centuries.

THE RISE OF FREE MEDIA: A BRIEF HISTORY
OF THE MICRO RADIO MOVEMENT

Pirate radio, that is to say illegal radio, has been around since the dawn of broadcasting. It has existed in many forms from student experiments, to radical politics, to libertarian free enterprise (Bender, 1988; Kuipers, 1989; Yoder, 1990). These stations were usually secret, operated by individuals or a few close friends. Most had a short life span. This was due to action by the FCC or, more likely, through technical failure or flagging interest by the operators themselves. A pirate radio subculture existed, based mostly around short-wave. However, what developed in the early 1990s deviated significantly from the unlicensed radio that had come before it. What changed things was the adoption of micro radio by a variety of activists who politicized the act of illegal broadcasting. Rather than an end to itself, activists saw radio as another tool in their kit. Over time, this movement built up to a point where it absorbed traditional American pirate radio into a national movement.

As I discussed earlier, the concept of free media has its origins in the Micro Radio Movement of the 1990s. Micro radio, while actually emerging in the middle to late 1980s, came into a wider realm shortly after the first Gulf War In 1990. If Kantako built the fire, it was Stephen Dunifer who lit the match. Dunifer, a lifelong activist living in Berkeley, CA, was outraged by the way the supposed "alternative" media covered the Gulf War. Even the traditional leftist bastion of Pacifica Radio was in disarray, embroiled in another round of factional fighting as a newly empowered board of directors sought to reign in the radicals at the network's individual stations. In 1993, Dunifer and some cohorts put Free Radio Berkeley on the air as an act of "electronic civil disobedience" (Coopman, 2000a).

Dunifer soon joined forces with the National Lawyers Guild's Committee for Democratic Communication and launched a challenge to the ban on low power radio. The court case, *Dunifer v. FCC* (No. C 94-03542 CW), was argued through petition and appeal from 1994 until 2000, when the 9th Circuit Court of Appeals finally ruled that he had no standing to challenge FCC regulations and enjoined him from broadcasting. What transpired over these six years was a far-ranging national battle over access to the radio spectrum. Ultimately, the grassroots movement that developed over these years drove the debate from obscurity to the national agenda. Micro radio was debated in the *New York Times,* discussed in Congress, denounced by the National Association of Broadcasters and National Public Radio, and spawned protests. It made allies of anarchists, churches, and small entrepreneurs. Thousands of acts of "electronic civil disobedience" across the nation overwhelmed the FCC and, together with public pressure, caused the agency to reverse itself and support the creation of a low power radio service. Despite heavy lobbying that resulted in Congress scaling back the new service (Radio Broadcasting Presentation Act, 2000), licensed Low Power FM became a reality in 2000. Even though they participated in this process, many stations still strongly opposed any type of licensing. Other stations would continue to broadcast illegally if denied a license, but would accept one if it were available. Dunifer exemplified the disdain for federal oversight. The only concession he was willing to make would be to send the FCC a postcard with a station's address, phone number, and frequency. Like many free radio advocates, he believes that dissent cannot be licensed (Coopman, 1999, 2000a; Howley, 2000).

The essential element that brought this huge social force together was the parallel development of the Internet. As computers became more commonplace and e-mail and Web browsers became accessible and easier to use, activists of all stripes began to see the advantages of fast and cheap communication. Many micro radio advocates got involved with radio to aid their activist activities. Groups such as Food not Bombs, combined with a select group of radical technicians with an interest in computers and radio, helped propel activism into the Information Age (Coopman, 2000a; Edmonson, 2000). The convergence of anarchist fueled activism and organizational structure, inexpensive computing power, fast communication via e-mail and listservs, easily learned HTML coding that spawned indexing websites, and audio compression that facilitated the sharing of content proved to be devastatingly effective. The efficiencies and economies of scale that reaped huge profits for industry also enabled a small number of media activists with scant resources to launch and maintain a national movement that eventually altered America's communication policy. Dunifer's rallying cry to "Free the Airwaves" escaped the photocopied pages of *Free the Airwaves* and was digitally blasted all over America (Coopman, 2000b, c; Dunifer, 1995).

Micro, Free, and Low Power Radio

In the beginning, all of the stations that came to be part of the movement for small community radio were micro radio stations. The idea of a small (micro) power transmitter was hardly revolutionary. The FCC had licensed 10-watt Class D stations in the past. It was how it was used that made the difference. As the Micro Radio Movement diversified, many stations had less and less in common other than the technology. The rebel philosophy was abandoned by many and rejected outright by others who wanted the stability of legal status. Some aspiring broadcasters even took pains to distance themselves from the unlicensed micro pioneers. At about the time of the first petition for a Low Power Radio Service, the term "micro radio" lost its descriptive utility. The press, academia, and participants in the movement have often used micro radio, free radio, and low power radio interchangeably. This is inaccurate and can be confusing. In order to accurately discuss the topic, it is important to clarify these different terms and place them within specific historical contexts. Micro radio, as coined by Kantako, describes the unlicensed radio stations that, beginning in 1986 and operating until 1998, coalesced into the national Micro Radio Movement. Low Power Radio (LPFM) is best reserved for stations that are licensed under the new service by the FCC. Free radio will describe stations that are unlicensed and are opposed to licenses on philosophical, ideological, or practical grounds. It is this latter category that interests us here.

FREE MEDIA

If we take this idea of free radio and apply it to all media, we arrive at the concept of "free media." There are three major attributes of what constitutes free media, most of these based in the free radio model discussed earlier. These are the freedom from/rejection of governmental regulation; freedom from/rejection of commercial or traditional funding constraints; and freedom from/rejection of organizational constraints. As my previous research indicates, my focus is mainly on broadcast media. However, the free radio model is applicable to any type of emergent media. It is important to note that in many cases, free media has a convergent property. Radio stations have websites and newsletters, newsletters have their own radio programs and so forth. To facilitate this type of convergence, the Radio4all website expanded to create the A-infos Radio Project (Radio4all.net). It is based on the idea of the A-infos Shop, a place for anarchists and free thinkers to meet and get free or at-cost books and propaganda. The Info

Shops grew out of the squatted anarchist centers of 1980s Britain (Atton, 2002). The A-infos Radio Project provides a library of free audio programming. Strictly noncommercial and nonproprietary, it allows people to upload as well as download programming. This greatly increased available programming for free radio, community stations, and noncommercial webcasters and gave those without a station the chance to share their views and culture. Many of the Independent Media Centers (IMC) include webcasting and audio elements; these in turn often wind up on the radio. So, an added element of free media is the freedom to use whatever means available to disseminate viewpoints, analysis, and culture.

Walker (2001) has discussed needed freedoms and applied them to the state of radio. He also describes three basic freedoms. Walker identifies the "Freedom to Choose" as the need for more diversity and media options. Next is the "Freedom to Create," which is the increased ability to make your own media. And finally, the "Freedom to Escape," the ability to break down the walls between producers and consumers. These certainly relate to the freedom from/rejection of governmental regulation, commercial, and organizational constraints. However, while Walker applies his general ideals to the reform of radio, I apply existing attributes of free radio to the broader concepts of all media.

FREEDOM AND REGULATION

Regulation or government sanction poses several problems for radical or fringe media, especially in broadcasting. Licenses are subject to specific rules, regulations, and qualifications for participants. There are requirements for having a certain federal tax status, the manner in which you must organize yourself, the amount of funding you must have, what you can and cannot say, whether you can take political stances, and who may participate. These are over and above the high financial costs of participating in the current licensing scheme. A good argument can be made that a certain level of regulation is needed to maintain order and the efficient use of scarce resources, like electromagnetic spectrum. The questions are whether or not the current system achieves these reasonable ends with the least amount of intervention and if it is applied evenly to all participants. An example of the latter being the "character" requirements for obtaining a broadcast license. Under current conditions someone like Dunifer who operated a 40 watt unlicensed radio station is deemed lacking character enough to deserve a license. Whereas General Electric, a company that has been convicted of several felonies and defrauding the U.S. government, is of sufficient good character to have dozens of licenses (Mokhiber & Weissman, 1999). While the Ruggiero decision (No. 00-1100) found a blanket ban on former radio pirates contained in the Radio Broadcasting Preservation Act of 2000 unconstitutional, it did not eliminate the FCC's character requirements for licensees.

Walker (2001) has argued that the regulatory scheme is not designed for the "necessity and convenience" of the public nor is it required for the efficient use of spectrum. The alleged chaos that predated regulation was vastly overstated, and there was sufficient evidence that broadcasters had implemented their own systems of compliance and control. What the federal government did by setting up the current scheme was to privilege certain powerful broadcasting interests and stifle dissent from overtly political stations, especially those of labor. The power of these incumbents was further made evident when NPR and the NAB convinced Congress that the FCC was incapable of adequately assessing the impact of the proposed LPFM service. It was the first time in the history of the FCC that Congress had ignored its technical expertise.

Legal and historical arguments aside, the advocates of free radio, and free media, believe that true cultural and political dissent cannot be contained within government regulatory structures. For them it's "no blood, no foul." If they can operate without interfering with others, they feel they should be left alone. The general adherence of free radio to this noninterference ethic is evidenced by the proportionally fewer cases of interference compared to licensed operators as well as the few cases of proven interference (Bilotta-Daily & Siska, 1999). Moreover, when notified of difficulties, there are many examples of stations shutting down immediately or, in the case of Free Radio Santa Cruz, moving to a new frequency to accommodate a new translator at the local NPR affiliate. The role and importance of this type of dissent is further explored in the conclusion.

FREEDOM AND FINANCING

The second major characteristic of free media is freedom from traditional funding constraints. Financing is arguably the biggest hurdle facing alternative or radical media. Often funding is derived from the same sources that fuel so-called mainstream media. Funding from the Corporation for Public Broadcasting (CPB), major foundations, business underwriters, or advertisers, is often what keeps the lights on. This type of funding always comes with strings attached and requires a certain level of regulatory legitimacy. Critics of these funding sources have equated it to poison or an addictive drug. An example is Pacifica Radio. The Pacifica Foundation, which holds the licenses of the five Pacifica Radio stations, was required to change the organizational structure of its board of directors in order to continue to qualify for CPB funding. These organizational adjustments shifted the balance of power from the individual stations to the board. Eventually, some board members were able to leverage this power in an attempt to exert tighter controls on the individual stations. This sparked a huge battle for control of the network. Essentially, it can be very difficult to challenge or critique a system that is financing you.

Historically, unconventional media was faced with the choice of getting traditional funding in order to produce quality content and production values comparable to commercial media, or eschewing this funding and settling for content and production values of lower quality. Moreover, even the physical act of producing media of any type required significant capitol. As Downing (2000) points out, the successful entrance into any of the mediums was usually a matter of timing. As early adopters prove a cutting edge medium, and a way to make profit is established, commercial interests are quick to move in and take over. For instance, early FM frequencies were considered worthless, and therefore were relatively easy to acquire. As the benefits of FM broadcasting became apparent, the price of these stations skyrocketed. Deregulation accelerated this trend. The flagship Pacifica station in Berkeley, CA, KPFA, was put into service before the FM band was broken up into reserved frequencies for noncommercial stations and open frequencies for commercial operations. Sitting on the commercial side of the band, KPFA is estimated to be worth upwards of $70 million.

Something that has altered this trend is the advancement of technology and the effects of the commodification of consumer electronics. Photocopiers, computers, software, scanners, digital audio, and video recorders are all becoming more accessible and affordable. The Internet now makes the movement and delivery of media of all types possible for very low costs. Web-based media sites, like the Independent Media Centers, run on open-source software and donated server space. Free radio is spared the dilemma of whether or not to accept funding from traditional sources by its illegality. However, there have been several cases of advertisers trying to buy time on popular pirate stations, and there was even an offer to a recently shutdown Black Cat Radio in Memphis, TN, to re-create the "pirate effect" on a local commercial station (they turned it down). In late 2001, the pioneering San Francisco Liberation Radio took a radical half step into the realm of sponsorship. Individual DJs can replace their dues to the station by getting sponsorships (twice normal dues) from local businesses that meet strict criteria. Station cofounder Richard Edmonson left the decision up to the collective. The station members felt that this was a way to support local independent businesses and help DJs with cash flow problems without compromising the integrity of the station.

The availability of cheap electronics and embracing of a DIY ethic has created a culture of self-sufficient free media. As with the free radio stations, these groups fund themselves through forming collectives where everybody contributes resources to make it happen. These groups hold benefits to raise money, ask listeners and readers for contributions and donations of materials, and form mutually beneficial relationships with activist groups. Many times key members are self-employed while others work regular jobs and spend any spare cash on producing media rather than consumer goods. Whether legal or illegal, free media has found the formula to get the message across without adopting the methods of their alternative media predecessors.

FREEDOM AND ORGANIZATION

Finally, there is the issue of the effects and constraints of organizational structure. Again, we look at the example of free radio. The challenges of operating a radio station with only volunteers are compounded by the threat of arrest and the lack of funding. These issues, combined with a high rate of turnover, make most organizational schemes incompatible. These factors resulted in organizational structures that are democratic, consensus based, or (usually) a combination of the two. The influence of activist organizational strategies pioneered by groups such as EarthFirst! were clearly influential. While there is much variation, there appear to be four main types of structures: the consensus collective, the democracy, public access, and the sole proprietor. First is the "consensus collective," where the group makes all major decisions. This is typical of many tight-knit stations usually founded on shared political or social principles, examples being Free Radio Cascadia and Free Radio Austin. The "democracy" type is where duties are delegated and these individuals or teams of individuals make day-to-day decisions with major issues being voted on by the station staff. Many stations combine elements of the collective model with this. Free Radio Santa Cruz and San Francisco Liberation Radio operate this way. Public access is a model where one or two people "own" the equipment and allow participation by others based on resource contribution and certain rules or guidelines. I have called this the San Marcos Model (1999) after uKind Radio in San Marcos, TX. And finally, there is the sole proprietorship. Derisively referred to as "Vanity Stations" by some, these often are more typical "old school" pirate radio operations. However, their contributions are often underestimated. Station P and Radio Anime are somewhat typical of these. What sets these models apart from most media operations is that the structure is dictated by different forces and therefore has different forms.

Epstein (2001) has compared the structures of the social movements of the 1990s, specifically the anti-globalization movement (or more accurately the globalization reform movement) to ideological anarchism. She identifies an anarchist "sensibility" or what I term "practical" anarchism. These techniques are based on egalitarianism and a commitment to consensus decision making. Although, in the case of free radio, the definition of consensus is often open to interpretation. Pete triDish, a founder of Radio Mutiny in Philadelphia, PA, and the Prometheus Radio Project, lamented the difficulties of making true consensus decision making work. In order to deal with obstructionists, or what he termed "the wing-nut factor," his collective developed the self-explanatory concept of "consensus minus one." In many cases, the unifying concept is consensus, but in operational reality many groups fall back to voting. Although, quite often, a super-majority of three-fourths is required to make decisions. There is also the reality that many people who wish to be involved do not want to be troubled with the day-to-day issues. They are only interested (if at all) in big issues, such as whether or not to shut down after a visit from the FCC or, more likely, what logo to use on station t-shirts. However, many of the characteristics that Epstein (2001) identifies, such as "decentralized organizational structure, based on affinity groups that work together on an ad hoc basis, and decision-making by consensus . . . egalitarianism; opposition to all hierarchies; suspicion of authority, especially that of the state; and commitment to living according to one's values" are clearly hallmarks of the free media concept (p. 1). Independent media activists sidestep the hierarchy issue by creating the term "whole-archy." Whole-archy describes and validates emergent leadership structures that are temporary and based on organizational needs. An example is having the most experienced technical person coordinate the technical crew.

These types of organizational structures make it difficult for authorities to deal with emergent free media, especially those that operate outside regulatory or legal boundaries. As I have discussed in previous research (Coopman, 1999), traditional controlling mechanisms are designed to deal with hierarchical entities with physical and monetary assets or at least clear leadership. Even in the case of Free Radio Berkeley, where Dunifer was clearly the instigator, the injunction and his departure from the collective only resulted in the shifting and renaming of the operation. From Free Radio Berkeley, to Tree Radio Berkeley, Radio Cedar Tree, and finally Berkeley Liberation Radio, the station is still in operation. In other cases, collective members split up and formed multiple free media groups.

Hamilton (2000) supports the concept that an organization's structure, specifically a media organization, dictates the way the organization behaves. Simply put, if you organize yourself like NBC, eventually you will behave like NBC. Alternative or radical media cannot be alternative or radical if its organizational structure is conservative. This idea is behind the differentiation between alternative media and free media. Free media is process based, chaotic, and in constant flux. It has no choice but to adapt to its circumstances. This environment is not conducive to pleasing investors or maintaining relationships with advertisers or institutions. *Mother Jones,* the *Nation,* or even such NPR fare as "This American Life" or "Latino USA" may, in fact, (at times) be radical, alternative, or cutting edge. But ultimately, organizational demands and their relation to financial and regulatory constraints explicitly and implicitly restrict them. Advertisers and underwriters (undertisers?) want to know the audience and how many are out there. They usually wish to be associated with a media environment that is conducive to consumerism. All these factors affect not just what gets disseminated, but even what gets investigated in the first place.

The primary factors that define free media are their operation outside regulatory forces, institutional independence, a primary dependence on self-funding, and novel organizational structures. In their comparison to other alternative media, these aspects are interrelated. Often regulatory requirements mandate certain organizational structures, as do funding sources. Contributors want to be able to write off donations on their taxes. Therefore an organization seeks nonprofit status, which in turn requires a board of directors-style structure. This shifts power away from the rank and file. The drive for consolidation and expansion of the organization's operation can also fuel a vicious cycle where money is needed for expansion and expansion is needed to attract more funding and so on. Free media's decentralized and distributed nature mostly precludes these pitfalls.

DISSENT, FREE MEDIA, AND DEMOCRACY

In this chapter I have discussed how free media emerged, what it is, and why it differs from alternative media. What I have not discussed, until now, is why free media? Why is free media worth discussing and what is its importance? The two answers to these questions deal with dissent and dissemination.

Dissent, in this context, the right to criticize existing authorities, institutions, and traditions, is critical in challenging unjust hierarchies and for promoting progressive social change (Shiffrin, 1999). This is not simply about criticizing some government policy or initiative. Dissent is about taking issue with fundamental aspects of our society. It is about questioning things such as our capitalist economic system or the influence of Christianity on culture. While it can be issue related, its power lies in critiquing the often-invisible systems and assumptions that form the foundation of our society. This is frightening to many people. However, it is important to remember that slavery and the subjugation of women were once considered bedrocks of our society, part of an invisible and unquestioned foundation on which our nation sat. Thoreau, an ardent abolitionist, said in 1863: "Those things which now most engage the attention of men [sic], as politics and the daily routine, are, . . . vital functions of human society, but should be unconsciously performed, like the corresponding functions of the physical body" (Thoreau, 1990, p. 90). Dissent questions this basic functionality and therefore is usually unpopular and often violently opposed. We are now finally at a point in our society that a person can (usually) stand on a street corner and say their piece (with some minor exceptions). In Thoreau's time, lecturing to a group, marching in the street, or publishing a broadside were the tools of informing the public. For the most part, they were the way the leaders of the day would speak to the public as well. However, in an era of mass communication where the leaders of culture, industry, and politics are able to reinforce their vision of societal truth to millions, how can the voice of the dissenter compete?

Ideas, without dissemination, are merely idle ramblings of discontent. The right to speak and the right to be heard have emerged as the cornerstone concepts of the First Amendment. The central idea is that in order for a free society to exist and develop, ideas must be allowed to be debated in an open and public forum. The hope was that by vigorous public debate, good ideas would be adopted and bad ideas would fall by the wayside. There was also the side benefit of keeping dissent in the open where the rulers could keep an eye on it. The U.S. Constitution protects us from having our speech suppressed simply because of its content (it's after you're done talking when the trouble starts). However, as those in the free radio movement discovered, while the government is not supposed to take you away for criticizing it, it can take you away for disseminating that criticism in an unapproved fashion.

Regulatory and economic constraints have done more to squelch dissent than the police or the courts. Forces such as market monopolization or technical standards create artificial scarcity and squeeze out the spaces for dissent to be heard. Mass media follow the Golden Rule: "Those who own the gold, make the rules," and its corollary, "Those with the most gold, make most of the rules." The more media you own, the more money you make, and the more money you make, the more you can afford to influence the rules to let you make and own more and so on. The ultimate example of this was the Telecommunications Act of 1996, perhaps the biggest act of corporate welfare in the history of the United States (McChesney, 1999; Tillinghast, 2000). Further, as mentioned earlier, the sheer power and influence of these forces were enough to change the course of Congress to override the FCC on Low Power Radio. Of the three technical studies done on LPFM, two concurred that it was technically feasible, one stated it was not. The FCC and proponents of LPFM conducted the two concurring studies. The opposing study was conducted by the National Association of Broadcasters (NAB) and supported by National Public Radio (NPR). Despite the preeminence of the FCC technicians, Congress ignored the FCC's expertise for the first time in its history. Congress chose to believe the broadcasting lobbies' minority study. It is this type of power and control that free media proponents cite when they elect to take themselves outside of a system that has no place for them.

Free media does not seek a handout, special treatment or status, or funding. Free media is about doing it yourself, DIY. As filmmaker and activist Michael Moore is apt to say: "Don't hate the media, become the media." Free media activists have found most media wanting and therefore set out to create their own. After over a decade of politicians extolling people to get off welfare, solve your own problems, and make something of themselves, a segment of society has done just that. Somehow I don't think this is what the bootstrap theorists had in mind. It is volunteerism run amok. Ameri-(hard)core, if you will. They are "social entrepreneurs," individuals and groups who take an entrepreneurial mindset and apply it to solving social issues and concerns (Gilmore, 2002). These individuals and groups, activists by design or happenstance, have simply stopped waiting around for their leaders to give them a better world. They have elected to act and create the world they wish to live in. The idea of free media really transcends just media. For this media activism flows from an underlying movement to retake culture and create a place beyond the corporate-socialist system and consumerism. It is as simple as the idea of seeing that something needs to be done, and doing it. The Santa Cruz Free School is an excellent example. A community driven skill-sharing network free of both bureaucracy and tuition, it joins other similar schools in Seattle and Portland. It was started by people used to the DIY ethos they learned as activists. Much like the free media discussed here, it operates on this theory of practical anarchism (Keast, 2002).

Free radio and free media emerged from activists' experience with groups such as Food Not Bombs (Edmonson, 2000). It came from the realization of the diverse elements of the Global Justice Movement that spurred the creation of the "Indymedia" system. The mainstream media was not covering issues that concerned many activists or, when they were covered, oversimplified or misrepresented them. Faced with this, a coalition of people decided to build their own media network. A network of Independent Media Centers would be assembled to disseminate information and analysis, not to make money. Begun at the 1999 World Trade Organization (WTO) protests in Seattle, the system of websites offering text, audio, video, and various associated print publications, webcasts, radio, and even satellite television spans the globe. In five years over one hundred independent media centers were operating on every continent. Each center is locally controlled with the network supplying the software and some technical support. The impact of these IMC's was illustrated by IMC Palestine's (located in Jerusalem) coverage of the Israeli Defense Force's incursions into the West Bank in the spring of 2002. With mainstream media banned from the area, this IMC was only source of news.

Shared skills, open-source software, and a wide variety of funding and finagling are creating a true alternative and an active, positive dissent to systems that people no longer are willing to support through silence. The development of free media will become a gauge of the health of political and cultural discourse.

REFERENCES

Atton, C. (2002). *Alternative media*. London: Sage.

Bender, H. A. (1988). The case of the *Sarah:* A testing ground for the regulation of radio piracy in the United States. *Fordham International Law Journal, 12,* 67–87.

Bilotta-Daily, D., & Siska, T. J. (1999, January/February). F.C.C.'s interference argument grounded: Commercial radio, not micropower, is more frequent hazard for aviation. *Fairness and Accuracy in Reporting*, 3–4.

Coopman, T. M. (Fall 1999). FCC enforcement difficulties with unlicensed micro radio. *Journal of Broadcasting and Electronic Media*, 43(4), 582–602.

———. (Winter 2000a). *Dunifer v. the FCC*: A case study of micro broadcasting. *Journal of Radio Studies*, 2(2), 287–309.

———. (2000b, May). Hardware handshake: Listserv forms backbone of national free radio network. *American Communication Journal*, 3(3) [online]. From http://acjournal.org/holdings/vol3/Iss3/articles/ted_coopman.htm.

———. (2000c, May). High speed access: Micro radio, action, and activism on the Internet. *American Communication Journal*, 3(3) [online] from http://acjournal.org/holdings/vol3/Iss3/rogue4/highspeed.html.

Downing, J. D. H. (2001). *Radical media: Rebellious communication and social movements*. Thousand Oaks: Sage.

Dunifer, Stephen. (1995, April/May). Seize the space! *Reclaiming the Airwaves*, 1.

Edmonson, R. (2000). *Rising up: Class warfare in America from the streets to the airwaves*. San Francisco: Librad Press.

Epstein, B. (2001, September). Anarchism and the anti-globalization movement. *Monthly Review*, 53(4), [online]. From http://www.monthlyreview.org/0901epstein.htm.

Fiske, J. (1996). *Media matters: Race and gender in U.S. politics* (revised edition). Minneapolis: University of Minnesota Press.

Gilmore, D. (2002, February 4). Rich, powerful listening to voices they once may have ignored. *San Jose Mercury News*, 1C–2C.

Hamilton, J. (2000, October) Alternative media: Conceptual difficulties, critical possibilities. *Journal of Communication Inquiry*, 24(4), 357–378.

Howley, K. (August 2000). Radiocracy rulz! Microradio as electronic activism. *International Journal of Cultural Studies*, 3(2), 256–267.

Keast, D. (2002, January 30–February 6). A is for anarchy. *Santa Cruz Metro*, 7–8.

Kiger, P. (2002, May 18). The private business of public radio. *Washington Business Forward* [online]. From http://www.bizforward.com/wdc/issues/2001-11/radio/.

Kuipers, D. (1989, April). A not so Jolly Roger: The silencing of "Radio Sarah": Radio New York International. *The Nation*, 559.

McChesney, R. W. (1999). *Rich media, poor democracy: Communication politics in dubious times*. New York: The New Press.

Mokhiber, R., & Weissman, R. (1999). *Corporate predators: The hunt for profits and the attack on democracy*. Monroe, MN: Common Courage Press.

Shiffrin, Steven, H. (1999). Dissent, injustice, and the meanings of America. New Jersey: Princeton University Press.

Smith, P. (Ed.). (1993). Thoreau, Henry David: Civil disobedience and other essays. New York: Dover Publications, Inc.

Soley, L. (1999). *Free Radio: Electronic civil disobedience*. Boulder: Westview Press.

Thoreau, H. D. (1993). Life without principle. In Smith (Ed.), *Henry David Thoreau: Civil Disobedience and Other Essays* (pp. 75–90). New York: Dover Publications.

Tillinghast, C. H. (2000). *American broadcast regulation and the first amendment: Another look.* Ames, IA: Iowa State University Press.

Walker, J. (2001). *Rebels on the air: Alternative history of radio in America.* New York: New York University Press.

Yoder, A. R. (1990). *Pirate radio stations: Tuning into underground broadcasts.* Blue Ridge Summit, PA: Tab Books.

Legal Documents

Greg Ruggiero v. Federal Communications Commission and United States of America, United States Court of Appeals for the District of Columbia Circuit, No. 00-1100 on Petition for Review of an Order of the Federal Communications Commission (February 8, 2002).

Radio Broadcasting Preservation Act of 2000.

United States v. Stephen Paul Dunifer, No. C 94-03542 CW, slip op. United States District Court for the Northern District of California (January 30, 1995).

14

Seize the Switches: TAO Communications, Media, and Anarchy

Jeff Shantz

A new (old) specter is haunting politics (again)—the specter of anarchism. Over the last six years, striking media coverage of angry, black-clad, balaclava-wearing youth demonstrating outside of global economic summits and political party conventions has suggested a return of the moral panic regarding anarchism that marked the turn of the last century. The actions attributed to so-called "black bloc" anarchists at global capitalist summits since the 1999 World Trade Organization (WTO) meetings in Seattle have returned anarchists to the headlines and landed them on the covers of *Time* and *Newsweek* in addition to a feature story on U.S. television's *60 Minutes II*. Also, police assaults on anarchists at economic summits, deploying pepper spray, tear gas, rubber bullets, and mass arrests, in addition to several shootings and even killings have suggested strongly to the general public that anarchists are something to be feared. That message has been reinforced in news media depictions of anarchists as "thugs" and "hooligans." Unfortunately, beyond the sensationalistic media accounts, very little is known about who anarchists are, what they think, or what their politics actually involve. Such radical, "underground" movements remain largely misunderstood by sociologists and popular commetators alike. This chapter will provide insights into anarchist ideas and practices as illustrated by a discussion of TAO Communications, an important anarchist media workers' collective.

Since the early 1990s, anarchism as a conscious political force has enjoyed a rather remarkable resurgence. Global economic transformations, along with major social dislocations and ecological crises, have encouraged a rediscovery of anarchism among people seeking alternatives to both capitalism and communism. The simultaneous collapse of state capitalism in the Soviet Union and the move of Western social democratic parties to the Right have left socialism discredited as an alternative to neoliberal capitalism. With the political Left in disarray, anarchism presents to many an overlooked alternative to both liberal democracy and Marxism.[1] Seattle, 1999, marked the emergence of the anarchists from their thriving underground presence to an international voice of dissent.

The lack of reasoned analysis of anarchist politics has meant that the actual practices and intentions of this major, and growing, contemporary movement remain obscured. Lost in sensationalist mainstream news accounts are the constructive practices undertaken daily by anarchist activists seeking a world free from violence, oppression, and exploitation. An examination of some of these constructive anarchist projects provides insights into real-world attempts to develop peaceful and creative social relations in the here and now of everyday life.

In order to bring their ideas to life, anarchists create working examples. To borrow the old syndicalist phrase, they are "forming the structure of the new world in the shell of the old."[2] These experiments in living, popularly referred to as "DIY" (Do-It-Yourself), are the means by which contemporary anarchists withdraw their consent from authoritarian structures and begin constructing other relationships. DIY releases counterforces, based upon notions of autonomy and self-organization as motivating principles, against the normative political and cultural discourses of neoliberalism. Anarchists create "autonomous zones,"[3] which are not about access to the state but about refusal of the terms of entry (e.g., nationalism, citizenship).

Communication across these diasporic communities is made possible, in part, by recent technological innovations (e.g., photocopiers, videocameras, Internet, and micro-transmitters). While remaining highly suspicious of the impacts of technology, its class-exclusivity, and its possible uses as a means of social control, anarchists have become proficient in wielding these technological products as tools for active resistance. In using these tools effectively anarchists have developed a busy presence on the Internet. Among the most important anarchist projects is TAO Communications, an organization that has played a major part in building global networks to counter capitalist globalism.

Castells, Yazawa, and Kiselyova (1996) identify the importance of symbolic politics for movements against global governance practices. Media skills are significant weapons in this age of mass rapid communication. For Castells, Yazawa, and Kiselyova (1996) such actions are necessary to impact the mainstream media, to bring people at large into the debate, and to build networks of resistance to the global order. It's in this respect that we might understand the significance of "counter-media" such as TAO within anarchist movements. Recognizing the limits of mainstream political channels from which they are, in any event, largely excluded, activists have decided to do it themselves. These various practices are all part of complex networks that are transnational, transboundary, and transmovement.

ANARCHY IS ORDER: THE ANARCHIST TRANSFER CULTURES

The word "anarchy" comes from the ancient Greek word "anarchos"and means "without a ruler" (Horowitz, 1964; Joll, 1964; Marshall, 1993; Woodcock, 1962). While rulers, not surprisingly, claim that the end of rule inevitably will lead to a descent into chaos and turmoil, anarchists maintain that rulership is unnecessary for the preservation of order. Rather than a descent into Hobbes' war of all against all, a society without government suggests to anarchists the very possibility for creative and peaceful human relations. Pierre-Joseph Proudhon neatly summed up the anarchist position in his famous slogan: "Anarchy Is Order."

Contemporary anarchists maintain a commitment to historic anarchist goals of creating a society without government, state, and private owner-ship of means of production in which people associate voluntarily. Indeed, the definition of anarchism presented by anarchists at recent gatherings highlights the inclusiveness of their conception of liberty.

Anarchy: A self governed society in which people organize themselves from the bottom up on an egalitarian basis; decisions made by those affected by them; direct democratic control of our workplaces, schools, neighborhoods, towns and bio-regions with coordination between differing groups as needed. A world where women and men are free and equal and all of us have power over our own lives, bodies and sexuality; where we cherish and live in balance with the earth and value diversity of cultures, races and sexual orientations; where we work and live together cooperatively. (*Active Resistance*)

Anarchists envision a society based upon autonomy, self-organization, and voluntary federation which they oppose to "the State as a particular body intended to maintain a compulsory scheme of legal order" (Marshall, 1993, p. 12). Contemporary anarchists focus much of their efforts on transforming everyday life through the development of alternative social relationships and organizations. They are not content to wait either for elite-initiated reforms or for future "post-revolutionary" utopias. If social and individual freedoms are to be expanded the time to start is today.

These are the building blocks of what anarchist sociologist Howard Ehrlich (1996) refers to as the anarchist transfer culture, an approximation of the new society within the context of the old. Within it anarchists try to meet the basic requirements of building sustainable communities. In this sense, anarchist autonomous zones are liminal sites, spaces of transformation and passage. As such they are important sites of re-skilling, in which anarchists prepare themselves for the new forms of relationship necessary to break authoritarian and hierarchical structures. Participants also learn the diverse tasks and varied interpersonal skills necessary for collective work and living. This skill sharing serves to discourage the emergence of knowledge elites and to allow for the sharing of all tasks, even the least desirable, necessary for social maintenance.

Anarchists encourage a cultivated "deepening" of knowledge as remedy to the anonymous, detached, knowledge broadening which they believe is endemic to conditions of postmodernity. This does not mean isolation or insularity, however. Rather, it speaks to social relations, whether local or federated, organized in a decentralized, grassroots manner. This new radicalism lives outside of the state and is organized toward self-reliance. Participants are encouraged to identify local problems, and to broaden and unite the individual "do-it-yourself" actions in which they are already involved, such as saving a park or cleaning up an abandoned lot. Lacking the drama of street clashes with police such small-scale actions of anarchists are almost never reported.

Anarchists see their efforts as laying the groundwork to replace state and capital with decentralized federations. Activists argue for the construction of "place" around the contours of ecological regions, in opposition to the boundaries of nation-states which show only contempt for ecological "boundaries" as marked by topography, climate, species distribution, or drainage. Affinity with bioregionalist themes is recognized in appeals for a replacement of nation-states with bioregional communities. While media create confusion about the message of anarchism, the anarchists "are clear on their objectives of building sustainable democratic grassroots communities that respect the environment and minimizing domination in any form" (Phillips, 2000, p. 44). For anarchists such communities might constitute social relations in an articulation with local ecological requirements rather than the bureaucratic, hierarchical interferences of distant corporate bodies.

MAINSTREAM MEDIA AND THE ANARCHISTS

The portrayal of anarchists and anarchism by mainstream media raises questions regarding access to "worldwide multimedia communications networks" in this post–Gulf War world of media manipulation. It also suggests to some commentators that in the age of flow through "smooth space," informational nodes may "displace boundaries and frontiers as the zones where practices of exclusion are concentrated" (Shapiro, 2001, p. 83).

Much research shows that mass media regularly provide coverage of political demonstrations that marginalizes protest groups (Duemler, 2000; McLeod & Hertog, 1992; Phillips, 2000). This has been glaringly apparent in news media coverage of the many demonstrations against global capitalism in North America over the past two years.[4]

Corporate media have labeled the protesters as unorganized groups of radical environmentalists, single-issue extremists, and directionless anarchists bent on disrupting social order. The extensive involvement of unions and labor in Seattle has generally been explained as a one-time aberration, and the global trade issues focusing on NAFTA and the WTO have been mostly forgotten. (Phillips, 2000, p. 43)

Recent studies of mass media reports of demonstrations have found that "news stories about protests tend to focus on the protesters' appearances rather than their issues, emphasize their violent actions rather than their social criticism, pit them against the police rather than their chosen targets, and downplay their effectiveness" (McLeod & Detenber, 1999, p. 3). For example, news reports of anti-globalization protests stress the appearances of "black bloc" members rather than the concerns that motivate them. Similarly emphasis is given to acts of property damage or conflicts with police. The issues raised by activists and the alternatives that they present are largely obscured.

In their study of the effects of television coverage of an anarchist protest, McLeod and Detenber (1999) have found that media reports that support the status quo significantly impact viewers' perceptions, leading them to be more critical of protesters, less critical of police, and less likely to support protesters' rights. Reports that support the status quo also produce lower estimates of protest effectiveness and estimations of newsworthiness. Protesters rarely are called upon to counter the status quo perspectives or even allowed to offer a response.[5] "As a result, protest coverage adopts 'official' definitions of the protest situation by focusing on questions of the 'legality of actions' as opposed to the 'morality of issues'" (McLeod & Hertog, 1992, p. 260). In the process, "news coverage will marginalize challenging groups, especially those that are viewed as radical in their beliefs and strategies" (McLeod & Detenber, 1999, p. 6).

At present, no groups are understood to be more radical than the "black bloc" anarchists of the global justice struggles. Likewise, no groups have been subjected more to marginalizing depictions than the anarchists. As McLeod and Detenber (1999, p. 19) note, "there is a pervasive social bias against anarchists. Anarchist movements are perceived, and in most cases misperceived, as groups that are against any and all laws." This is nothing new, of course. Chomsky (1998, p. 184) and Hong (1992) remind us that the specter of the anarchist or communist agitator has long been a favored trope of North American propaganda.

The shadowy figure of the anarchist bomber remains one of the most popular means for instilling fear and insecurity in people. In popular news accounts, the threat of anarchy is still used to conjur images of violence, chaos, destruction and the "collapse of civilization" (Marshall, 1993). Never mind that few anarchists ever have advocated violence, let alone engaged in terrorist acts (Bookchin, 1995; Kornegger, 1996; Woodcock,

1962). Chomsky (1998, p. 185) identifies this overplaying of anarchist violence as a technique of marginalizing people, separating them from struggles to improve their lives and keeping them from working together by creating divisions. This point is exemplified by the media preoccupation with violence at recent demonstrations and the attribution of that violence to "anarchists" regardless of the actuality of events. While focusing on the motivations, concerns, and issues behind demonstrations might highlight similarities with demonstrators, the context-free attention to violence makes such connections more difficult.

ANARCHY AND THE NET

Mainstream media reports have depicted anarchists as anti-modern Luddites out to stop the flow of progress and human development. Such views overlook the richly constructive aspects of actual anarchist practice. As Phillips (2000, p. 44) notes, a closer look shows that the anarchists "have successfully used the Internet and satellite links to stream e-mail, radio, and TV images throughout the world, and continue to work toward building real news systems independent of corporate media." Recognizing that corporate media are not likely to give up their control over information flows, anarchists have relied on the do-it-yourself principles that underlie much of their work. A main outlet for this DIY[6] media has been the Internet.

Some, like Kuehls (1996), suggest that the emergence of "flows" such as satellite communications and the Internet provide spaces for an enactment of politics outside of the bounded spaces of states. These "smooth" spaces are said to offer great opportunities for activism beyond sovereign territories. Indeed, as tools for organizing, "the new technologies are doubtless powerful, rendering international communication rapid, easy, and cheap, and creating the possibility of international bulletins and appeals that make the old telephone trees look rather quaint" (Hirshkop, 1998, p. 212). The Internet has been especially crucial for organizing and communicating among grassroots activists over the past decade. It has provided an important space for activists limited by traditional media channels that would otherwise not be available to them. Examples of significant efforts on the Net abound in recent years. Human rights organizations, environmentalist groups, immigration and refugee networks, and labor unions have used the Net to share information, strategize, and coordinate efforts across borders (Drew, 1997).

Perhaps the most striking instance of a skillful traversing of "smooth space" are the now legendary communiqués of the Zapatistas of Chiapas, Mexico. The poetic and poignant messages, especially those attributed to Subcommandante Marcos, inspired activists across the globe and helped to build strong solidarity networks to support the Zapatistas and to try to build on their example in local struggles.

Another influential example of creative Internet work involved Radio B92, an independent broadcaster in Belgrade, Serbia, briefly shut down by the Milosevic regime for reporting on mass demonstrations against the government in 1996. With the transmitter shut down, the staff of B92 converted audio reports to computer audio files and were able to get their message out to a worldwide audience over servers provided by Progressive Networks of Seattle. Notably, anarchists played a large part in the networks that emerged to support both Radio B92 and the Zapatistas. The organizing that has taken place around protests against the meetings of capitalist globalizers underscores the possibilities for use of the Internet as an important means of communication.

However, "smooth space" also is occupied by those who would seek to contain open communications and limit participation and the creation of new political projects. The utopian vision of the Internet as a realm of democracy and mutualism contrasts starkly with the rapid commercialization of the Net (McChesney, 1997).[7]

When the very structure of a society depends upon a lack of democracy, however, democracy will depend upon a fight, and upon social forces with the interests, will, and intelligence to struggle for it. Technology will doubtless have a role in this struggle, but it offers no shortcuts: one cannot buy democracy off a shelf or download it from a Website. It demands courage, fortitude, and political organization, and, as far as we can see, Microsoft has yet to design a software that can deliver these. (Hirschkop, 1998, p. 217)

Political organization is exactly what the tireless activists of TAO Communications are attempting to build. For more than six years this group of activists has played a major part in organizing global anarchist networks.

THE ANARCHY ORGANIZATION: TAO COMMUNICATIONS[8]

> Every tool is a weapon if you hold it right.
> —*Ani DiFranco*

TAO Communications has its prehistory in the Media Collective, a Toronto discussion circle formed in 1994 that was more a situationist happening than a formal collective. In the cross-fertilization that occurred at monthly meetings, Food Not Bombs fed people, musicians met and played, rooftop gardeners shared seeds and tips, organizers of subway parties plotted, and many guerrilla performances and cultural deconstructions took place. As often happens in such bubbling cauldrons of creativity, cracks soon appeared and in January of 1996 the Media Collective was laid to rest. TAO Communications was one of the fragments picked up and reworked by anarchists, hackers, and slackers and has since grown far beyond its Toronto roots to encompass a global network.

Organizers called themselves TAO as an acronym for mythical collectives of "The Anarchy Organization" (as if there could ever be one with a capital T), or "Those Amazing Orangutans," or "Tasty Apples and Oranges." More seriously, the name alludes to non-Western anti-authoritarian traditions, which preexist Proudhon finding the word anarchy by centuries. The idea was to avoid capture by definition and state recognition; to stay active and keep moving, always changing (Lilley, personal communication, January 27, 2002).

During the late 1990s Internet hype had become sheer mania. Its supposed vast, open, equal playing field was covertly but consistently being undermined by corporate privatization of the telecom infrastructure.

It was also an idea at the time that the Internet was vast and open and resistant to censorship. As mostly tech workers, these anarchists had seen through the "California ideology" of Net hype that valorized shiny, new, victimless speed capitalism. It was important before the window closed and the networks were completely carved up into proprietary corporate fiefdoms to secure any and all worker-owned and operated access. (Lilley, personal communication, January 27, 2002)

TAO wanted to push against that closing window by opening up sourcecode and access, securing all worker-owned and operated access, and cultivating an internationalist network based on mutual aid rather than profit. TAO workers wanted to maintain autonomy and to extend support, infrastructure, and relative security to radical communications. As secretaries and coders for student, labor, and enviromental groups, the emphasis was on social struggle, on bodies in the streets, rather than so-called "virtual" reality. TAO travelling organizers denied the Internet's existence, and talked instead about ownership of the means of production and other such sticky aspects of old-fashioned materiality.

We understood that Article 19 of the Universal Declaration of Human Rights (the freedom to hold opinions without interference and seek, receive, and impart information and ideas through any media and regardless of frontiers) was in itself too much ideal, and not enough assertion, so we formed a 10-point program of concrete demands, based on the Black Panther Party's. (Lilley, personal communication, January 27, 2002)

Several projects were carried forward or initiated to win these demands. Among the most important of these has been A-Infos. A-Infos was a mailing list culled from postal addresses the Toronto publication *Anarchives* had gathered since the 1960s, joined with the e-list established by the I-AFD in Europe, and supported by Freedom Press, which has operated out of London since Kropotkin and others began it in the 1880s. A-Infos is now carried on its own server within the TAO matrix, and its multiple lists and digests distribute news "by, for, and about" anarchists to over 1,200 subscribers in twelve languages, with substantial daily traffic, as well as print and radio reproduction around the world. A-infos has become the most important daily news source on anarchist activities. It has been crucial in posting anarchist calls for participation in anti-globalization protests years prior to Seattle and continuing to today.

Other projects supported by TAO include: The Student Activist Network, the Direct Action Media Network (an unfortunately defunct precursor to the Indymedia conglomerate), and PIRG.CA (public interest research groups). Solidarity work has been done with the Ontario Coalition Against Poverty, Esgenoopetitj (colonial name: Burnt Church) First Nations, CUPE 3903 (strike-winning teaching assistants at York University), and numerous groups formed to oppose Bush's war mobilization after September 11. From the original single machine, TAO now operates at least eight computers, serving the needs of over 1,000 members, a spread of organizations and individuals, who self-manage thousands of lists, hundreds of web pages, as well as databases for progressive projects. Besides basic shell access without advertisements or space quotas, organized TAO workers are able to offer secure access to Web-based e-mail and Internet Relay Chat.

In 1999, TAO workers joined the Industrial Workers of the World (IWW) with the intention of forming a branch among telecom workers in the Toronto area. TAO workers believed that this would solidify syndicalist and cooperative structures, help with the rotation of job tasks, improve benefits for TAO workers, and generally raise class consciousness, particularly in the online arena where labor is too often made invisible and victimized by speed need.

In Barcelona in 1936, anarchist liberation of the city was greatly assisted by the daring seizure of the Telephone Exchange. Currently technology is used more as a tool of fascist repression, of surveillance and control, than of the kind of liberation TAO seeks. It will be ever more important to organize workers under that panoptic gaze, from the call centres now set up inside prison walls to the young women assembling chips in Malaysia, if we are ever to win our freedom. Seize the switches! (Lilley, personal communication, January 27, 2002)

Though much attention to anarchism comes from propaganda of the deed, or sabotage, most anarchists still recognize publication and communication are quite important to a winning strategy. "To publicly claim responsibility for our actions and offer explanation, to organize greater strength, shape context and record our history, it's the ability to publish that often raises the stakes and pushes us forward" (Lilley, personal communication, January 27, 2002). That may be partly why libertarians of all stripes took so quickly to the Internet and why its language of openness and freedom without censorship has become a target for commodification by the corporate colonizers of the Internet.

The anarchists of TAO Communications do not view the Internet as the "vehicles of new and more democratic social and political relationships" (Hirschkop, 1998, p. 208). It is simply one possibly useful tool, the usefulness of which will be determined by the ways in which it is wielded and the character of the forces wielding it. The recent protests against global capital have situated the Internet as an important tool used by activist organizations, but only within the context of actual movements "on the ground."

ANARCHY AND DIY NETWORKS

Castells, Yazawa, and Kiselyova (1996, p. 22) suggest that marginal movements are typically rendered invisible by corporate mass media until they "explode in the form of media events that call public attention, and reveal the existence of profound challenges to everyday normalcy." Yet these dramatic mobilizations are merely the surface manifestations of much larger movements composed of various emergent processes and practices. These networks "act as 'cultural laboratories' in which new collective identities are formed" (Purdue, Dürrschmidt, Jowers, & O'Doherty, 1997, p. 647).

Anarchism consists of networks of autonomous communications. Influential anarchist writer Hakim Bey refers to these autonomous networks as "the Web." The current forms of the Web consist of the networks of zines and marginal publications, pirate radios, websites, listservers, and hacking. Bey argues (1991, p. 110) that at this point the Web is primarily a support system capable of sharing information from one autonomous zone to another. Despite his use of the conventional terminology of "the Web," Bey is at pains to make clear that what he is speaking of does not refer solely to computer technology. The information webwork of anarchy uses the tools of mass technology for ends that are communitarian rather than private, asserting use value over exchange value.

The Web provides logistical support for the autonomous zones, but, even more fundamentally, it also helps bring the autonomous zone into being. In Bey's view the autonomous zone "exists in information-space as well as in the 'real world'" (1991, p. 109). The Web, in part, makes up for the lack of duration and locale experienced by many autonomous zones. These networks make up the anarchist underground of the "future in the present." Its significance rests not in the specifics of technology, but in "the openness and horizontality of the structure" (Bey, 1991, p. 11). As Plows (1998, p. 155) notes, the decentralized, fluid structure of DIY webs "allows actions to happen rapidly and spontaneously, without the limitations of the top down approach." The avoidance of hierarchical approaches helps to avoid some of the problems that have "broken the militancy of other . . . revolutionary groups" (Plows, 1998, p. 155). Anarchist networks reject pyramidal and centralized power structures and offer an alternative social organization that values instead, cooperation, and self-management. One result of the flexible and participatory structures characterizing DIY is that, as Plows (1998, p. 155) suggests, "An initially small and local campaign has the potential to become the focus for a large-scale national protest site in the time it takes to network the information."

CONCLUSION

Anarchists recognize the processes by which some ideas gain ascendance while others are marginalized. They know that access to corporate media is by no means "free and equal." Anarchists share with many academic media critics an understanding of mainstream media as geared to the interests of established corporate powers.

The question of hegemony attempts to address "which specific ideologies, representing the interests of which specific groups and classes will prevail at any given moment, in any given situation" (Hebdige, 1993, p. 14). Anarchist communications may be understood as acts of counterhegemony that contest the views and practices of dominant institutions such as global trade bodies, multinational corporations, and neoliberal governments. Not only are these acts aimed at providing a sense that things can be done differently, they are also aimed at real practices of transformation of social relations. They show that hegemony can be challenged and resistance is not necessarily recuperated (Hebdige, 1993, pp. 16–17).

Shared views and practices help to forge solidarity among participants, "provided that there are some outlets which publicize group activities and issues, legitimate anarchist organizations and coordinate group members, thereby reducing the fear of isolation. This function may be provided by alternative media" (McLeod & Hertog, 1992, p. 272). This may happen not only by helping to construct a sense of community and by improving the knowledge shared by anarchists but also "by linking anarchist and other 'radical' movements nationally and internationally. It also provides 'mobilizing information' about future anarchist events" (McLeod & Hertog, 1992, p. 272). All of this can contribute to the constitution of movements and the challenging of hegemonic perspectives and practices.

The media work to return, symbolically at least, cultures of resistance to the hegemonic meaning structure. Members of resistance cultures are made to fit in the places where common sense would have them (as children, malcontents, or trouble-makers) (Hebdige, 1993, p. 94). These practices of marginalization can have the familiar effects of "dividing to conquer" potential allies.

In the process, the protesters are isolated from the "general public" even though they may share some views and concerns with significant portions of the population. In essence, the media coverage may discourage interest and participation in such protest activities and thereby inhibit the growth of critical social movements. (McLeod & Hertog, 1992, p. 273)

Anarchists do not resist mass media by asking for improved representation but by telling their own stories themselves. They present counter-media, to the major mass media, which show little respect for the lives, feelings, and experiences of the marginalized. This is done not only to counter hostile or inaccurate media representations but to share ideas, build solidarity, and develop strategies for social change. This contributes to a measure of control over means of production and reproduction and encourages the construction of participatory and democratic cultures and the breakdown of divisions between producer and consumer. It is the active creation of a participatory democratic culture.

Following Castells, Yazawa, and Kiselyova (1996), one might suggest that anarchist movements respond to the processes of social exclusion and cultural alienation currently associated with global processes of governance by challenging the global order and asserting counterpractices. Attempts are made to (re)construct cultural meaning through specific patterns of experience in that participants create meaning against the logics of global intrusions that would render them meaningless. Radical social movement alliances are largely engaged in transforming the normative cultural and political codes of emerging global relations. Anarchy encourages a critical reconceptualization of politics as currently constituted. It offers a glimpse of politics that refuse containment by any of the containers of conventional politics, whether by states or mass media. Anarchist movements may further challenge the meanings of territoriality and sovereignty in the current context. Such manifestations may open spaces for a (re)constitution of politics by destabilizing tendencies toward enclosure of any totalizing discourse such as "globalization" or "free trade."

The reemergence of anarchism is important in the possibilities it raises— there is always the chance that they will remain possibilities only. This uncertainty derives partly from activists' rejection of legitimizing mechanisms and externally imposed definitions. It remains to be seen if these developments are suggestive of any durable breakout from established categories.

Marginal struggles open spaces for experimentation in lived experiences. Through the construction of "futures in the present" they nurture possibilities that cannot be contained within conventional notions of politics. The emergence of subterranean radicalisms, which receive scant attention even within critical works, open cracks in the walls of the political. "Interests and groups defined as marginal because they have become 'disturbances' in the system of social integration are precisely the struggles which may be the *most* significant from the point of view of historical emancipation from social hierarchy and domination" [emphasis in original] (Aronowitz, 1990, p. 111). Anarchy asks us why we should assume that a "globalized civil society" will be any better than the civil society that brought poverty, homelessness, racism, and ecological annihilation in the first place.

NOTES

1. Even contemporary Left writers who are otherwise aware of alternative movements and radical politics are often dismissive of anarchists. Hirschkop (1998, pp. 212–213) refers to "would-be cyber-anarchists," using a popular mainstream media technique to denigrate activists while questioning their motives for organizing on the Net: "Reading the exclamations of the technologically enthused, however, one senses that what excites them is not what the Internet can do for the *sober and responsible citizen,* but the dizzying possibilities it opens up for those of a *mischievously anarchistic* bent" [emphasis added].

2. This phrase is found in the "Preamble" to the Constitution of the Industrial Workers of the World (IWW).

3. This term was popularized by anarchist writer Hakim Bey in his influential book *T.A.Z.: The Temporary Autonomous Zone, Ontological Anarchy, Poetic Terrorism.*

4. As Edward Herman (1998, p. 202) makes clear, this is no coincidence: "It may be worth noting that the transnational media corporations have a distinct self-interest in global trade agreements, as they are among their foremost beneficiaries" (Herman, 1998, p. 202). Today, six firms control the majority of market share in daily newspapers, magazines, television, radio, books, and motion pictures in the United States (Duemler, 2000, p. 47).

5. In Herman's (1998, p. 194) view: "The power of the U.S. propaganda system lies in its ability to mobilize an elite consensus, to give the appearance of democratic consent, and to create enough confusion, misunderstanding, and apathy in the general population to allow elite programs to go forward."

6. The "Do-it-Yourself" ethos has a long and rich association with anarchism. One sees it in Proudhon's notions of People's Banks and local currencies (see, Proudhon, 1969), which have returned in the form of LETS (Local Exchange and Trade Systems). In North America, nineteenth-century anarchist communes, such as those of Benjamin Tucker, prefigure the A-zones and squat communities of the present day.

7. We should bear in mind Edward Herman's (1998) notes of caution regarding the threat to democratic use of new technologies by corporate concerns for profit and business influence on the flows of information. "Although the new technologies have great potential for democratic communication, left to the market there is little reason to expect the Internet to serve democratic ends" (Herman, 1998, p. 201).

8. This section would not have been possible without the participation of TAO worker P. J. Lilley.

REFERENCES

Aronowitz, S. (1990). *The crisis in historical materialism.* Minneapolis: University of Minnesota Press.

Bey, H. (1991). *T.A.Z.: The temporary autonomous zone, ontological anarchy, poetic terrorism.* Brooklyn: Autonomedia.

Bookchin, M. (1995). *Social anarchism and lifestyle anarchism: An unbridgeable chasm.* Edinburgh: AK Press.

Castells, M., Yazawa, S., & Kiselyova, E. (1996). Insurgents against the global order: A comparative analysis of the Zapatistas in Mexico, the American militia and Japan's AUM Shinrikyo. *Berkeley Journal of Sociology.* Summer, 21–59.

Chomsky, N. (1998). Propaganda and control of the public mind. In R. W. McChesney, E. M. Wood, & J. B. Foster (Eds.), *Capitalism and the information age: The political economy of the global communication revolution* (pp. 179–189). New York: Monthly Review Press.

Drew, J. (1997). Grassroots activism in the electronic age. In D. Hazen & J. Winokur (Eds.), *We the media: A citizens' guide to fighting for media democracy* (p. 189). New York: The New Press, 189.

Duemler, D. (2000). The right to be heard: Creating a social movement for the 21st century. *Social Policy, 31*(2), 45–51.

Ehrlich, H. J. (1996). How to get from here to there: Building revolutionary transfer culture. In H. J. Ehrlich (Ed.), *Reinventing anarchy, again* (pp. 331–349). Edinburgh: AK Press.

Hebdige, D. (1993). *Subculture: The meaning of style.* London: Routledge.

Herman, E. S. (1998). The propaganda model revisited. In R. W. McChesney, E. M. Wood, & J. B. Foster (Eds.), *Capitalism and the information age: The political economy of the global communication revolution* (pp. 191–205). New York: Monthly Review Press.

Hirschkop, K. (1998). Democracy and the new technologies. In R. W. McChesney, E. M. Wood, & J. B. Foster (Eds.), *Capitalism and the information age: The political economy of the global communication revolution* (pp. 207–217). New York: Monthly Review Press.

Hong, N. (1992). Constructing the anarchist beast in American periodical literature, 1880–1903. *Critical Studies in Mass Communication, 9*, 110–130.

Horowitz, I. L. (Ed.). (1964). *The anarchists.* New York: Dell.

Joll, J. (1964). *The anarchists.* New York: Grosset and Dunlap.

Kornegger, P. (1996). Anarchism: The feminist connection. In H. J. Ehrlich (Ed.), *Reinventing anarchy, again* (pp. 156–168). Edinburgh: AK Press.

Kuehls, T. (1996). *Beyond sovereign territory: The space of ecopolitics.* Minneapolis: University of Minnesota Press.

Marshall, P. (1993). *Demanding the impossible: A history of anarchism.* London: Fontana Press.

McChesney, R. (1997). The Internet and the digital revolution. In D. Hazen & J. Winokur (Eds.), *We the media: A citizens' guide to fighting for media democracy* (pp. 178–180). New York: The New Press.

McLeod, D. M., & Detenber, B. (1999). Framing effects of television news coverage of social protest. *Journal of Communication, 49*(3), 3–23.

McLeod, D. M., & Hertog, J. K. (1992). The manufacture of 'public opinion' by reporters: Informal cues for public perceptions of protest groups. *Discourse and Society, 3*(3), 259–275.

Phillips, P. (2000). Mainstream corporate media dismiss democracy. *Social Policy, 31*(2), 43–44.

Plows, A. (1998). Earth First!: Defending mother earth, direct-style. In G. McKay (Ed.), *DiY culture: Party and protest in nineties Britain* (pp. 152–173). London: Verso.

Proudhon, P.-J. (1969). *Selected writings of Pierre-Joseph Proudhon.* Garden City: Anchor Books.

Purdue, D., Dürrschmidt, J., Jowers, P. & O'Doherty, R. (1997). DIY culture and extended milieux: LETS, veggies boxes and festivals. *The Sociological Review*, 645–667.

Shapiro, M. J. (2000). National times and other times: Re-thinking citizenship. *Cultural Studies, 14*(1), 79–98.

Woodcock, G. (1962). *Anarchism: A history of libertarian ideas and movements.* New York: World Publishing.

15

Become the Media:
The Global IMC Network

Dorothy Kidd

> The Seattle IMC and the growing Independent Media Center Network
> represent a new and powerful emerging model that counters the trend
> toward the privatization of all public spaces by expanding our capacity
> to reclaim public airwaves and resources.
> —*Seattle IMC Brochure, 2001*

INTRODUCTION

Over 110 centers, in thirty-five countries, have joined the Independent Media
Center (IMC) Network since the first IMC was started in Seattle in late 1999
to publicize the campaigns against the World Trade Organization (WTO).
These multimedia sites provide a real-time alternative to corporate and state
media sources about the continuing battles against corporate globalization,
as well as campaigns for peace and social justice. However, more than just a
platform for counter-information, the IMC Network operates with a different mode of representation, in a new kind of communications commons.[1]

Each Indy Media site operates autonomously, without an hierarchical
command, unlike the broadcast model where representation is centrally controlled and managed. Rather than commodifying information and selling it
through multiple branded channels, the IMC Network creates a very different kind of synergy between producers and audiences. Rather than a journalism of a professional corps, Indy Media promotes the do-it-yourself
approach, as encapsulated in an early banner on the Italian site: "Don't Hate

the Media—Become the Media." Their innovation of "open publishing" allows anyone with Internet access to represent themselves directly. As well, all site visitors are encouraged to become their own news editors, actively selecting their own information from a diversity of news, commentary and analysis, resource links, and interactive discussion opportunities from around the world.

This new communications commons survives against and within an encroaching global enclosure of information. Corporate and state powers are moving to exploit, incorporate, and privatize the rich resources of the Internet, and to marginalize and demonize sites and perspectives that oppose neoliberalism. The IMC itself has been a focus of this repression, during the Free Trade Area of the Americas (FTAA) protests in Quebec City in the spring of 2001, the G8 meetings in Genoa, and the European Union meetings in Spain (Alzaga, 2002; Herndon, 2001; Starhawk, 2001). The IMC Network is resisting this enclosure, acting to open up and circulate a vision of democratic organization and participatory communication worldwide.

Since my first observations of the Seattle IMC during the WTO protests, and through face-to-face, e-mail and telephone conversations, interviews, and meetings, I have been struck by the scope and scale of achievement. This chapter argues that the IMC's convergent technology, its participatory organization and mode of production, and its connection to a new global social justice movement makes it less vulnerable than earlier communications commons, such as the international community radio and TV networks in which I participated.[2]

THE REVOLUTION OF THE RICH AGAINST THE POOR[3]

The earliest English commons were eroded in a protracted and often bloody struggle that took place from the late 1400s to the early 1800s, ushering in the grand transformation to European global capitalism. During the fifteenth century, often considered a golden age for English labor, the majority were small farmers who worked the land under a system of open fields and common rights. They held customary right, or "copyhold" to a part of the feudal estate, as a sort of sub-tenant. They also shared the use of untitled village land, marsh, forest, and water holdings in common with other small and medium-sized farmers and tenants (Travis, 2000, p. 5). This shared use allowed them to meet some or all of their daily needs, while at the same time providing important cultural and social values over which they had some control.

The English commons were not ideal democratic societies. Many rural families were poor and subject to the domination of the feudal landlords via rents, levies, tributes, and taxes. However, within the commons, landlord rule was usually not enforced every day. Instead, commoners developed sophisticated interpersonal and community communication to manage their shared resources, using a "rich variety of institutions and community sanctions which . . . effected restraints and stints upon use" (Thompson, 1991, p. 131). The English words "communication" and "democracy" both originated during this period of complex negotiations of customary rights and commons obligations. *Communication* meant "to make common to many," while *democracy* derives from the sixteenth century when it meant "the rule of the comminaltie," the popular power of the multitude, implying the suppression of rule by the rich (Williams, 1976, p. 93).

The enclosures were the first project of capitalist accumulation that laid the basis for the "great transformation" from a feudal agricultural economy to an industrial economy (Polanyi, 1944). One of the least discussed, and greatest impacts, was on the common people, who were dispossessed from their rural communities, and who, without their shared usage and subsistence practices, were compelled to move to look for waged work in the towns and cities of Europe, and then in the new colonies of the Americas. This project, of expropriation and exploitation of lands, and clearing of commoners, was then extended to Ireland, Scotland, and Wales and, even more brutally, throughout the Americas, Africa, and Asia.

Begun by the wool lobby, and eventually endorsed by English Parliamentary writ, the means of restructuring included engineering and highway projects, surveillance, the imposition of new work disciplines, and criminalization of those who resisted, as well as new systems of thought and governance. All of these early modes of structural adjustment were met with extraordinarily widespread and diverse resistance, a diversity of tactics that parallels those in use by social justice movements today. These ranged from moral and legal appeals, parliamentary petitions, and lobbying, to fence breaking, arson and systematic trespass, and direct uprisings and riots among commoners, sailors, slaves, military personnel, and sex trade workers. As the enclosures went global, so, too, did the rebellions, and new commons sprang up throughout the new colonies (Linebaugh & Rediker, 2000).

The metaphors of the commons and enclosures have recently been given new currency in debates over globalization and development, global communication, and the Internet. The tragic view of the commons has been reinvoked by neoliberal economists, arguing, as did Adam Smith and the first feudal landlords, that the resource be enclosed under private corporate control in order to stop its unregulated overuse and make it more efficient (Travis, 2000). A second school describes the commons as a "public" resource, which should be managed by state or multilateral international institutions, or public-private partnership. However, a growing number are challenging these arguments, proposing commons regimes as alternative modes of ownership, governance, and communications to corporate and state systems. This vision was drawn on by several of the players in the global justice movement that came of age in Seattle, and that influenced the IMC.

SEATTLE: A NEW NAME FOR AN OLD CAMPAIGN

"Seattle" was the culmination of at least two decades of organizing against the current program of corporate capitalism, variously called neoliberalism, or globalization, whose planks include corporate downsizing, structural adjustment programs (SAPs), privatization and deregulation of public institutions, and free trade and other capital-friendly agreements. Movements of the Right and Left had critiqued the Bretton Woods Institutions, the World Bank, International Monetary Fund, and the newly named WTO, since the 1960s. However, not until the 1980s, and the dissemination of horror stories related to debt-imposition, structural adjustment programs, and the huge dams and mega-projects, did widespread protests target these multilateral institutions and their policies (Cleaver, 1999, p. 8).

The imposition of neoliberal policies during the 1980s displaced thousands from their lands and livelihoods in southern countries and dismantled already bare community infrastructures and social support systems (G. Dalla Costa, 1995). Rural and urban self-help organizations acted to create their own modes of survival, of water, electricity, health, food, and community development, often assisted by a rapidly growing cadre of middle-class professionals from nongovernmental organizations (NGOs), who had stepped in to fill the vacuum left by the state (Alvarez, 1998; Riaño, 1994). Together these popular organizations, NGOs, and activists from the Left, trade union movement, and women's movements protested the global policies of national governments, multilateral organizations, and corporate players in the street, at multilateral forums and through their own communications systems.

Many groups were supported by, or had generated their own alternative media, of newsletters and magazines, low power and community radio, and video and film documentaries. These media featured news reports and analyses, and individual testimonies and stories, often directly from those involved, in contrast to the marginalization of these stories in the corporate media. However, the circulation of these alternative representations was often very local and sporadic due to the lack of resources and of means of distribution.

The development of computer-mediated communications and the Internet provided a new communications technology for production and distribution. During the mid-1980s, NGOs began to adopt these new technologies, which provided them with low-cost access to extensive resources at a global reach and speed, dramatically transforming the possibilities for political organization and action (Eagleton-Pierce, 2001; Smith, 2001). By the late 1980s, a number of international computer networks were formed, such as Greenet, Peacenet, Labornet, and Women's Net, allied with the Association of Progressive Communicators (APC). By 1995, there were eighteen international member networks, in use by 30,000 community activists, educators, policymakers, and nonprofit organizations (Ribeiro, 1998, p. 336).

The vector of organization and mobilization was from south to north. The coalition began with austerity protests in Latin America, the Caribbean, the Middle East, Africa, and Eastern Europe. In the late 1980s, they spread to Western Europe and Canada in demonstrations against privatization, deregulation, and continental standardization reinforced through the Europe Union and the North American Free Trade Agreement (NAFTA). This nascent cross-border organizing continued in face-to-face meetings during multilateral conferences such as the Rio Conference on the Environment in 1992, the Social Development Summit in Copenhagen, and the Beijing Women's Conference in 1995; and in actions against free trade policies such as the North American Free Trade Agreement (NAFTA), the Multilateral Agreement on Investment (MAI), and the Asia Pacific Economic Conference (APEC). After a decade, in no small part reinforced and circulated through this growing alternative communications, mass protests against "corporate globalization" finally reached the United States in Seattle in 1999 (Starr, 2000, p. 46).

THE NEW ENCLOSURES

Two schools characterized this global battle as a renewed conflict between commons and enclosures. One group were longtime critics of international development programs that promoted Western capitalist models. Gustavo Esteva from Mexico and Vandana Shiva from India highlighted the creativity of ordinary people, maintaining their commons heritage amidst their displacement from their lands, traditional knowledges, and ways of life (Esteva, 1993; Shiva, 1994). In 1993, the British magazine, *The Ecologist,* documented a dizzying variety of commons regimes—trees, forests, land, minerals, water, fish, animals, language, time, radio wavelengths, silence, seeds, milk, contraception, and streets—working outside the institutions of both market and state, to create or "defend, open democratic community institutions that ensure people's control over their own lives" (1993, p. 175). An active contributor to the International Forum on Globalization, Vandana Shiva has written: "[W]hat will be the human costs of new enclosures being carved out for privatization of living resources and water resources? . . . Intellectual property rights and water privatization are new invisible cages trapping humanity" (Shiva, 2002, p. 3).

Another school of autonomist Marxists described the neoliberal project as a new enclosure (Midnight Notes, 1992). They documented the commoners' insurrections that connected rioters and protesters from Venezuela, Zambia, South Africa, Algeria, and West Africa, to Europe and North America in the 1980s (Caffentzis, 1995, pp. 34–35; G. Dalla Costa, 1995). They recast the historical thread between commoners, sailors, slaves, sex workers, and soldiers on both sides of the Atlantic during the first centuries of European colonialism (Linebaugh & Rediker, 2000). Mariarosa Dalla Costa described the bridge "thrown through space and historical time" linking the Zapatista "struggles against continued 'primitive' expropriation of the land to those against the post-Fordist expropriation of labor that brings with it the progressive dismantlement of the public system of social rights and guarantees" (M. Dalla Costa, 1994, p. 11). A new global solidarity network of communication and action had emerged, interweaving indigenous movements, workers, ecological movement militants, women's groups, and human rights activists. The bridge between these groups was the continuing struggles for the commons, whose public spaces and ecology provided the possibility of "life, of beauty and continual discovery" (M. Dalla Costa, 1994, p. 13). This new set of commons, three Midnight Notes collaborators wrote, was not about defending "what remains from the past, or what was created under variants of twentieth-century socialism, but . . . to create a multiplicity of mutually supportive new commons" (Neill, 2001, p. 136).[4]

Teasing out these analyses before Seattle, Nick Dyer-Witheford and I reframed the discussion about contemporary communications. "Our new commonwealth . . . is the creation of a 'communications commons'—a counterproject against capital's attempts to 'enclose' the immaterial territories of airwaves, bandwidths, and cyberspaces in the same way it once enclosed the collective lands of the rural commons." The development of new networks of autonomous media, including the alternative press, community radio, public-access TV, micropowered radio, and grassroots computer networking, needs to advance beyond the state-operated public broadcasting favored by an earlier generation of Left media activists (Dyer-Witheford, 1999, p. 203).

THE CYBER COMMONS

More recently, Lawrence Lessig and David Bollier have used the metaphors of the commons and enclosure to describe the resource sharing and social relations of the Internet (Bollier, 2002; Lessig, 2001). Lessig describes the Internet as an "innovation commons," whose open architecture was defined by a freely exchanged layer of "code," or software, providing the logic for the privatized physical layers, or hardware, and the information, or "content." This mix of commons and enclosed layers arose during the Internet's incubation and development among the publicly funded research environment of the U.S. Military's Advanced Research Project Agency (ARPA). Within the network of university research centers associated with ARPA, computer scientists and graduate students developed a social ethos of cooperative design and information sharing. Operating with public money, they exchanged ideas to create a flexible technical architecture, whose Open Source code allowed any end user to develop, improve, and freely share the code, even as it scaled to a size millions of times larger (Bollier, 2002, p. 102). Using easily replicable and shared digital code, the resource was enhanced, rather than limited, through increasing participation (Bollier, 2002, p. 37). By the 1990s, hundreds of individuals and groups, loosely collected in the Open Source movement, shared new software and hardware and created new operating protocols of intellectual property, such as the General Public License, or copyleft, to facilitate their free distribution and prevent their enclosure through privatization (Bollier, 2002, p. 29). While some of these "geeks" or "techies" went on to become entrepreneurs, the early work of this dispersed corps led to a wide variety of computer software and hardware, operating systems, and networks (Bollier, 2002; Witheford, 1997).[5]

This new international class of knowledge workers operates with a concept of collective intelligence antithetical to proprietary ideas of intellectual property (Bosma et al., 1999; Castells 2001). Their mantra is that "information is free" and that technology is a means to liberate information; their role is to allow information to circulate freely without the gatekeepers of nation-state or corporate domain (Castells, 2001, p. 33). While few describe themselves as commoners, many articulate their work in terms of breaking the corporate enclosure of the Internet, or contributing to democracy (Pahati, 2002). Regardless of their self-definition, the Open Source movement and the hacker's movement have had a profound impact on the Net, working to keep the open architecture and challenging the new corporate enclosures, now enforced through U.S. regulation (Dyer-Witheford, 2002). Many of the IMC Tech crew are the next generation of the Open Source movement.

During the 1990s, the Internet commons was threatened as the dominant model of cyberspace shifted from "publicly funded" information sharing to one of private commercial gated space (Menzies, cited in Murphy, 2001b, p. 5). The majority of sites are no longer the .orgs and .govs that operate a decentralized communications network. Much of the traffic is now dominated by the .coms, and the broadcast model, where a small number of global media giants control the cable and telephone distribution pipelines into the Net, the service providers, the most popular sites, and the intellectual property rights on online content. However, this move to fence off or enclose the Net under corporate control has met resistance. A growing number of groups, in the United States and elsewhere, are intervening against state and corporate encroachment, promoting commons-inflected policies and encouraging the development and circulation of Open Source materials.[6] Also, maverick groups and individuals continue to hack the enclosures of corporate systems, as well as defy the privatization of content and software (Witheford, 1997).

SEATTLE INDEPENDENT MEDIA CENTER

The Seattle Indy Media Center represented a leap forward for the communications commons. The global justice movement had engendered many critical collaborations among independent media producers, as well as communications networks among social movements of women, labor, indigenous people, and peace activists (Kidd, 2003). However, many of these efforts had been stymied by the difficulties of sustaining long-term collaborations without stable financing, production facilities, or mechanisms for distribution and promotion; the craft separation into specific media technologies and practices; and rivalries for resources.

The Seattle IMC brought together three sets of commoners from earlier struggles over the cyber and terrestrial commons: techies from the Open Source movement, activist media producers, and social activists from the global justice coalition. Working collaboratively, they overcame some of the earlier technical limits to production, distribution, and as importantly, reception, as real-time audio, text, photos, and video clips circulated horizontally, with few gatekeepers, with a global reach. As well, like every other commons, their contribution was not merely the sum of their technical assets, but their social organization, as they drew on a legacy of organizational and communications skills developed by earlier social movements and media activists (Herndon, 2001).

The initial project wisely drew from activists in several alternative media networks, extending invitations to participate very early on in the planning, fund-raising, and gathering of production equipment.[7] More seasoned media activists worked together with newer producers and activists, using both old and new media. Tom Poole, of Deep Dish TV, said: "In the early '90s, we all knew about each other but folks were more factionalized. Now you can see that there's a more collective effort" (Rinaldo, 2000). The storefront, filled with an array of multimedia equipment and a constant stream of personnel, and only a whiff of tear gas away from the street demonstrations, allowed for bridges between different media, different organizations, and different generations.

The convergence of new and old technologies and platforms allowed for a variety of distribution strategies. The Internet site was supplemented with a daily printed newsheet, live coverage from a downtown micro-radio transmitter, a daily National Radio Project program distributed via satellite, and conventional mail to community radio stations throughout North America. The collaboratively produced "The Showdown in Seattle: Five Days That Shook the WTO," was circulated via the website, as well as via satellite distribution to cable and public television stations, and over land through schools and colleges, labor, and community centers around the world.

The IMC also took advantage of the advancements in digital production equipment. The new lightweight digital cameras and audio recorders are cheap, easy to work with and edit, and can broadcast instantaneously. Eric Galatas from Free Speech TV thinks that television will change dramatically as a result. "There are so many people now picking up DV [digital video] cameras, getting their hands on iMacs or G4s and editing great videos," he said. "I think we're going to look back on this period as a launch pad for an entirely new way of making and distributing television" (Rinaldo, 2000).

Birthed in the high-tech incubator of Seattle, the IMC drew on funds and technical resources. Many of the talented young techies had developed their expertise using peer-to-peer technologies and collaborative protocols in the Open Source movement. Mathew Arnison of the Community Activist Technology (CAT) group in Sydney, Australia, provided the "open publishing" software. Many sites still operate on the same ISP and use Open Source software (Arnison, 2001). The global support crew remains indispensable. Via cyberspace, and often from day jobs in the corporate high-tech world, they share the support and improvement of sites and the network as a whole.

The strength of the Seattle IMC was not just its command of powerful technologies, but the surprise and freshness of their emerging paradigm of autonomous communications (Uzelman, 2002, pp. 85–86). Not only were they independent of the management and ownership of corporate and state media, they also were experimenting with new logics and languages of news, breaking with the professional practices and rational discourses of mainstream news, of much alternative media production, and of the principal NGOS at the Seattle protests (Uzelman, 2002; Wall, 2003).

On the production side of the communications relation, their do-it-yourself approach featured the volunteer crew bringing witness directly from the demonstrators, with the minimum of managing and packaging. On the reception side, their address to audiences was not the come hither tease of network news, drawing the consumer to the ad, but much less mediated and more dialogical, activist to activist, encouraging audiences to provide their own wrap, links, and often background and context.

THE GLOBAL NETWORK

On a radio panel, Sheri Herndon (2002) said: We need a new understanding . . . of how our solidarity can create a network. A lot of time [people] think of [indymedia] as a digital network . . . a digital network is not going to be a threat to the status quo and corporate power. Where the threat is is that we are organizing a coordinated social network and that means improving our communications from the many, to the many and to all the nodes.

The IMC Network has grown very rapidly and become a critical resource for activists and audiences around the world, providing an extraordinary bounty of news reports and commentaries, first-person narratives, longer analyses, links to activist resources, and interactive discussion opportunities. In the beginning, they focused primarily on mobilizations at multilateral summits of neoliberal governance. At each of these meetings, they provided innovative coverage, which often included collaborative initiatives with other media and social movement activists. As the Network has added new member sites, it has widened the scope of its coverage to include local, national, and international campaigns around all of the myriad issues associated with the global justice movement.

Success has not been without external and internal challenges. Increased visibility has brought more attention from national and international security agencies, and both organized and random spammers and hate-mail posters. The IMC crews continue to operate as witnesses at demonstrations, providing a thin skin of protection against greater police violence and a photographic and audio record for the legal teams. However, after the confrontation between demonstrators and police during the spring 2001 FTAA meeting in Quebec City, the FBI raided the Seattle site, based on information from the Canadian Security Force (CSIS). During the Genoa Meeting of the G8 in Genoa, Italy, the Italian police attacked the IMC, beating and arresting everyone inside (Halleck, 2002; Starhawk, 2001). Six months later, riot police stormed into centers around Italy, ostensibly to provide evidence about the violence at the summit. In advance of the meetings of the European Union in Barcelona, Spain, in 2002, the Spanish police announced their tracking of the IMC site, with those of other alternative information networks (Alzaga, 2002). Three sites in Europe have been shut down, either temporarily or permanently, because of legal action: IMC Switzerland 2 because of a lawsuit against the site carrying a cartoon that was perceived as anti-Semitic; IMC Norway because of an alleged copyright violation; and IMC Netherlands because of their link to a German site that authorities had shut down because of that site's earlier posting of an article detailing methods for stopping trains carrying nuclear waste (Roving, 2002).

As troublesome have been the constant inundations to the sites, individual sites, and especially the global Israel and Palestine IMCs, have been systematically hacked. Many others have been plagued with racist, right-wing, or hate-filled commentaries. Solving these problems has not been without controversy, as many have argued against any new gates or gatekeeping protocols. The Open Publishing function has not been withdrawn, but many site crews have become more selective of content, relegating the hate mail to inner or hidden pages, with or without some kind of rating system. In April 2002, partly in response to the spamming problem, a global network decision was made to replace the open IMC homepage newswire with a center page of the most significant stories from sites around the world. This trend toward selection, or at least ranking, of content could lead to a professionalization of new writing and editing (Meikle, 2002a). Or, it could lead to a much more peer-to-peer network, in which audiences are enlisted more actively in curating and editing stories (Meikle, 2002a). The question posed by Sheri Herndon of the original Seattle IMC is whether the IMC crews should be editors or librarians (Herndon, 2003).

The expanded horizon for production and distribution has limited the battles over the resources for media representation, but not eliminated

them. The decentralized network model, and the focus on days of action, dispersed around the globe, helped share the work, which was often made possible through the formation of small, closely knit teams working all out for short periods. However, this carnivalesque pace of production and dependence on individual volunteers is hard to sustain. Those people able to volunteer and to work within the existing social milieu tend to represent a small minority of young, white, male North Americans and Europeans (Rinaldo, 2000). This tendency has been, to an extent, exacerbated by the existing gendered, class, and racialized divisions of labor among media and Internet aficionados, and continues to be an issue of contention in meetings and listserves (Rinaldo, 2000).

Several sites and the Network as a whole have dealt with these problems in creative ways. Many centers carry material from other local alternative and independent media "in an effort to diversify content and promote alternative media as a whole" (Shumway, 2002, p. 9). Local IMC collectives are also working more closely with activist groups outside the white-dominated circles of the global justice movement. For example, in New York, they feature the work of activists involved in the Diallo police brutality case, housing, and AIDS. In Los Angeles, they work in collaboration with Latino community groups. In San Francisco, the site owed its origins to our initiative to bring together activist groups working on key regional issues, such as housing, the prison industrial complex, and the growing response to corporate media dominance (Messman, 2001, Personal Observation).

Since then, a new San Francisco collective has developed a number of special series with groups organizing around the forest, energy, and labor. Following the initial attack on Iraq in the spring of 2003, the San Francisco IMC became a fulcrum of the days of action of the peace movement. Looping cell phones, the micro-powered radio station, San Francisco Liberation Radio, video cameras, and the website, they went around the corporate media blockade to create a real-time discussion between demonstrators in the street, independent and mainstream reporters, and site users in the Bay area and around the world (Angulo, 2003).

In Latin America, the IMC sites all draw on existing social activist groups and communications media. Latin America has a strong tradition of social movement activism and communication. However, telephone lines, computers, Internet access, and volunteer time are limited to a tiny fraction of urban, professional, and upper classes. As Luz Ruiz of Chiapas Media put it, "Most people in Chiapas don't have access to water, let alone the Internet" (Ruiz, 2003). Tim Russo of Chiapas Media told me, "The Internet just doesn't cut it for getting information back to the communities. . . . What is important in solidarity in the south is not so much how to produce information, but how to train people to produce information for themselves, and this is different than what a lot of other indymedia's [in the United States] think"

(Personal Interview, 2002). The Chiapas IMC produces and distributes much of their content using radio, audio cassettes and video, with the Internet primarily for national and international distribution.

In Brasil, they also mix old and new media. In Rio de Janeiro, the IMC has taken video documentaries from favela to university to foster discussion of the upcoming Free Trade Area of the Americas (FTAA) agreement. In Porto Alegre, they use the Internet to gather and circulate news, which is then sent to a network of free and community radio stations. In Sao Paolo, the IMC set up a free Internet center to enable poor people to access it. They also take the video documentaries of demonstrations and land occupations to the neighborhoods, setting up monitors for everyone to watch. Almost all of the IMC centers also distribute printed news-sheets that are photocopied and posted on walls all over the city, because of lack of funds for printed copies (Ortellado, 2003).

Inspired by "Seattle" the Argentina MC grew in fits and starts until the surge of organizing against the national government, and IMF policies, in December of 2001. Since then, a collective has developed that is much more rooted in the ongoing popular struggles in locked out and operating workplaces, neighborhood assemblies, and among the traditional Left parties and independent political and cultural organizations. While they encourage news reports, announcements, and commentaries via their website, they also work off-line, coordinating shows of videos and photos, and workshops on the Internet, journalism, and popular education (Boido, 2003).

Nevertheless, there will have to be very creative solutions to overcome the huge inequalities of resources that exist between North and South, urban and rural, professional and poor, and men and women. One of the important steps, confirmed by Luz Ruiz, is to encourage much more "south–south collaboration: so that she and others from the global south can share experiences, expertise, and connections for their very different contexts (Personal Interview, 2002).

The real tragedy of the European commons was the commoners' limited resources; defenselessness against the combined forces of the wool industry, Parliament, and armed might; and isolation. In contrast, the IMC's global network of dispersed sites, their rapid circulation of information between them, and their connection to the global social justice movement should make the IMC Network much more resistant to enclosure. This will require a commitment to strengthening the connections among news producers, movement groups, and audiences alike, to create a communications commons among all the social networks organizing for a different world vision.

NOTES

1. An earlier work, "Talking the Walk: The Media Enclosures and the Communications Commons," elaborates on the communications commons regimes used by community-based local radio stations (Kidd, 1998).

2. For a discussion of these earlier alternative media networks, see the first and second editions of John Downing's *Radical Media* (1984, 2001), Clemencia Rodriguez's (2001) *Fissures in the Mediascape*, Alfonso Gumucio Dagron's (2001) *Making Waves: Stories of Participatory Communication for Social Change*, and Dee Dee Halleck's (2002) *Hand-Held Visions: The Impossibilities of Community Media*. See also Bruce Girard, Ed. (1992), *A Passion for Radio*, about the World Association of Community Radio (AMARC), and Nancy Thede and Alain Ambrosi, Eds. (1991), *Video: The Changing World*.

3. From the title of a talk given by Vandana Shiva, produced for Alternative Radio Productions by David Barsamian, 1994.

4. There is also an overlap between the work of these groups. Mariarosa Dalla Costa draws on the work of Vandana Shiva, and Gustavo Esteva's work appears in the latest Midnight Notes collection about the Zapatistas (2001).

5. "ARPA-funded labs also gave rise to some of the most important computing innovations of the past generation: electronic mail and e-mail lists, word processing programs, the computer mouse and the Windows computing environment" (Bollier, 2002, p. 103). Outside ARPA, computer techies, working with community-based organizations across North America and Europe developed a wide variety of computer software, hardware, and operating systems, as well as facilitating the movement of free and community nets (Castells, 2001; Gutstein, 1999).

6. See, for example, Meikle, 2002, p. 107; Prelinger, 2002, pp. 263–278; Rheingold, 2003, pp. 203–205.

7. Among these contributors were NY-based Paper Tiger, Changing America, and Free Media Alliance; San Francisco-based Whispered Media, Berkeley Free Radio, the National Radio Project, and Corpwatch; national projects Deep Dish TV, Free Speech TV, Democracy Now, and Fairness and Accuracy in Reporting (FAIR); and international projects Radio for Peace International and Media Island International.

REFERENCES

Alvarez, S. E. (1998). Latin American feminisms "go global": Trends of the 1990s and challenges for the new millennium. In S. E. Alvarez, E. Dagnino, & A. Escobar (Eds.), *Cultures of politics/politics of cultures: Re-visioning Latin American social movements*. Boulder, CO: Westview Press.

Alzaga, L. (2002). Rebellion among the surveilled webs. Znet interactive. http:zena.secureforum.com/interactive/content/display.

Angulo, S. (May 14, 2003). Personal Interview.

Arnison, M. (June 2001). Decisions and diversity: Sydney Indymedia volunteer, Version 0.2. http://www.cat.org.au/maffew/decisions.html.

Boido, P. (May 2003). Indymedia Argentina. Presentation to Our Media Conference 3, Barranquilla, Colombia. URL: ourmedianet.org/eng/om2003/papers2003/Boido_OM3.pdf.

Bollier, D. (2002). *Silent theft: The private plunder of our common wealth*. New York and London: Routledge.

Bosma, J. P., van Mourik Broekman, T. Byfield, M. Fuller, G. Lovink, D. MaCarty, P. Schultz, F. Stalder, M. Wark, & F. Wilding. (1999). *Read me!* Filtered by Net Time: ASCII Culture and the Revenge of Knowledge. Brooklyn: Autonomedia.

Caffentzis, G. (1995). The fundamental implications of the debt crisis for social reproduction in Africa. In M. Dalla Costa & G. Dalla Costa (Eds.), *Paying the price: Women and the politics of international economic strategy.* London: Zed Books.

Castells, M. (1997). *The information age. Economy, society and culture. Volume II: The power of identity.* Oxford: Blackwell Publishers.

———. (2000). *The rise of the network society.* Oxford: Blackwell Publishers.

———. (2001). *The Internet galaxy: Reflections on the Internet, business and society.* Oxford: Oxford University Press.

Cleaver, H. (1995). The electronic fabric of struggle. Online. Internet. Available: http://www.eco.utexas.edu/faculty/Cleaver/zaps.html.

———. (1999). Computer-linked social movements and the global threat to capitalism. Online. http://www.Eco.utexas.edu/faculty/Cleaver/hmchtmlpapers.html.

Dagron, A. G. (2001). *Making waves: Stories of participatory communication for social change.* New York: The Rockefeller Foundation.

Dalla Costa, G. (1995). Development and economic crisis: Women's labour and social policies in Venezuela in the context of international indebtedness. In M. Dalla Costa (Ed.), *Paying the price: Women and the politics of international economic strategy.* London and New Jersey: Zed Books.

Dalla Costa, M. (1994). Development and reproduction. *Common Sense 17,* 11–33.

Downing, J. (1984). *Radical media: The political organization of alternative communication.* Boston: South End Press.

Downing, J. with T. V. Ford, G. Gil, & L. Stein. (2001). *Radical media: Rebellious communication and social movements.* Thousand Oaks: Sage.

Dyer-Witheford, N. (1999). *Cyber-Marx: Cycles and circuits of struggle in high-technology capitalism.* Urbana: University of Illinois Press.

———. (2002). E-capital and the many-headed hydra. In G. Elmer (Ed.), *Critical perspectives on the Internet.* Lantham, MD: Rowman & Littlefield.

Eagleton-Pierce, M. (Sept. 2001). The Internet and the Seattle WTO protests. *Peace Review. Special issue: Social justice movements and the Internet, 13*(3), 331–338.

Ecologist, The. (1993). Whose common future? Reclaiming the commons. Philadelphia and Gabriola Island, B.C.: New Society Publishers.

Esteva, G. (1993). Development. In W. Sachs (Ed.), *The development dictionary: A guide to knowledge and power.* London and New Jersey: Zed Books.

Ford, T. V., & G. Gil. (2001). Radical Internet use. In J. Downing et al. (Eds.), *Radical media: Rebellious communication and social movements.* Thousand Oaks, London and New Delhi: Sage Publications.

Girard, B. (Ed.). (1992). *A passion for radio.* Montreal: Black Rose Books.

Gutstein, D. (1999). e.con: How the Internet undermines democracy. Toronto: Stoddart.

Halleck, D. D. (2002). *Hand-held visions: The impossibilities of community media.* New York: Fordham University Press.

Herndon, S. (20 July 2001). Telephone Interview.

———. (May 2003). Panel Presentation to "Our Media." Barranquilla, Colombia.

Independent Media Center Brochure. (2001). Seattle, WA: Independent Media Center.

Kidd, D. (1998). Talking the walk: the media enclosures and the communications commons. Dissertation. Simon Fraser University.

Kidd, D. (2003). Indymedia.org: A new communications commons. In M. McCaughey, & M. Ayers (Eds.), *Cyberactivism: Online activism in theory and practice.* New York: Routledge.

Lessig, L. (1999). *Code and other laws of cyberspace.* New York: Basic Books.

———. (2001). *The future of ideas: The fate of the commons in a connected world.* New York: Random House.

Linebaugh, P., & M. Rediker. (2000). *The many-headed hydra: Sailors, slaves, commoners, and the hidden history of the revolutionary Atlantic.* Boston: Beacon Press.

Madison IMC. (2002). Independent media journalists discuss the past, present, and future of Indymedia. www.madison.indymedia.org/newswire/display_any/3637.

Martinez, E. (2002). Where was the color in Seattle? In M. Prokosch & L. Raymond (Eds.), *The global activist's manual.* New York: Thunder Mouth Press/Nation Books.

Meikle, G. (2002). *Future active: Media activism and the Internet.* New York: Routledge.

———. (2002a). Indymedia and the new Net news. *M/C Journal.* www.journal.media-culture.org.au/0304/02-feature.html.

Menzies, H. (2001). On digital public space and the real tragedy of the commons. In M. Moll & L. Regan-Shade (Eds.), *e-commerce vs. e-commons: Communications in the public interest.* Ottawa: Canadian Center for Policy Alternatives.

Messman, T. (2001). Justice journalism: Journalist as agent for social change. *MediaFile, 20*(4), 1.

Midnight Notes Collective. (1992). *Midnight oil: Work, energy, war 1973–1992.* Brooklyn NY: Autonomedia.

Midnight Notes. (2001). *Auroras of the Zapatistas: Local and global struggles of the fourth world war,* 2nd ed. Brooklyn: Autonomedia.

Murphy, B. (2001). Propagating alternative journalism through social movement cyberspace: The appropriation of computer networks for alternative media development. In Eglash et al. (Eds.), *Appropriating technology: Vernacular science and social power.* University of Minnesota Press.

———. (2002). Towards a critical history of the Internet. In G. Elmer (Ed.), *Critical perspectives on the Internet.* Rowman & Littlefield.

Neeson, J. M. (1993). *Commoners: Common right, enclosure and social change in England, 1700–1820.* Cambridge: Cambridge University Press.

Neill, M. (2001). Rethinking class composition analysis in light of the Zapatistas. In Midnight Notes (Ed.), *Aurora of the Zapatistas: Local and global struggles of the fourth world war.* Brooklyn, NY: Autonomedia.

Ortellado, P. (May 2003). Panel Presentation to Our Media Conference. Barranquilla, Colombia.

Pahati, O. (January 24, 2002). Digital pirates and the "Warez'Wars." Alternet.

Paton, D. (December 3, 1999). War of the words: Virtual media versus mainstream press. *Christian Science Monitor.*

Pavis, T. (2002). Modern day muckrakers: The rise of the Independent Media Center movement. *OnLine Journalism Review.* USC Annenberg.

Pfaffenberger, B. (Dec. 13, 1999). In Seattle's aftermath: Linux, independent media and the survival of democracy in *Linux Journal*, www.linuxjournal.com/article.

Polanyi, K. (1944/1957). *The great transformation*. Boston: Beacon Press.

Prelinger, R. (2002). Yes, information wants to be free, but how's that going to happen? Strategies for freeing intellectual property. *The Anti-Capitalism Reader*. New York: Akashic Books.

Rennie, E. (2002). Community media: Fenced off or walled out? Finding a space for community in the new media environment. Presented to IAMCR, Barcelona.

Rheingold, H. (2003). *Smart mobs: The next social revolution*. Cambridge, MA: Perseus Publishing.

Riaño, P. (Ed.). *Women in grassroots communication: Furthering social change*. Thousand Oaks, CA: Sage.

Ribeiro, G. L. (1998). Cybercultural politics: Political activism at a distance in a transnational world. In S. Alvarez, E. Dagnino, & A. Escobar (Eds.), *Cultures of politics/politics of cultures: Revisioning Latin American social movements*. Boulder: Westview Press.

Rinaldo, R. (2000). Pixel visions: The resurgence of video activism. Online. Internet. Available www.Lip.org.

Rodriguez, C. (2001). *Fissures in the mediascape: An international study of citizen's media*. Cresskill, New Jersey: Hampton Press.

Roving. (Posted June 15, 2002). Indymedia three years on. Article #647. www.indymedia.org.

Ruiz, L. (July 8, 2002). Personal Interview. San Francisco.

———. (May 2003). Panel Presentation to Our Media Conference. Barranquilla, Colombia.

Russo, T. (July 8, 2002). Personal Interview. San Francisco.

Shiva, V. (1993). Resources. In W. Sachs (Ed.), *The development dictionary: A guide to knowledge and power*. London and New Jersey: Zed Books.

Shiva, V. (1994). The recovery of the commons, a public lecture. Alternative Radio Productions. David Barsamian.

———. (2002). Terrorism as cannibalism. www.zmag.org.

Shumway, C. (2002). Participatory media networks: A new model for producing and disseminating progressive news and information. http://www.reclaim the media.org/stories.php?/story=02/05/216042306.

Smith, J. (Spring 2001). Cyber subversion in the information economy. *Dissent*, 48–52.

Starhawk. (2001). Lifelong activism: Finding the courage, tenacity and love. In N. Welton & L. Wolk (Eds.), *Global uprising: Confronting the tyrannies of the 21st century*. Gabriola Island, B.C.: New Society Publishers, pp. 262–264.

Starr, A. (2000). *Naming the enemy: Anti-corporate movements confront globalization*. London and New York: Zed Books.

Tarleton, J. (Winter 2000). Protesters develop their own global Internet news service. *Mark Nieman Reports, 54*(4) 53.

Thede, N., & A. Ambrosi. (1991). *Video: The changing world*. Montreal: Black Rose Books.

Thompson, E. P. (1968). *The making of the English working class*. Harmondsworth, England: Penguin Books.

———. (1991). *Customs in common*. London: Merlin Press.

Travis, H. (Spring 2000). Pirates of the information infrastructure: Blackstonian copyright and the First Amendment. *Berkeley Technology Law Journal,* *15*(2) 777.

Uzelman, S. (2002). Catalyzing participatory communication: Independent media centre and the politics of direct action. M.A. Thesis, Simon Fraser University.

Wall, M. (2003). Press conferences of puppets: NGOS' vs. street groups' communication in the battle of Seattle. *Javnost/The public. 10*(1), 1–16.

Williams, R. (1976). *Keywords: A vocabulary of culture and society.* New York: Oxford University Press.

Witheford, N. (1997). Cycles and circuits of struggle in high-technology capitalism. In J. Davis, T. Hirschl, & M. Stack (Eds.), *Cutting edge: Technology, information, capitalism and social revolution.* London: Verso.

16

The IMC Movement Beyond "The West"[1]

John D. H. Downing

INTRODUCTION

The confrontation that raged in Seattle on November 30, 1999, and the days following between city, state, and federal law enforcement officers, and activists of many stripes contesting the World Trade Organization's power, policies, and its Council of Ministers' secretive dealings, was a pivotal transition in the growing international movement contesting global neoliberalism (Cohen & Rai, 2000; O'Brien et al., 2000). As Petrella, Udry, and Aguitton (1996, p. 59) put it:

What has been built in the last thirty years is not a globalized economy but the world capitalist archipelago of islands—large and small—in which are concentrated the global scientific and technical capacity (over 92% of world R&D spending, more than 90% of patents and installed digital capacity), the financial power and the symbolic and media power of the current epoch.

In that confrontation in Seattle, the roles of the then brand-new Independent Media Center and of "radical media" of many kinds were of the highest importance. They enabled the opposition organizers to

- Prepare the ground politically and logistically for the demonstrations months beforehand.
- Field at least a hundred or more on-the-spot videographers, audio-interviews, and still photographers among the demonstrators to pool their reportage inside the protest, not at a distance behind police lines.

- Bypass corporate media in order to inform the global public at the time why the protests were taking place, and afterwards about repressive police and jailhouse actions against demonstrators.
- Facilitate widespread international discussion of the issues thereafter.

At the media heart of this political activity during the demonstrations and over the years following—but not in a directive sense—was Seattle's Independent Media Center. In later confrontations in 2000—during the World Bank meeting in Washington D.C., in April, during the Organization of American States meeting in Windsor, Ontario, in June, during the U.S. Republican and Democratic Parties' nomination conventions later that year, during the IMF and World Bank meeting in Prague in November, and over the months that followed in still other places where transnational capital's representatives foregathered to forge their policy priorities—Independent Media Centers have emerged as a dynamic and original force (Downing, 2002a, 2002b).

By "radical media" (Downing, 2001)—or "citizens' media" (Rodríguez, 2001)—I refer to those small-scale media of many technical and genre formats that have no allegiance to corporate, religious, or governmental authority, but rather set out to suborn an oppressive status quo and propose defenses and alternatives to it. Typically they operate as an alternative public sphere in close relationship to political and social movements, a major instance during the Second Cold War having been the Western European anti-nuclear movements' media of the 1980s (Downing, 1988). Currently there is evident a strongly renewed interest in their operation (also Atton, 2001; Couldry, 2000; Fairchild, 2001; Gumucio Dagron, 2001; Halleck, 2001; Hamilton, 2000; Linder, 1999), even though commentators obsessed with bigness tend to note them, if at all, as being of very marginal interest.

In fact, as I have argued at some length in Downing (2001), their historical and contemporary roles within all kinds of social movements have been far greater than our static notions of mainstream media and their quantifiable "audiences" would suggest. Rodríguez (2001), similarly, argues strongly that the analytical frames we use to study large-scale media prompt misguided and irrelevant research questions concerning radical media. A study such as Sreberny-Mohammadi and Mohammadi's (1994) of small-scale media in the Iranian revolutionary movement of the late 1970s testifies to the folly of marginalizing such movement media, as does the long-term impact of *samizdat* through the 1970s and 1980s in the former USSR.

THE GROWTH OF INDEPENDENT MEDIA CENTERS

In less than three years since Seattle, IMCs have mushroomed. As of September 2002, there were some ninety worldwide. They were concentrated mostly in the "West" (i.e., the United States [about 50], Canada [10], Europe [about 20], and Australia and Aotearoa/New Zealand [4]). Usually they began in the process of protest movements organizing a major local confrontation with one or other agency or forum for transnational corporate policymakers, and then they continued on afterwards as a communication node for news about global neoliberal strategies and decisions, and for local conflicts over labor, human rights, and environmental issues in particular.

Their principal technology consisted of a website maintained on one or more servers. However, given the possibilities enabled by digital communication technologies, they mostly functioned as much more than just an informational website in the classic "Seek-and-you-shall-find" printed text mode. Many of them provided photo archives, audio interviews, video files, searchable archives, and a large array of easy hyperlinks to all the other IMCs and to a slew of additional radical organizations and media projects. Many provided real-time video- and audio-streaming of ongoing moments in street confrontations between anti-capitalist[2] demonstrators and the police. In the Seattle case, and in some others (e.g., Genova 2001, São Paulo 2001), video-documentaries were subsequently edited together from the footage shot by many different videographers recording the street contestations and downloaded at the IMC locale.[3] In addition, the IMC websites provided scope for ongoing discussion of both strategies and tactics of the movements, and diagnoses of neoliberal policy initiatives.

The IMCs mostly offered a mode of political communication substantially different from older models of radical movement media, not only technologically but also politically.

Technologically the difference is obvious, not least in the mesh of media technologies enabled by digital platforms. One feature of this mesh is worth emphasizing, namely the use of still photos, sometimes of demonstrations, sometimes of police repression, sometimes of artwork such as murals, graffiti, or newspaper cartoons. High resolution close-up color images of protest actions or of cartoons, that can often be enlarged to fill the entire monitor screen, can serve as an extremely arresting and effective use of the computer medium. If technical facilities include projection on to a large screen for a sizable audience, even more so. Carlini (1996, p. 227) has argued that this expansion from purely textual materials risks moving users toward "less reflective" and more image-centered appropriations of content, but his argument seems to neglect the potential for focusing very reflectively on gripping images that Web technology permits precisely because it is possible to stare at them for as long as one wishes, and to summon them back on to the screen with a few key-strokes.

Politically speaking the IMCs' model of organization was neither Leninist nor Social-Democratic, taking those terms to signify quasi-military and hierarchical in the first case, and legislative/parliamentary in the second. There are so many mistaken preconceptions and alarmist notions about anarchism that one hesitates to use the term; but stripped of its individualistic and terroristic gloss, as of its association with a chaotic disregard for organization, it comes closest to fitting the reality, even though far from a label all IMC activists would adopt for themselves (Downing, 2003). But the IMC ethos and modus operandi were very much ones of providing an *enabling* forum and technical services for a variety of political action groups committed to the centrality of effective mediated communication to their struggles. IMCs sought to impose no central editorial control, and actively encouraged members of the public to post their views and responses.[4] At the same time, in news reporting their general philosophy was to *combine* passion and the quest for accuracy, rather than seeing them as antithetical, as more traditionally minded journalists would tend to do.

Overall, the IMC philosophy was nicely encapsulated in a logo developed by the Italy IMC: Don't Hate the Media—Become the Media!

IMCs BEYOND THE METROPOLITAN NATIONS

The huge inequity between communication technology provision and use in the metropolis, and its availability in the rest of the planet (Hamelink, 2000, pp. 55–106), obviously reproduced itself in the predominant growth of IMCs, in the first three years of their development, within the United States of America, Canada, Europe, and Australia/New Zealand. On one level, this is encouraging, in that there is growing opposition within affluent nations to the damage their corporate elites wreak internationally. On the other hand, the need of communication technologies to assist in political mobilization is not a whit less acute in weak-economy zones of the planet than it is in the OECD countries.

This chapter will focus on a number of the IMCs that have been set up outside the high-income countries: Argentina, Brazil, Colombia, India, Israel, Mexico, Nigeria, Palestine, Russia, South Africa, Uruguay.[5] The inclusion of some of these, such as Israel or Russia, may not fit the definition of classically poor nations such as Paraguay, Myanmar, and Mali, but in every case there is acute, sometimes savage, economic and political conflict involved in which the constructive potential of IMCs could certainly be utilized. At the same time, this is a preliminary analysis of a very new phenomenon. Some of these IMCs were only set up in 2002. It is also only glancingly a user-study, for although it is characteristic of IMCs to encourage postings from activists, and in that sense one can get some flavor of the local involvement from those postings, it would require major resources to assess in each one of these cases just to what degree the IMC in question was truly at the heart of the struggle for political and economic solutions useful to a majority of people. The discussion of each site will proceed according to a regional rather than alphabetical plan.

India (www.india.indymedia.org). November 2000 was the starting date. This was initially one of the most active of the IMCs focused upon here.

As of March 2002 its archives already held sixty-six pages, with about ten postings per page. By September 2002 the flow had slowed somewhat. Its content focused overwhelmingly on India, with rather little about neighboring Pakistan, Bangladesh, Nepal, and Sri Lanka. There were some postings relating to Palestine, Afghanistan, U.S. corporate imperialism, and other non-Indian themes.

The language used was English, meaning that the website contents would be accessible in principle to about 100 million Indian citizens. Whether the avoidance of the other official national languages held further political implications is an interesting question for further research.

Most postings were by citizens resident in the country, although there was a scattering of contributions from the diaspora and from non-native India-watchers in Canada, Australia, England, and elsewhere. Contributors' political line was strongly in favor of Dalit and Adivasi[6] rights, and both news items and postings commented in shock at the explosions of bloody communal violence between Hindus and Muslims that swept Ahmedabad and some other cities in February 2002, as well as in outrage at the active connivance of Gujarat State's BJP government in the slaughter. Voices on the site also spoke out vigorously against the growing practice of female foeticide by Indian parents following amniocentesis procedures, and against the huge Narmada dam project, comparable in scope to China's Three Gorges dam, and its negative environmental and social impact. In September there was a series of postings attacking the government's settlement with Dow Carbide, the successor company to Union Carbide whose Bhopal disaster had killed and maimed so many twelve years previously, a settlement significantly reducing the firm's financial liability to the maimed survivors and the bereaved families.

The threat of a nuclear confrontation with Pakistan in mid-2002 and the ongoing question of Kashmir received less attention than might have been anticipated. There were some rather windy and sententious postings from the Madarai Collective, a group quite often posting to the Indymedia site, but surprisingly these made no reference to the Indian government's long history of suppressing Kashmiri rights and of violently repressing political protest. The notion that Kashmiris might mostly prefer to be more autonomous, directly ruled neither by India nor Pakistan, was not addressed.

The political tone was that of a fairly generic far Left, not identified with any particular grouping or party and not engaging in sectarian polemics. Attitude toward the national BJP governing elite was unremittingly hostile, routinely described as "our fascist government."

The Mumbai site (www.mumbai.indymedia.org) opened in June 2002. Its postings mostly addressed the Dow Carbide cutback in compensation, but were not many in number through September of that year. It was running a little less than one news story of some kind per day, and had a handful of magazine articles as well. It is worth mentioning, if only to stress that all ninety IMC sites were not operating at anything like identical levels of intensity.

Russia (www.russia.indymedia.org). The site was not explicit at the time of writing about the identity of the collective that ran it, though its general orientation appeared to be anarchist. There were no postings listed before March 2002. The text was mostly in Russian, with some links in English to Seattle Indy Media. It had a mixed news magazine and breaking news format, with article-length commentaries about once a month—for example, one on the anti-corporate protests at the Barcelona EU summit (3/16/02), another describing a press conference and public forum held by lawyers representing skinheads accused of racist attacks in the Moscow suburb Tsaritsyno a year earlier (March 6, 2002).

Shorter postings to the right of the page, in the standard Indymedia format, addressed a variety of foreign and domestic issues: the NATO summit in Prague, Greek anarchist protests, a critique of corporate media coverage of the Barcelona summit and another one of advertising directed at children, a hunger strike by a civil rights activist in Kazakhstan, a protest against the psychiatric hospital detention of an anarchist activist named Novozhilov, anti-McDonalds actions, demonstrations in Quito against the Free Trade Association of the Americas, some Kaliningrad environmentalists denouncing Baltic Sea water pollution. There seemed considerably less energy and focus in spring 2002 than was visible in the initial phase of the India IMC, or the two next examples, though by fall 2002 there were on average several postings a day. In August-September, topics also included an event in Strasbourg expressing opposition to the war in Chechnya, a demonstration outside MVD headquarters in Moscow against the policy of stopping Chechen refugees from returning to Chechnya, and commentary on savage police violence against punk rock bands in the repressive neighboring regime of Belarus.

Israel (www.indymedia.org.il). Begun in September 2001 and based in Tel Aviv, this IMC focused for its first year pretty well exclusively on the Palestinian–Israeli conflict.[7] The site was definitely energetic, creating some fifty postings a day in March 2002, and in September major postings every two to three days. Divisions or conflicts internal to Israeli society (e.g., over religious observance, Ashkenazi–Sephardi relations, the very large new Russian-origin community) were rarely commented upon or analyzed, though one of the exceptions was an item posted in August 2002 on the government's refusal to allow in a group of Eritrean and Ethiopian asylum-seekers, despite its being a signatory to world refugee and human rights conventions. Some postings were by Arab analysts, such as Brenda Awad's (March 15, 2002) describing the Israeli military's attacks on civilians in the Occupied Territories, others by international commentators. The site maintained postings in English, Hebrew, and Arabic.

Critiques of Israeli government policy toward Palestine were energetic and searching, including some based upon readings of Herzl, the ideological founder of Zionism, and of the political and economic policies pursued by the first Zionist settlers in the 1880s. There were also debates, for example over the March 2002 Saudi Arabian proposal for a final settlement of the Israeli–Palestinian conflict. About two to four postings were appearing a day in spring 2002, some of them reprinted from other sources such as the Israeli left-leaning daily *Haaretz* and *Al Ahram,* Egypt's newspaper of record.

The site maintained close links with the Israeli activists in Peace Now and with the Israeli human rights advocacy group, B'Tselem, and reproduced their press statements and research documents. At the same time, the approach to human rights went well beyond simply a tragic list of those killed and maimed and addressed four-square the political dimension involved, namely the Occupation, and what the site's contributors fairly uniformly identified as Premier Sharon's and other leaders' determination to maintain the conflict at a steady high temperature, including continuously expanding the settlements (thirty-four new ones in the twelve months since Sharon's February 2001 election). Prominence was given to the Refusenik Watch tally of the growing number of Israeli soldiers refusing to serve in the Occupied Territories while pledging to defend the pre-1967 borders. An ongoing daily headcount was maintained at the site of such individuals—over 400 as of fall 2002.

One posting by a university professor (March 17, 2002) noted a survey showing that the Sharon and Netanyahu factions in the political class were far ahead of most Israeli opinion, for only 24 percent of Israelis wanted to keep all the settlements intact, while 32 percent wanted to see them all wound up entirely. He questioned why it was that such information was so little available in Israel's mainstream media. A U.S. analyst posted an article reviewing Israel's nuclear weapons arsenal and strategy (March 21, 2002). Uri Avnery, long-term leader of Peace Now, argued that "denial, misrepresentation and liquidation" constituted the standard three-phase strategy used by successive Israeli administrations to scotch any attempts at peace negotiations, and warned that it would be the way the Saudi peace initiative would be handled (March 4, 2002).

In May 2002 the collective was subjected to police harassment, in the shape of the Computer Crimes division demanding to know about an article received but not published some six weeks previously, alleging that mass murder units were being developed by the Israeli government capable of killing four thousand people an hour. Like many of the other Indymedia sites, the Israel site held to a minimal editorial interference policy, based on the following criteria for what it would block: (1) direct calls for violence; (2) directly racist statements; (3) publications that attempt to directly market goods; and (4) information which can be proven to be false. The fact this posting had only been seen by and was only accessible to members

of the editorial board was easily ascertainable, and thus the police intervention represented the second time in two months that attempts had been
made to intimidate Israel Indymedia.

Palestine (www.jerusalem.indymedia.org). This site was officially opened
only on March 22, 2002. It functioned in English and Arabic. Its organizers described themselves as mostly refugees from areas occupied by Israel,
and as wanting to set up "a truly free forum for the Palestinian people who
choose to participate." They went on to state:

> Our mission is to help Palestinian activists organise, motivate and inform. We want
> to help people develop the art of story telling and debate. We want to be a catalyst
> for those stories to reach into other media and parts of the planet. We want to break
> down barriers and encourage the flow of information from people with both good
> and bad stories to tell, to the people we know are out there who want to hear them.
> We want to create a physical and virtual space that creates a sense of achievement
> and reflection but is vibrant and open enough to attract people who are interested
> in activism; while remaining practical and focussed to encourage all people in our
> audience to contribute.

During the Israeli military assault on Ramallah and the Palestinian
Authority leadership's compound at the end of March 2002, the IMC site
was active along with its Israeli counterpart in giving repeated updates on
events, as well as marking protests around the world, especially in Europe
and the United States. News was given prominence of Israeli soldiers firing
on ambulances and of Israeli refusals to allow the Red Cross to the zone of
fighting. One of the news photographs reproduced of the international
protests featured women demonstrators in Boston, Massachusetts, holding
a placard with the words *Jewish Women for Justice in Israel/Palestine*.
Another press photograph showed Neturei Karta International, a strictly
Orthodox Jewish group opposed to Zionism, publicly burning an Israeli
flag, and announcing in a press statement:

> The Zionist experiment has reached its inevitable conclusion. Death tolls mount and
> no viable solution is in sight. Slowly the Jewish people are awakening to the reality
> of Zionism, its rejection of Torah views of exile and redemption, combined with its
> aggressive stance towards Gentiles in general and Palestinians in particular. By burn-
> ing the Israeli flag we are symbolically declaring that the Israeli state, contrary to its
> absurd claims, is not representative of the Jewish people. In fact, its denial of our
> faith and its brutalization of the Palestinian people, renders it antithetical to Judaism.

By fall 2002 the site included regular updates from Palestinian cities cut
off from each other by the occupation and the curfew: Bethlehem, Gaza,
Hebron, Jenin, Nablus, Ramallah, and Tulkarm. It carried an open peace-
focused letter from a Jewish American to Palestinian academic and activist
Hanan Ashrawi (though he misspelt her name as Asharwi), some items from

the left-leaning Israeli daily *Haaretz* and one from *Newsweek* on the U.S. role in supporting Saddam Hussein in earlier years. There was evidence, however, that rightist activists were trying hard to drown the debate site with saturation postings sneering at any and all claims for Palestinian rights: On 9/15/02 alone, "Average Jeff" contributed seventeen such out of forty-nine postings, and a number of others were in the same vein. It was not clear why they permitted individuals like "Average Jeff" to crowd up their site.

However, as of late August 2002, reports began to surface that the site was in danger of being taken over by orthodox Marxists from the Popular Front for the Liberation of Palestine, who were refusing involvement to any who did not share their beliefs. At the time of writing this situation had not been resolved. If so, it is a real pity, another chapter in leftist political machinations. Initially the Palestinian site was clearly run by people refusing the slide into racist rage that dominated much public opinion in both nations during the second Intifada. These lone voices in the midst of war hysteria are both brave and visionary, and represent a major lifeline to the future. But at times we have no need of the state or of corporate power to subvert our best efforts.

Nigeria (www.nigeria.indymedia.org). The first posting was dated November 5, 2001. The collective behind this IMC appeared to be dominated by Earth First! Nigeria. The language was only English, which along with Pidgin is the nearest to a lingua franca that the country currently has. The site thanked activists in the Urbana-Champaign IMC in the United States for their technical help.

A majority of postings were not about Nigeria, but those that did focused particularly upon the continuing ecological damage caused in the oil-rich Delta region by Shell, Chevron, Mobil, and Texaco; the lethal violence regularly meted out to protesters by the Nigerian Army units posted to guard the oil company sites, a repression that the companies piously claimed was none of their making; women's protests against Chevron; widespread protests across Nigeria against the sharp hike in gasoline prices in December 2001, representing a step toward an economic order more acceptable to the IMF, but deeply angering to ordinary Nigerians who for four decades since Independence have seen their oil riches vanish into their own tyrants' and oil company pockets; and a lengthy Human Rights Watch report on positive and negative developments in Nigeria.

There was rather little news about the rest of the continent, sadly reiterating a very common phenomenon throughout Africa as also of Latin America, namely the continuing news deficit about both nearby and more distant neighbor nations. There was one posting from the Kenyan newspaper *The Nation* covering a slum area women's protest in Nairobi against the eruption of inter-tribal violence, but in a sense this posting confirmed the standard press pattern: no background, no follow-up, news of tragedy and violence only.

While editorial controls are light to nonexistent in many IMCs, in this instance they seemed absent, and thus permitted some real cranks to share their weirdness with others. An example is the posting from a self-styled pastor of the Global Crusaders Church Incorporated from Benin City, who claimed at great and semiarticulate length how he had personally foiled twenty-seven military coups, and complained bitterly that President Obasanjo had never taken the trouble to thank him. There was even a white supremacist and anti-semitic posting permitted.

As of the time of writing, the Nigerian IMC was the weakest of those studied for this chapter, even though it had a couple of postings a day of various kinds.

South Africa (www.southafrica.indymedia.org). This IMC emerged in the runup to the World Conference Against Racism in Durban in August 2001. Most of the postings were about local points of social struggle, though these were explicitly tied in with global capitalism. Prominent among them were South Africa's terrifying AIDS crisis and TAC, the Treatment Action Campaign that was challenging President Mbeki's resolute determination to avoid confronting the AIDS issue. Also prominent were news items covering evictions for nonpayment of services/utilities bills (e.g., in Delft South in the Western Cape), or for squatting, in Valhalla Park, Cape Town, where the city council had allocated land and promised housing, but where when none was forthcoming the residents organized their own, along with basic services, including toilets. Other posts dwelt on water cutoffs for nonpayment—for example, in Tafelsig, Western Cape, where residents protesting with burning tires were attacked with police batons and rubber bullets, and a number were hospitalized.

There were posts on other issues, whether Palestine, South Korea, or Spain, but once again remarkably little if any coverage at all of the rest of the African continent.

When describing economic struggles of the kind noted previously, the tone of the posts was reasonably descriptive. There was considerable vituperation, however, not merely for President Mbeki in relation to the AIDS crisis, but more generally for what was described as the "coalition" among the African National Congress/South African Communist Party and labor union federation COSATU, which the South African IMC defined as simply stooges of transnational corporate capitalism. There was a sectarian tone to the language reminiscent of ultra-leftist splinter grouplets of the 1970s, a sense that the more superciliously and utterly dismissive the tone, the closer the world would draw to a definitive solution to its problems. One letter critiquing this style and attacking the collective for claiming the IMC mantle to legitimize themselves was published on the site (9/7/01), but otherwise it continued pretty well unabated.

On the other hand, some useful materials also found their way on to the site, such as a very good critique of the claim frequently heard in the white community that South Africa is suffering from a "culture of nonpayment" for utilities or for rented accommodation dating back to the apartheid era confrontations. It was provided by a Queens University, Ontario, academic living in Canada, not by a local, but was a lot stronger and more useful than a number of the local postings.

Unfortunately the South African IMC also appeared somewhat weak in comparison to some of the others we are reviewing here. By fall 2002, though, its pace had quickened, and it took in a series of protests held around the time of the World Summit on Sustainable Development in Johannesburg. Postings compared the repression of these and other local citizens' protests about living conditions with apartheid-state tactics.

Mexico. There were three IMC sites in Mexico: the first in San Cristóbal de las Casas, Chiapas, established in February 2001, the second in Mexico City,[8] founded in June 2001, and the third in Tijuana founded in April 2002.

The Chiapas site [www.chiapas.indymedia.org], as of fall 2002, ran its feature columns quite often in both Spanish and English (the latter a little fractured, but fully understandable). Its focus was in substantial part on indigenous rights, the Zapatista movement, the federal and local state's attempts to repress it, including by paramilitary groups, and on the immediate southern region of the country. A number of postings later in 2002 attacked President Vicente Fox's proposed Puebla-Panamá Plan, in the government's view an attempt to stimulate development under Mexican hegemony both of southern Mexico and of Central America. For the Chiapas site collective, this signified a corporate onslaught that would be most likely to reduce living standards for the majority.

The Mexico City site (www.mexico.indymedia.org) ran articles, lengthy audio interviews, and still photos, including photos of political murals and a file of 100 photos of March 2002 demonstrations in Monterrey against the UN conference on world poverty, which it defined as a pretense at making constructive policies to address the situation. It made much of the demonstration's principal slogan, "We don't want them to give us a hand unless they get off our backs!" (No queremos que nos den una mano si no que nos la quiten de encima!).

The site also carried materials such as a map specifying the geographical disposition of the military within the State of Chiapas, articles on protests by Chicano activists in Los Angeles and New York City, a leaked Canadian government document setting out intelligence definitions of anti-WTO activists, and an article (in English) claiming the 9/11 attacks on the World Trade Center were actually committed by the U.S. government (though not with any anti-Semitic content). Many posts were offered in both Spanish and English, and occasionally one from a Brazilian source would be in Portuguese.

Rather like the Russian IMC in this regard, only seemingly with more energy behind it, the Mexico City IMC was organized like a news magazine, mostly offering long-ish articles. These included translations into English from the leftist Mexican weekly *La Jornada,* frequent translations from Zapatista communiqués, and translations of Chomsky into Spanish. There were intermittent postings from elsewhere in the Americas, namely Brazil, Colombia, Bolivia, Puerto Rico, Haiti, the United States, and still further afield from Egypt, Sweden, Switzerland, and elsewhere. Other postings concerned events in Argentina, Palestine, Ecuador, and elsewhere. There were a great number of postings on 9/11, perhaps reflecting Mexico's geographical and—post-NAFTA—political proximity to the United States.

Colombia (www.colombia.indymedia.org). There was no clear indication when this IMC started, but the first posts appeared to date from May 2001. As of March 2002 there were about six to nine short posts a day, mostly in Spanish, a few in English. By September of the same year there was usually one feature posting a month, usually focusing on general themes, the Free Trade Association of the Americas project, the significance of May 1, and a local anti-corporate globalization project in the northernmost province of the country.

February 2002 was dominated by one domestic issue, namely the sudden cancellation of peace negotiations by Colombian President Pastrana with FARC, the leading guerrilla group (Fuerzas Armadas Revolucionarias Colombianas), which had been in armed conflict with successive governments for many years previously. The aborted negotiations were followed very swiftly by—obviously carefully preorchestrated—military swoops and sweeps in many parts of the country. The involvement of the U.S. military, initially under the banner of the so-called "War on Drugs," and then inexorably against the guerrillas in a scenario that resembled the Salvadoran situation at the end of the 1970s, was a further dimension of the crisis. The site carried a chronology of the peace process to date, statements on the breakdown of negotiations from Pastrana, by the FARC, by the former Peace Assembly, and by a group called Peace Colombia. Overall the critical civil war situation, with its long historical roots, not surprisingly dominated the site, in a way reminiscent of the Palestinian and Israeli IMCs.

The other issue that dominated postings earlier in the month was the World Social Forum meeting in Porto Alegre, Brazil. The site carried lengthy dossiers on three issues addressed in Porto Alegre that especially closely concerned Colombians, namely labor issues, foreign debt issues, and biogenetics. These were not the only foreign materials on the site, but even there the primary focus was on Latin America, with occasional postings about countries further away, such as Nepal or the Philippines.

Again like some other sites, editorial intervention was minimal, and one day in March 2002 the site carried a warning repeated in four subsequent posts from long-term neo-fascist U.S. activist Lyndon Larouche, warning that the U.S. government was on the edge of taking over the government of Argentina. But such nonsense was relatively rare on this site.

Brazil (www.brasil.indymedia.org). The first Brazilian IMC began in São Paulo during the mobilization against the Free Trade Association of the Americas summit in Québec City in April 2001. Although the Québec City demonstrations—and the huge wall built to keep the demonstrators from communicating directly with the summiteers—received the most international media attention, the São Paulo confrontation was a major event as well, marked by equally vigorous police repression of the demonstrators.

The Brazil IMC was very active. It particularly featured a great number of still photos, and a substantial number of magazine-length articles. Each day brought two to three news updates. The basic news items were available in English, Spanish, and even Esperanto—a throwback to the tradition of some anarchist groups a hundred years ago—as well as Portuguese. It ran special dossiers on the Argentine crisis and the Middle East crisis, and maintained a calendar of meetings of global corporate powerholders (the World Bank, the FTAA, the UN, G8, the Council of Europe, etc). It ran hyperlinks to articles by Tariq Ali, Naef Al-Zari, M. A. Bastenier, Mauricio Campos, Noam Chomsky, Eduardo Galeano, Antonio Martins, José Saramago, and others.

Its scope was Latin American, hemispheric and global, as well as national. Internationally, for example, it ran material from a variety of sources noting the instant use of the 9/11 attacks by governments around the world as a rationale for repressing their opposition movements. As regarded Brazil, it particularly focused on the long-running Landless Movement of agricultural workers in the country's northeast, and on urban squatters' and homeless people's movements.

However, its emphasis on visual imagery was particularly strong, carrying pungent cartoons by the Lebanese-Brazilian artist Latuff, one of which was entitled Boomerang Politics and showed the World Trade Center towers being hit, not by planes, but by two boomerangs, each one labeled American Interventionism. Another, entitled "Gotcha!" (Te peguei!), showed Uncle Sam carrying two enormous pistols with tags dangling from them portraying the black-on-yellow nuclear radiation symbol, but gasping with pain and in shock as a plane slams into his testicles. The Brazil IMC had also produced a twenty-two minute documentary on the FTAA confrontation in São Paulo, entitled, "It didn't start in Seattle, it won't end in Québec" (Não começou em Seattle, não vai terminar em Québec)—a nice indirect reminder that the anti-corporate movement is global, not merely North American. As of fall 2002, it was running twenty posts a day on average, focusing on the national economic crisis and movements contesting capitalist solutions to it. But there were also posts on the tense situation in Colombia, on police invasion of a micro-radio station premises in Rio de

Janeiro, and on the Johannesburg Summit. The site ran little or nothing on the impending national elections that fall, which foreign corporate media seemed only able to define as a gripping suspense story (would the socialist activist candidate Luiz Ignacio da Silva, known as Lula, change his spots or not?). For Indy Media Brazil, the dynamics of the economic and political situation could in no way be reduced to that pathetic reduction of the process to the viewpoint of a single presidential candidate.

Argentina (www.argentina.indymedia.org). This IMC began about the same time as the Brazil IMC, specifically on April 7, 2001. It was the most active, at the time of writing, of all the IMCs discussed in this chapter, claiming 18,000 archived items, and showing twenty-four lead entries on the single day of March 28, 2002, alone. Since Argentina has become the supreme icon of the failure of free-market fundamentalism, reneging on a foreign bank debt of $US141 billion despite having pegged its peso to the U.S. dollar for almost a decade, and since it has a highly educated and urbanized public, it is fitting that the Argentina IMC should be such a center of energy. Its focus was almost entirely on Argentina, which in Latin American circles might be sniffed at as cultural narcissism only too typical of the country, but its location in the eye of the neoliberal needle meant that its experience and the outcome of its public mobilizations were of vital interest globally. Just as Iran and Vietnam in the 1970s were the supreme failed test-cases of U.S. foreign politics and economic policy, of the U.S. corporate elite's collaboration with high-level repression and corruption, so Argentina became the transnational corporate elite's analogous successor nation in the zeroes of the new century.

The Argentina IMC collective defined their mission thus:

Indymedia has no fixed offices or facilities; from a *locutorio*,[9] from a house, from a borrowed computer, Indymedia is growing and multiplying every day, allowing expression to all tendencies, but without subordinating itself to any of them in particular . . . and emphasizing those which are at the heart of things.

The collective also cited with approval both the Chiapas Indymedia self-description as "the voice of the voiceless" (la voz de los que no tienen voz), and the insistence of Rodolfo Walsh, a famous and courageous Argentinean journalist who ran a clandestine news service at the outset of the military dictatorship in 1976–1983 and was killed by the junta in 1977, that "every human being is a reporter" (cada persona es un corresponsal).

Argentina throughout the life of the IMC was marked not only by economic disruption and public protests against it, but also by a growing popular revulsion with the whole political class and its performance stretching back to the days of the military dictatorship. This revulsion had been fed by public confessions and revelations in the later 1990s from and about former torturers, the military top brass that directed them, and the sequestration of their victims' infant children. A pattern of street protests emerged known as *escraches* (Kaiser, 2002), in which the demonstrators would converge on a former torturer's house and publicly denounce him, writing huge graffiti on the walls and throwing cans of red paint against his building. The Argentina IMC covered these escraches with both text and photos, for example one in which a former torturer had been admitted to hospital and the demonstrators outside the building shouted "Clap your hands, clap your hands, keep on clapping, the bastard Bergés has to die!" (Aplaudan, aplaudan, no dejen de aplaudir, Bergés hijo de puta se tiene que morir!).

As the Argentinean economic and political crisis wore on, the site continued in very high gear, defining its mission as giving hope to people who were perpetually being told by mainstream media, "You're fucked, and you can't do anything to change it" (Estás jodido y no podés hacer nada para cambiarlo). Instead they concentrated their information on the numerous challenges to state and corporate policies throughout the nation, including the success of a Mapuche Indian community in getting a snowboarding resort closed because of its ecological damage.

Before leaving the Argentina IMC, a couple of technological observations are in order: The server this IMC used was actually located in the state of Colorado, USA, and a new one was in the process of being configured with help from Indymedia San Francisco. This is an index of two things: both the mixture of politically specific location and placelessness characterizing digital media—IMCs in particular (Downing, 2002b)—and global solidarity between activists.

Uruguay (www.uruguay.indymedia.org). The first postings appear to have been in January 2002. Although its initial productivity was nowhere near Indymedia Argentina's, there were several postings a day as of March 2002. By fall 2002 however, as Uruguayans found themselves dragged more and more rapidly into the economic meltdown affecting Argentina, the pace had quickened, with four to five daily postings. There seemed to be particular interest in audio-files in the Uruguay IMC, with six available at the time of writing: two on Italy, one on Guatemala, one on the casualties in Afghanistan, and two with Uruguayan themes (Sara Méndez, a child of disappeared parents from the military dictatorship era, managed to establish her true parents by DNA testing; and political contests leading up to Uruguay's elections).

Unlike the Argentina IMC the Uruguay IMC initially focused very intensively on international issues, Argentina itself, Colombia, Puerto Rico, Zimbabwe, the second Asia Pacific International Solidarity conference in Sydney, Australia, and global corporate elite meetings in Fortaleza, Brazil, or the UN "poverty" meeting in Monterrey, Mexico. The collective also provided news of meetings to challenge the status quo, such as the "Reclaim Your Media" demonstration of 20,000 strong in Rome against the virtual one-person media monopoly of Italian premier Berlusconi, and the World

Social Forum meeting in Porto Alegre. A few postings were in Portuguese or in English.

By fall 2002 topics included protests against the use of genetically modified foods; defense of community radio stations, which were being blamed by the government for encouraging looting of supermarkets during the economic crisis; and once more the story of the detained and disappeared in Uruguay. The first page carried a listing of first national and then international events of importance with hyperlinks to each.

CONCLUSION

Briefly, we have seen the considerable variety of emphases and levels of energy that have been in play in these non-"Western" Independent Media Centers. They are a very recent but particularly interesting phenomenon in terms of challenges to the strategic failures of corporate media and the difficulty of grassroots movements in finding ways to circulate their views and experiences horizontally, especially on a global scale. As the examples previously cited illustrate, each Indymedia site embraces the local and the global in different proportions, but mostly tries to act as a service operation rather than with any aims at hegemonic influence over political movements.

The concentration of IMCs in either affluent nations or among users with fairly high educational levels—which often implies an affluent family background, given the normal class structure of educational provision—means they are not instantaneously the property of the poorest or the most powerless. At the same time, they do establish *international political connectivity* of a kind not tied in most cases to a particular political party or sect, and therefore much more open to debate and the working through of different emphases and strategies. It is to be hoped that they will consolidate and proliferate, both.

A question that must be left hanging, but that is of central importance, is the role women play in these centers. I will close on a tantalizing note by observing that in all the Spanish-language Latin American IMCs, where there is a box to click on for further information called "About Us," it is written in every case Acerca de Nosotr@s—Spanish rigorously distinguishes gender, but takes the masculine as inclusive, which would normally mean writing Nosotros. In each case however the address symbol is used for the final vowel, visually combining Nosotros (males, or inclusive) and Nosotras (women). For some people in these IMCs, at least, the linguistic reinforcement of gender hegemony is to be resisted as well.[10] An encouraging small sign.

NOTES

1. An earlier version of this chapter was presented at a conference on international and intercultural communication at the Beijing Broadcasting University Institute in March 2002.

2. I say "anti-capitalist" because "anti-globalization" can easily be misread as globalophobia, which is typically not a vice of these movements, as the IMCs' stress on international information and solidarity makes very clear.

3. E.g., *Showdown in Seattle* (Indymedia, 2000) and *This Is What Democracy Looks Like* (Big Noise Films, 2000).

4. Inevitably, extremist rightists in the United States sought to abuse this openness in order to push their destructive agenda. The response, after considerable debate on the website, was to install a quasi-editorial function, namely to file those postings to a separate folder so that the public could inspect them at any time if it wished. In the context of a very active free political speech lobby in the United States, this was an imaginative technical solution to balancing the two objectives entailed.

5. Between the first version of this chapter, presented to a conference at the Beijing Broadcasting Institute in April 2002, and the revised version for this volume completed in September, new IMCs opened up in Mumbai, Jakarta, Quito, Tijuana, Bolivia, and Rosario, Argentina. Given their recency at the time of writing, I have only added in the Mumbai site, at the editors' suggestion, so as to be able to review its approach to the high-intensity conflict between the Indian and Pakistani governments during 2002.

6. *Dalit,* members of the caste referred to often as "Untouchables," and *Adivasi* are one of the tribal groups fighting to realize their rights under India's constitution.

7. An exception was an article on the proposed Mediterranean Free Trade Zone (3/10/02) by Friends of the Earth Middle East.

8. As with a number of IMCs, clicking on About Us reveals a short statement of media philosophy and priorities but very little about the protagonists themselves. I deduced the site was in Mexico City because of words in a report on the demonstrations against the UN World Poverty Conference in Monterrey in March 2002, where the writer was acknowledging the anxiety of some demonstrators from Mexico City before the event that the very conservative city might be hostile to *chilangos,* the standard and generally unflattering Mexican term for people from Mexico City (drawing on the usual stereotypes in any country of capital city denizens). In fact they were very pleasantly surprised by the warmth with which they were greeted, but the use of the term indicated the normal location of these IMC activists.

9. "In the 00s" became a term in Argentina to describe little storefront businesses where people could make phone calls, national or international, some serving also as Internet centers. Their growth was a response to the privatization of telecommunications and the consequent high cost of home phone service. My thanks to Professor Susana Kaiser of the University of San Francisco for clarifying this word for me.

10. The Brazil IMC avoids the issue by entitling the box "About the IMC."

REFERENCES

Atton, C. (2001). *Alternative media.* London, UK: Sage Publications Co.

Carlini, F. (1996). *Internet, Pinocchio e il Gendarme: le prospettive della democrazia in rete.* Roma: Manifestolibri.

Cohen, R., & Rai, S. M. (Eds.). *Global social movements.* London UK: The Athlone Press.

Couldry, N. (2000). *The place of media power: pilgrims and witnesses of the media age.* London, UK: Routledge.

Downing, J. (1988). The alternative public realm: the organization of the 1980s antinuclear press in West Germany and Britain. *Media, Culture & Society, 10*(2), 163–181.

———. (2001). *Radical media: Rebellious communication and social movements.* Thousand Oaks, CA: Sage Publications Inc.

———. (2002a). Independent Media Centers: A multi-local, multi-mediatic challenge to global neoliberalism. In Marc Raboy (Ed.), *Global media policy.* Luton UK, Luton University Press.

———. (2002b). *The Indymedia phenomenon: Space-place-democracy and the new Independent Media Centers,* presented at the BOGUES: Globalisme et Pluralisme conference in the University of Québec, Montréal, April 2002: http://www.er.uqam.ca/nobel/gricis/even/bog2001/b2_pr_f.htm.

———. (2003, Forthcoming). The Independent Media Center movement and the anarchist socialist tradition. In N. Couldry & J. Curran (Eds.), *Contesting media power.* Lanham, MD: Rowman & Littlefield.

Fairchild, C. (2001). *Community radio and public culture.* Cresskill NJ: The Hampton Press.

Gumucio Dagron, A. (2001). *Making waves: Participatory communication for social change.* New York: Rockefeller Foundation.

Halleck, D. D. (2001). *Handheld visions.* New York: Fordham University Press.

Hamelink, C. (2000). *The ethics of cyberspace.* London, UK: Sage Publications Co.

Hamilton, J. (2000). Alternative media: Conceptual difficulties, critical possibilities. *Journal of Communication Inquiry, 24*(4), 357–378.

Kaiser, S. (2002). Escraches, demonstrations, communication and political memory. *Media, Culture & Society 24*(4), 499–516.

Linder, L. R. (1999). *Public access television: America's electronic soapbox.* Westport CT: Greenwood Publishing Group.

O'Brien, R., Goetz, A. M., Scholte, J. A., & Williams, M. (2000). *Contesting global governance: Multilateral economic institutions and global social movements.* Cambridge UK: Cambridge University Press.

Petrella, R., Udry, C. A. & Aguiton, C. (1996). Espropriati del mondo, costruiamo insieme un'altra globalizzazione. In F. Houtart & F. Polet (Eds.), *Globalizzazione delle Resistenze e delle Lotte: l'altra Davos.* (pp. 53–61) Bologna: Editrice Missionaria Italiana.

Rodríguez, C. (2001). *Fissures in the mediascape.* Cresskill NJ: The Hampton Press.

Sreberny-Mohammadi, A., & Mohammadi, A. (1994). *Small media, big revolution: Communication, culture and the Iranian revolution.* Minneapolis: University of Minnesota Press.

Index

260

Index

About the Editors and Contributors

TED M. COOPMAN is a community and media activist and scholar. He has written extensively on the Micro Broadcasting Movement, media regulation and law, activists' use of the Internet, media democracy, and dissent. His research has been featured in the *Journal of Broadcasting and Electronic Media,* the *Journal of Radio Studies,* and the *American Communication Journal.* His book reviews have appeared in several journals, including the *Southern Journal of Communication.* He serves on the board of directors of the American Communication Association (ACA) and has acted as book review editor for its journal. He is a member of the Santa Cruz Independent Media Center collective and operates Rogue Radio Research, a resource and information guide for Free Radio and Low Power FM. He holds an M.S. in Mass Communications from San Jose State University and currently is a student in the Communication doctoral program at the University of Washington.

SASHA COSTANZA-CHOCK is a graduate student at the Annenberg School for Communication, University of Pennsylvania. He studies political economy of communication with a focus on the use of new technologies by social movements. Costanza-Chock also works with Hip Hop Against Infinite War (www.bignoisefilms.com/infinitebeatz) and Communication Rights in the Information Society (www.crisinfo.org). e-mail: schock@asc.upenn.edu

JOHN D. H. DOWNING teaches in the Radio-Television-Film Department at the University of Texas at Austin. As of late 2002, he was editing an

Encyclopedia of Alternative Media (Sage Publications Inc., California) and completing a book, *Representing 'Race,'* written jointly with Charles Husband of Bradford University, U.K., on fresh and comparative approaches to the study of racism, ethnicity, and media (Sage Publications Co., U.K.).

PATRICK F. GILLHAM is a doctoral candidate in Sociology at the University of Colorado in Boulder. His research focuses on the influence of social movement organizational attributes on role and tactical decisions during contentious episodes against the WTO, World Bank, and IMF. Other work includes examination of high-risk participation in the environmental movement and explaining shifts in the global justice movement and policing following the September 11, 2001, terrorist attacks on Washington, D.C. and New York City.

DOROTHY KIDD is active in the growing media democracy movement. She teaches Media Studies at the University of San Francisco. Her historical study about international community radio producers is called *Talking the Walk: The Media Enclosures and the Communications Commons.* An earlier report on the IMCs is included in the forthcoming Martha McCaughey and Mike Ayers (ed.), *Cyberactivism: Critical Theories and Practices of On-line Activism* (Routledge).

LOUISE LECLAIR, a communications representative with the Canadian Union of Public Employees (CUPE) in Burnaby, B.C., took an educational leave in 2002 to complete a master's degree at Simon Fraser University. She has written numerous pamphlets, articles, and radio and television spots in her more than thirty years of working in advertising, government, cultural, and labor communications. Political activism has driven most of her career changes.

GARY T. MARX is Professor Emeritus at M.I.T. He received his Ph.D. from the University of California, Berkeley. He is the author of *Protest and Prejudice, Undercover Police Surveillance in America* and co-editor of *Undercover: Police Surveillance in Comparative Perspective.* Publications and reports related to his chapter can be found at garymarx.net.

EMMA MILLER previously worked for eight years as a social worker with children and families in Lanarkshire, Scotland. Since 1999 she has been a member of the Glasgow University Media Group, Glasgow University, Scotland. She currently is writing her doctorate on audience responses to television coverage of developing countries.

ANDY OPEL is an assistant professor in the Department of Communication at Florida State University, teaching documentary video production and media studies. His work has appeared in *Enviropop: Studies in Environmental Rhetoric and Popular Culture* and *The Journal of American Culture*. His research interests include the intersection of consumer culture and the environment as well as the emerging media and democracy movement.

DONNALYN POMPPER is an associate professor in the Department of Communication at Florida State University. Prior to earning a Ph.D. in Mass Media and Communication, she worked in print journalism covering environmental issues in the Philadelphia-New Jersey area, as well as in corporate and agency marketing communications. Her research agenda involves social risk, gender-ethnicity issues, collective memory, and computer-assisted textual analysis. Her research has appeared in *Enviropop: Studies in Environmental Rhetoric and Popular Culture, Environmental Communication Yearbook, The West Wing: The American Presidency as Television Drama,* the *Journal of Public Relations Research, Public Relations Review, Media History Digest,* and *Journalism and Mass Communication Quarterly.*

ILIA RODRÍGUEZ is an assistant professor of mass communications at St. Cloud State University in Minnesota, where she teaches journalism and media studies. Her scholarly interests include journalism history, international communication, and minorities in media. Her research has been published in *Gazette: The International Journal for Communication Studies* and *The Howard Journal of Communications.*

JEFF SHANTZ is a Ph.D. candidate in Sociology at York University in Toronto, Canada. His writings have been published in journals, including *Feminist Review, Capital and Class, Critique of Anthropology* and *Environmental Politics,* as well as in numerous newspapers and magazines. He co-hosts the anti-poverty report on CHRY community radio.

NANCY SNOW is assistant professor of communications at California State University, Fullerton, and adjunct professor at the Annenberg School for Communication, USC. She is former associate director of the UCLA Center for Communications and Community, a media advocacy research and training organization.

ANNE MARIE TODD earned her Ph.D. from the University of Southern California's Annenberg School for Communication. She currently is an assistant professor at San Jose State University.

AUDREY VANDERFORD is a doctoral student in the Comparative Literature Program at the University of Oregon. Her work examines the performance of political protest in radical environmentalist and anarchist movements, and she has published articles on pie-throwing, treesitting, and street theatre.

KARIN WAHL-JORGENSEN is a Lecturer in the School of Journalism, Media and Cultural Studies at Cardiff University, Wales, U.K. Her work has been published in journals including *Critical Studies in Media Communication, Journalism & Mass Communication Quarterly, Journalism, Journalism Studies, Mass Communication & Society, Javnost/The Public, Journal of Communication Inquiry,* and the *Peace Review.* She also has contributed to edited volumes on *Gender, Politics and Communication* and *The Idea of Public Journalism.* Her research focuses on citizenship, democracy, and the media. She is book reviews editor for *Social Semiotics.*

ÅSA WETTERGREN is a doctoral student in Sociology at Karlstad University, Sweden. Her research agenda includes contemporary resistance, and understanding how emerging resistance movements and forms of protest, such as culture jamming, are contingent upon present sociocultural discourses.